A PRACTICAL APPROACH TO

PLANNING LAW

A PRACTICAL APPROACH TO

PLANNING LAW

Fourth Edition

Victor Moore LLM, Barrister

Professor of Law, University of Reading

BLACKSTONE
PRESS LIMITED

This edition published in Great Britain 1994 by Blackstone Press Limited, 9-15 Aldine Street, London W12 8AW. Telephone: 081-740 1173

ISBN: 1 85431 355 X

First edition 1987
Second edition 1990
Third edition 1992
Reprinted 1993
Fourth edition 1994

Typeset by Montage Studios Limited, Tonbridge, Kent
Printed by Bell and Bain Ltd., Glasgow

Contents

19   Listed buildings and conservation areas   335

20   Ancient monuments and areas of archaeological importance   363

21   Minerals   369

22   The control of outdoor advertisements   374

23   Trees   380

24   Conservation of Natural Habitats   384

25   Remedies for adverse planning decisions   388

Preface

Since the Third Edition of this book was published in 1992, most of the changes made to the Town and Country Planning Act 1991 have been the subject of judicial or other interpretation. Indeed, in the two years ending March 1994, there have been no fewer than 429 challenges by statutory review procedure to Ministerial decisions. In addition, the number of challenges to local authority decisions by judicial review continues to rise. Meanwhile, parallel to this judicial activity, the flow of new or revised guidance from the Department of the Environment continues unabated, along with numerous proposals for further amendments to the planning law system which can only lead to the subject becoming even more complex than at present.

Mention should also be made of the unsatisfactory state of the law with regard to planning obligations and the extent to which community benefits can be lawfully taken into account in determining planning applications. In this new edition, I have tried to bring readers up-to-date as far as possible with these developments.

Professor Victor Moore
September 1994

Preface to the First Edition

Given the large number of excellent books available on the subject of planning law, some excuse is obviously needed to justify this new addition to existing literature.

The invitation to write a book of no more than 350 pages, including appendices, on the subject and without the use of footnotes, proved to be a challenge impossible to resist.

In the pages that follow therefore, I have tried to prune what is an extremely difficult and complex subject down to its basic principles. I have attempted to describe planning law and its administration in both simple and practical terms, and resisted the temptation to stray too far into technical details or to refer to judicial decisions which have made occasional departures from those basic principles.

Two aspects, however, must be drawn to the reader's attention. First, limitations of space has meant this book does not deal with the law and practice in Scotland, which, although substantially similar to that for England and Wales, has a number of significant differences. Secondly, the book has anticipated the bringing into force of the changes made to the law by the planning provisions of the Housing and Planning Act 1986. It is expected, however, that the provisions of the Act not yet in force will be brought into force by commencement order before the year has run its course.

Lastly, after years of promise, a new General Development Order is expected to be promulgated shortly. But as anyone interested in the use and development of land will know, if a publication in this subject were to await the translation of all proposals into reality, no books on planning law would be published at all.

October 1987

Table of Cases

Table of Statutes

European Community Legislation

Table of Statutory Instruments

ONE
Historical introduction

Before there existed any public control over the use and development of land, landowners were free to use their land in any way they wished, subject only to any limitations in the grant under which they held it and to obligations placed upon them at common law. In essence, therefore, provided an owner acted within the limitation of his estate or interest and committed no nuisance or trespass against his neighbour's property, he was free to use his land for the purpose for which it was economically best suited. Today, most societies require not only that this freedom be restricted for the public good, but also that the use to which land is put should be determined by the long-term interests of the community as a whole rather than as a consequence of the incidence and spread of individual land ownership.

Although as early as the middle of the 19th century, public health legislation in Great Britain had been passed to remedy the worst effects of insanitary housing conditions, it was not until 1909 that an attempt was made to deal with more general land use problems such as the separation of incompatible uses or the lack of amenity land. The Housing, Town Planning etc. Act 1909 was primarily concerned with housing in that it gave wide powers to local authorities to build new houses and to clear existing substandard housing. Section 54 of that Act, however, gave local authorities the power to prepare schemes:

as respects any land which is in course of development or appears likely to be used for building purposes, with the general object of securing proper sanitary conditions, amenity, and convenience in connection with the laying out and use of the land, and of any neighbouring lands.

Here was the beginning of planning law. Yet from the start it was plagued by a number of problems, many of which have recurred and remained unresolved to the present day.

Section 54 of the 1909 Act was discretionary in that local authorities were not required to prepare schemes, merely empowered to do so. The Housing,

Town Planning etc. Act 1919, attempted to remedy that defect by requiring the council of every borough or urban district with a population of over 20,000 to prepare schemes for land in the course of development or likely to be used for building purposes. Despite the fact that in 1919 Parliament set a time limit for the preparation of these schemes, the time-limit had to be extended on a number of occasions as authorities found that the formidable task of preparing schemes could not be accomplished within the time set for doing so.

Although in 1919 the time taken to prepare schemes may have been exacerbated by the shortage of people possessing the necessary technical skills, the problem of delay has never been satisfactorily resolved. Under the Town and Country Planning Act 1947, local planning authorities were required within three years to submit to the Minister a development plan for their area. Most authorities found they were unable to do so within that period. Then, under the Town and Country Planning Act 1968, although no time-limit was laid down for the submission of structure plans to the Secretary of State, it took some 14 years before the last structure plan was submitted to him for approval. Similar delay problems continued to apply to proposals for the alteration or replacement of development plans.

Unfortunately for the planning process, development pressures often build up faster than planners can plan. Hence the more outdated a development plan may be, the less relevant it becomes to making decisions about the use and development of land and the greater the pressure on authorities to rely on non-statutory plans or to make land use decisions on an individual and *ad hoc* basis.

Another problem with the 1909 Act was that before a scheme could be implemented it had to be approved by central government and an opportunity given to people to object to its provisions. The difficulty in this area is that democracy and speed do not always go hand in hand, and if the public are to be given the right to influence the content of the scheme or plan, the preparation and approval or adoption process is by that much delayed. Later legislation has perpetuated the right of the public to object to proposals in any development plan submitted for approval or adoption. Under the Town and Country Planning Act 1947, the Minister was required to consider any objections made to a development plan submitted to him for approval. Under the Town and Country Planning Act 1968, he was required to consider any objections made to a structure plan submitted to him for approval. Now the Town and Country Planning Act 1990 requires each local planning authority to consider objections made to the content of development plans prepared by the authority.

The third problem to arise under early planning legislation came to be known as the compensation/betterment problem. Planning control can affect property values for better or worse, and the problem that needed to be solved was how to treat those whose land had either decreased in value (the compensation aspect), or increased in value (the betterment aspect) due to a scheme. The early legislation allowed local authorities to recover from owners 50 per cent of any increase in the value of land due to the making of a scheme. At the same time, it gave owners a right to receive compensation from the authority for any decrease in the value of their land. Under the Town and Country Planning Act 1932, the amount of betterment which a local authority could recover from owners was increased from 50 to 75 per cent. In addition, however, the owner was given the right to require payment to be deferred until he had actually realised the increased value through the sale of the land or its development. If this did not happen within five years as regards land zoned for industrial or commercial purposes, or 14 years in any other case, no betterment at all was payable.

The operation of these provisions proved disastrous. A local authority wishing to control the development of land in their area might find themselves faced with a heavy liability for compensation which they would have difficulty in meeting unless they were also prepared to allow some development in the area. On the other hand, a local authority not wishing to restrict development in their area might hope to obtain a considerable sum by way of betterment from owners, without any liability to pay compensation. As it turned out, however, the collection of betterment proved to be almost impossible, mainly because of the lapsing provisions previously referred to.

The failure to deal satisfactorily with the financial consequences of land use planning meant the failure of land use planning itself. It has been estimated that after more than a quarter of a century of effort the number of schemes which were prepared and approved under the 1909 Act and subsequent legislation could be counted on the fingers of one hand!

The advent of the Second World War presented an opportunity to consider whether a more effective system for the control of land use could be found. The opportunity had been taken to set up a number of bodies charged with investigating particular facets of the land-use system. The three main reports produced by this exercise were the Barlow Report, the Scott Report and the Uthwatt Report.

The Barlow Report This was the report of the Royal Commission on the Distribution of Industrial Population (Cmd 6153). It was set up in 1937 under the chairmanship of Sir Montague Barlow, to enquire into the causes of the geographical distribution of the industrial population, to consider the social, economic and strategic disadvantages resulting from the concentration of industry and industrial population in cities and regions and to consider what methods should be taken to counteract them. The report advocated the dispersal of industry from congested urban areas and the progressive re-development of those areas wherever necessary. The aim of dispersal advocated in the report was accepted by the government, with the acknowledgement that it had a specific role to play in deciding where new industry was to be located. The legislation that followed was to adopt a carrot-and-stick approach. Under various Industry Acts, industry was given financial incentives to locate in particular areas. Under planning legislation, industrial development could occur in an area only if the developer had obtained from central government a certificate (called an industrial development certificate) that the development was consistent with the proper distribution of industry. Today, although some of the financial incentives remain, the industrial development certificate procedure has been abandoned and the relevant statutory provisions repealed.

The Scott Report   This was a report of a Committee on Land Utilisation in Rural Areas (Cmd 6378). It was set up under the chairmanship of Lord Justice Scott to consider the problems of piecemeal development of agricultural land and the unrestricted development of the coastline. One of the Committee's recommendations was that sporadic building in the countryside should be controlled and planning schemes designed so as to direct all new settlers into country towns and villages except where they could advance some decisive reason why they should be housed in the open countryside.

The Uthwatt Report   This was the report of the Expert Committee on Compensation and Betterment (Cmd 6386) under the chairmanship of Mr Justice Uthwatt. The main feature of this report was an examination of the problem of compensation and betterment. In so doing it identified the twin concepts of shifting value and floating value.

The idea behind the concept of shifting value was that planning control does not reduce the total sum of land values, but merely redistributes them by increasing the value of some land whilst decreasing the value of other land. Because of this it was possible for one authority to find themselves paying compensation for restrictions on development, whilst a neighbouring authority could recover betterment because of those same restrictions. The lesson to be learnt, therefore, was that financial arrangements to deal with the compensation/betterment problem could not be dealt with at a local level.

The idea behind the concept of floating values was that potential value is by nature speculative. Development may take place on parcel A or parcel B. The prospect floats over both parcels. The value of any parcel of land is obtained by estimating whether the development is likely to take place on one parcel of land or on some other. Where planning restrictions are imposed on land and owners are given the right to claim compensation for any loss so caused, they will tend to assume that but for those restrictions the floating value would settle on their land, rather than on the land of their neighbours. The result was that owners claiming compensation would tend to overestimate the prospect of the development taking place on their land, so that in total, all claims for compensation over an area could far exceed the actual loss of development value suffered.

Town and Country Planning Act 1947   All three reports contributed significantly to the system of land use control established by the Town and Country Planning Act 1947. The Act came into effect on 1 July 1948. The essential features of that Act were as follows:

(a)   It created local planning authorities and required each authority to prepare a development plan for their area indicating the manner in which they proposed land in their area should be used, whether by development or otherwise, and the ways by which any such development should be carried out.

(b) All land was made subject to planning control, not just land within a scheme prepared by the authority. As a result, apart from minor development, any person wishing to develop land had first to obtain express planning permission to do so from the local planning authority. In deciding whether to grant permission, the authority were to be guided by the provisions of the development plan.

(c) Wide powers were given to local planning authorities to deal with development carried out without planning permission.

(d) Wide powers were given to local planning authorities to secure the preservation of trees and buildings of architectural or historic interest and to control the display of advertisements.

(e) If a person was granted planning permission for any development falling outside the existing use of his land, he had to pay a development charge to the State equal to the value of that permission.

(f) If a person was refused planning permission for such development, no compensation was paid for that refusal.

(g) To compensate landowners affected by (e) and (f) above who may perhaps have purchased their land before the Act came into force at a price reflecting its value for development, the Act set up a fund of £300 million. Any owner who could prove that his land had depreciated as a result of the 1947 Act could make a claim against the fund for the difference between the value of the land for existing use purposes and its value on the assumption the Act had not been passed. Payments from the fund were to be made in 1954.

It will be seen that the financial provisions of the Act ((e) to (g) above), effectively dealt with the problems examined by the Uthwatt Committee. The sum of £300 million was an estimate of the total development value of land nationally, and claims against the fund were, if necessary, to be scaled down, so that in total they added up to that sum. Furthermore, since the fund was administered by central government, local planning authorities were now free to make planning decisions without any regard to the economic or financial consequences of so doing.

Most of the financial provisions of the 1947 Act have now been dismantled. In particular, the Town and Country Planning Act 1953 abolished the development charge. Although further attempts were made by the Land Commission Act 1967 and the Development Land Tax Act 1976 to recoup for the community part of the development value of land which would otherwise accrue to the owner, no special tax on development value now exists, although an owner may be liable to pay capital gains tax on such value if he realises a capital gain on the disposal of his land.

It will be remembered that the 1947 legislation contained no provision for the payment of compensation to a landowner refused planning permission for development which fell outside the existing use of his land. When the development charge was abolished in 1953, it was decided to maintain that rule, so that in general since the 1947 Act no compensation has been payable for any loss incurred by the refusal of planning permission for such development, or indeed for the grant of planning permission made subject to conditions.

This general rule, however, was subject to one exception. An owner could claim compensation if he or his successors in title could show the existence of a claim made under the 1947 Act against the £300 million fund in respect of loss suffered as a result of the Act. In such rare cases, the compensation was limited to the amount of the claim or the amount of the loss due to the planning decision, whichever was less. Even this exception however, has now been abolished. The Planning and Compensation Act 1991 repealed almost all existing statutory provisions providing for the payment of compensation for adverse planning decisions.

With regard to the non-financial provisions of the 1947 Act, the elements of the system established at that time have withstood the passage of time. Although numerous changes and improvements have been made to the statutory provisions since that date, the basic scheme of the legislation remains the same.

Changes since 1947   Among the many changes made since 1947 mention might be made of:

(a)   The major reorganisation of local government in 1974 leading to changes in the number of local planning authorities and their respective functions.

(b)   The introduction in 1968 of a new type of development plan to replace those prepared under the 1947 Act.

(c)   The progressive strengthening of the provisions for enforcing planning control.

(d)   The strengthening of the provisions relating to the preservation of buildings of special architectural or historic interest.

Yet despite the continued reverence of the law to the basic elements of the system as introduced in 1947, the law has become not only more complex, but also considerably more disparate in its application. Today, quite apart from the normal technicalities of the law and its procedures, a landowner wishing to develop his land may have additionally to consider such matters as: whether his land is within an enterprise zone, a simplified planning zone, a national park, an area of outstanding natural beauty, a conservation area or a site of special scientific interest; whether the current development plan for the area is the new-style development plan or a combination of the old and the new-style development plan; and if the latter, and they happen to conflict with each other, which plan is to prevail; whether the development proposed is permitted under the Town and Country Planning General Development Order or some special development order; and whether there is a building on the land of special or architectural interest, or a tree protected by a tree preservation order, or the land contains a scheduled monument.

Town and Country Planning Act 1990   Town and country planning legislation has been consolidated previously in the Town and Country Planning Act 1962, and again in the Town and Country Planning Act 1971. Since that date, planning legislation has been amended frequently. So much so, that in 1989, the Government decided to ask the Law Commission to consolidate the legislation yet again. It was decided that the consolidation should involve four separate Acts of Parliament. Consolidation of legislation does not involve changes in the substance of the law. In this case, however, the opportunity was taken to correct a number of anomalies and inconsistencies of a technical nature. Subject to these changes however, the Acts restated existing law. The four Acts, which all received the Royal Assent on 24 May 1990 are:

Town and Country Planning Act 1990
This Act consolidated certain enactments relating to town and country planning but excludes special controls in respect of buildings and areas of special architectural and historic interest and in respect of hazardous substances, with amendments to give effect to recommendations of the Law Commission.
Planning (Listed Buildings and Conservation Areas) Act 1990
This Act consolidated certain enactments in relation to special controls in respect of buildings and areas of special architectural or historic interest, with amendments to give effect to recommendations of the Law Commission.
Planning (Hazardous Substances) Act 1990
This Act consolidated certain enactments relating to special controls in respect of hazardous substances, with amendments to give effect to recommendations of the Law Commission.
Planning (Consequential Provisions) Act 1990
This Act makes provision for repeals, consequential amendments, transitional and transitory matters and savings in connection with the consolidation of enactments in the Acts mentioned above, including provisions to give effect to the recommendations of the Law Commission. This Act is largely concerned with ensuring continuity. Thus, for example, it provides that any document made, served or issued after the coming into force of the consolidating Acts which refer to an enactment repealed by the consolidation is to be construed as referring to the corresponding provision of the relevant new Act. In addition, for the most part, statutory instruments made under the old legislation continue to have effect as though made under the new consolidating Acts.

With the exception of the Planning (Hazardous Substances) Act 1990, most of the provisions of the Acts came into force on 24 August 1990. Hereinafter, the main Act, the Town and Country Planning Act 1990, will be referred to simply as 'the 1990 Act'.

Planning and Compensation Act 1991   Because it is not possible to make substantial changes to legislation in a consolidation Act, the need to make a number of important changes to planning law had to await separate amending legislation. The Planning and Compensation Act 1991 received the Royal Assent on 25 July 1991. As its name implies, it amended the law relating to both planning and the assessment of compensation for the compulsory acquisition of land. With regard to planning, the Act made important changes to the law relating to development plans, the definition of development, appeals, enforcement notices, listed buildings and other specific matters. Those changes have been incorporated in the text that follows.

TWO

Planning organisation

From its very beginning in 1909, planning legislation has given to local authorities direct power and responsibility for carrying on the day-to-day administration of land use control. Central government's role in the administration of planning began as, and has since remained, the supervision and coordination of the way in which those powers and responsibilities are exercised.

There are, of course, many bodies with a role to play in the field of town and country planning. Basically, however, planning organisation has two main tiers, a central government tier under the mantle of the Secretary of State, and a local government tier in the shape of local planning authorities.

2.1 The Secretaries of State

Nowhere in the law is there to be found any general statement of the responsibilities of the Secretary of State. The duty imposed on a predecessor, the Minister of Town and Country Planning, which was set out in the Minister of Town and Country Planning Act 1943, 'of securing consistency and continuity in the framing and execution of a national policy with respect to the use and development of land throughout England and Wales', was repealed in 1970. One should shed no tears. The duty imposed was too vague and too wide to be legally enforceable. It did represent, however, a statement of the political responsibility of that Minister to Parliament; and in that same sense, the statement, though now unwritten, describes the political responsibility of the Secretary of State.

Under our governmental system there is more than one Secretary of State. Yet in law his office is one and indivisible, so that any one Secretary of State may exercise the powers of any other. The functions of any particular Secretary of State, however, are allocated to him by Order in Council made under the Ministers of the Crown Act 1975. In this way, in the field of planning law, the Secretary of State for the Environment assumes these powers in relation to England. In Wales, the powers are assumed by the Secretary of State for Wales, and in Scotland, by the Secretary of State for Scotland.

As far as England is concerned, the Secretary of State for the Environment is presently assisted in the exercise of his powers and functions by three Ministers of State. They are the Minister for Local Government and Planning, the Minister for Housing, Inner Cities and Construction and the Minister for Environment and Countryside. There are also two Parliamentary Under-Secretaries of State, each with special responsibilities, one of whom is responsible for the handling of government business in the House of Lords.

These arrangements, however, are political arrangements allowing for the sharing of departmental responsibilities between a number of Ministers in the same Department of State. They in no way affect the particular powers and functions which in law are placed exclusively upon the Secretary of State.

Following the creation of a new Department of National Heritage in May 1992, responsibility for the listing of historic buildings in England passed to the Secretary of State for National Heritage. Controls over works to historic buildings, however, remain the responsibility of the Secretary of State for the Environment. The Secretary of State for National Heritage is also responsible for scheduling ancient monuments and granting scheduled monument consents; repair notices and associated compulsory purchase orders; and policy, procedures and reserve powers in respect of the designation of conservation areas.

The organisation of planning administration places the Secretary of State for the Environment at the apex of a pyramid of power. Despite many attempts made over the years to shift more of the responsibility for planning decisions from central to local government, planning organisation remains a hierarchy of centralised pontification, with the Secretary of State the supreme central pontiff. So it is that, however small a parcel of land may be, the final say in determining the use to which that land can be put is given, in law, to the Secretary of State.

Governmental powers and duties are broadly analysed as being of three kinds, namely legislative, administrative and judicial. So too, may the powers and duties of the Secretary of State under planning legislation be analysed.

2.1.1 Legislative powers

Despite the length of the 1990 Act, many of its provisions are no more than general statements of principle. The Secretary of State, however, is given power by the Act to fill in the detail by making regulations or orders. Under s. 333 of the 1990 Act, the power to make regulations and many of the more important orders are exercisable by statutory instrument. The use of this power is subject to varying degrees of parliamentary control or scrutiny. Statutory instruments are normally required to be laid before Parliament for a period of 40 days. The more important statutory instruments also require an 'affirmative resolution' of both Houses of Parliament during that period before they come into effect. With others, the statutory instrument comes into effect automatically, unless during that period either House of Parliament passes a 'negative resolution' preventing it from doing so. Finally, some statutory instruments have merely to be laid before Parliament, thus avoiding any more formal parliamentary control.

Under the 1990 Act, most statutory instruments containing *regulations* are subject to the negative resolution procedure. So too are most statutory instruments containing a *development order.* Most other statutory instruments containing orders, however, including the important Town and Country Planning (Use Classes) Order, have merely to be laid before Parliament. Two of the main statutory instruments made by the Secretary of State are:

(a) *Town and Country Planning (Use Classes) Order 1987.* This order (see Appendix B) specifies 15 'use classes' for the purpose of s. 55(2)(f) of the 1990 Act. Its significance is that where buildings or other land are used for a purpose within any of the classes specified in the Order, the use of the buildings or other land for any purpose within the same class is not to be taken to involve development.

(b) *Town and Country Planning General Development Order (GDO).* This order has two main functions. First, it deals with the procedure to be followed when an application is made for planning permission, or an application made to determine whether or not a proposed activity would be lawful etc., as well as many other procedural matters. Secondly, it specifies a number of classes of development which are permitted to be undertaken on land without the need to obtain express permission to do so from the local planning authority. Such development is referred to as 'permitted development'.

The power of the Secretary of State to make these orders, though subject to varying degrees of parliamentary control, shows the extent of his legislative power. By reducing the number of 'classes' in the Use Classes Order, or by extending the content of a class, he can reduce the number of activities which constitute development and therefore require planning permission. By widening the scope of the development permitted by the GDO, he can remove activities which constitute development from the general control of local planning authorities. It is significant that when he last made major amendments to the GDO in 1981, it was estimated that its effect was to reduce the number of applications for planning permission made to local planning authorities by some 15 to 20 per cent.

The Secretary of State also has power under s. 59 of the 1990 Act to make a special development order. Unlike a general development order which will normally apply to all land, a special development order grants planning permission only for the development of the land specified in the order. Although until quite recently this power had been used sparingly, its scope can be illustrated by the case of *Essex County Council v Ministry of Housing & Local Government* (1967) 18 P & CR 531. An inquiry had been held into objections to the possible choice of Stansted as the site of the third London airport. After the inquiry the government announced its intention to grant planning permission for the development of the site to the British Airports Authority by means of an order made under what is now s. 59 of the 1990 Act. Since the public inquiry, the Minister had taken into account further questions of fact, and the county council claimed that in accordance with the rules of natural justice the Minister was not entitled to make an order until he had received and considered representations made to him on the new facts. In an action against the Minister the council asked, *inter alia,* for a declaration that the action of the Minister in purporting to decide to grant planning permission for the development was *ultra vires,* void and of no effect. In an application to have the writ and statement of claim struck out, the Minister claimed that they disclosed no reasonable cause of action, were frivolous and vexatious and an abuse of the process of the court. In granting the application, the court held that the power of the Minister to make a special development order under the section was a purely *administrative legislative power,* for the exercise of which he is responsible to nobody except Parliament, and that no duty was imposed on him to act judicially before making an order under the section.

What the court was here recognising was that the decision to grant planning permission by a special development order was an administrative act, but one exercised by the Minister in a legislative form.

The following are examples of the use made of special development orders in recent years:

(a) *Town and Country Planning (Vauxhall Cross) Special Development Order 1982 (SI No. 796).*   This order granted planning permission for office development at what was known as the 'Green Giant' site at Vauxhall, London. The order was made following the holding of an architectural competition to determine the most appropriate design for office development at one of the capital's most important sites.

(b) *Town and Country Planning (Telecommunication Network) (Railway Operational Land) Special Development Order 1982 (SI No. 817).*   This order granted planning permission to lay cables (to be used for the carrying of cable television) along the route of railway lines. The grant of planning permission in this way thus relieved cable television operators from having to make an express application for planning permission to every local planning authority through whose land a cable was to run.

(c) *Town and Country Planning (NIREX) Special Development Order 1986 (SI No. 812).*   This order granted planning permission, subject to conditions, to a body called United Kingdom Nirex Ltd for the carrying out of development for the purpose of investigating the suitability of four specified parcels of land for use for the deposit of low-level radioactive waste. This order was made because of the fear that if an application for planning permission were required to be made for such development, local planning authorities might refuse permission, not because of objections to the limited nature of the investigatory work to be carried out, but because of the long-term consequences for the area if the investigatory work were to show that the land was suitable for the deposit of such waste. The development for which planning permission was granted by this special development order was in fact later abandoned by Nirex, on the ground that there was now no economic advantage in having a specific site for the shallow disposal of low-level waste.

(d) *Town and Country Planning (Trafford Park Urban Development Area) Special Development Order 1987 (SI No. 738).*   This order permits within the urban development area, development in accordance with proposals submitted to the Secretary of State by the Urban Development Corporation and approved by him under s. 148(1) of the Local Government, Planning and Land Act 1980. Similar orders permitting development in accordance with proposals made to the Secretary of State, have been made with regard to other Urban Development Corporations.

Mention should also be made of the following bizarre, but perfectly legal use of the Secretary of State's power to grant planning permission by special development order.

In 1977 an application for planning permission was made to construct an oxide fuel reprocessing plant at Windscale (now known as Sellafield) in Cumbria. Because of the public concern over the proposed development, the Secretary of State 'called in' the application for his own decision rather than leave the decision to be made by the local planning authority. Then, following a public local inquiry into the application and objections made to it, the Inspector recommended that, subject to conditions, the application should be granted. Normally, the Secretary of State would have done no more than decide whether or not to accept his Inspector's recommendation. In this instance, however, he considered that Parliament should be able to express a view on the proposed development. He decided, therefore, to refuse the application for planning permission. In so doing, he avoided any objections which might arise as a result of his quasi-judicial role in the planning process. The parliamentary debate was then able to take place without giving rise to an obligation on the Secretary of State to reopen the inquiry if fresh evidence was forthcoming during the course of the debate. The Secretary of State then granted, by special development order (Town and Country Planning (Windscale and Calder Works) Special Development Order 1978 (SI No. 523)), planning permission for the very same development which he had earlier refused, with the parliamentary debate taking place on a 'prayer' against the order.

A somewhat different procedure was followed, however, with regard to the decision on an application by the Central Electricity Generating Board to build a nuclear power station at Sizewell, in Essex. After receiving the report of the Inspector, both Houses of Parliament were given an opportunity to debate the report and the issues involved. In the debate in the House of Commons, the Secretary of State made it clear that he was there to listen to the views which would be expressed and that he had no intention of commenting or making observations on the report. Shortly after the debate had been held the Secretary of State proceeded to grant planning permission for the development proposed.

2.1.2 Administrative powers
Although local planning authorities are the primary bodies responsible for the day-to-day administration of planning, the Secretary of State has wide power to ensure that they act in accordance with his general policy. He also has wide power to enable him to supervise and coordinate their individual activities. In addition, he provides general guidance and advice to local planning authorities on how they should exercise their powers.

The basic document through which the Secretary of State exercises general policy control is the development plan for an area. Under early planning legislation he was required to approve all development plans prepared by local planning authorities. When the 'new-style' development plans prepared under Part II of the 1990 Act were introduced in 1968, he was required to approve only the structure plan part, which he could do in whole or in part and with or without modifications or reservations. Now, under the Planning and Compensation Act 1991, county planning authorities have been given the power to *adopt* their own structure plans. The Secretary of State's policy control over a structure plan's content, however, is secured by the requirement in a new s. 31(6)(a) of the 1990 Act, that in formulating the general policies to be included in a structure plan, the authority must have regard to specified matters including 'any regional or strategic planning guidance given by the Secretary of State to assist them in the preparation of the plan'. The Secretary of State's policy control over the content of a structure plan is also secured by giving him power, in a new s. 35A(1) of the 1990 Act, to direct that all or any part of the proposals in a structure plan shall be submitted to him for his approval.

Although the Secretary of State has never had general power to approve the local plan part of the 'new-style' development plans prepared under Part II of the 1990 Act, his policy control over their content has always been secured by a reserve power to call in a local plan for his approval, and by the overriding requirement that proposals in a local plan should be in general conformity with the structure plan for the area.

The position is somewhat similar in Greater London and the metropolitan areas. The Local Government Act 1985, which abolished the Greater London Council and the metropolitan county councils, provides for the preparation by the London boroughs and metropolitan districts of a new kind of development plan, to be called the unitary development plan. The unitary development plan is not 'approved' by the Secretary of State, but instead 'adopted' by the authority that prepared it. The Secretary of State's control over policies contained in the plan is again secured by his power to call in any part of the plan for his own approval, and the requirement that in formulating the general policies to be contained in Part I of the plan, the authority should have regard to any strategic guidance given to them by the Secretary of State to assist them in the plan's preparation.

The powers of the Secretary of State also extend to determining appeals made under s. 78 of the 1990 Act against the refusal by a local planning authority to grant planning permission, or against a decision to grant planning permission subject to conditions. In the year 1993/94, the Secretary of State for the Environment (or an Inspector acting on his behalf), determined 14,113 appeals (about 3.7 per cent of the total number of applications made) under the provisions of s. 78 of the 1990 Act, of which no less than 35.2 per cent were allowed. This is in marked contrast to the 25 per cent success rate which was common in the mid 1970s, and the change may be due to an increase in the number of refusals of planning permission by local planning authorities.

It may perhaps be that local planning authorities did not always take cognisance of the guidance given by the Secretary of State in para. 15 of an earlier PPG 1: General Policy and Principles, issued in January 1988, that:

There is always a presumption in favour of allowing applications for development, having regard to all material considerations, unless that development would cause demonstrable harm to interests of acknowledged importance.

When PPG 1 was revised in March 1992, the underlying rationale for the presumption in favour of development was expressed in para. 5 in a slightly different form as follows:

The planning system should be efficient, effective and simple in conception and operation. It fails in its function whenever it prevents, inhibits or delays development which should reasonably have been permitted. It should operate on the basis that applications for development should be allowed, having regard to the development plan and all material considerations, unless the proposed development would cause demonstrable harm to interests of acknowledged importance.

The Secretary of State is also required under s. 174 of the 1990 Act, to determine appeals made against enforcement notices served by local planning authorities; and in doing so, he may uphold, quash or vary the enforcement notice, and may, in appropriate circumstances, grant planning permission for the development to which the notice relates. In the year 1993/94, the Secretary of State for the Environment (or an Inspector acting on his behalf), determined 4,032 appeals against enforcement notices, of which 2,454 were upheld, 530 varied and 1,048 quashed.

Under the 1990 Act, the Secretary of State determines appeals against decisions of local planning authorities in many other areas, including decisions relating to certificates of lawfulness of existing use or development (s. 191), certificates of lawfulness of proposed use or development (s. 192), the display of advertisements (s. 220), and the cutting down, topping or lopping of trees the subject of a tree preservation order (s. 208). He may also be required to confirm orders made by local planning authorities revoking or modifying a planning permission previously granted (s. 97), orders requiring a use of land to be discontinued or the alteration or removal of buildings or works (s. 102) and notices requiring that development begun but not completed should be completed (s. 94). It should be noted that in the period between April 1979 and December 1988, the Secretary of State confirmed 1,300 revocation orders under the provisions of what is now s. 97 of the 1990 Act.

Under s. 77 of the 1990 Act, the Secretary of State may 'call in' applications for planning permission for his own determination, rather than allow them to be determined by the local planning authority. The power is used very selectively, the Secretary of State exercising the power only if planning issues of more than local importance are involved.

The reasons given by the Secretary of State for exercising his call-in power have included green-belt considerations, conflicts with development plan policies, the loss of prime-quality agricultural land and local authority development proposals which have generated controversy. Specific instances where the Secretary of State has exercised his call-in power have included proposals for development at Windscale (mentioned above), the redevelopment of Spitalfields Market, Stamford Bridge football stadium, extensions to airport capacity at Stansted and London (Heathrow), proposals for the construction of an aerodrome for use by short take-off and landing (STOL) aircraft on land in the London Docklands and later, proposals to extend the runway and to install runway approach lighting. More recently, he has called in for his own decision the application by the British Airports Authority to build a fifth terminal at London (Heathrow) Airport. In England in 1993/94, 99 applications for planning permission were called in by the Secretary of State under this power.

In addition to the power to call in applications for planning permission for his own decision, the Secretary of State also has power under the Planning (Listed Buildings and Conservation Areas) Act 1990 to call in for his own decision applications made to the local planning authority for listed building consent.

Associated with the Secretary of State's power to call in applications for his own determination, is his power under the GDO to give a direction to local planning authorities restricting their power to grant planning permission for development, either indefinitely or for a specified period of time. Such directions are made with regard either to a class of application or to an application for a specific site. The purpose appears to be to protect the Secretary of State's right to call in the application by giving him time to consider whether or not he should in fact exercise that power. A direction so given, however, does not take away the power of the local planning authority to refuse to grant planning permission for the development proposed. Occasionally too, the power is used to safeguard land from development, where the land is needed for further public works such as roads or other transport facilities. In England in 1990/91, a total of 182 directions were issued by the Secretary of State under this power; and 70 of the planning applications called in by the Secretary of State followed the issue of such directions.

In addition, under the GDO, the Secretary of State may give directions to a local planning authority requiring the authority to consult with authorities, persons or bodies named in the direction before granting planning permission. The authority named in the direction may well be the Secretary of State. In this way the body consulted is formally made aware of particular planning applications. In cases where the Secretary of State is required to be consulted, he may decide to use his powers either to give a direction to the local planning authority, or decide without more to call in the application for his own decision under s. 77.

An example of the exercise by the Secretary of State of his powers under this provision is the requirement that local planning authorities consult him on any applications for development comprising gross shopping floor space of 20,000 square metres or more and prohibiting the grant of planning permission for such development until at least 21 days after the consultation. Consultation is not required, however, where the local planning authority decides to refuse the application.

The relevant direction, the Town and Country Planning (Shopping Development) (England and Wales) (No. 2) Direction 1993 is contained as an Annex to Circular No. 15/93.

Mention should also be made of the Secretary of State's wide default powers (e.g., under s. 51 of the 1990 Act in relation to development plans and ss. 100 and 104 in connection with the revocation of planning permission and the discontinuance of a use). Although default powers are rarely exercised, the powers allow him to impose a particular course of action on a local planning authority. According to statistics given to Parliament, default powers to revoke the grant of planning permission by local planning authorities were exercised by the Secretary of State on 18 occasions between 1955 and 1973. In 1991, he was reported as having given notice to the Borough of Poole that he was considering whether or not to revoke the deemed planning permission granted by the borough to itself for residential development on land which formed part of a site of special scientific interest. In the same year, the Secretary of State issued a direction that planning permission granted by Wealden District Council for a dwelling house be revoked after two previous applications for similar developments on the same site had been refused by the council and, on appeal, by the Secretary of State.

More recently in the autumn of 1992, the Secretary of State decided to hold an administrative inquiry into the operation of the planning system by North Cornwall District Council. The terms of reference of the inquiry were 'to consider the issues which have been raised about the administration of the planning system in North Cornwall and to make recommendations on any desirable changes in the formulation of policy or in procedures'. Quite separately from the setting up of this inquiry, the Secretary of State also announced he was considering whether it would be expedient for him to exercise his powers under ss. 100 and 104 of the 1990 Act to make orders revoking two planning permissions previously granted by the council and/or requiring the discontinuance of use or the removal of buildings or works. The action arose because of a number of complaints made about the consistency of planning decisions made by North Cornwall District Council. The council had been criticised by the Local Government Ombudsman over particular planning decisions, and the District Auditor had also made criticisms in a public interest report. Such criticisms had been the subject of wider public comment with the showing of a Channel 4 TV programme 'Cream Teas and Concrete' in December 1991, which had featured specific cases.

The report of the inquiry set up by the Secretary of State in 1992 and published towards the end of 1993, found that the North Cornwall District Council had granted planning permission for sporadic development in the open countryside on an inconsistent basis and contrary to national planning guidance and approved policies in the county structure plan. The report also criticised inappropriate decisions by the council and its committees, the lack of formally adopted policies, inadequate publicity arrangements and a number of procedural problems. Following government concern over the operation of planning control in North Cornwall, and the setting up of the inquiry, the Secretary of State exercised his power in August 1993 to revoke a planning permission granted for a farmer's retirement house in North Cornwall as being contrary to planning policy, and in another case took steps to require the carrying out of landscaping and further works to the exterior of an agricultural dwelling in order to minimise its effect on an Area of Outstanding Natural Beauty.

It appears, however, that the grant of planning permission for development contrary to planning policy guidance may occur in areas other than North Cornwall. Following criticism by the Commission for Local Administration in Wales and the Welsh Affairs Select Committee of the House of Commons of similar practices by local planning authorities in the principality, the Secretary of State for Wales thought it appropriate to write to all Welsh local planning authorities to remind them of the need to be fair and consistent in the treatment of planning applications.

In order to inform others about his policies and to lessen the need for him to use the powers he possesses (e.g., by keeping to a minimum the number of appeals made to him from decisions of local planning authorities), the Secretary of State issues Circulars, guidance notes on planning policies, White Papers and other policy statements. The importance to local planning authorities and others who are concerned with the use and development of land of Circulars and guidance notes containing the Secretary of State's policy on major planning issues cannot be overestimated.

In 1988, the Secretary of State began to issue Planning Policy Guidance notes (PPGs), to provide guidance on general and specific aspects of planning policy, and Minerals Planning Guidance notes (MPGs) to provide advice on the control of minerals development. PPGs and MPGs aim to provide concise and practical guidance on planning policies, in a clear and accessible form. Since 1988, the role of Departmental Circulars has been restricted to giving advice on legislation and procedures. In addition, the Secretary of State now also issues Regional Planning Guidance (RPGs) to provide guidance to local planning authorities on regional planning policies.

The following are the PPGS, MPGs and RPGs issued and in force:

Planning Policy Guidance Notes

PPG1   **General Policy and Principles (January 1988) (Revised March 1992)**
        Outlines the planning framework and the purpose of the planning system. Contains a general statement of planning policy.

PPG2   **Green Belts (January 1988)**
        Explains the purpose of the Green Belts and the need for a general presumption against inappropriate development within Green Belts.

PPG3   **Housing (January 1988) (Revised March 1992)**
        Sets out the Government's policies on the provision of housing land and emphasises the key role of the planning system in meeting the demand for housing.

PPG4   Industrial and Commercial Development and Small Firms (November 1992)
Emphasises the importance of a positive approach towards development which contributes to national and local economic activity.

PPG5   Simplified Planning Zones (November 1992)
Explains the working of this special procedure for facilitating development or redevelopment in designated areas by removing the need for a planning application for certain types of development proposals.

PPG6   Town Centres and Retail Developments (July 1993)
Provides policy guidance on planning aspects of retail development and all developments in town centres.

PPG7   The Countryside and Rural Economy (January 1992)
Contains advice on non-agricultural development in the countryside, including new uses of agricultural land and buildings, housing and the special restrictions which apply in some areas.

PPG8   Telecommunications (December 1992)
Gives comprehensive advice on planning aspects of telecommunications development.

PPG10   Strategic Guidance for the West Midlands (September 1988)
PPG11   Strategic Guidance for Merseyside (October 1988)
PPG12   Development Plans and Regional Planning Guidance (February 1992)
Underlines the importance which the Government attaches to up-to-date local plans as the basis for sound and effective planning control and urges local authorities to extend the coverage of statutory local plans.

PPG13   Transport (March 1994)
Provides advice on how local authorities should integrate transport and land-use planning.

PPG14   Development on Unstable Land (April 1990)
Seeks to clarify the position with respect to all forms of instability and their consideration within the planning system.

PPG15   Planning and the Historic Environment (September 1994)
PPG16   Archaeology and Planning (November 1990)
Sets out the Secretary of State's policy on how archaeological remains on land should be preserved or recorded and gives advice on the handling of archaeological remains under the development plan and control systems.

PPG17   Sport and Recreation (September 1991)
Describes the role of the planning system in safeguarding open space with recreational value.

PPG18   Enforcing Planning Control (December 1991)
This note revises previous Ministerial policy guidance about enforcement previously contained in Circulars, on the coming into force of new enforcement provisions introduced in the Planning and Compensation Act 1991.

PPG19 **Outdoor Advertising Control (March 1992)**
Gives advice on how advertising control should be exercised.

PPG20 **Coastal Planning (September 1992)**
Encourages local planning authorities to draw up plans to protect the best of the coastline by directing development towards areas that are already built up.

PPG21 **Tourism (November 1992)**
Explains the economic significance of tourism and its environmental impact, and therefore its importance in land-use planning. It explains how the needs of tourism should be dealt with in development plans and in development control.

PPG22 **Renewable Energy (February 1993)**
Describes the various renewable forms of energy; explains renewable energy's potential role in tackling greenhouse gas emissions; sets out the relevant instruments of policy, including the Non-Fossil Fuel Obligation; outlines relevant environmental protection legislation; gives a statement of general planning aims; explains how local planning authorities should include renewable energy policies in their plans, and advises them to consider what contribution their area might make; notes the considerations which should apply when it is intended to locate renewable energy installations in designated areas; explains when environmental assessment is required; sets out the environmental implications of renewable energy; and refers to planning conditions, temporary permissions and other consents/permissions.

PPG23 **Planning and Pollution Control (July 1994)**
Provides guidance on the relevance of pollution control to the exercise of planning functions. It advises on the relationship between authorities' planning responsibilities and the separate statutory responsibilities exercised by local authorities and other pollution control bodies, principally under the Environmental Protection Act 1990 and the Water Resources Act 1991.

Minerals Planning Guidance

MPG1 **General Considerations and the Development Plan System (January 1988)**
Covers the general principles and policy considerations of minerals planning with specific advice on the development plan system.

MPG2 **Applications, Permissions and Conditions (January 1988)**
Provides guidance on planning applications for minerals development, planning permissions and the imposition of planning conditions.

MPG3 **Coal Mining and Colliery Spoil Disposal (July 1994)**
Provides advice to mineral planning authorities and the coal industry on how to ensure that the development of coal resources

and the disposal of colliery spoil can take place at the best balance of social, environmental and economic cost, whilst ensuring that extraction and disposal are consistent with the principles of sustainable development.

MPG4   **The Review of Mineral Working Sites (September 1988)**
Provides guidance on the review of mineral working sites, including the compensation implications.

MPG5   **Minerals Planning and the General Development Order (December 1988)**
Provides guidance on those aspects of the General Development Order which are of special relevance to minerals interests.

MPG6   **Guidelines for Aggregates Provisions in England (April 1994)**
Provides advice to mineral planning authorities and the minerals industry on how to ensure that the construction industry continues to receive an adequate and steady supply of minerals at the best balance of social, environmental and economic costs, whilst ensuring that extraction and development are consistent with principles of sustainable development.

MPG7   **The Reclamation of Mineral Workings (August 1989)**
Gives advice on planning considerations, consultations and conditions which are relevant to the reclamation of mineral workings.

MPG8   **Planning and Compensation Act 1991: Interim Development Order Permissions (IDOs) — Statutory Provisions and Procedures (September 1991)**
Advises on the procedures to be followed in applying for registration of IDOs.

MPG9   **Planning and Compensation Act 1991: Interim Development Order Permissions (IDOs) — Conditions (March 1991)**
Gives guidance on the type of conditions to be applied to IDO permissions.

MPG10   **Provision of Raw Material for the Cement Industry (November 1991)**
Advises Mineral Planning Authorities and the industry on what needs to be done to ensure that there is an adequate and continuous supply of raw material to maintain production in a manner which has full regard to the environment.

MPG11   **Control of Noise at Surface Mineral Workings (April 1993)**
Advises mineral planning authorities and the mineral industry on how environmental performance can be improved by the control of noise from mineral operations.

MPG12   **Treatment of Disused Mine Openings and Availability of Information on Mined Ground (March 1994)**
Develops the guidance given in PPG14 on broad planning and technical issues in respect of unstable land with reference to problems caused by disused mine openings.

Regional Planning Guidance

RPG1   Strategic Guidance for Tyne and Wear (June 1989)
RPG2   Strategic Guidance for West Yorkshire (September 1989)
RPG3   Strategic Guidance for London (September 1989)
RPG4   Strategic Guidance for Greater Manchester (December 1989)
RPG5   Strategic Guidance for South Yorkshire (December 1989)
RPG6   Regional Planning Guidance for East Anglia (July 1991)
RPG7   Regional Planning Guidance for the Northern Region (September 1993)
RPG8   Regional Planning Guidance for the East Midlands Region (March 1994)
RPG9   Regional Planning Guidance for the South East Region (March 1994)

(Regional Planning Guidance has also been issued as PPGs; namely PPG10 and 11 (see above).)

The policy contained in Guidance Notes constitutes a material consideration which local planning authorities, and indeed the Secretary of State himself, must take into account in exercising their planning powers. This aspect is dealt with in Chapter 11.

Although Circulars containing the Secretary of State's views on the meaning and effect of new legislation are helpful to an understanding of the law, they are not authoritative interpretations of the law, since the courts are the only body with power to do this.

2.1.3 Judicial powers

Although as stated above, the interpretation of the law is a matter for the courts, the Secretary of State has power in specific situations to make preliminary determinations of law. In dealing with an appeal against an enforcement notice, for example, he may have to decide whether the activity enforced against is development and thus a breach of planning control. He also has power to determine whether or not a particular activity constitutes development in dealing with an appeal made to him against a determination made by a local planning authority as to whether or not a proposed activity would be lawful or on an appeal against an enforcement notice under s. 174, where the ground of appeal is that the matters in the notice do not constitute a breach of planning control. These matters are essentially matters of law, which the person affected and the local planning authority may either decide to accept or to challenge in the courts.

Although the occasions when the Secretary of State acts judicially may be few, he frequently has to act in a quasi-judicial capacity. It is now established law that in dealing with such matters as appeals from the decisions of local planning authorities, the Secretary of State is acting in a quasi-judicial capacity and thus bound to observe the rules of natural justice. These rules provide considerable procedural safeguards for the parties involved in the appeal and ensure that the parties are given what has been described by the House of Lords as a 'fair crack of the whip'. The matter is dealt with more fully in Chapter 17.

2.2 Local planning authorities

2.2.1 County planning authorities and district planning authorities
In most of England and Wales the powers conferred by the 1990 Act on the local planning authority are exercisable by two local authorities, namely by the county council as the county planning authority for their area and by the district council as the district planning authority for their area.

This dual responsibility for the exercise of planning powers in any area, however, does not occur in Greater London and the metropolitan areas. Following the abolition of the Greater London Council and the metropolitan county councils on 1 April 1986, the only local authorities with power to act as the local planning authority in those areas are the London boroughs and the metropolitan districts respectively.

The division of responsibility between the county planning authority and the district planning authority in areas outside Greater London and the metropolitan counties is discussed later.

2.2.2 Joint planning boards
In order to provide cohesion in the administration of planning functions over a wider area than that administered by a single county or district planning authority, s. 2 of the 1990 Act allows the Secretary of State to constitute a joint board as the county planning authority for the areas or parts of the areas of any two or more councils, or as the district planning authority for the areas or parts of the areas of any two or more districts. Under the section, such boards are bodies corporate, with perpetual succession and a common seal. Only two joint boards have so far been established, both covering national parks. They are the Lake District Special Planning Board and the Peak District Joint Planning Board. Both Boards act as the local planning authority for their particular areas, exercising both development plan and development control functions.

2.2.3 Urban development corporations
In addition to county councils, district and joint planning boards, a non-elected authority may be given power to act as a local planning authority for an area.

Under part XVI of the Local Government, Planning and Land Act 1980, the Secretary of State is empowered, subject to approval by both Houses of Parliament, to make orders designating urban development areas and to set up urban development corporations (UDCs) to secure the regeneration of those areas. So far, the criteria adopted for the selection of such areas have been the level of unemployment, the amount of derelict and vacant land and the extent to which public sector funds will lever private sector investment to regenerate the area. Under the Act, UDCs have general powers to acquire, hold, manage, reclaim and dispose of land, to carry out building and other operations and to provide services and infrastructure.

Under s. 149 of the 1980 Act, the Secretary of State may, by order, provide that a UDC shall be the local planning authority for the whole or any portion of its area, for such purposes of Part III of the 1971 Act (now Part III of the 1990 Act) (i.e., development control functions), and in relation to such kinds of development, as may be prescribed. Under s. 7(1) of the 1990 Act once such an order has been made, the UDC is to be the local planning authority for the area in place of any authority who would otherwise be the local planning authority for the area, in relation to such kinds of development as are specified in the order.

Under the 1980 Act, UDCs were set up for the dockland areas of Liverpool and London. In both cases, the development corporation was made the local planning authority for its area for the purposes of Part III of the 1971 Act. This arrangement led to some difficulty, since local authorities in the area continued to retain responsibility for the preparation of development plans. Such plans play a major part in the way in which development control functions are exercised under Part III. Conflict can easily arise (and has done so), where a development corporation's view of the action needed to secure regeneration of the area is different from the local authority's view of the policy needed to achieve that end. An example of the tension between a local authority and UDC can be seen in R v Secretary of State for the Environment, ex parte Southwark London Borough Council [1987] JPL 587.

It should also be noted that under s. 148 of the 1980 Act, a UDC may itself submit proposals to the Secretary of State for the development of land within the urban development area. The section further provides that where he approves such proposals, he may make a special development order granting planning permission for the development of land in accordance with those proposals. Where this is done, no application for planning permission needs to be made for the development in question.

Under the original provisions of the 1980 Act, a UDC could only be set up for land in a metropolitan district or inner London borough. This legislative barrier to the setting up of urban development corporations in non-metropolitan areas was removed by the Housing and Planning Act 1986. Now, in addition to the two dockland areas of Liverpool and London, UDCs have been set up in the Black Country, Greater Manchester (Trafford Park), Tyne and Wear, Teesside, Cardiff Bay, Central Manchester, Leeds, Sheffield, Bristol, Birmingham Heartlands and Plymouth.

It should be noted that there are important differences in the way UDCs operate. Unlike elected local authorities, they are not subject to the provision of the Local Government (Access to Information) Act 1985, so the public has fewer legal rights with respect to access to meetings, reports and documents of UDCs than they would otherwise have. One or two UDCs, however, have agreed agency arrangements with local authorities whereby the latter process and determine planning applications.

UDCs, unlike local authorities, are not accountable to the electorate. Members are appointed by the Secretary of State, and although some 'local authority' membership of a corporation is regarded as essential, the majority of members are drawn from the private sector. UDCs are, however, within the responsibilities of the Parliamentary Commissioner for Administration, and the Local Commissioner (for planning matters) and they are required to submit an Annual Report and Statement of Accounts to Parliament.

There are also differences between UDCs and local authorities with regard to compulsory purchase. Normally, local authorities acquiring land for development or redevelopment are able to support their case for confirmation of a compulsory purchase order with specific proposals for the land in question. The Secretary of State will normally expect to see a detailed land use plan supporting the acquisition. It is recognised, however, that in the special circumstances in which UDCs operate, it may not always be possible or desirable to make specific proposals beyond a general framework for the regeneration of the area, and the Secretary of State will have regard to those circumstances when required to confirm any compulsory purchase order. (See Circular No. 23/88.)

When a UDC is acquiring land, the normal rules for assessing compensation apply. But this includes the application of the notorious s. 6 of the Land Compensation Act 1961, which in effect provides that no account is to be taken of any increase in the value of the interest being acquired, where this is due to the scheme of the acquiring authority. Since the London Docklands UDC was created in 1981, property values have increased substantially. At risk from the operation of s. 6, therefore, is the landowner who bought land in, say, 1984, at a price which reflected the UDC's presence in the area, which is then compulsorily acquired by the UDC at a later date. Because of the operation of s. 6, the compensation paid for the land may not equal the price paid for the land in 1984 by the purchaser.

Unlike enterprise zones, no fixed life has been set for UDCs though it is expected that the UDCs at Bristol and Leeds will be wound up shortly, and the remainder (apart from Birmingham Heartlands and Plymouth) in the period from 1997 onwards.

2.2.4 The Urban Regeneration Agency

Part III of the Leasehold Reform, Housing and Urban Development Act 1993 establishes, as a body corporate, the Urban Regeneration Agency. The Agency's main object is to secure the regeneration of land in England which is suitable for regeneration and which is vacant or unused; in an urban area and underused or ineffectively used; or is contaminated, derelict, neglected or unsightly. The Agency is given wide powers, which include a power to acquire, hold, manage, reclaim, improve, develop, redevelop and dispose of land. Under s. 170 of the 1993 Act, the Secretary of State is given power to designate urban regeneration areas, which are intended to be similar to urban development areas designated under the Local Government, Planning and Land Act 1980 (see 2.2.3), save that the regeneration of the area will be carried out by the Urban Regeneration Agency rather than a specially created Urban Development Corporation. Where the Secretary of State has exercised his powers to make a designation order, the order may provide that the Agency shall be the local planning authority for the whole or any part of the designated area for such purposes of Part III of the 1990 Act and ss. 57 and 73 of the Planning

(Listed Buildings and Conservation Areas) Act 1990 as may be specified in the order; and in relation to such kinds of development as may be so specified. Under a new s. 8A of the 1990 Act, where a designation order transfers any of the planning functions mentioned above to the Agency, the body which would otherwise be the local planning authority for the area in question may no longer exercise those functions.

2.2.5 Enterprise zone authorities

Under s. 179 of and sch. 32 to the 1980 Act, the Secretary of State is given power to designate, by order, an area of land as an enterprise zone. Enterprise zones were originally conceived as experimental. The hope was that by removing certain tax burdens and by relaxing or speeding up a number of administrative controls, private sector industrial and commercial activity within the zones would be encouraged. In December 1987, it was announced that there would be no general extension of the enterprise zone experiment except in exceptional circumstances. Since then, however, a number of other enterprise zones have been designated. More recently, in March 1994, the Secretary of State announced that the European Community had accepted proposals for three new enterprise zones in East Durham, East Midlands and the Dearne Valley, and that he expected the zones to be designated in the autumn of 1994 once arrangements were in place to ensure EC restrictions applied on State aid to industry in the zones.

Schedule 32 provides that each enterprise zone should be administered by an enterprise zone authority. Furthermore, s. 6(1) of the 1990 Act provides that an order made under sch. 32 may provide that the enterprise zone authority shall be the local planning authority for the area for such purposes of the Planning Acts, and in relation to such kinds of development as may be prescribed by the order. The order may also provide that the enterprise zone authority shall be the local planning authority for the area covered by the scheme to the extent mentioned in the order, to the exclusion of the body which would otherwise be the local planning authority for the area. In most cases this terminology will be no more than a cosmetic necessity. Although an enterprise zone may have been prepared by a county council or urban development corporation, most have been prepared by the appropriate district councils.

Schedule 32 also provides that the designation order should specify the period for which the area is to remain an enterprise zone. So far all the designation orders have limited the life of the zone to 10 years from the date of the order. The following table gives the date of designation of each zone.

Name of enterprise zone	Date of designation
Belfast	21 August 1981
Clydebank (City of Glasgow)	18 August 1981
Clydebank District	3 August 1981
Corby	22 June 1981
Dale Lane and Kinsley (Wakefield)	23 September 1983
Delyn	21 July 1983
Dudley	10 July 1981

Name of enterprise zone	Date of designation
Dudley (Round Oak)	3 October 1984
Glanford (Flixborough)	13 April 1984
Hartlepool	23 October 1981
Inverclyde	3 March 1989
Invergordon	7 October 1983
Isle of Dogs	26 April 1982
Lanarkshire	1 February 1993
Langthwaite Grange (Wakefield)	31 July 1981
Londonderry	13 September 1983
Lower Swansea Valley	11 June 1981
Lower Swansea Valley (zone Number 2)	6 March 1985
Middlesbrough (Brittania)	8 November 1983
Milford Haven	24 April 1984
North East Lancashire	7 December 1983
North West Kent (zones Number 1-5)	31 October 1983
North West Kent (zones Number 6 and 7)	10 October 1986
Rotherham	16 August 1983
Salford Docks/Trafford Park	12 August 1981
Scunthorpe	23 September 1983
Speke (Liverpool)	25 August 1981
Sunderland	27 April 1990
Tayside	9 January 1984
Telford	13 January 1984
Tyneside	25 August 1981
Wakefield	23 September 1983
Wellingborough	26 July 1983
Workington (Allerdale)	4 October 1983

It will be seen that some of the first enterprise zones created no longer exist, and that the life of many others is now drawing to a close. According to the seventh annual report on enterprise zones published by the Department of the Environment in August 1993, 25 enterprise zones remain designated covering 3,623 hectares.

The benefits available to both new and existing industrial and commercial business located in an enterprise zone for the 10-year period are as follows:

(a)   Under sch. 32 to the 1980 Act, occupiers of industrial and commercial properties are exempt from liability to pay rates. Where property is used for both domestic and business purposes, the rateable value of the property is divided between the two elements and the business part is exempt.

(b)   Section 74 of the Finance Act 1980 applies and extends to enterprise zones the provisions of the Capital Allowances Act 1968 (now consolidated as the Capital Allowances Act 1990). The effect of this is to allow 100 per cent initial capital allowances for capital expenditure incurred in the construction, extension or improvement of industrial and commercial buildings or structures during the life of an enterprise zone; and for such expenditure incurred in the following 10 years under a contract entered into during the life of the zone.

(c)   The power of industrial training boards under s. 4 of the Employment and Training Act 1981 to impose an industrial training levy on employers does not extend to employers located in an enterprise zone.

(d)   Consideration by Customs and Excise of applications made for consent to the opening of a 'customs warehouse' within an enterprise zone are given priority. So too are applications for 'inward processing relief', a relief given from payment of customs and other duties on goods processed within the United Kingdom but imported from and then exported to countries outside the European Community.

As far as planning control is concerned, s. 82 of the 1990 Act provides that the adoption or approval of a simplified planning scheme has effect to grant in relation to the zone, planning permission for development specified in the scheme or for development of any class so specified. Hence an express application for planning permission is not necessary for such development. In England and Scotland, enterprise zone schemes grant planning permission for all development save that specified in the enterprise zone scheme. In Wales, however, the schemes specify only those types of development for which planning permission is given. Enterprise zones frequently have subzones. These are areas within the zone where the full range of planning permission granted by the scheme may not be appropriate, as where, for example, there is need to safeguard an area around an existing hazard or to protect the amenity of an adjacent residential area.

Enterprise zone schemes often exclude from the general grant of planning permission development where specific control remains necessary to protect health and safety and for the control of pollution. Hence an application for planning permission is normally required to be made for the construction of buildings or use of buildings or land in enterprise zones for the following purposes:

(a)   Special industrial uses listed in use classes V to IX (inclusive) of the schedule to the Town and Country Planning (Use Classes) Order 1972.

(b)   The storage, manufacture, processing and/or use of specified hazardous substances.

(c)   Factories, magazines and stores which require licensing under the Explosives Act 1875.

(d)   Any development or use which requires licensing under the Nuclear Installations Act 1965.

(e)   Storage, disposal, treatment or recycling of waste other than as a use ancillary to permitted development.

Various other types of development may be excluded from the general grant of planning permission in order to reflect the local circumstances within the individual scheme. These exclusions may include such things as scrapyards, mineral development, caravan sites, outdoor markets, fun-fairs, residential accommodation, shops over a certain size or buildings over a certain height.

Enterprise zone schemes granting planning permission may also specify conditions or limitations to which the permission is subject, as, for example, a condition requiring prior approval for the location of junctions on distributor roads, or the approval of design and landscaping for development on land forming the boundary of a subzone.

The relaxation of planning controls in enterprise zones applies only to removing the need to apply for express planning permission. There is no relaxation in the law relating to the protection of listed buildings or trees, nor to the statutory provisions governing the stopping up or diversion of highways, footpaths or bridleways.

There are two further aspects of enterprise zones which should be mentioned. First, since most of the zones were created, the Town and Country Planning (Assessment of Environmental Effects) Regulations 1988 (SI No. 1199) applying a European Community Directive, require environmental assessment to be carried out on certain development projects specified in the Schedules to the Regulations. Although the Regulations do not affect enterprise zones already created, should any new ones be created, the scheme would have to make specific provision to allow that process to be carried out, by omitting from the development for which planning permission is given, any development to which the Regulations apply.

Secondly, a problem could arise when an enterprise zone scheme comes to an end. The problem is that since planning permission is granted by the scheme, development commenced but not completed when the scheme comes to an end would cease to benefit from that planning permission. The 1990 Act seeks to overcome that difficulty by providing that where a scheme ceases to have effect, planning permission under it shall also cease to have effect except in a case where the development authorised by it has been begun. Under existing planning law, development can be begun by the mere digging of a trench. In such cases the local planning authority can use its powers to secure completion of the development by the service of a completion notice under s. 94 of the 1990 Act. The difficulty, however, is that outside enterprise zones, the development for which planning permission has been granted will be evidenced by documentary records, including the grant of express planning permission. Where planning permission has been granted by an enterprise zone scheme, however, no documentary evidence as to the precise form of development permitted by the scheme will be available, so that it may be difficult to determine whether or not that development has been completed.

2.2.6 Housing action trusts

Under s. 62 of the Housing Act 1988, the Secretary of State is given power to establish housing action trusts. The purpose of these trusts is to secure the improvement of local authority housing stock which may be transferred to them in their area, and then hand them over to other owners and managers. Under s. 67 of that Act, the Secretary of State may by order, provide that for such purposes of Part III of the 1990 Act (development control) and ss. 67 and

73 of the Planning (Listed Buildings and Conservation Areas) Act 1990 (publicity for applications for planning permission affecting the settings of listed buildings or conservation areas), and in relation to such kinds of development as may be specified in the order, a housing action trust shall be the local planning authority for the whole or part of its area.

Under s. 8 of the 1990 Act, where such an order is made, the trust shall be the local planning authority for such area, in place of any authority who would otherwise be the local planning authority for that area in relation to the development, as may be specified in the order.

2.2.7 Broads Authority
Under the Norfolk and Suffolk Broads Act 1988, a Broads Authority was established with a general duty to manage the Broads for the purposes of conserving and enhancing the natural beauty of the Broads; to promote the enjoyment of the Broads by the public; and to protect the interests of navigation. Under s. 5 of the 1990 Act, the Broads Authority is made a local planning authority for the Broads for certain limited purposes (mainly with regard to trees and rights of entry) and the sole district planning authority in relation to many other provisions of the Act such as those relating to the preparation of local plans and development control.

2.2.8 Division of planning powers between the county planning authority and the district planning authority
Bodies that may be a local planning authority within an area are thus county councils, district councils, joint planning boards, urban development corporations, enterprise zone authorities, housing action trusts and the Broads Authority. The main functions of local planning authorities are twofold; namely the preparation and maintenance of a development plan for their area, and development control, which includes such matters as the determination of applications for planning permission and the service of enforcement notices.

In those parts of the country where there is both a county planning authority and a district planning authority for an area, the basic scheme of the 1990 legislation is to distribute planning powers and functions in the area between the two main authorities in the following way.

2.2.8.1 Development plans

(a)   The county planning authority is required to prepare and maintain a structure plan for their area. In addition, the county planning authority, as the mineral planning authority for the county, is required to prepare a minerals local plan for their area. Furthermore, under a new provision introduced by the Planning and Compensation Act 1991, the county planning authority is required to prepare a waste local plan, either separately or as part of a joint waste and minerals local plan.

(b)   The district planning authority is required to prepare and maintain a local plan for their area.

2.2.8.2   Development control

(a)   The county planning authority are mainly responsible for development control functions within their area in respect of 'county matters'. County matters are defined in para. 1 of sch. 1 to the 1990 Act and include the winning and working of minerals and the operational development of land situated partly within and partly outside a national park. Within England, the development of land relating to the deposit of refuse or waste material is also a county matter (see the Town and Country Planning (Prescription of County Matters) Regulations 1980 (SI No. 2010)).

(b)   The district planning authority are mainly responsible for all other development control functions within their area. Development control includes not only the determination of applications for planning permission and related matters, but also the enforcement of planning control.

It will be seen that in the division of planning responsibility between the two tiers of local government, one of the most important tasks allocated to a county planning authority is the exercise of responsibility for minerals and mineral extraction. Because county planning authorities administer an area much larger than that administered by a district planning authority, the county is better able to make decisions about mineral extraction in a dispassionate way. Mineral extraction is a kind of development which no one is keen to have on his doorstep. The allocation of responsibility reflects the fact that the county planning authority are much less likely to be influenced by strong local objection to such development than would the district planning authority. Hence because of their role in this area, the county planning authority must prepare a minerals local plan for their area as well as exercise development control functions over mineral extraction.

Recent statistics show that 478,000 applications for planning permission were made to district planning authorities in England in 1993/94, as against 2,045 applications made to county planning authorities. Most of that number related to applications for mineral development and the deposit of waste. Not surprisingly, only about eleven per cent of applications determined by counties are done so within the statutory eight-week period.

2.2.9   Greater London and the metropolitan areas
From 1 April 1986, different arrangements exist with regard to the exercise of planning functions in Greater London and the metropolitan areas. Section 1 of the Local Government Act 1985 abolished on that date the Greater London Council and the metropolitan county councils. As a consequence the Act provides for the transfer of most functions previously exercised by the Greater London Council and the metropolitan county councils to the appropriate London borough or metropolitan district. Within the Greater London and metropolitan areas, therefore, the normal system of local planning administration involving a distribution of functions between county planning authorities and district planning authorities has been replaced by a unitary system, whereby the London boroughs and metropolitan districts exercise all the

functions of a local planning authority within their areas, subject only to the special arrangements for urban development corporations and enterprise zones.

The Local Government Act 1985 also introduced a new type of development plan, called a 'unitary development plan', to be prepared in those areas by the appropriate London borough or metropolitan district. This is dealt with fully in Chapter 4.

THREE
Simplified planning zones

3.1 The concept

The Housing and Planning Act 1986 gave local planning authorities power to designate simplified planning zones in their area. The power is now to be found in ss. 82 to 87 of the 1990 Act.

Simplified planning zones (SPZs) are an extension of the planning regime which has been pioneered in enterprise zones. By granting planning permission for development specified in the SPZ scheme, developers can know with certainty the precise type of development that can be carried out within the zone without having to make (and pay for) a planning application. This secures that the work and expense associated with the preparation, making, processing and determination of applications for planning permission are thereby saved.

SPZs cannot be set up in national parks, conservation areas, the Broads, areas of outstanding natural beauty, land identified in a development plan as part of a green belt or land forming part of an area of special scientific interest under s. 28 or 29 of the Wildlife and Countryside Act 1981.

Under s. 82 of the 1990 Act, an SPZ is an area in respect of which an SPZ scheme is in force. The adoption or approval of an SPZ scheme operates to grant in relation to the zone, or to any part of it specified in the scheme, planning permission for the development specified in the scheme or for the development of any class so specified. The section also provides that any planning permission granted under an SPZ scheme may be unconditional, or subject to such conditions, limitations or exceptions as may be specified in the scheme.

Schemes prepared under these provisions may be either general or specific. A general scheme will grant a general or wide permission for almost all types of development, but list exceptions where an application for planning permission will be required. A specific scheme will identify the specific type or types of development permitted and any limitations imposed. An application for planning permission would then have to be made for any development not specified in the scheme.

As with enterprise zone schemes, an SPZ scheme may include subzones, where the full range of planning permission available elsewhere in the zone may be curtailed. Examples of subzones might include health and safety subzones around hazardous installations or contaminated land, or where an SPZ adjoins a residential or other environmentally sensitive area. Most SPZs are likely to be designated in older urban areas where a stimulus is needed to promote regeneration of the area and to encourage economic activity.

3.2   Use of SPZ schemes

According to advice given by the Secretary of State, SPZs may be used in the following diverse circumstances:

(a)   Where a development plan makes provision for development in an area for the first time — for example, a new 'industrial park' — the development plan will establish the allocation of the land for development, leaving an SPZ scheme to grant planning permission to allow the development to take place.

(b)   Where an old industrial estate has become obsolete and needs to be replaced, an SPZ scheme can be drafted to permit a wide range of extensions, changes of use and redevelopment.

(c)   Where a large disused site, such as former railway sidings in a central location, can be used for mixed industrial, warehousing, commercial and retailing development, a general SPZ scheme could grant planning permission for the widest possible range of development.

(d)   Where a large tract of land in a single ownership is awaiting redevelopment, an SPZ scheme can be used to grant planning permission for one predominant use such as housing with local shops and community amenities or for mixed commercial development.

(e)   Where an area has been selected for large-scale residential development, an SPZ scheme can lay down broad objectives and essential design criteria, leaving freedom to the developer to decide such things as the exact mix of dwelling types, the layout, landscaping, elevation and choice of materials.

(f)   Where an authority have prepared a development brief for a particular site, setting out the kinds of development the authority would like to see take place, an SPZ scheme can be prepared granting planning permission for that development.

The Secretary of State also considers that SPZ schemes can be used in association with grants and incentives which are available to both the public and private sector to stimulate redevelopment and urban regeneration. These grants include City Grant and Derelict Land Grant.

These examples apart, the Secretary of State envisages SPZs as also being used to provide better coordination between development and the provision of supporting infrastructure, to assist in the refurbishment of old industrial areas, to enhance sales of underused publicly owned land and assist in the redevelopment and rehabilitation of inner city housing areas.

3.3   Duration of an SPZ scheme

Section 85 of the 1990 Act provides that an SPZ scheme shall take effect on the date of its adoption or approval and last for a period of 10 years from that date. At the end of that period the scheme, and the planning permission it grants, will cease to have effect. If, however, at the end of that period, development authorised by the permission has been begun, it may be completed. If it has been begun but completion is unreasonably delayed, the authority may serve a completion notice under the provisions of s. 94 of the 1990 Act. The provisions of s. 56 of the 1990 Act apply in determining when development authorised by an SPZ scheme has been begun. (These provisions are dealt with later in Chapter 13.)

3.4   Preparation of schemes

Section 83 of the 1990 Act provides that every local planning authority shall consider in which part or parts of their area it is desirable to create an SPZ scheme and to keep that question under review. If an authority do consider it desirable, they are then obliged to make a scheme.

So far, only a few simplified planning schemes have been adopted. The first was in Derby and covered 18 acres of derelict land one mile south of the city centre and adjacent to Derby County Football ground to provide over 300,000 sq. ft. of industrial and office space accommodating several hundred jobs. The scheme grants planning permission for the erection of buildings and use of land for Business, General Industrial and Storage or Distribution uses (covered respectively by Classes B1, B2 and B8 of the Use Classes Order). The permission granted is subject to a number of conditions. Within the zone there are a number of subzones, where the full range of permission granted elsewhere in the zone is restricted.

The second simplified planning zone was designated for Willowbrook, Corby, by the Corby District Council. The scheme grants planning permission for General Industrial and Storage and Distribution uses (covered respectively by Classes B2 and B8 of the Use Classes Order). As with the Derby zone scheme, the permission granted is subject to conditions (e.g., re vehicular access, height of buildings, etc.) and contains a subzone where permission is granted for Business use and for no other purpose.

According to a consultation paper issued by the government in August 1990, there were then only three adopted SPZ schemes in England and Wales, though a number of others were being actively pursued. By the end of December 1992, only six had been adopted, three in England and three in Scotland. The consultation paper issued in August 1990 claimed that research had shown that procedures for creating SPZ schemes were widely perceived as being cumbersome and time-consuming and that this may have dissuaded some authorities and developers from embarking on their preparation. The paper proposed, therefore, that the procedures for the adoption of an SPZ should be streamlined.

Prior to the Planning and Compensation Act 1991, the procedure for the preparation and adoption of SPZ schemes was similar to that required for local plans and unitary development plans. The procedure was dealt with in sch. 7 to the 1990 Act and regulations made thereunder.

As a result of criticism in the consultation paper of the procedures involved in the preparation and adoption of SPZs, the Planning and Compensation Act 1991 made a number of modifications to the statutory provisions by amending sch. 7 to the 1990 Act. In addition, a new set of regulations, the Town and Country Planning (Simplified Planning Zones) Regulations 1992 (No. 2414), now supplements the 1990 primary legislation. In brief the procedure now requires: .

(a)   the local planning authority keeping under review the desirability of creating SPZs in their area;

(b)   where the authority propose to make or allow a scheme, the authority consulting specified persons and bodies (reg. 3);

(c)   the authority making copies of the proposal available for inspection and giving notice of it in the prescribed form (reg. 4);

(d)   an opportunity being given for objections to be made in writing to the local planning authority (reg. 5);

(e)   the consideration of objections, which may be by way of local inquiry or other hearing (reg. 7);

(f)   the consideration by the authority of the report of the person appointed to hold the inquiry or hearing, where an inquiry or hearing has been held (reg. 8);

(g)   if no inquiry or hearing has been held the consideration of objections by the authority (reg. 9);

(h)   the preparation of a statement by the authority of the decision reached following (f) or (g) above, and of the reasons for the decision (regs 8 and 9);

(i)   the adoption by the local planning authority of the authority's proposals and the giving of requisite notice of so doing (reg. 11).

Unlike the procedures for local plans and unitary development plans, anyone can request a local planning authority to make or alter an SPZ scheme. If the authority are requested to do so but refuse, or do not decide to do so within three months, that person may require the authority to refer the matter to the Secretary of State. The Secretary of State may then direct the authority to make or alter a scheme.

As with development plans, the Secretary of State may direct the authority preparing a scheme to consider modifying it. He also has the power to direct the authority to submit the scheme to him for his approval.

FOUR
Development plans

4.1 Introduction

Development plans play a vital part in the system for the control of development. They constitute the main backcloth against which applications for planning permission are determined and decisions are made on whether or not to issue an enforcement notice to terminate unauthorised development. The strength of the development plan system is that it ensures that there is both a rational and a consistent basis for making those decisions.

It should be emphasised that development plans are not prescriptive. They act only as a guide to the way in which development control functions are exercised. They do not, for example, guarantee that an application for planning permission for development which conforms with the provisions of the development plan for an area will necessarily be granted.

Development plans have a further but more limited purpose, namely the coordination of those functions which influence the scale, location and timing of the development or redevelopment of land, particularly with regard to the extent and availability of the necessary infrastructure.

Although the primary purpose of development plans has remained constant from the first moment an obligation was placed on all local planning authorities to prepare them following the Town and Country Planning Act 1947, the form and content of development plans has undergone considerable change. There are in fact three different types of development plan system, each of which may influence the way in which development control functions under the 1990 Act are exercised. The three types are:

(a)   Development plans prepared under provisions contained originally in the Town and Country Planning Act 1947, and now colloquially referred to as 'old-style' development plans.

(b)   Development plans prepared under provisions contained originally in the Town and Country Planning Act 1968, and now colloquially referred to as 'new-style' development plans.

(c)   Unitary development plans prepared under the provisions of the Local Government Act 1985, following the dissolution of the Greater London Council and the Metropolitan County Councils in April 1986.

4.2   Old-style development plans

The Town and Country Planning Act 1947 provided that as soon as may be after the appointed day (1 July 1948), each local planning authority should carry out a survey of their area and, within three years, or such extended period as the Minister might allow, submit to him a report of the survey together with a development plan for their area. The purpose of the survey was to assemble and collate information about the area to form the basis for the preparation of the authority's plan for that area.

The purpose of the old-style development plan was to indicate the manner in which the local planning authority proposed that land in their area should be used, whether by the carrying out thereon of development or otherwise, and the stages by which such development should be carried out. In addition, the Act provided that a plan might in particular define the sites of proposed roads, public and other buildings and works, airfields, parks, pleasure grounds, nature reserves and open spaces, or allocate areas of land for use for agricultural, residential, industrial or other purposes of any class specified in the plan. The development plan could also define as an area of comprehensive development, an area which in the opinion of the authority should be developed as a whole for the purposes of dealing with extensive war damage, bad lay-out, or obsolete development, or for the purpose of relocating population or industry or replacing open space in the course of the development or redevelopment of an area. The statutory basis for the continuing but declining authority of old-style development plans is now to be found in sch. 2 to the 1990 Act.

The 1947 Act recognised the ever-changing nature of land use planning by imposing on each local planning authority a duty, once in every five years, to carry out a fresh survey of their area, and to submit to the Secretary of State a report of the survey, together with proposals for any alterations or additions to the plan which appeared to them to be required. Following the decision made in 1968, however, to concentrate resources on preparing the new-style development plans rather than on updating the old, the law was amended to provide that proposals for altering or adding to the old-style development plans should not be made without the approval of the Secretary of State.

4.2.1   Content, form and procedure
The form and content of the old-style development plan were largely determined by regulations made under the 1947 Act. The appropriate Regulations provided that the plan was to consist of a basic map (drawn to a specified scale) and a written statement which would include a summary of the plan's main proposals and the stages by which any development proposed therein was to be carried out. In addition, the plan could include such other maps as the authority considered appropriate. As regards the procedure for the

plan's preparation and approval, local planning authorities were required by the Act to consult with any district council within their area before they prepared a development plan, and to give the district council an opportunity to make representations to them before the plan was submitted to the Minister for his approval. There was no requirement at this stage that the local planning authority should consult with other bodies or persons on any matter which the authority proposed should be included in the plan.

On the submission of the development plan by the local planning authority to the Minister, the authority were required to give public notice of that fact by advertisement in the *London Gazette* and in at least one newspaper circulating in the area concerned. Members of the public then were given an opportunity to object or make representations to the Minister about its content. Thereafter the Minister was required to hold a local inquiry or other hearing before deciding whether he should approve the plan, which he could do either with or without modification.

4.2.2 Defects of the old-style development plan system

By the mid 1960s, it had become clear that the development plan system established under the 1947 Act was failing to meet current needs. One of the main difficulties was that the content of the old-style development plans had been based on the two assumptions: that the population would remain stable and that there would be little growth in the volume of motor traffic. In fact, both these assumptions proved to be false. An increase in the population which followed the end of the Second World War had led to an increase in the demand for hospitals, schools and housing. An increase in the standard of living in the same period had led to an increase in the number of motor vehicles using the roads, to a need for investment in a new road programme to accommodate those vehicles, and thus to the growth of development pressure on land where it had never previously existed. In theory at least, it should have been possible for the old-style development plans to be amended to accommodate the changes that were then taking place. In practice, however, this proved to be impossible because of the rapid pace of change and the law's requirement that the same administrative procedures be followed for proposals to amend development plans as were required for their original preparation.

In addition, however, the old-style development plans had a further and more fundamental defect. The plans concentrated on land use, and did so in excessive detail. The concentration took place at the expense of many other factors which help to shape the environment but also require to be integrated into land use planning, such as national investment programmes and social and economic objectives. Indeed, in retrospect it seems unlikely that a single document would ever be able to perform both functions adequately.

Against this background, in 1964 the Government set up a Planning Advisory Group comprising officers of local government, the professions and departments concerned to advise it on the future of the development plan system. Its report, *The Future of Development Plans*, published in 1965, recommended the gradual adoption of a new 'two-tier' development plan system. Most of the report's recommendations were given effect in the Town and Country Planning Act 1968; and later consolidated, first in the Town and Country Planning Act 1971, and now in the 1990 Act.

4.3 New-style development plans

The statutory provisions relating to the two-tier development plan system which was introduced into the law by the Town and Country Planning Act 1968 are now to be found in Part II of the 1990 Act and the associated Town and Country Planning (Development Plan) Regulations 1991 (SI No. 2794) (the Development Plan Regulations). The essence of the system is the creation of a single development plan for an area having two tiers, namely, a structure plan tier and a local plan tier, with each tier performing a different but related function.

The purpose of the structure plan tier of the development plan is to sketch general lines of development in an area with a broad brush. Basically, structure plans are concerned with land use, but deal with it in terms of policies applicable to the major land uses such as employment, housing, education and recreation, and, in particular, transport policy and lines of communication within the area and in relation to neighbouring areas. Structure plans set out policies and proposals of structural or strategic importance for an area. They also provide important links between national economic and social planning and local land use planning. Because structure plans deal with policies and proposals for a wide area in very general terms, they do not deal with individual properties or show the precise boundaries of areas where particular policies apply.

Local plans, on the other hand, are much more detailed than their parent structure plan. They deal with local issues, but within the context of the policies set out in the structure plan. They develop and apply the policies of the structure plan in force for the area, and show how these policies relate to precisely defined areas of land. Local plans, where they are in force, also provide the basis for the exercise of a local planning authority's development control functions. In addition, by allocating sites for particular purposes, they can form the basis on which the development or redevelopment of an area can proceed.

Originally, three types of local plan were envisaged:

(a) *District plans.* These plans varied widely in the size of the area they covered. Their purpose was to deal with the comprehensive planning of areas where change was likely to take place in a piecemeal fashion over a long period of time. Although this type of plan was identified by name in the first set of regulations that were made dealing with the new-style development plan system, later regulations contained no such reference. Such plans became merely local plans.

(b) *Subject plans.* These plans dealt with a particular land use issue arising in an area. Typically, subject plans might deal with such matters as mineral extraction, derelict land reclamation or recreational facilities in rural areas.

(c) *Action area plans.* The original legislation provided that a local planning authority's general proposals contained in a structure plan should indicate any part of the area covered by the plan (which it described as an action area), which the authority had selected, for commencement during a prescribed period, for comprehensive treatment, in accordance with a local plan prepared for the selected area as a whole, by development, redevelopment or improvement of the whole or part of the area selected. Under earlier regulations, a local plan prepared for an action area was to be known as an action area local plan. The purpose behind the requirement that action areas be indicated in the structure plan was to give early notice to developers and others that an area had been selected for rapid and intense change by way of development, redevelopment or improvement. Under the Local Government, Planning and Land Act 1980, however, the obligation to indicate action areas in a structure plan was abandoned in respect of all structure plans approved or amended after 13 November 1980. Thereafter, until special types of local plan were abolished by the Planning and Compensation Act 1991, an action area plan could be prepared by a local planning authority without any earlier indication in a structure plan that they would be doing so. Now, under the latest statutory provisions, a local plan may 'designate' any part of the authority's area as an action area which they have selected for comprehensive treatment by development, redevelopment or improvement during a prescribed period. An action area is thus to be part of the local plan for the area but without its own specific plan.

The 'new-style' development plan system created in 1968 envisaged that whereas the whole of the area of a local planning authority would be covered by one or more structure plans, local plans would not necessarily cover the whole of the area covered by a structure plan. Under the relevant provisions of the Act, the district planning authority was required merely to keep under review the need for, and adequacy of, local plans for their area.

On the other hand, different types of local plan could be prepared for the same area. Nothing in the legislation, it seemed, prohibited the preparation of, say, both a district plan and a subject plan for the same area. Indeed, the 1990 Act specifically provided that different local plans could be prepared for different purposes for the same area.

4.4   Defects of the new-style development plan system

Although work had begun in 1971 on the preparation of the first structure plans, it was not until 1985, some 14 years later, that all the 82 'first-generation' structure plans which were to cover England and Wales had been approved. Subsequently, local planning authorities have been engaged in preparing for the Secretary of State's approval alterations to these structure plans; and in a few cases, their complete replacement.

According to a consultation paper issued by the Department of the Environment in 1986, one of the main reasons for the slowness in preparing and approving structure plan proposals was that many of the written statements and explanatory memoranda were much longer than they actually needed to be.

In the first round of approved structure plans, several of the plans contained more than 100,000 words of policies and explanatory material. Many of them were also found to contain an inordinately large number of 'policies'; typically more than 100, but in one case 250. Overall, most of the structure plans submitted for approval contained development control policies of excessive length, leading to many modifications having to be made by the Secretary of State.

A second difficulty causing delay in the preparation and approval of structure plans was a widespread tendency for some local planning authorities to include policies in them that had little or nothing to do with land use planning or the physical environment. Examples of irrelevant policies in structure plans submitted for approval included those relating to building design standards, storage of cycles, the development of cooperatives, racial or sexual disadvantage, standards of highway maintenance, parking charges, the location of picnic sites and so-called 'nuclear-free zones'. In all these cases, approval by the Secretary of State was delayed by the need to delete or modify these proposals from the submitted structure plan.

As far as local plans are concerned, the consultation paper said that, by March 1986, only 474 local plans had been adopted. These comprised 315 district plans, 42 subject plans and 37 action area plans. The average time between the deposit and the adoption of local plans was about 20 months. Although the Secretary of State regarded many local plans as too detailed and containing policies unrelated to the purposes of development plans, the main reason for delay in the adoption of local plans was seen as the length and complexity of the procedures for preparing them and the relationship between local plans and structure plans. Unless the Secretary of State had directed that an expedited procedure be used, local plans could not be adopted until the relevant structure plan policies have been approved or altered.

The defects of the new-style development plan system led local planning authorities to begin to rely on non-statutory plans and policies to guide development in their areas, rather than take the formal steps of altering an existing development plan or preparing a new one. The result was that the public were denied the right to object to these plans and policies as they were not subject to the rigours of an independent examination in public, or to a public local inquiry.

The consultation paper proposed, therefore, the abolition of structure plans and the creation of a new single-tier development plan to be prepared by each district council for the whole of their area, in a form similar to local plans. Although there are a number of important differences, the proposals were similar to the new system of unitary development plans introduced for Greater London and the metropolitan areas of England by the Local Government Act 1985.

The proposals were carried forward a step further with the publication in January 1989 of a White Paper, *The Future of Development Plans* (Cm 969). The White Paper envisaged a wider role for regional planning guidance, and contained proposals, since abandoned, that the present system of structure and local plans be replaced by statements of county planning policies and district development plans. In this way it was hoped to provide a clearer policy framework for local planning decisions; to simplify and speed up the preparation and review of plans; and to define the responsibilities of counties and districts more clearly.

Soon after, because many of the proposals in the White Paper required legislation, the government issued planning policy guidance intended to advance proposals which could be implemented administratively and without legislation. These included:

(a) Greater coverage of regional planning guidance by the Secretary of State.

(b) Retaining structure plans but bringing forward alterations and replacements of structure plans where these plans were seriously out of date, in parallel with the new regional guidance.

(c) Replacing structure plans which cover only part of a county area with a single concise structure plan covering a whole county.

(d) Restricting the scope of future structure plans by ensuring they concentrate only on key land issues. Structure plans it was thought, should contain policies on new housing, green belts and conservation, the rural economy, major industrial, office, retail and other employment-generating development, strategic highway and other transport facilities, mineral working, waste disposal, and tourism, leisure and recreation.

(e) Avoiding at the planning application or appeal stage, a re-examination of the merits of stated policies set out in regional guidance and structure plans.

4.5 Changes to the new-style development plan system

The government eventually decided upon the major legislative changes needed to the development plan system, which it introduced in the Planning and Compensation Act 1991. The legislative basis of the new-style development plan system in Part II of the 1990 Act, has now been amended by ss. 26 and 27 of the 1991 Act. The main changes are as follows.

4.5.1 Structure plans

County councils are required to prepare (where they have not already done so) a *single* structure plan to cover the whole of their area. Under the old provisions of the 1990 Act, local planning authorities were able, with the consent of the Secretary of State, to prepare a structure plan for part of their area. This has meant that a number of authorities now have more than one structure plan covering their area. The Planning and Compensation Act 1991 introduces a new subsection (7) into s. 31 of the 1990 Act, requiring authorities in that position to prepare proposals for a single replacement structure plan to cover the whole of the authority's area.

County councils are now allowed to adopt their own structure plans instead of having to refer them (as in the past) to the Secretary of State for his approval. Under the old provisions of the 1990 Act, structure plans prepared by county planning authorities or a joint or special planning board were required to be approved by the Secretary of State. The 1991 Act introduces new ss. 32 to 35C into the 1990 Act to allow proposals for the alteration or replacement of structure plans to be adopted by the authorities who prepared them. The new sections also deal with the procedures to be followed by authorities in preparing their structure plans, in considering objections to them and, if necessary, holding an examination in public, before the plans are finally adopted.

Many of the provisions in the new ss. 32 to 35C of the 1990 Act rewrite previous provisions found in the Act, but adapted to reflect the new powers of county planning authorities and joint or special planning boards to adopt their own proposals. However, the new sections also contain new provisions to ensure that the Secretary of State has the necessary powers to ensure the proper discharge of his responsibilities to Parliament for the framing and execution of a national land use policy. In particular the following changes should be noted:

(a)   The Secretary of State may by regulation prescribe the particular land use matters with which the general policies and proposals in a structure plan are to be exclusively concerned (new s. 31(4)). Such regulations may make different provisions for different cases and shall be subject to any direction given in a particular case by the Secretary of State (new s.31(9)).

(b)   In formulating the general policies to be included in a structure plan, the relevant authority is required to have regard to specified matters including 'any regional or strategic planning guidance given by the Secretary of State to assist them in their preparation of their plan' (new s. 31(6)(a)).

(c)   An authority wishing to prepare proposals for the alteration or replacement of a structure plan which the Secretary of State has previously called in and approved, in whole or in part, must first obtain the consent of the Secretary of State to do so (new s. 32(3)).

(d)   Under the old provisions of the 1990 Act, a local planning authority preparing proposals for the alteration or replacement of a structure plan for its area, was required to take steps to ensure that adequate publicity was given to those proposals. Under the 1991 Act, that requirement has been removed from the body of the 1990 Act. Instead, the local planning authority must comply with any requirements imposed by regulations made by the Secretary of State under s. 53 of the 1990 Act (new s. 33(1)). The effect of this change is to take the provisions relating to the 'pre-plan public participation process' out of the primary legislation and allow it to be dealt with in secondary legislation. The regulations which have been made re-enact the main provisions previously found in the 1990 Act, but subject to modification aimed at reducing the amount of publicity given to proposals at that stage and allowing local planning authorities greater flexibility to decide on the appropriate level of publicity and consultation required.

(e)   Because the Secretary of State is no longer required to approve an alteration or replacement of a structure plan, he is given an express right to object to such proposals, so long as he does so in accordance with the relevant regulations (new s. 33(5)).

(f)   The Secretary of State is given power at any time during the period between the sending to him of a copy of the authority's proposals and their adoption, to direct the local planning authority to modify its proposals in such respects as are indicated in the direction (new s. 35(2)). This provision was already available to the Secretary of State with regard to local plans and unitary development plans.

(g) The Secretary of State is given power at any time during the period between the sending to him of a copy of the authority's proposals and their adoption, to direct that all or any part of the proposals shall be submitted to him for his approval (new s. 35A(1)). The effect of such a direction is to prevent the local planning authority taking any further steps for the adoption of any of the proposals until the Secretary of State has given his decision on the proposals or the relevant part of the proposals (new s. 35A(2)(a)). Furthermore, once called in, the proposals or the relevant part of the proposals are not to have effect unless approved by the Secretary of State (new s. 35A(2)(b)). Having called in the proposals for his own decision, the Secretary of State may reject the proposals or approve them in whole or in part and with or without modifications or reservations (new s. 35A(4)).

(h) The new provisions require a local planning authority to hold an examination in public into any matter affecting their consideration of proposals to alter or replace a structure plan which they consider 'ought to be examined'. The power is similar to that given to the Secretary of State under the old provisions of the 1990 Act. However, because of the power now given to county planning authorities and joint and special planning boards to adopt their own structure plan proposals, the Secretary of State is empowered to direct a local planning authority to cause an examination in public to be held into those matters affecting their structure plan proposals which are specified in the direction (new s. 35B(1)). Similarly, if the Secretary of State calls in structure plan proposals for his own decision, he is given the power to hold an examination in public into such matters as he specifies (new s. 35B(2)). As in the past any examination in public, whether held at the behest of the Secretary of State or the local planning authority, is to be conducted by a person or persons appointed by the Secretary of State (new s. 35B(3)). Where the local planning authority hold an examination in public into matters affecting their proposals, the person or persons conducting the examination will make a report to the authority, who must then consider the report and decide what action to take, if any, on the report's recommendations.

As with the old procedures, no one has a right to be heard at an examination in public. Attendance depends upon an invitation. Under the new provisions, however, the local planning authority have the power to invite any person to take part in the examination, subject, of course, to the overriding right of the person conducting the examination to invite additional participants to take part. Where, however, the examination in public follows the call-in of structure plan proposals by the Secretary of State the power to invite any person to take part in the examination in public lies with the Secretary of State, not with the local planning authority (new s. 35B(5)).

(i) The Secretary of State is given a new power, exercisable after consultation with the Lord Chancellor, to make regulations with respect to the procedure to be followed at any examination in public (new s.35B(6)).

4.5.2   Local plans

Every local planning authority in a non-metropolitan area must now prepare a *single* local plan covering the whole of their administration area (new s. 36(1)). Previously, local planning authorities had a power, but not a duty to prepare local plans. As stated earlier, this discretionary element led to local planning authorities relying on non-statutory local plans when making development control decisions, rather than submit their detailed policies to the time-consuming process of the formal adoption procedures required by the Act.

Under the old law, a 'local plan scheme', prepared by the county planning authority in consultation with the district planning authority, determined which authority were to be responsible for preparing any particular local plan. Because of the duty now placed upon district planning authorities to prepare districtwide local plans, the provisions relating to the preparation of local plan schemes have now been repealed.

The basic relationship between a structure plan and a local plan is to remain the same. Hence the statute continues to provide that 'a local plan shall be in general conformity with the structure plan' (new s. 36(4)). Similarly, the statute contains provisions whereby the county planning authority may issue a certificate of conformity. However, it is now provided that the county planning authority must supply the district planning authority with either a statement that the local plan or the proposals are in general conformity with the structure plan, or a statement that they are not in such conformity (new s. 46(2)). Where a statement of non-conformity is given, the 1990 Act now provides that it shall be treated by the district planning authority as an objection made to the provisions of the local plan (new s. 46(4)).

As previously indicated, under the old law, a separate local plan (called an action area plan) could be made in respect of any area of land identified by the local planning authority as an action area. Now, however, the 1990 Act provides that the local plan may designate any part of the authority's area as an action area. If an action area is so designated, the local plan must contain a description of the treatment proposed by the authority for that area (new s. 36(7) and (8)). This means that in future there will be no more local plans prepared specifically for action areas.

Under the old law, policies for the mining and working of minerals were contained within local plans or in a specific type of local plan called a subject plan. Under amendments made by the Planning and Compensation Act 1991, it becomes the duty of the mineral planning authority to prepare a plan, to be known as a 'minerals local plan' for its area, formulating the authority's detailed policies for its area in respect of the winning and working of minerals or the deposit of mineral waste (new s. 37(1) and (2) of the 1990 Act). Since the mineral planning authority for an area in non-metropolitan areas is the county planning authority, minerals local plans will in future be 'county-wide' plans, covering the whole of the administrative area of the county.

As with the procedure for the alteration or replacement of a structure plan, a local planning authority, in preparing a local plan, is required to take steps to ensure that adequate publicity is given to its proposals. As with the new regime relating to structure plan proposals, the 1991 Act removes that obligation from the body of the 1990 Act. Instead, the local planning authority must now comply with any requirement imposed by regulations made by the Secretary of State under s. 53 of the 1990 Act (new s. 40(1)). Regulations now made re-enact the main provisions previously found in the 1990 Act but subject to modifications aimed at reducing the amount of publicity given to proposals at that stage and by allowing local planning authorities greater flexibility to decide on the appropriate level of publicity and consultation required.

4.6   Structure plans (the new provisions)

4.6.1   The survey
As with the old-style development plans, the new-style development plans are based upon a survey. Section 30 of the 1990 Act provides that a local planning authority shall keep under review the matters which may be expected to affect the development of their area or the planning of its development; and may, if they think fit, at any time institute a fresh survey of their area examining those matters. Section 30 indicates a number of particular matters the authority are required to examine and keep under review. These include:

(a)   The principal physical and economic characteristics of the area of the authority and, so far as they may be expected to affect that area, of any neighbouring areas.

(b)   The size, composition and distribution of the population of that area.

(c)   The communications, transport system and traffic of that area and, so far as may be expected to affect that area, of any neighbouring area.

(d)   Such other matters as may be prescribed or as the Secretary of State may in a particular case direct.

In addition, the Secretary of State may prescribe or direct particular matters to be surveyed, though no such prescriptions or directions are currently in force.

Originally it was necessary for the local planning authority to prepare a report of the survey and to publish the report at the same time as the authority were giving publicity to the matters they proposed to include in a structure or local plan. The report was also required to be sent to the Secretary of State with any structure plan sent to him for approval. In the view of the Secretary of State, those requirements led to work at the survey stage being over-elaborate. Accordingly, there is now no obligation on an authority to prepare a report of any fresh survey they may carry out or to publish it or send it to the Secretary of State.

4.6.2   Continuity, form and content
Section 31(1) of the 1990 Act provides that each structure plan approved by the Secretary of State under the Town and Country Planning Act 1971 shall continue in force after the commencement of the 1990 Act. Since the whole of the country is now covered by approved structure plans, the provisions that follow are mainly applicable to proposals to alter an approved plan, or

proposals for replacement of a plan. Indeed, s. 32 of the 1990 Act provides that a local planning authority may at any time prepare proposals for the alteration to the structure plan for their area, or for its replacement. An authority may not, however, without the consent of the Secretary of State, prepare proposals in respect of a structure plan if the plan or any part of the plan has been approved by the Secretary of State following a direction from him (under s. 35A of the 1990 Act) that the proposals be submitted to him for approval. In addition, the Secretary of State is given power to direct an authority to prepare proposals for the alteration or replacement of a structure plan within a specified period.

Note that s. 31(7) provides that where there is a structure plan relating to part of the area of the local planning authority, the authority shall, within such period (if any) as the Secretary of State may direct, prepare proposals for replacing those structure plans with a single structure plan relating to the whole of their area.

The content and form of a structure plan are determined by its function, and broad policies and proposals are best described in words. Hence s. 31(2) of the 1990 Act provides that:

A structure plan shall contain a written statement formulating the authority's general policies in respect of the development and use of land in their area.

In addition s. 31(3) of the 1990 Act requires a structure plan to include policies and proposals in respect of:

(a) the conservation of the natural beauty and amenity of the land;
(b) the improvement of the physical environment; and
(c) the management of traffic.

In formulating their general policies for inclusion in the plan, s. 31(6) requires authorities to have regard to:

(a) any regional or strategic guidance given by the Secretary of State;
(b) current national policies;
(c) the resources likely to be available; and
(d) such other matters as the Secretary of State may prescribe or direct.

In addition, in formulating their general policies, the Town and Country Planning (Development Plan) Regulations 1991 (the 'Development Plan Regulations') require authorities to have regard to:

(a) social and economic considerations;
(b) environmental considerations; and
(c) any policies and proposals of an urban development corporation which affect, or may be expected to affect, their area.

Although the form of the structure plan is a written statement, s. 31(5) of the 1990 Act provides that the structure plan should also contain such diagrams, illustrations or other descriptive or explanatory matter in respect of the general policies and proposals as may be prescribed; and such other matters as the Secretary of State may, in any particular case, direct. The Development Plan Regulations provide that a structure plan shall contain a diagram, called a key diagram, illustrating the general policies formulated in the plan's written statement. The Development Plan Regulations go on to provide that a structure plan may also contain an inset diagram, drawn to a larger scale than the key diagram, illustrating the application of the general policies to part of the area covered by the structure plan. It is significant that the regulations go on to provide that no key diagram or inset diagram contained in a structure plan 'shall be on a map base'. This provision thus helps to prevent the identification on a structure plan of any particular parcel of land.

Under s. 32(5) of the 1990 Act, any proposals for the alteration or replacement of a structure plan must be accompanied by an explanatory memorandum. This explanatory memorandum must summarise the reasons which in the opinion of the local planning authority justify each of their proposals; any information on which the proposals are based; the relationship of the proposals to general policies for the development and use of neighbouring land which may be expected to affect the area to which the proposals relate; and may contain such illustrative material as the authority think appropriate.

The explanatory memorandum is not a part of the structure plan though a copy has to be made available for inspection by the public along with the authority's proposals for the alteration or replacement of a structure plan; and a copy has to be sent to the Secretary of State along with the authority's proposals. Moreover, it was held in *Holden v Secretary of State for the Environment* [1994] JPL B1 that the explanatory memorandum does not form part of the relevant development plan for the purposes of s. 54A of the 1990 Act (see later).

4.6.3 Preparation and approval

4.6.3.1 Predeposit consultation Under the system for the preparation of old-style development plans, the local planning authority were required to consult only with district councils in their area about the content of the plan before submitting it to the Minister for his approval. By 1968, however, it was thought that the public and others should be able to influence the content of the development plan before the authority had become committed to any specific solution to the planning problems of their area, and before they took formal action to secure the plan's approval. The provisions relating to the preparation of the new-style development plans reflect this approach.

Section 33(1) of the 1990 Act now provides:

When preparing proposals for the alteration or replacement of a structure plan for their area and before finally determining their contents the local planning authority shall—

    (a) comply with—
       (i) any requirements imposed by regulations made under section 53; and

(ii)   any particular direction given to them by the Secretary of State with respect to a matter falling within any of paragraphs (a) to (c) or (e) of subsection (2) of that section; and

(b)   consider any representations made in accordance with those regulations.

Regulation 10 of the Development Plan Regulations provides that:

(1)   When preparing proposals for a statutory plan or for the alteration or replacement of such a plan, . . . and before finally determining the contents of the proposals, the local planning authority shall consult—

(a)   the Secretary of State for the Environment and the Secretary of State for Transport, in England, or the Secretary of State for Wales, in Wales;

(b)   any other local planning authority for the area covered by the proposals;

(c)   any local planning authority for an area adjacent to the area covered by the proposals;

(d)   except in the case of structure plan proposals, the council of any parish or community for the area covered by the proposals;

(e)   the National Rivers Authority;

(f)   the Countryside Commission and the Nature Conservancy Council for England, in England, or the Countryside Council for Wales, in Wales;

(g)   the Historic Buildings and Monuments Commission for England, in England.

(2)   The local planning authority shall consider any representations made by the consultees before finally determining the contents of the proposals.

(3)   The local planning authority shall prepare a statement of any other persons they have consulted when preparing their proposals, in addition to those listed in paragraph (1), and of any steps they have taken to publicise their proposals and to provide persons with an opportunity of making representations in respect of those proposals.

It will be seen that in addition to the list of prescribed consultees in reg. 10(1), local planning authorities are also given a discretion to consult others. The view taken by the government is that authorities should use their judgment to determine what degree of publicity and consultation is appropriate, so allowing them flexibility to tailor their approach according to circumstances. Clearly proposals for a replacement structure plan may warrant wider publicity and consultation than proposals for a relatively minor alteration to an existing plan. Nevertheless, local planning authorities will be expected to consult organisations with a particular interest in the proposals, including conservation and amenity groups and businesses, development and infrastructural interests.

It should be noted that reg. 10 refers to proposals for the preparation of a 'statutory plan'. A statutory plan is defined in the regulations as a 'unitary development plan, structure plan, local plan, minerals local plan or waste plan'. Hence the provisions of reg. 10 relating to pre-deposit consultation apply to all such plans.

4.6.3.2   The deposit of proposals   Section 33(2) of the 1990 Act provides that where an authority have prepared proposals for the alteration or replacement of a structure plan, they shall:

(a)   make copies of the proposals and the explanatory memorandum available for inspection at such places as may be prescribed by . . . regulations;
(b)   send a copy of the proposals and the explanatory memorandum to the Secretary of State; and
(c)   comply with any requirements imposed by those regulations.

Regulation 11 of the Development Plan Regulations provides that an authority shall make the proposals available for inspection at the authority's principal office and such other places within their area as they consider appropriate; give notice of the fact by advertisement in the prescribed form; and give notice in similar form to any consultee under reg. 10(1). The proposals made available for inspection must be accompanied by the explanatory memorandum, and a statement prepared by the local planning authority of persons consulted (other than those specifically identified in the regulations) together with steps taken by the authority to publish their proposals and to provide persons with an opportunity to make representations in respect of those proposals.

Each copy of the proposals made available for inspection or sent to the Secretary of State in accordance with s. 33(2) must state the prescribed period within which objections may be made to the authority. Regulation 12 of the Development Plan Regulations provides that:

The period within which objections and representations may be made to the local planning authority with respect to proposals for . . . the alteration or replacement of a [structure] plan, made available for inspection under section . . . 33(2)(a) . . . shall be six weeks beginning with the date on which a notice given pursuant to regulation 11(1)(b) is first published in a local newspaper.

The regulation also provides that objections and representations shall be made in writing and addressed to the local planning authority in accordance with the details given in the published notice.

Section 33(5) of the 1990 Act provides that persons who may make objections in accordance with the regulations include, in particular, the Secretary of State.

The authority must, of course, consider objections made in accordance with the Act and Regulations. Accordingly, s. 33(6) of the 1990 Act provides that the proposals shall not be adopted by the authority until after they have considered any objection made in accordance with the regulations or, if no objections are made, after the expiry of the prescribed six-week period.

It will be seen that the regulations allow 'representations' as well as objections to be made with respect to proposals for the alteration or replacement of a structure plan. Regulation 12(3) requires the local planning authority to consider in addition to any objections made, any representations made in accordance with the regulation.

4.6.3.3 Adoption of proposals Section 35(1) of the 1990 Act provides that:

> ... the local planning authority may by resolution adopt proposals for the alteration or replacement of a structure plan, either as originally prepared or as modified so as to take account of—
>
> (a) any objections to the proposals; or
> (b) any other considerations which appear to them to be material.

Section 35B(1) of the Act, however, provides that before adopting proposals for the alteration or replacement of a structure plan:

> ... the local planning authority shall, unless the Secretary of State otherwise directs, cause an examination in public to be held of such matters affecting the consideration of the proposals as—
>
> (a) they consider ought to be so examined; or
> (b) the Secretary of State directs.

Two other matters should be noted. First, s. 35B(3) provides that an examination in public shall be conducted by a person or persons appointed by the Secretary of State for that purpose. This provision is intended to ensure that the person or persons appointed should be independent of the local planning authority. Secondly, s. 35B(4) provides that no person shall have a right to be heard at an examination in public. Under s. 35B(5), however, the right of the local planning authority to take part is recognised, as is the overriding power of the person or persons holding the examination in public to invite any person to take part.

It is for the local planning authority, however, to make the initial decision as to the matters with which the examination in public will be concerned; and also the persons invited to take part in it. Under reg. 15 of the Development Plan Regulations, the local planning authority must give notice of this information by advertisement at least six weeks before the opening of the examination in public; and the notice must invite representations to be made to the local planning authority on both the list of matters selected and the persons invited to take part.

As regards the selection of matters chosen for examination and the participants invited to take part in the examination in public, the Code of Practice on Development Plans (included as Annex A to Planning Policy Guidance PPG 12: Development Plans and Regional Planning Guidance) says:

33 In the case of *structure plans,* where an examination in public is to be held, the planning authority should select only those issues arising on the deposited proposals on which they need to be more fully informed by means of public discussion in order to reach their decisions. All objections and representations will be looked at to see whether they give rise to issues which should be selected for examination.

34 This material will also help to identify those authorities, organisations and individuals whom the authority should consider inviting to take part in the examination. The basic criterion in selecting participants will be the significance of the contribution which they can be expected to make to the discussion of the matters to be examined, either from their knowledge or from the views they have expressed.

35 As the purpose of an examination in public is to discuss the selected issues, rather than to hear objections, it is not intended that all those who have objected should be invited to the examination. It is also unlikely that all those whose objections or representations relate to issues selected for discussion will be invited to take part. The aim will be to select participants (whether statutory bodies, interest groups or individuals) who between them represent a broad range of viewpoints and have a relevant contribution to make. Participants will not necessarily be just those who made objections or representations. As already noted ... the authority should make the list of issues and those who have been invited to participate available for inspection when the EIP is advertised.

36 There will be an opportunity for those who wish to send written comments about the selection of matters and participants to do so. The notice will state that comments may be made within 28 days. Any comments made within this period will be considered and the authority, after consulting the chairman, may add or make changes to the list. However, since the published selection will have been made on the basis of the additional information considered necessary to enable the authority to take a decision on the deposited proposals, it is not normally likely that many changes will be necessary. The Secretary of State has a reserve power to direct the authority to include issues for consideration at an EIP if he considered it necessary to do so.

It has always been the intention and the form, that the person or persons (colloquially referred to as the panel) holding the examination in public should be as independent as possible, which explains the overriding power of the panel to invite persons to take part in the examination in public who have not been invited to do so by the local planning authority.

The examination in public was a new kind of forum created by the Town and Country Planning Act 1972 as a result of the unique and special character of structure plans. Under the old-style development plan system, objectors to the plan were given an unfettered right to attend a local inquiry held into it by the Secretary of State. Had that right been made available for the new-style structure plans, the length of each inquiry might have been considerably prolonged by the duplication of evidence given by individuals making similar objections. In addition, it was feared that the nature of the structure plan might itself lead to an increase in the number of objectors, and therefore to an increase in the number who might wish to attend the subsequent local inquiry. Hence the traditional forum for considering the authority's plan and objections to it was redesigned and given the new name of examination in public to distinguish it from the more traditional form of a local inquiry; and along with it the introduction of a process of selection for objectors and others wishing to attend.

4.6.3.4 The panel   In the past where the Secretary of State decided to hold an examination in public, he normally proceeded to appoint three persons to conduct the examination, one of whom he appointed as chairman. The chairman was normally an independent person with a wide range of relevant experience in central or local government or in the professions concerned with land use. Quite frequently, he or she was a lawyer and a member of the Local Government and Planning Bar.

One of the other two members of the panel was likely to be a senior official from the appropriate regional office of the Department of the Environment, and the third member a senior Inspector from the Planning Inspectorate of the Department. Exceptionally, the Secretary of State could appoint assessors to assist the panel in cases where expert knowledge in a specialist field was essential.

The role of the panel was to examine the matters selected for discussion to ensure that all information needed to reach a decision on the proposals had been made available. The current Code of Practice says that the panel will, apart from the Chairman, normally have only one other member, but exceptionally it may be necessary to appoint a third member, with the agreement of the authority. Unlike the traditional public local inquiry, the examination in public does not proceed by way of an examination-in-chief where the proposals are presented, followed by cross-examination of those presenting them and then possibly their re-examination. For this reason, although it is open to participants to be accompanied or be represented by professional advisers, the practice has not been encouraged.

According to the Code of Practice:

> 57   The examination will take the form of a probing discussion, led by the Chairman and the other member(s) of the panel, with the county planning authority and other participants. As a general rule, the Chairman will draw attention to those issues on which information and clarification are required, taking into account any statements submitted by participants. Participants may be invited to enlarge on their objections or statements or to question other participants, but the ordering of the discussion will be a matter for the Chairman.
>
> 58   The Chairman will ensure that the selected issues are examined in appropriate depth to enable the panel to make recommendations. Although the Chairman may sometimes consider it necessary to discuss the detailed

implications of the structure plan general policies and proposals, the panel will, in reporting to the planning authority, confine their recommendations to the level of detail appropriate to the structure plan.

59   The panel will not have counsel to assist them, and it is not necessary for participants to be professionally represented. Participants should not feel at a disadvantage if they are not professionally represented, or that their contribution will not be effectively made without such representation. The panel will take an active part in the discussion: if they consider that participants (whether a group or an individual) have a relevant point or argument which has not been developed sufficiently, the panel may take it up and pursue it.

60   It will be open to participants to be accompanied at the examination by professional or other advisers; to have their contributions made on their behalf; and to arrange for persons with special knowledge of a subject to take part in the discussion on their behalf. If a participant's place at the table is to be taken at any point by an adviser acting on behalf of the individual or group, this should be arranged with the Chairman.

61   An issue to be discussed may involve the interests of a Government department (including the Department of the Environment). Where it is considered that the department concerned can make a useful contribution to the discussion, they will be invited to send a participant. He or she will be there to explain the department's views about the structure plan proposals which concern them, and to give appropriate information; the representative may explain departmental policies and their relevance, but will not be required to discuss their merits.

At the end of the examination in public, the report of the panel, together with its recommendations, is sent to the local planning authority. The authority must then give consideration to them before deciding whether or not to adopt the proposals, either as originally prepared or with modifications.

4.6.3.5   Ministerial intervention   As well as having the power to object to proposals for the alteration or replacement of a structure plan, the Secretary of State has power under s. 35 of the 1990 Act, if it appears to him that the proposals are unsatisfactory, to direct the authority to modify the proposals in such respects as are indicated in the direction. An example of the use of this power occurred in early 1994, when the Secretary of State directed the Peak Park Joint Planning Board to include in its revised structure plan a requirement that the Board should 'have regard to the need to maintain a stock of permitted reserves [i.e., an aggregates land bank] appropriate for the National Park area ... unless exceptional circumstances prevail'. In addition to this power, under s. 35A of the 1990 Act, the Secretary of State may, at any time before the local planning authority have adopted their proposals, direct that all or any part of the proposals shall be submitted to him for approval. Where the Secretary of State uses this power, he may approve the proposals in whole or in part and with or without modifications or reject them.

4.6.3.6 Modification of proposals Regulation 18 of the Development Plan Regulations provides that where:

... a local planning authority proposing to modify proposals ... for the alteration or replacement of a [structure plan] (whether to comply with a direction given by the Secretary of State or on their own initiative) shall, unless they are satisfied that the modifications they intend to make will not materially affect the content of the proposals—

(a) prepare a list of the modifications with their reasons for proposing them;
(b) make copies of that list available for inspection at any place at which the plan proposals have been made available for inspection;
(c) give notice by local advertisement in [the prescribed form]; and
(d) serve a notice in similar form on any person who has objected to, or made a representation in respect of, the plan proposals in accordance with these regulations and not withdrawn the objection or representation.

The need to advertise proposed modifications to a structure plan is regarded by the courts as important. In October 1990, in an unreported decision, the High Court quashed by consent, two policies in the Lancashire Structure Plan on the ground that there had been a failure to advertise the proposed modifications as required by the then Structure and Local Plan Regulations.

The period within which objections and representations may be made to the local planning authority in respect of proposed modifications is six weeks from the date notice was first published in a local newspaper. The regulations require the objections and representations to be made in writing.

In dealing with the consideration of objections, the Code of Practice, which applies here equally to objections to proposed modifications to any statutory plan, says:

68 When the objection period has expired, the planning authority must consider all the objections made and decide whether it is necessary to hold an inquiry or reopen the EIP. If they decide to propose further modifications, either directly in response to objections or following receipt of an Inspector's/panel recommendations (if there is an inquiry or reopened EIP), these must be advertised in accordance with the procedure described above. If, however, the authority decide that no further modifications materially affecting the content of the plan need to be contemplated, they will give another notice of their intention to adopt the plan after 28 days.

69 An inquiry (or reopened EIP) into (or in connection with) objections will be necessary only in exceptional circumstances, and it will not normally be necessary to hold a further inquiry into matters already considered. That includes instances where there are objections to modifications *not* proposed by an authority in response to an Inspector's/panel report. The Secretary of State advises planning authorities to hold an inquiry (or reopen the EIP) where objections raise matters which were not at issue at all at the earlier

stage. This may arise, for example, if it is proposed to substitute an entirely different proposal for one which was in the plan as considered earlier, so that the objections made to the proposed modification include new evidence. It may also arise if, on consideration of objections, the authority are disposed to withdraw, or significantly alter, a proposed modification. If the original modification was put forward to meet an objection, it may be inappropriate to withdraw it without giving the original objector an opportunity to consider and comment on the new arguments put forward. If an authority decide not to hold an inquiry or to reopen the EIP to consider (or in connection with) objections to proposed modifications, the Secretary of State may direct them to do so.

70   If the planning authority hold an inquiry or reopen the EIP, they must carry out the same procedure for giving public notice as they did for the original inquiry or EIP. At the end of the process the Inspector (or EIP Chairman) reports to the planning authority who then decide what action to take on each of the recommendations. The authority must prepare a statement of their decisions on each recommendation and give their reasons for reaching them, paying particular attention to any recommendation they do not accept.

Paragraph 69 of the Code of Practice advises that a decision to hold a fresh inquiry should only be taken in exceptional circumstances. In *British Railways Board* v *Slough Borough Council* [1993] JPL 679, the High Court quashed part of the authority's local plan on the ground that the refusal of the authority to hold a fresh inquiry had been unreasonable, given that after the Inspector conducting the inquiry into the plan had proposed modifications to the authority's proposals for the use of a particular piece of land, the authority had proposed yet another modification to the proposals for the use of the land. In that case the proposed modification was a completely different proposal from that considered at the inquiry. There had, in effect, been a volte face by the Council on the appropriate use of the land after the holding of the inquiry.

4.6.3.7   The adoption   Under reg. 20 of the Development Plan Regulations, when a local planning authority resolve to adopt proposals for the alteration or replacement of a structure plan, the authority must:

(a)   publish a notice once in the *London Gazette* and for two successive weeks in at least one local newspaper stating the date on which the plan was adopted, and the date when it became operative (copies of this notice, together with copies of the plan as adopted and copies of the reports and other relevant documents, must be made available for inspection at the authority's office); and

(b)   send an individual notice to anyone who asked to be notified of the adoption of the plan and to the Secretary of State.

4.7 Local plans (the new provisions)

As indicated earlier, local plans set out, within the general context of the structure plan, detailed policies and specific proposals for the development and use of land. The content of a local plan is an important guide in the making of planning control decisions. Local plans also enable local communities to participate in decisions about where development should be accommodated in their area. For this reason, the Planning and Compensation Act 1991 has made the preparation of a district-wide local plan mandatory, in place of the previous discretionary power to prepare a local plan, which if exercised, might have been exercised for only part of the area of the district planning authority.

4.7.1 Form and content

Section 36(1) of the 1990 Act provides that the local planning authority shall, within such period (if any) as the Secretary of State may direct, prepare for their area a plan to be known as a local plan.

In addition, s. 39 provides that a local planning authority may at any time prepare proposals for alterations to the local plan for their area, or for its replacement. Any proposals for the alteration of a local plan may relate to the whole or part of the area to which the plan relates. By s. 36(2) of the 1990 Act, a local plan shall contain a written statement formulating the authority's detailed policies for the development and use of land in their area.

Section 36(3) provides that the policies in the local plan shall include policies in respect of:

(a) the conservation of the natural beauty and amenity of the land;
(b) the improvement of the physical environment; and
(c) the management of traffic.

In formulating their detailed policies the authority is required to have regard to such information and other considerations as the Secretary of State may prescribe or, in a particular case, direct; and the provisions of any enterprise zone scheme designated under the Local Government, Planning and Land Act 1980 (s. 36(9)).

The section expressly excludes from inclusion in a local plan, policies in respect of the winning and working of minerals and policies in respect of the depositing of refuse waste materials other than mineral waste. This is because the 1990 Act requires the preparation of separate minerals local plans and waste local plans (see below).

In addition, a local plan may designate any part of the authority's area as an action area, i.e., an area which is to be treated comprehensively by development, redevelopment or improvement (or partly by one and partly by another method) commencing during a prescribed period. If an area is so designated, the plan must contain a description of the treatment proposed by the authority. Under the Development Plan Regulations the prescribed period is 10 years from the date the plan was first made available for inspection.

Although it is provided that a local plan should contain a written statement etc., it must also contain:

(a) a map illustrating each of the detailed policies, and
(b) such diagrams, illustrations or descriptive matter in respect of policies as may be prescribed,

and may contain such descriptive or explanatory matter as the authority think appropriate.

The Development Plan Regulations specify that the map included in a local plan should be called the proposals map and should be a map of the authority's area reproduced from, or based upon, an Ordnance Survey map and should show national grid lines and reference numbers. Furthermore, the regulations provide that policies for any part of the authority's area may be illustrated instead on a separate map on a larger scale than the proposed map, to be called an inset map.

Under the Development Plan Regulations, a local plan must contain a reasoned justification of the policies formulated in the plan. The reasoned justification should contain a statement of the regard which the local planning authority have had in formulating their policies to any enterprise zone scheme in their area; and in the case of a local plan containing waste policies, the regard had in formulating those policies to policies in any waste disposal plan and the reason for any inconsistency between the two plans (see below).

4.7.2   Preparation and approval

4.7.2.1 Pre-deposit consultation The provisions relating to local plans in this respect, found in s. 40(1) of the 1990 Act, replicate the provisions found in s. 33(1) relating to the pre-deposit consultation requirements for proposals to alter or replace a structure plan (see 4.6.3.1 above). Likewise, the references there made to reg. 10 of the Development Plan Regulations in dealing with alterations or replacement of structure plans, apply equally to proposals to prepare, alter or replace a local plan.

4.7.2.2 The deposit of proposals As with the provisions relating to predeposit consultation, the provisions relating to the deposit of proposals contained in a local plan in s. 40(2) to (7) replicate almost in their entirety the provisions found in s. 33(2) relating to the deposit of proposals for the alteration or replacement of a structure plan (see 4.6.3.2).

Likewise the references there made to regs. 11 and 12 of the Development Plan Regulations in dealing with alterations or replacement of structure plans, apply equally to proposals to alter or replace a local plan.

4.7.2.3 Adoption of proposals Section 43 of the 1990 Act provides that:

(1) ... the local planning authority may by resolution adopt proposals for a local plan or for its alteration or replacement, either as originally prepared or as modified so as to take account of—

(a) any objections to the plan; or
(b) any other considerations which appear to them to be material.

As stated, however, s. 40(7) provides that a local plan or proposal for its alteration or replacement shall not be adopted by the authority under s. 43 until:

(a) after they have considered any objections made in accordance with the regulations; or
(b) if no such objections are made, after the expiry of the prescribed period.

Unlike proposals for the alteration or replacement of a structure plan where the local planning authority must cause an examination in public to be held, s. 42 of the Act provides:

(1) Where any objections have been made, in accordance with the regulations, to proposals for a local plan or for its alteration or replacement copies of which have been made available for inspection under section 40(2), the local planning authority shall cause a local inquiry or other hearing to be held for the purpose of considering the objections.
(2) The local planning authority may cause a local inquiry or other hearing to be held for the purpose of considering any other objections to the proposals.
(2A) No local inquiry or other hearing need be held under this section if all persons who have made objections have indicated in writing that they do not wish to appear.

By reg. 14 of the Development Plan Regulations a local planning authority must:

... at least six weeks before the opening of any local inquiry or other hearing which they cause to be held to consider objections to proposals for a statutory plan or for the alteration or replacement of a statutory plan made available for inspection under section ... 40(2)—

(a) give any person who has objected to, or made a representation in respect of, the proposals in accordance with these regulations and not withdrawn the objection or representation, notice of the time and place at which the inquiry or other hearing is to be held, the name of the person appointed to hold it, and its purpose; and
(b) in the case of a local inquiry, give notice of that information by local advertisement.

The regulation also provides that a local inquiry shall be held in public.
Where an inquiry is held, it is conducted by an Inspector appointed by the Secretary of State. Although the Act provides for regulations to be made to allow the local planning authority to nominate the person appointed to hold the inquiry, no regulations to permit this have yet been made. The reason for this is that there is (at present) little public confidence in the ability of a local

planning authority to appoint a person having the kind of independence which is associated with those now appointed by the Secretary of State, most of whom are members of the Department's Planning Inspectorate.

No regulations have ever been made prescribing the procedure to be followed at any public local inquiry or hearing. The procedure is to a great extent governed by the Code of Practice on Development Plans contained in Annex A to Planning Policy Guidance, PPG12: Development Plans and Regional Planning Guidance, published in February 1992. Although the code has no statutory force, compliance with it reduces the prospect of a subsequent legal challenge being made to a plan based upon an allegation that objections have not been fairly considered or that there had been a breach of natural justice. The code is not exhaustive, however, and situations may sometimes arise which the code does not cover. In *R v Wakefield Metropolitan District Council (ex parte Asquith)* [1986] JPL 440, the local planning authority had prepared three, virtually identical draft local plans covering the whole but different parts of their area. The plans were identical in the sense that they each contained a 'policy section' intended to indicate the authority's general planning policy throughout their area. They decided that they should hold public local inquiries into each of the three plans. After considering the relevant statutory provisions and consulting the Secretary of State, the authority decided first to hold an inquiry into the policy sections of the plans, and then two other Inspectors would be appointed and different inquiries would be held into the specific aspects of each of the three plans. It was also arranged that these two additional Inspectors would attend the 'policy' inquiry beforehand as observers. As a matter of urgency the applicants sought judicial review to challenge this procedure. Dismissing the application, Woolf J held that the legislation allowed such a pattern of inquiries, that the objectors did not need to be consulted about setting up the inquiries and that the procedure to be used was not a breach of natural justice. With the requirement now being that a local planning authority must prepare a district-wide local plan for its area, the circumstances mentioned in the *Wakefield* case are not likely to arise again, save perhaps where an authority is preparing both a waste local plan and a minerals local plan.

4.7.2.4 Adoption procedure   At the close of the public local inquiry, the Inspector conducting the inquiry will report to the local planning authority. Regulation 16 of the Development Plan Regulations provides that:

(1)   Where a local planning authority cause a local inquiry or other hearing to be held ... the authority shall, after considering the report of the person holding the inquiry, other hearing or, ... as the case may be, prepare a statement of—

(a)   the decisions they have reached in the light of the report and any recommendations contained in the report; and
(b)   the reasons for those decisions.

(2) Where a list of proposed modifications to the statutory plan proposals is made available for inspection under regulation 18(1) after the statement of decisions and reasons is prepared, the report mentioned in paragraph (1) and that statement shall be made available for inspection from the date on which, and at the places at which, the list is made available for inspection.

As with proposals for the alteration or replacement of a structure plan, a local planning authority may propose, after considering the report of the Inspector, to modify their proposals for the alteration or replacement of a local plan.

In doing so, the authority must comply with the provisions of reg. 18 of the Development Plan Regulations which apply equally to local plans (see 4.6.3.6).

As with structure plans, the period within which objections and representations may be made to the local planning authority in respect of the proposed modification is six weeks from the date notice was first placed in a local newspaper. The regulations require objections and representations to be made in writing. The authority have a discretion as to whether to hold a further public local inquiry. In deciding whether or not to do so, they will no doubt be guided by paras. 68 to 70 of the Code of Practice on Plan Preparation (see 4.6.3.6).

4.7.2.5 The adoption As with proposals relating to structure plans, reg. 20 of the Development Plan Regulations provides that when a local planning authority resolves to adopt proposals for a local plan or for the alteration or replacement of a local plan, the authority should:

(a) publish a notice once in the *London Gazette* and for two successive weeks in at least one local newspaper stating the date on which the plan was adopted, and the date when it became operative (copies of this notice, together with copies of the plan as adopted and copies of the reports and other relevant documents, must be made available for inspection at the authority's office); and

(b) send an individual notice to anyone who asked to be notified of the adoption of the plan.

4.7.2.6 Certificate of conformity The 1990 Act contains a number of provisions designed to protect the integrity of the two-tier development plan system.

Section 36(4) of the 1990 Act boldly states:

A local plan shall be in general conformity with the structure plan.

To be doubly sure of the effectiveness of this provision, however, s. 46 of the Act provides that an authority responsible for the local plan shall not proceed to the pre-deposit consultation process required by s. 40 unless the county planning authority have issued a certificate that the proposals conform generally to the structure plan. The procedure involves the district planning authority serving on the county planning authority a copy of the plan or proposals. The county planning authority must then issue a statement that the plan or proposals are in general conformity; or that they are not in such conformity. In the case of the latter, the statement must specify the respects in which the plan or proposals are not in such conformity; and that statement must then be treated by the local planning authority as a statutory objection to the plan or proposals.

Although the requirements that a local plan should be in general conformity with the structure plan will normally prevent any conflict arising between the two, s. 46(10) of the 1990 Act provides that if a conflict does arise, the provisions of the local plan shall prevail over the structure plan. The provision does not apply, however, where a structure plan has been altered or replaced, and the planning authority have notified the district planning authority of that fact and of any local plan which, in their opinion does not so conform.

4.7.2.7 Secretary of State's power to call in As with applications for planning permission where the Secretary of State has a right to call in the application for his own determination, the Secretary of State has the right to call in a local plan proposal for his approval. Section 44(1) of the 1990 Act provides:

> After copies of proposals have been sent to the Secretary of State and before they have been adopted by the local planning authority, the Secretary of State may direct that the proposals or any part of them shall be submitted to him for his approval.

With regard to that subsection, s. 44(2) of the 1990 Act further provides that if the Secretary of State issues a direction in accordance with s. 44(1):

> (a)   the authority shall not take any further steps for the adoption of any of the proposals until the Secretary of State has given his decision on the proposals or the relevant part of the proposals; and
> (b)   the proposals or the relevant part of the proposals shall not have effect unless approved by him and shall not require adoption by the authority under section 43.

The power to call in a local plan proposal is only likely to be used in a limited range of circumstances. It is likely that the Secretary of State would only consider it appropriate to do so:

(a)   where the plan (i.e. local plan proposals) raises issues of national or regional importance; or
(b)   where the plan (i.e. local plan proposals) gives rise to substantial controversy, for example, extending beyond the area of the plan-making authority.

The Secretary of State may also call in local plan proposals for his consideration where the local planning authority have failed to modify them to take into account an objection made by the Ministry of Agriculture, Fisheries and Food (s.44(3)).

Once local plan proposals have been called in by the Secretary of State, he may, under s. 45 either approve them or reject them.

The power to call in local plan proposals under this provision and then to reject them has only been used on a limited number of occasions. In January 1986 the Secretary of State gave a direction to the London Borough of Southwark that the North Southwark Local Plan should not have effect unless approved by him. According to the Secretary of State, he took the action because of conflict between the local plan and national policies on industrial development. He also considered that as proposed to be adopted, the local plan was inconsistent with the objects and general powers of the London Docklands Urban Development Corporation to secure regeneration of its area.

After considering the plan, the Inspector's report of the public local inquiry and the council's decision on that report, he decided to use his power under the section to reject the plan. In doing so, the Secretary of State said he considered the plan conflicted both with government policies spelt out in Circulars and the approved Greater London Development Plan. He also noted that the plan was opposed in general to private investment in the area and was critical and hostile to the objectives of the development corporation. He considered that these defects, which the council were not prepared to rectify, were of such a nature as to flaw fundamentally the plan as a whole.

Another example occurred in 1987. Then, at the same time as Merton London Borough Council were considering proposals for a Wimbledon Town Centre Local Plan, the Secretary of State had to consider two competing applications for planning permission for the development of the town centre, only one of which was favoured by the council. One of the applications he was considering on appeal following the refusal of the application by the council. The other he was considering following his decision to call-in the application for his own determination. As things stood there was thus a danger of inconsistency between his decision on the applications and the council's decision on the local plan.

The Secretary of State decided, therefore, to call-in the local plan in order that he could consider it at the same time as he was considering the Inspector's report following the public inquiry into the appeal and called-in application. His reason for so doing was to consider whether any action was necessary to bring about consistency as between the local plan and the specific decisions on the applications; and, if so, what steps should be taken to achieve that consistency.

In addition to the two cases mentioned above, the Secretary of State has for environmental and highway reasons also called in a local plan for Berwick-upon-Tweed and a local plan for the London Borough of Lewisham. A further eight local plans prepared by former metropolitan county councils were called in by the Secretary of State in 1986 to enable them to be carried forward to approval following the abolition of those counties.

The 1990 Act also gives a reserve power to the Secretary of State to enable him to direct a local planning authority to consider modifying one or more of its local plan proposals (s. 43(4)). This power allows the Secretary of State to direct an authority to alter part of their plan and might be appropriate where the part appears to be seriously at variance with national policy.

4.8 Further proposals to improve the local plan process

It was intended that the new system of district-wide local plans introduced by the Planning and Compensation Act 1991 would be in place by the end of 1996. By early 1994, however, it had become apparent that some slippage in the timetable had occurred. It seemed that the enhanced status of local plans (arising no doubt from the impact of the new s. 54A of the 1990 Act) had resulted in more interest in local plan preparation from landowners, developers and the public than had previously been the case. Accordingly in March 1994, the government issued a consultation paper in which it made a number of proposals for speeding up the local plan process. These included removal of excessive detail from local plans; the provision of a standard form of objection; a requirement that each objection duly made should relate to a single policy; the encouragement of greater use of written representations; the earlier organisation of inquiries; the greater use of pre-inquiry meetings; a firmer agenda for inquiries; requiring inspectors to provide a stronger lead on issues to be discussed at the inquiry; the provision of shorter Inspectors' reports; and earlier response by authorities to the report.

Some of these proposals, if agreed, could be implemented through administrative changes. Others, however, would require changes to be made to primary or secondary legislation.

4.9 Minerals local plans and waste local plans

In addition to structure and local plans, local planning authorities may also be required to prepare minerals local plans and waste local plans.

4.9.1 Minerals local plans

Until the Planning and Compensation Act 1991, policies for the winning and working of minerals were contained either within local plans or in a specific type of local plan called a subject plan. Now under amendments made by the 1991 Act, a duty is placed on mineral planning authorities (see Chapter 21) to prepare a plan, to be known as a 'minerals local plan' for their area, formulating the authority's detailed policies for their area in respect of the winning and working of minerals or the deposit of mineral waste. Since the mineral planning authority for non-metropolitan areas is the county planning authority, minerals local plans will in future be 'county-wide' plans covering the whole of the administrative area of the county. It should be noted that there is no power to prepare minerals local plans in metropolitan areas; hence policies for the winning and working of minerals or the deposit of mineral waste must be contained in the unitary development plans for those areas.

Under the new s. 37 of the 1990 Act substituted by the Planning and Compensation Act 1991, a minerals local plan 'shall contain a written statement formulating the authority's detailed policies for their area in respect of development consisting of the winning and working of minerals or involving the depositing of mineral waste'. A minerals local plan must also contain a map illustrating each of the detailed policies in the plan and such diagrams, illustrations or other descriptive matter in respect of the policies as may be prescribed. It may also include such descriptive or explanatory matter as the authority think appropriate. The new section also requires a minerals local plan to be in general conformity with the structure plan. In most other respects, the same procedures apply to the adoption of minerals local plans, as apply to the adoption of local plans generally.

4.9.2 Waste local plans

The Planning and Compensation Act 1991 introduced a new statutory requirement for local plan coverage of development involving the depositing of refuse or waste materials (other than mineral waste). In metropolitan areas, policies in respect of development involving the deposit of refuse or waste materials are contained in unitary development plans. Elsewhere, applications for planning permission for development involving the deposit, treatment, storage, processing and disposal of refuse or waste materials, other than mineral waste, are decided by county planning authorities. A new s. 38 of the 1990 Act, inserted into the Act by the 1991 Act, now requires county planning authorities either to prepare a separate waste local plan, or to combine it with their minerals local plan.

The purpose of a waste local plan is to address the land-use implications of the authorities' waste policies, including, for example, the need for sites and facilities in particular areas and suitable locations for such sites having regard to geological and hydrological considerations.

Waste local plans should be distinguished from waste disposal plans, which are plans drawn up by waste regulation authorities under the Control of Pollution Act 1974. Waste disposal plans are concerned with the types and quantities of waste circulating in an area and the facilities available for their disposal. Waste local plans must have regard to waste disposal plans and any inconsistencies between them justified in the reasoned justification for the waste local plan.

As with minerals local plans, the same procedures apply to the adoption of waste local plans as apply to local plans.

4.10 Unitary development plans

Following the abolition of the Greater London Council and the metropolitan county councils by the Local Government Act 1985, the existing two-tier system of local planning authorities in Greater London and the metropolitan area of England was reduced to one. From 1 April 1986, the London boroughs and the metropolitan districts began to exercise all the functions of the local planning authority in their areas.

The Local Government Act 1985 also made provision for the introduction in the Greater London and metropolitan areas of new 'unitary development plans' (UDPs). The authority for these plans is now contained in Part II of the 1990 Act. Each local planning authority in these areas is to prepare a new UDP for their area. It should be noted that the Secretary of State may direct a local planning authority to prepare a UDP within a specified period. That power can be used to ensure the preparation at the same time of a cluster of UDPs which, together, will cover a much larger area than that covered by a plan prepared by any individual local planning authority.

The essence of the new UDP is that it is prepared in two parts. Part I contains the authority's general policies for their area, whilst Part II formulates those policies in detail.

In the White Paper, *The Future of Development Plans* (Cm 569), published in January 1989, the government stated its intention to harmonise the terminology and detailed procedures for plan-making in the metropolitan areas and London with what was proposed for the rest of England and Wales. The White Paper stated that the aim would be to provide, so far as it was possible to do so, 'uniform, or closely comparable procedures, for the preparation and adoption of development plans throughout England and Wales, so as to assist public understanding of the system and its effective operation'. Changes made by the 1991 Act to the procedures for the preparation and adoption of UDPs implement that intention.

The main changes made to the UDP procedures by the 1991 Act are as follows:

(a) The 1990 Act has been amended to give the Secretary of State power to make regulations prescribing the particular aspects of development and land use with which the general policies in Part I of the UDP are to be exclusively concerned (new s. 12(3B)). This provision is similar to one that now covers structure plans and, as in that case, is designed to help the local authority to concentrate on key strategic issues in formulating general policies to be included in the plan.

(b) The 1991 Act amended the 1990 Act by revising the list of matters to which a local planning authority are required to have regard in formulating their general policies in Part I of the UDP. In particular, the amendment allows the Secretary of State to prescribe additional matters that local planning authorities are required to take into account (new s. 12(6)).

(c) The provisions relating to UDPs in the 1990 Act are now modified as regards the pre-plan public participation process, and the procedures to be followed on deposit of the plan. As regards the former, the requirement to give adequate publicity to matters which the authority propose to include in the plan etc., which was previously found in the body of the 1990 Act, has, as with structure and local plan proposals, now been removed from the Act and is dealt with by the Development Plan Regulations.

As regards changes made to the deposit procedure, the 1991 Act amended the 1990 Act to require the local planning authority to comply with any requirements imposed by the regulations. These regulations require an authority to notify people and organisations whom they believe may wish to make representations about the proposals in the plan, that the plan has been placed on deposit. In addition, the regulations provide for the making of representations (as distinct from objections) to proposals in the UDP at the deposit stage. Any representations made, therefore, might include representations in support of the local planning authority's proposals.

Section 12(3) of the 1990 Act now provides:

Part I of a unitary development plan shall consist of a written statement formulating the authority's general policies in respect of the development and other use of land in their area.

Under s. 12(3A), those policies must include policies in respect of:

(a)   the conservation of the natural beauty and amenity of the land;
(b)   the improvement of the physical environment; and
(c)   the management of traffic.

Section 12(3B), however, provides that regulations may prescribe:

the aspects of such development and use with which the general policies in Part I of a unitary development plan are to be concerned, in which case the policies shall be concerned with those aspects and no others.

Section 12(6) further provides:

In formulating the general policies in Part I of a unitary development plan the authority shall have regard to—

(a)   any regional or strategic planning guidance given by the Secretary of State to assist them in the preparation of the plan;
(b)   current national policies;
(c)   the resources likely to be available; and
(d)   such other matters as the Secretary of State may prescribe or, in a particular case, direct.

Section 12(4) of the 1990 Act provides:

Part II of a unitary development plan shall consist of—

(a)   a written statement formulating in such detail as the authority think appropriate ... their proposals for the development and use of land in their area;
(b)   a map showing those proposals on a geographical basis;
(c)   a reasoned justification of the general policies in Part I of the plan and of the proposals in Part II of it; and
(d)   such diagrams, illustrations or other descriptive or explanatory matter in respect of the general policies in Part I of the plan or the proposals in Part II of it as the authority think appropriate or as may be prescribed.

Provision is also made for the local planning authority to designate in Part II of the UDP any Part of the authority's area as an action area. They must also take into account in preparing the plan the provisions of any scheme under sch. 32 to the Local Government, Planning and Land Act 1980 relating to land in their area which has been designated as an enterprise zone.

Paragraph 4(1) of Part I of sch. 2 to the 1990 Act further provides that Part II of the plan shall include any local plans in force at the time when the UDP is prepared, but subject to any alterations which may be set out in Part II of the plan.

As might be expected, the Act requires that the proposals in Part II of a UDP shall be in general conformity with Part I; and that a UDP shall not be adopted unless Part II of the plan is in general conformity with Part I.

The procedures for the preparation of UDPs have always been based closely upon the procedures for the preparation of local plans. Thus s. 11 gives a discretion to the authority to institute a survey of their area. A duty is also placed on an authority preparing a UDP, and before finally determining its contents, to carry out pre-deposit consultations.

As with local plan preparation, the procedure involves the local planning authority having to consider any objections made to a UDP and to hold a local inquiry or other hearing for that purpose, to which the Tribunal and Inquiries Act 1992 is to apply (ss. 15(1) and 16).

As with the procedure for the preparation and adoption of local plans, the Secretary of State has a power to call in the UDP for his approval (s. 18). He may do this for the whole or a Part of the UDP, at any time between it being placed on deposit and a copy being sent to the Secretary of State, and its adoption by the local planning authority. If the Secretary of State exercises his power of call-in, the local planning authority must not take any further steps in connection with the adoption of the plan until he has given his decision on the plan or the relevant Part of it; and the plan or relevant Part of it will have no effect unless it is approved by him. It seems that the power of call-in extends not only to the whole or Part of the UDP, but to part of any of the two Parts of the UDP. So the Secretary of State may, for example, call in only the transport policies contained in Part I of the UDP in order to ensure that they are compatible with national transport policies. He may then proceed to approve that part of Part I which contains the transport policies, leaving the remainder of Part I and Part II of the UDP to be adopted by the local planning authority. If, however, the Secretary of State has approved the whole or part of Part I of the UDP with modifications, the local planning authority may be required to make modifications to Part II of the UDP in order to make Part II conform generally to Part I.

4.10.1 Transitional arrangements
Schedule 2 to the 1990 Act provides that the development plans in force in the area of any local planning authority in Greater London and the metropolitan counties shall continue in force for that area until a UDP for that area has become operative. Development plans likely to be in force will be the structure plan, any local plan and any old-style development plan. Hence the

above-mentioned development plans continue in force until a UDP has been adopted or approved for the appropriate area. As far as local plans are concerned, however, those in force in an area when a UDP is adopted or approved are automatically made part of Part II of the UDP, subject only to any proposals the local planning authority may bring forward for their alteration, repeal or replacement, which must be specified in Part II of the UDP. The intention is that Part II of the UDP will list the local plans to be included, but will give details of any proposed alterations or replacements. These alterations etc. will then be subject to objections, and any that are made will have to be considered at a local inquiry or other hearing along with any other objections to the UDP.

4.11 Judge in their own cause

It is sometimes claimed that in allowing a local planning authority to adopt their own plans, the legislature has made the authority a judge in their own cause. To some extent there may be truth in this claim, but it should be noted that there are a number of restraints in the preparation and adoption process which inhibit the way in which the discretion given to a local planning authority is exercised. First, there is the safeguard of publicity for the authority's proposals required by the 1990 Act, (ss. 33 and 40), for structure and local plans respectively. Secondly, proposals in a local plan must be in general conformity with the structure plan (ss. 36(4) and 46). Thirdly, if objections are duly made and not withdrawn, the local planning authority must hold an examination in public or a public local inquiry or other hearing to consider them (ss. 35B and 42(2)). Fourthly, the examination in public or local inquiry or hearing is conducted by an independent Inspector and the procedure made subject to the Tribunals and Inquiries Act 1992 (ss. 35(8) and 42(6)). Fifthly, the Secretary of State is given power to call in development plan proposals for his own approval (ss. 35A and 44).

Despite these restraints, however, it is still possible for a local planning authority to adopt policies in the face of sustained and prolonged opposition from local objectors. This is seen in the case of *R v Hammersmith & Fulham London Borough Council (ex parte People before Profit Ltd)* [1981] JPL 869.

The applicants were an association of persons who had objected to proposals in a local plan for the redevelopment of Part of Hammersmith Broadway. A public local inquiry had been held into their objections, and the Inspector conducting the inquiry had found almost entirely in their favour. After considering the Inspector's report and his recommendations, however, the local planning authority resolved to reject them. The authority also resolved to grant planning permission for the development of the site in accordance with the proposals in the plan that the Inspector had criticised.

The Divisional Court refused the applicants leave to apply for judicial review to quash the resolutions to reject the Inspector's recommendations and to grant planning permission for the development on the ground that the authority had kept throughout within the law, and that the applicants had no reasonable case which would entitle the court to quash the decision. In giving judgment, Comyn J said that one consequence of this unhappy case was to lead him to believe that public inquiries very often had no useful purpose at all. He went on to say that he was slightly perturbed to think that a public inquiry of up to a month's length would take place and its findings be so favourable and yet the authority could dismiss it virtually out of hand.

In this case the local planning authority had the law on their side. In the absence of any call-in by the Secretary of State, the authority were the political monarch in their own area and were taking what had become a political decision. Research in this area shows that 90 per cent of the recommendations made by Inspectors following inquiries into local plans are accepted by the local planning authority. Where they have not done so, the issues have usually been minor and have related to the application of policy to specific sites. In considering this aspect, however, it should be remembered that the Secretary of State, in determining applications for planning permission (either after call-in or on an appeal against an adverse decision by the local planning authority), may well take into account any recommendations made by an Inspector following an inquiry into a local plan which the local planning authority have decided to reject unless, that is, the new s. 54A prevents such a course.

4.12 Meaning of the term 'development plan'

The development plan is rarely a single document. Once the changes to the development plan system introduced by the Planning and Compensation Act 1991 have been implemented, the development plan for an area will be:

    (a)   In non-metropolitan areas:

        (i)   the structure plan;
        (ii)   the local plan;
        (iii)   the minerals local plan; and
        (iv)   the waste local plan.

    (b)   In metropolitan areas: the unitary development plan.

Until the plans required by the 1991 Act have been prepared and adopted, it may be necessary both in metropolitan and non-metropolitan areas to take into account development plans approved or adopted under previous statutory provisions such as the 'old-style' development plans.

4.13 Legal effect of a development plan

The end-product of the plan-making process is to provide, as far as possible, a concise statement of the policy framework within which development in any area is to be controlled or allowed. This aim is reflected in a number of statutory provisions found in the 1990 Act and elsewhere. The main provisions are:

    (a)   In dealing with applications for planning permission, s. 70(2) of the 1990 Act requires that the local planning authority 'shall have regard to the provisions of the development plan, so far as material to the application, and to any other material considerations'.

The precise meaning of the phrase 'shall have regard to the provisions of the development plan' has been judicially considered on a number of occasions. In *Simpson* v *Edinburgh Corporation* 1961 SLT 17, Lord Guest said that the expression 'shall have regard to' did not in his view mean 'slavishly adhere to'. According to his Lordship, the phrase requires the local planning authority to consider the development plan, but it does not oblige them to follow it. He went on:

> In view of the nature and purpose of a development plan . . . I should have been surprised to find an injunction on the planning authority to follow it implicitly, and I do not find anything in the Act to suggest that this was intended. . . . It was also pointed out that if the phrase was mandatory, then the addition of the words 'to any other material considerations' . . . would, if the development plan and other material considerations were inconsistent, face the planning authority with an impossible task of reconciling the two. . . . The [local] planning authority are to consider all the material considerations, of which the development plan is one.

The view expressed by Lord Guest in *Simpson* v *Edinburgh Corporation* was considered and followed in *Enfield London Borough Council* v *Secretary of State for the Environment* [1975] JPL 155, where Melford Stevenson J refused to quash a grant of planning permission given by the Secretary of State for industrial development in the green belt contrary to the provisions of the development plan which he had approved. The court held that the words 'have regard to' did not make adherence to the plan mandatory.

The Planning and Compensation Act 1991 may now have altered the significance of this provision. Section 26 of the 1991 Act provided that the following provision should be added at the end of Part II of the 1990 Act:

> 54A. Where, in making any determination under the planning Acts, regard is to be had to the development plan, the determination shall be made in accordance with the plan unless material considerations indicate otherwise.

The likely effect of this new provision is discussed further in Chapter 11. It should be noted, however, that the new provision affects the interpretation placed upon the term 'provisions of the development plan' not only in the determination of applications for planning permission, but also in the other circumstances listed in paras (b) to (e) below.

(b) Where planning permission for development is necessary and has not been obtained, s. 172(1) of the 1990 Act requires the local planning authority, in considering whether to issue an enforcement notice requiring the breach to be remedied, to have 'regard to the provisions of the development plan and to any other material considerations'.

(c) In considering whether to revoke or modify a permission granted for development on an application made under Part III of the 1990 Act, s. 97 of the Act requires the local planning authority to have regard 'to the development plan and to any other material considerations'.

(d) In considering whether to make an order requiring discontinuance of the use of land or the removal or alteration of buildings or works, s. 102 of the 1990 Act requires the local planning authority to have regard 'to the development plan and to any other material considerations'.

(e) In exercising powers under s. 226 of the 1990 Act to compulsorily acquire land in connection with development and for other planning purposes, a local authority is required, in considering whether land is suitable for development, redevelopment or improvement, to have regard, *inter alia*, 'to the provisions of the development plan, so far as material' and 'to any other considerations which would be material for the purpose of determining an application for planning permission for development on the land'.

(f) The interests of owner-occupiers of land may be 'blighted' where an indication has been given in a development plan that land may be required for some public purpose. In such cases, Part VI of the 1990 Act allows the owners of certain interests in land so affected to serve 'blight notices' on the appropriate authority requiring the authority to purchase their interests.

(g) Where land is being acquired by a public authority for some public purpose, the compensation paid for the interest acquired is normally based on its market value. In order to assist in the determination of that value, the Land Compensation Act 1961 provides that the parties may assume that, were it not for the acquisition, planning permission would have been granted for development of a specific kind. Some of these assumptions about planning permission depend directly upon the provisions of the development plan.

4.14 Legal challenge to development plans

Under the provisions of s. 287 of the 1990 Act, any person aggrieved by a unitary development plan or a local plan, or by any alteration or replacement of any such plan or structure plan, may question its validity by application to the High Court. The grounds of challenge under the section, however, are limited to two, namely, that the plan, alteration, repeal or replacement is not within the powers conferred by Part II of the 1990 Act, or that any requirement of Part II or of any regulations made thereunder has not been complied with. A further limitation on the use of this power is that the person aggrieved must make the application within six weeks from the date of publication of the first notices of the plan's approval or adoption or its alteration or replacement. The period of six weeks means precisely six weeks and not a day more. After the six-week period has elapsed, it is no longer possible to challenge the validity of the action taken. This is the result of s. 284(1) of the 1990 Act which provides that, except as provided under s. 287, the validity of a structure plan, local plan or unitary development plan or any alteration or replacement of any such plan, 'shall not be questioned in any legal proceedings whatsoever'.

On an application under s. 287, the High Court may, if satisfied that what has been done is outside the powers conferred by Part II of the 1990 Act, or that the interests of the applicant have been substantially prejudiced by the failure to comply with the requirements of Part II or the regulations thereunder, wholly or partly quash the plan, or as the case may be, the alteration or replacement either generally or in so far as it affects the property of the applicant. The court also has the power, by interim order, wholly or partly to suspend the operation of the plan until the final determination of the proceedings.

Similar provisions applied to old-style development plans (although they are no longer being brought up to date) and will, as indicated, apply to the new unitary development plans when adopted.

Since 1984, there have been a growing number of challenges to the validity of new-style development plans. Apart from the cases already referred to, the more important are as follows.

In *Edwin H. Bradley & Sons Ltd* v *Secretary of State for the Environment* (1982) 47 P & CR 374, the main allegation made was that in approving a structure plan with modifications, the Secretary of State had failed to comply with his duty under what is now s. 35(10) of the 1990 Act to give 'such statement as he considers appropriate of the reasons governing his decision'. Gildewell J held that the Secretary of State was entitled to give 'short reasons' for his decision, so long as he had complied with the tests laid down in *Re Poyser & Mills' Arbitration* [1964] 2 QB 467, and given reasons which were adequate and intelligible. His lordship found that the Secretary of State had done so.

In *Barnham* v *Secretary of State for the Environment* [1985] JPL 861, however, the Secretary of State had approved an alteration to a structure plan in a way that made it conflict with policy guidance contained in a government Circular. Farquharson J held that he should have referred to that guidance in the statement of reasons for his decision, and that the failure to do so was a breach of his duty under what is now s. 35(10). Accordingly, his lordship quashed part of the alterations to the structure plan which the Secretary of State had approved.

In *Fourth Investments Ltd* v *Bury Metropolitan Borough Council* [1985] JPL 185, McCullough J held that the Inspector who had conducted the inquiry into a local plan had erred in failing to balance the local green-belt significance of the applicant's land against the possibility that further land than that already allocated in the plan for housing might be needed in the future, and that in that event the applicant's land might be required for that purpose. In quashing the policy in the local plan in so far as it related to the applicant's land, McCullough J held that on the Inspector's findings (or on his inability to make findings far enough into the future) about housing land requirements and upon his findings about the green-belt significance of the applicant's land, the chances that the land might be needed for future housing were sufficiently high for it to have been wrong to have given the land a green-belt notation in the plan.

Probably the most important legal challenge made to the provisions of a development plan occurred in *Westminster City Council* v *Great Portland Estates plc* [1985] AC 661. There the respondent company challenged both the industrial and the office policies contained in the Westminster City local plan. With regard to industrial development, the general policy was that applications for planning permission for new industrial floor space and the creation of new industrial employment were to be encouraged. That general policy was modified, however, in the case of applications for planning permission to rehabilitate or redevelop existing industrial premises. There, the authority's general policy was supplanted where it was considered necessary to maintain the continuation of industrial uses important to the diverse character, vitality and functioning of Westminster. The policy was intended to protect 'specific industrial activities' from redevelopment. The company challenged this latter aspect as being outside the purposes of planning law. The essence of its argument was that the protection of specified industrial activities was not a policy concerned with the development and use of land, but one concerned with the protection of particular users of land. It was irrelevant, it was claimed, to have regard in this way to the interests of individual occupiers.

Giving the only speech, but one concurred in by all the other Law Lords, Lord Scarman adopted the general principle enunciated by Lord Parker CJ in *East Barnet Urban District Council v British Transport Commission* [1962] 2 QB 484 that, in considering whether there had been a change of use, 'what is really to be considered is the character of the use of the land, not the particular purposes of a particular occupier'. It was a logical process, Lord Scarman thought, to extend the ambit of that statement to the formulation of planning policies and proposals. However, like all generalisations, he said, the statement of Lord Parker had its own limitations. Personal circumstances of the occupier, personal hardship, the difficulties of business which are of value to the community were not to be ignored in the administration of planning control.

Lord Scarman thought the human factor was always present, though indirectly as the background to the consideration of the character of land use. Yet in exceptional or special circumstances it would have a direct effect. But such circumstances, he said, fell to be considered not as a general rule but as exceptions to a general rule to be met in special cases. Such cases *may* be mentioned in a plan, he said, but it would only be necessary to do so where prudent to emphasise that, notwithstanding the general policy, exceptions could not be wholly excluded from consideration in the administration of planning control. He therefore disagreed with the view of the Court of Appeal that the council's real concern was the protection of existing occupiers. He thought the council had made a strong planning case for its proposal, and that the linkage (i.e., between the general policy and the exceptions) was 'a powerful piece of positive thinking within a planning context'. Accordingly the challenge to the industrial policy failed.

As regards the challenge to the authority's office policy, the plan had divided the City of Westminster into two zones, a 'central activities' zone and elsewhere. The policy was expressed in the plan as being 'to guide office development to location within the central activities zone'. Elsewhere, in order to ensure that land use and development were compatible with residential use, the policy was to prescribe (almost) any office development, save in exceptional or special circumstances. The plan had stated that those exceptional circumstances were to be set out in non-statutory guidelines to be prepared after consultation following the adoption of the plan.

In quashing the office policies in the plan, Lord Scarman held (after admitting that the point had caused him some difficulty) that the authority had failed to comply with the duty imposed on them to formulate in the plan its development and land use proposals. The authority had, he said, 'deliberately omitted some'. By so doing they had deprived persons such as the respondent company from raising objections and securing a public inquiry into such objections.

A further argument raised by the respondent company in its challenge to the office policies in the plan, namely, that in commenting upon the Inspector's report the authority had failed to give an adequate statement of their reasons for rejecting his views and recommendations, was rejected by their lordships.

The decision of the House of Lords is important for a number of reasons. First, as regards the extent to which the personal circumstances of an occupier or the character of an occupier can be taken into account, which until this decision had never been clear. It was no doubt partly legal uncertainty on this point that led the Secretary of State at one time to decline to approve policies in a number of structure plans which sought to restrict the occupation of new residential development to local persons. More importantly, however, the judgment strengthens the hand of local planning authorities wishing to protect from redevelopment the many and varied small businesses found in inner city areas, be it the bookshop, the violin maker or the local store.

Secondly, the judgment makes clear that the duty of a local planning authority to formulate in a plan 'their proposals for the development and other use of land' means all proposals, not merely some of them. Other proposals, it seems, cannot be left to influence development control decisions from the sidelines if they are proposals capable of being included in the plan. It would appear that the decision does not impede the utility of non-statutory local plans, provided that the policies contained in the non-statutory plan are policies which have been formulated after the adoption of the local plan.

Any non-statutory local plan may continue to be a material consideration to be taken into account by an authority in exercising its planning control functions. But there must be a considerable moral obligation on authorities to put a non-statutory local plan on a more formal basis by taking formal steps to include the policies in the non-statutory local plan in the adopted statutory local plan by amending the latter.

FIVE

Definition of development
1: Operational development

5.1 Need for planning permission

Section 57(1) of the 1990 Act provides that, subject to the following provisions
of that section, 'planning permission is required for the carrying out of any
development of land'. This planning permission may be granted following the
determination of an express application for permission made to the local
planning authority for the area in which the land is situated. In other cases,
however, it is not necessary for an express application to be made. This is
because planning permission for the development in question may have been
granted by a development order (such development is generally known as
'permitted' development), or by some specific statutory provision (as in the
case of enterprise zones or simplified planning zones), or be deemed to have
been granted (as in the case of the display of advertisements) under other
powers contained in the Act, or authorised by some Private Act of Parliament.

5.2 Definition of development

The term 'development' is central to the power of local planning authorities to
control the use and development of land. It is defined in s. 55 (see Appendix A)
and in s. 336(1) (the interpretation section) of the 1990 Act. Section 55(1)
contains the central core of the definition and provides that development may
take one of two forms, namely, 'the carrying out of building, engineering,
mining or other operations in, on, over or under land' or 'the making of any
material change in the use of any buildings or other land'.

   The scheme of the Act is to keep these two forms of development separate
and distinct. So in order to prevent confusion which might otherwise arise
between the two forms by way of overlap, s. 336(1) of the 1990 Act provides
that the expression 'use' in relation to land, 'does not include the use of land for
the carrying out of any building or other operations thereon'. Hence, any

planning permission granted solely for the making of a material change in the use of land or buildings will not authorise the carrying out of an operation on the land in order to secure the better enjoyment of the new use. On the other hand, the Act recognises that the enjoyment of a building erected under a grant of planning permission will almost inevitably involve a change in the use of the land on which the building has been erected. Accordingly, s. 75(2) of the 1990 Act provides that:

Where planning permission is granted for the erection of a building, the grant of permission may specify the purposes for which the building may be used.

Section 75(3) then goes on to say:

If no purpose is so specified, the permission shall be construed as including permission to use the building for the purpose for which it is designed.

The two forms of development, namely, a building, engineering, mining or other operation or a material change of use, are often referred to as two limbs in order to emphasise their related but independent characteristics. The first limb is often referred to as 'operational development'.

Although the core of the definition is contained in s. 55(1) of the 1990 Act, it is qualified by important provisions contained in subsections (2) to (5) of that section. Subsection (2) lists three operations (paras (a) to (c)), three uses (paras (d) to (f)) and then one further operation (para. (g)) added to the subsection by the Planning and Compensation Act 1991, which are not to be taken to involve the development of land. Subsection (3) lists two uses which, for the avoidance of doubt, are declared to involve a material change of use. Subsection (4) amplifies the meaning of the term mining operations; subsection (4A) brings certain fish-farming activities within the definition of development; and subsection (5) provides that the display of certain advertisements shall constitute a material change of use.

5.2.1 Building operations

As already stated, the first part of the definition of development is the 'carrying out of building, engineering, mining or other operations in, on, over or under land'. Subsection (1A) of s. 55 of the Act provides that the term 'building operations' includes:

(a) demolition of buildings;
(b) rebuilding;
(c) structural alterations of or additions to buildings; and
(d) other operations normally undertaken by a person carrying on business as a builder.

Two points about this definition should be noted. First, the use of the word 'includes' shows that the words that follow are not exhaustive of its meaning; secondly and somewhat surprisingly, the erection of an entirely new building is not specifically mentioned as being within the term. It seems fairly clear, however, that such activity must fall within the concluding clause of the definition as being work normally undertaken by a person carrying on business as a builder.

5.2.1.1 Buildings As recognised in the definition given to the words 'building operations', the work done will normally involve work to a 'building'. The meaning of the word 'building', therefore, may also be relevant to the question of whether a particular activity constitutes development. 'Building' is defined in s. 336(1) to include 'any structure or erection, and any part of a building, as so defined, but does not include plant or machinery comprised in a building'. The word 'building' therefore, has been given in this context a wider meaning than is normally given to it in everyday parlance. It will thus include 'erections' which may not normally be regarded as 'buildings'.

As might be expected, therefore, a number of significant judicial decisions have been made on its precise meaning and application.

In *Buckinghamshire County Council* v *Callingham* [1952] 2 QB 515 the Court of Appeal held that the model village and railway at Bekonscot near Beacons-field was a structure or erection, and therefore a building within the meaning of that word. In *James* v *Brecon County Council* (1963) 15 P & CR 20, however, it was held that a battery of six swing-boats erected at a fairground was not a structure or erection. An important factor in that decision was that the entire battery could be dismantled by six men in no more than half an hour.

Thus in determining whether a structure or erection exists, factors likely to be considered dominant by the courts are size and permanence. That much seems clear from two of the most important judicial decisions made in this area.

In *Cheshire County Council* v *Woodward* [1962] 2 QB 126, a coal merchant installed a coal hopper and conveyor equipment in his coal yard without first obtaining a grant of planning permission to do so. The hopper, which was some 16 to 20 feet in height and mounted on wheels, traversed and delivered coal to stationary lorries beneath. An enforcement notice was then served on behalf of the county council alleging a breach of planning control and requiring the removal of the hopper and conveyor.

The coal merchant appealed to the Minister against the enforcement notice and the Minister, after holding an inquiry, accepted the recommendation of the Inspector and quashed the notice. The Council then appealed to the High Court on the point of law that the Minister had erred in holding that the installation was not development. In dismissing the appeal, Lord Parker CJ said:

... the Act is referring to any structure or erection which can be said to form part of the realty, and to change the physical character of the land.

It seems, however, that an object may be affixed to land and not be a building, or not be affixed to land and be a building. According to Lord Parker CJ in *Cheshire County Council* v *Woodward:*

The mere fact that something is erected in the course of a building operation which is affixed to the land does not determine the matter. Equally, as it seems to me, the mere fact that it can be moved and is not affixed does not determine the matter ... There is no one test; you look at the erection, equipment, plant, whatever it is, and ask: in all the circumstances is it to be treated as part of the realty? So here, ... one must look at the whole circumstances, including what is undoubtedly extremely relevant, the degree of permanency with which it is affected.

The decision in *Cheshire County Council* v *Woodward* was later considered by the courts in *Barvis Ltd* v *Secretary of State for the Environment* (1971) 22 P & CR 710. In this case the appellant company had erected at its depot a mobile crane normally used by it for erecting pre-cast concrete structures on contract sites. The crane was some 89 feet high and ran on a steel track permanently fixed in concrete. The crane could be dismantled in sections and re-erected, but took several days to do so. The local planning authority maintained that the erection constituted development and served an enforcement notice on the appellant requiring its removal. Following an appeal, the notice was upheld by the Secretary of State. The appellant company then challenged the decision of the Secretary of State in the High Court. It maintained that the crane was intended to be moved on and off land as requirements demanded; that it was not fixed to the land, nor did it form part of the realty. Furthermore, its degree of permanence was slight and had not altered the physical character of the land. Dismissing the appeal, Bridge J said he did not wish in the slightest degree to question the validity or usefulness of the tests propounded in *Cheshire County Council* v *Woodward*, which he considered it might be necessary to apply in a borderline case. He felt, however, that here it was not necessary to apply the tests propounded in that case. One must ask, he said:

... was the crane, when erected, a 'building' within the definition ... ? 'Building' includes any structure or erection. If, as a matter of impression, one looks objectively at this enormous crane, it seems to me impossible to say that it did not amount to a structure or erection.
... in my judgment, this crane was not the less a structure or erection by reason of its limited degree of mobility on rails on the site, nor by reason of the circumstance that at some future date, uncertain when it was erected, the appellants contemplated that it would be dismantled. ...

In *R* v *Swansea City Council (ex parte Elitestone Ltd)* (1993) 66 P & CR 422, the question arose whether chalets were buildings and therefore capable of being protected from demolition by conservation area status. The Court of Appeal considered the chalets were buildings and that the degree of permanence was a highly material factor in so deciding. Other significant facts may, however, be size and composition by components.

Despite what was said in *Cheshire County Council* v *Woodward* and *Barvis Ltd* v *Secretary of State for the Environment* one can envisage many situations in which the question of whether or not an object is a structure or erection will be finely balanced and where it may be difficult to decide on which side the scales should be brought down.

It should be remembered here that the decision-making processes in the planning law field allow the Secretary of State, in determining such matters as appeals against enforcement notices or the refusal of an authority to issue a certificate of lawfulness of a proposed use or development under s. 192 of the 1990 Act, to make an initial determination on whether or not a particular activity constitutes development. Although this is a determination on a point of law, landowners and local planning authorities may be willing to accept his decision and be reluctant to pursue the matter further by challenging his decision in the courts. Hence, the Secretary of State's decision in a particular case is often final.

In that capacity, he has held that such things as a carport, a Portakabin, an inflatable whale (erected on a pier at a seaside resort), a plastic tree (erected in the children's playing area in the grounds of a public house) and a steel frame supporting a polythene cover over a swimming-pool were structures or erections and thus within the definition of a building. From a practical point of view, it should also be borne in mind that the General Development Order grants planning permission for such minor matters as the erection or construction of gates, fences, walls or other means of enclosure. However, this is not in itself conclusive proof that in law such work necessarily constitutes a building operation: the content of an order made under the Act cannot be used to try to discover the meaning of the Act itself.

5.2.1.2 Building operations which are not development Mention was made earlier that s. 55(2) of the 1990 Act specified three operations (paras (a) to (c)) and three uses (paras (d) to (f)) and then a further operation (para. (g)), which were not to be taken to involve the development of land. The operation mentioned in paragraph (a) is:

the carrying out for the maintenance, improvement or other alteration of any building of works which—

(i)   affect only the interior of the building, or
(ii)   do not materially affect the external appearance of the building,

and are not works for making good war damage or works begun after 5th December 1968 for the alteration of a building by providing additional space in it underground.

This provision makes it clear that it is not development to remove, say, an internal wall of a building. The provision however, is sometimes misunderstood. There are many activities which may affect only the interior of a building or do not materially affect its external appearance. These activities will not constitute development, not because of the provisions in s. 55(2)(a) but because the work involved does not constitute a building operation. In other words, one must first consider whether the work involved falls within the meaning of development as defined in ss. 55(1) and 336(1). If it does, one has then to consider whether it is excluded from that definition by being an activity which falls within s. 55(2)(a). Thus it is not development to replace a broken pane of glass in the window of a dwellinghouse. The reason is that it is not an operation as defined in ss. 55(1) and 336(1), and the fact that the replacement does not materially affect the external appearance of the building is not relevant.

The value of following this approach is best seen with regard to the concluding provision in s. 55(2)(a), namely the words 'and are not ... works begun after 5th December 1968 for the alteration of a building by providing additional space in it underground'. These words were introduced into the law by the Town and Country Planning Act 1968. The need to do so arose from the wishes of a provincial department store to extend its premises. Being unable to do so either upwards or outwards, it decided to obtain the additional space it needed by excavating downwards. On the completion of the work and the opening of the store's household basement the additional custom generated by the extension caused considerable congestion in the surrounding streets.

The work done by the store was not development and the local planning authority were powerless to prevent it. Although it constituted a building (and possibly also an engineering) operation under s. 55(1), it was excluded from the definition of development by virtue of being work for the alteration of a building which affected only its interior. During the passage of the 1968 Act through Parliament, the opportunity was taken to close this lacuna in the law by, as it were, excluding that exclusion for the future.

Thus after 5 December 1968, work of this kind requires planning permission. Such work would be a building operation, but one to which the provisions of para. (a) of s. 55(2) would not apply.

The question of whether or not carrying out works for the maintenance, improvement or other alteration of a building materially affects the external appearance of the building is one which will normally be determined by the local planning authority or, on appeal, by the Secretary of State. In one rare case, however, the question was determined by the courts.

In *Kensington & Chelsea Royal London Borough Council* v *C. G. Hotels* [1981] JPL 190 the owners of a West London hotel installed floodlights without planning permission. The local planning authority then served an enforcement notice requiring their removal. Some of the floodlights were attached to the basement area of the hotel; others simply stood under their own weight on first floor balconies but were not attached to the building other than by the electricity supply cable.

The owners had appealed to the Secretary of State and an Inspector, acting on his behalf, had concluded that there was no breach of planning control and quashed the notice. In dismissing an appeal against the decision of the Secretary of State, the Divisional Court held that assuming, without actually deciding, that the installation of floodlights constituted development within s. 55(1) of the 1990 Act, the placing of electric cables and floodlights in position and the fixing of some of them to the building, did not 'materially affect the external appearance of the buildings'. If the external appearance of the building had been materially affected, it was caused by the running of electricity through the cables, not by the positioning and fixing of the floodlights.

5.2.1.3 The problem of demolition The problem of whether or not the demolition of a building *simpliciter* constitutes development has for many years been uncertain yet important. 'Building operations', it may be recalled, is defined in s. 55(1A) to include 'demolition of buildings; rebuilding; structural alterations of or additions to buildings; and other operations normally undertaken by a person carrying on business as a builder'.

Prior to the 1991 Act, the definition of building operations (previously found in s. 336(1) of the Act) did not include 'demolition of buildings' and this led to much uncertainty.

The leading case in this area was without doubt that of *Coleshill & District Investment Co. Ltd* v *Minister of Housing & Local Government* [1969] 1 WLR 746. The facts are particularly crucial to the decision. A site had consisted of six separate buildings used during the last war as an ammunition depot. Four of the buildings had been used as magazines, the other two for the storage of explosives. Around each building was a blast wall 9 feet in height. Against each wall and on its outside was a sloping embankment of rubble and soil extending out about 8 feet from the base. The functional relationship between the wall with its embankment and the buildings which it surrounded is only too self-evident.

There was no dispute between the parties that the original use having been discontinued, the six buildings had an existing use for storage purposes. The appellant company wished to remove the embankments and walls. As a first step it started to remove the embankments. Following complaints by residents, the local planning authority served an enforcement notice on the company requiring it to cease the removal. The company, having taken the view that this activity did not constitute development and that no planning permission was necessary, appealed against the enforcement notice to the Minister, who refused to grant planning permission for the development and upheld the notice.

The company had also wished to demolish the walls. It therefore applied to the local planning authority, under what was then s. 64 of the 1990 Act, for a determination whether that operation would constitute development. Having heard nothing from the authority within the period prescribed for doing so, the company appealed to the Minister against non-determination of their application. The Minister then determined that the removal of the walls would constitute development and that planning permission was required. Thus, by two separate procedural routes, the Minister had given a decision that the removal of the embankments and walls constituted development. In the High Court the company again contended that an act of demolition was not development. The case eventually reached the House of Lords. Their lordships thought that the question of whether demolition was or was not development was a neat and arresting question, but not one that needed to be answered on the facts of the case. According to their lordships, the true path of inquiry was not to crystal-gaze or to ask hypothetical questions. One had to see exactly what had been done, and then see whether it came within the statutory definition of development. They pointed out that it was unnecessary (and possibly misleading) to give work a single label like demolition, and then try to apply the definition to that label. Their lordships were clearly right. Nothing is to be gained by asking, for example, whether renovation, or repair, or rehabilitation constitutes development.

The House of Lords went on to find that the Minister had made no error of law in holding:

(a) that the blast walls and embankments were an integral part of the buildings and that the removal of the blast walls would constitute a building operation; and

(b)   that the removal of the embankments was an engineering operation.

The decision has proved difficult to interpret. There is no doubt that an important feature of the case was the upholding of the Minister's finding that the blast walls and embankments formed an integral part of the buildings. Hence it was inevitable that their removal would constitute development, since a building operation was then defined in s. 336(1) to include 'structural alterations . . . to buildings'.

The decision thus raised the important question of whether or not it would be development to remove the whole of a building or a building complex. Leaving aside the possibility that its removal might constitute an engineering operation (see 5.2.2) it is difficult to see how, if the whole of a building were demolished, it could be said to be 'a rebuilding operation, a structural alteration or an addition to a building'. It could be, however, that the courts would regard that activity as an 'other operation normally undertaken by a person carrying on business as a builder'. No one, it seems, could be sure. There was an *obiter* statement which suggested that, unless the total removal of a building constituted an engineering operation, the work would not be regarded as development. In *Iddenden* v *Secretary of State for the Environment* [1972] 1 WLR 1433 the appellant had demolished a Nissen hut and workshop and erected in its place a new building. The local planning authority had served an enforcement notice upon him requiring him to demolish the new building which had been erected without planning permission. Iddenden claimed that the notice was invalid because it did not also require him to re-erect the buildings he had demolished. It was held that the local planning authority had a discretion to decide what steps were required to restore the land to its condition before the development took place. They could if they wished, decide that all that was necessary was the pulling down of the new building. That effectively disposed of the appellant's argument. For good measure, however, Lord Denning MR added that 'Whilst some demolition operations may be development . . . the demolition of buildings such as these was not'. In other words, it was not a breach of planning control to remove these old buildings.

The difficulty of knowing whether or not the law regarded the *total* demolition of a building as development had important consequences for development control. The demolition of buildings sometimes took place in order to remove an impediment to the grant of planning permission for the redevelopment of the land on which the building stands. Planning permission, for example, might be refused for the redevelopment of land with an existing community use such as shops and theatres, because of a desire to retain those uses; and this even though the redevelopment proposal was in accordance with the provisions of the development plan for the area. If the shops and theatres are first demolished, no valid reason then exists for the refusal of the permission. Nowhere has this been more of a problem than with regard to buildings having some architectural or historical interest, but which are not considered to possess such special qualities as to warrant their inclusion in the statutory list of buildings (called listed buildings) kept by the Secretary of State under the provisions of s. 1 of the Planning (Listed Buildings and Conservation Areas) Act 1990. The significance of this is that if the buildings were within the list they could not be demolished without listed building consent to do so first being obtained. It often happens that once an application for planning permission is made for redevelopment of land on which there stands a building which, although not listed, has some architectural or historical interest, the application will generate suggestions that the building has sufficient special qualities to warrant it being added to the list, and so subject to the special protection which is given to listed buildings. If it is added, the prospect of obtaining listed building consent to its demolition to enable the redevelopment to go ahead is not likely to be high. It follows, therefore, that in these situations there is pressure on landowners and developers to first demolish the building and then make an application for planning permission for the redevelopment of the land on which it stood. In this way no one is alerted to the possibility that an important building would be lost to the public heritage if planning permission was granted, and by the time the public are alerted, it has already been lost.

It should be noted, however, that under s. 74 of the Planning (Listed Buildings and Conservation Areas) Act 1990, it is an offence to demolish a building in a conservation area without consent (see Chapter 19).

In recent years, further concern has been expressed over the wanton demolition of existing houses, prior to the submission of applications for planning permission for residential development of the land on which the houses stood with much higher housing densities. In a consultation paper issued in 1989 by the Secretary of State, various ways to deal with this problem were canvassed.

As it so happened, the Secretary of State's consideration of the views expressed by consultees was quickly overtaken by events. In *Cambridge City Council* v *Secretary of State for the Environment* (1991) 89 LGR 1015, Mr David Widdicombe QC, sitting in the High Court as a deputy judge, described the question whether demolition was development within the Act as 'a question which like a ghost has haunted planning law for many years. . . . The time has now come when the ghost must be laid to rest'. He then went on to hold that the demolition of houses was a 'building operation' being (as per the definition in s. 336(1)) an 'other operation normally undertaken by a person carrying on business as a builder'. Although an appeal against that decision was subsequently allowed by the Court of Appeal (1992) 90 LGR 275, the government decided after the High Court decision to include a provision in the Planning and Compensation Act 1991 amending the definition of building operations, then contained in s. 336(1) of the 1990 Act, to include the 'demolition of buildings' and to include that definition in the body of s. 55.

Since, however, few problems have arisen with the demolition of buildings other than dwellinghouses, the 1991 Act has given the Secretary of State power to make directions enabling him to provide that the demolition of particular types of building is not to involve development. Thus the following new paragraph (g) was added to the three operations listed in s. 55(2) (in paras (a) to (c)) which are *not* to be taken to involve development:

... the demolition of any description of building specified in a direction given by the Secretary of State to local planning authorities generally or to a particular local authority.

The Secretary of State has now made the Town and Country Planning (Demolition — Description of Buildings) (No. 2) Direction 1992, published as an Annex to Circular No. 26/92, 'Planning Controls over Demolition'. The effect of the Direction, which came into force on 27 July 1992, is to provide that the demolition of the following types of building shall *not* be taken to be a building operation:

(a) Listed buildings, buildings in conservation areas and any building which is a scheduled monument as defined in the Ancient Monuments and Archaeological Areas Act 1979. The demolition of all such buildings is subject to control under other legislation.

(b) A building of less than 50 cubic metres (when measured externally). Clearly this is intended to be a *de minimis* provision.

(c) Any building other than a dwellinghouse or a building adjoining a dwellinghouse. Thus buildings used as offices, factories, shops or warehouses are outside the definition of development.

It should be noted that for the purposes of the Direction, the term 'building' includes each house in a pair of semi-detached houses, and every house in a row of terrace houses (whether or not, in either case, the house is in residential use). The term does not, however, include any gate, fence, wall or other means of enclosure. On the other hand, the term 'dwellinghouse' *includes* a residential house or hostel, and a building containing a flat.

The new control over demolition is intended in the main to apply to the demolition of dwellinghouses and of buildings adjoining dwellinghouses. However, because the demolition of most dwellinghouses does not justify the full application of these new controls, the Secretary of State has, with one important exception, exercised his power to amend the General Development Order to grant planning permission for the demolition of all buildings which are not already excluded from control by the Direction described above. With that one exception, namely, where a building has been made unsafe or uninhabitable, either through deliberate action or neglect by anyone having an interest in the land on which the building stands and the building can be made secure through temporary repairs or support, the demolition of a dwellinghouse or of a building adjoining a dwellinghouse is permitted development by virtue of the Order. Before such permitted development rights may be used, however, the Order provides that the developer must first apply to the local planning authority for a determination of whether the prior approval of the authority is required as to the *method* of the proposed demolition and any proposed restoration of the site. The authority are then given 28 days to consider the matter. If the developer is not notified within the 28-day period that prior approval is required, he may proceed to demolish the building in accordance with the details submitted by him to the authority in his application for the determination. If, on the other hand, the authority require prior approval to be obtained before demolition, the only remedy available to the developer is to seek that prior approval and then, if approval should not be given, to appeal to the Secretary of State.

The purpose of this prior-approval requirement is to give local planning authorities the opportunity to regulate the details of demolition in order to minimise the impact of that activity on local amenity. It must be emphasised, however, that the need to seek prior approval does not in fact prevent demolition from taking place. In order to do that, there must be in place an Article 4 direction (see Chapter 7), withdrawing the permitted development right.

It should be noted too that the prior-approval procedure described above, does not apply where demolition:

(a)   is urgently necessary in the interest of health or safety, on condition that the developer gives a written justification of the demolition to the local planning authority as soon as reasonably practicable after the demolition has taken place; or

(b)   takes place on land for which planning permission for redevelopment has been granted or deemed to be granted; or

(c)   is required as a result of a demolition order, made under Part IX of the Housing Act 1985, or in a clearance area declared under s. 289 of the same Act; or

(d)   is required as a result of an enforcement notice issued under Part VII of the Town and Country Planning Act 1990; or

(e)   is required as a result of an order requiring the removal of the building made under s. 102 of the Town and Country Planning Act 1990 which has been confirmed; or

(f)   is required by virtue of a planning agreement or obligation made under s. 106 of the Town and Country Planning Act 1990; or

(g)   is required or permitted under any other legislation.

The above changes do not affect the need to obtain planning permission for any demolition which amounts to an engineering operation; or indeed for the partial demolition of a building if that can be regarded as a 'structural alteration' to a building. To that extent, the decision of the House of Lords in the *Coleshill* case continues to be relevant.

5.2.2 Engineering operations

The 1990 Act gives little guidance on the meaning of the expression 'engineering operations' save that s. 336(1) provides that it includes 'the formation or laying out of means of access to highways'. It will be recalled that in *Coleshill & District Investment Co. Ltd v Minister of Housing & Local Government* [1969] 1 WLR 746, the House of Lords found that the Minister had not erred in law in holding the removal of an embankment to be an engineering operation. In this case it was shown that the removal of the embankment would require many lorries to be used over a prolonged period to transport the debris away from the site. On the other hand, the removal of a mere shovelful of earth from one spot to another is unlikely to be considered an engineering operation. Somewhere in between lies the demarcation line that separates an activity which is not an engineering operation from one which is. The meaning of the term has until recently received little judicial consideration. The absence of judicial guidance led at one time to much uncertainty and inconsistency in cases where the term had to be applied. In 1983, however, the meaning of the term was clarified by the decision in *Fayrewood Fish Farms Ltd v Secretary of State for the Environment* [1984] JPL 267, in which the High Court had to consider whether the excavation and removal of topsoil for the purpose of extracting underlying gravel constituted an 'engineering operation'. The Secretary of State had thought that it did. In remitting the matter back to the Secretary of State with the opinion of the court, Mr David Widdicombe QC, sitting as a Deputy High Court judge, accepted that the Secretary of State was basically right to hold that engineering operations called for engineering skills, but that he had gone too far in requiring that there had to be a 'specific project which is of sufficient predetermined size and shape that a conception of the finished project can be illustrated on a plan or drawing'. In his view, the term 'engineering operations' should be given its ordinary meaning in the English language. It must mean, he said, 'operations of the kind usually undertaken by engineers, i.e., operations calling for the skills of an engineer'. These would normally be civil engineers, but could be traffic engineers or other specialist engineers who applied their skills to land. It did not mean, he said, 'that an engineer must actually be engaged on the project, simply that it was the kind of operation on which an engineer could be employed, or which would be within his purview'.

In the exercise of his appellate functions, the Secretary of State for the Environment has held that the removal of part of an embankment supporting a railway bridge and the deposit of subsoil and topsoil on land constituted an engineering operation [1983] JPL 616. Although the deposit of refuse or waste materials on land is regarded by the 1990 Act as being, if anything, a material change of use, it was suggested by the High Court in *Ratcliffe v Secretary of State for the Environment* [1975] JPL 728 that the deposit of refuse could amount to an 'engineering operation'.

Whatever the meaning of the term 'engineering operation' its compass is limited by the provisions in paras (b) and (c) of s. 55(2) of the 1990 Act, the two remaining operations specified in that subsection as not to be taken to involve the development of land. The provisions are as follows:

(b) the carrying out on land within the boundaries of a road by a local highway authority of any works required for the maintenance or improvement of the road;

(c) the carrying out by a local authority or statutory undertakers of any works for the purpose of inspecting, repairing or renewing any sewers, mains, pipes, cables or other apparatus, including the breaking open of any street or other land for that purpose.

As regards the activity mentioned in paragraph (b), it should be remembered that, particularly in country areas, the boundaries of a road may frequently be much wider than that part of the road which is actually 'made up'. This provision enables the local highway authority, therefore, to make important alterations to the line of a road by such activities as ironing out a curve or removing old walls and hedges, without the need to apply for planning permission to do so. This freedom from planning control is compounded by a provision in the General Development Order. The Order grants planning permission for 'the carrying out by a local highway authority on lands outside but adjoining the boundary of an existing highway of works required for or incidental to the maintenance or improvement of the highway'. Although the local highway authority would, unless it already owned adjacent land, have to purchase it from the owner before being able to avail itself of the permission granted by the order, the two provisions taken together give a wide latitude to highway authorities to alter the lay-out of a road without the public being able to influence its proposals.

It will be recalled that s. 336(1) provides that engineering operations includes 'the formation or laying out of means of access to highways'. It would seem, therefore, that the simple driving of a vehicle on to the highway is not in itself an engineering operation. However, under the Highways Act 1980 the highway authority has power to erect fences or posts to prevent access to the highway from adjacent land.

Prior to the Planning and Compensation Act 1991, doubts existed about the extent to which fish farming constituted development, and thus an activity subject to development control.

Section 14 of the 1991 Act inserted into s. 55 of the 1990 Act a new subsection (4A) to bring fish tanks (cages) in inland waters within the definition of development. The new subsection (4A) provides:

Where the placing or assembly of any tank in any part of any inland waters for the purpose of fish farming there would not, apart from this subsection, involve development of the land below, this Act shall have effect as if the tank resulted from carrying out engineering operations over that land; and in this subsection—

'fish farming' means the breeding, rearing or keeping of fish or shellfish (which includes any kind of crustacean and mollusc);
'inland waters' means waters which do not form part of the sea or of any creek, bay or estuary or of any river as far as the tide flows; and
'tank' includes any cage and any other structure for use in fish farming.

Allied to the decision to make the placing or assembly of fish tanks development, the government amended the General Development Order to provide that such activity should be permitted development under the Order when carried out on land outside national parks. However, under the Order, a person wishing to exercise such permitted development 'rights' must give prior notice to the local planning authority. This prior-notification procedure allows the local planning authority to decide within a period of 28 days whether or not they wish to make the activity subject to their prior approval. If the authority do so decide, it allows them to exercise control over the siting and appearance of the development.

5.2.3 Mining operations
As originally enacted the definition of development contained no definition of the term 'mining operations'. In s. 336(1) however, minerals are defined to include 'all minerals and substances in or under land of a kind ordinarily worked for removal by underground or surface working, except that it does not include peat cut for purposes other than sale'.

The Town and Country Planning (Minerals) Act 1981 amended the definition of development by adding a new provision. This is now contained in s. 55(4) which states:

For the purposes of this Act mining operations include—

(a)   the removal of material of any description—

(i)   from a mineral-working deposit;
(ii)   from a deposit of pulverised fuel ash or other furnace ash or clinker; or
(iii) from a deposit of iron, steel or other metallic slags; and

(b) the extraction of minerals from a disused railway embankment.

The 1981 Act was passed after the government had considered the report of the Stevens Committee on Planning Control over Mineral Workings. Concern was there expressed about whether the definition of development and particularly mining operations, was wide enough to include the recovery of material originally removed or extracted from the land and then deposited on it, such as a slagheap from a coal-mine or a coal deposit on a railway line. The amendment made to the definition of development by the 1981 Act makes clear that this and other like activities over which there was similar doubt now fall within that definition.

5.2.4 Other operations

It is clear that there must be some restriction on the words 'other operations'. As was pointed out by the House of Lords in *Coleshill & District Investment Co. Ltd* v *Minister of Housing & Local Government* [1969] 1 WLR 746, the use of the words 'building, engineering, mining or other operations', makes it clear that not every operation constitutes development since to hold otherwise would be to render the words 'building, engineering and mining' superfluous. Their lordships also pointed out that since 'mining' operations differed substantially from 'building' operations, it was not possible for a single genus to fit all three words. Accordingly 'other operations' could not be construed *eiusdem generis*. Their lordships all agreed, however, that there must be some restriction on the meaning of 'other operations'; that it must be construed by reference to building, engineering and mining, and that the maxim *noscitur a sociis* might apply even though it is not *eiusdem generis*. Lord Pearson also suggested that although no single genus would fit all three preceding words, it was possible that there were three separate genera, and that 'other operations' would connote an activity similar to 'building operations', or to 'engineering operations' or to 'mining operations'.

In *Cambridge City Council* v *Secretary of State for the Environment*, the Court of Appeal, having concluded that there had been no evidence before the deputy judge upon which he had been entitled to make a finding of fact that the demolition of the houses in question constituted work normally undertaken by a person who carried on business as a builder, went on to consider whether the work constituted an 'other operation' on land. On the basis of authority (i.e., the *Coleshill* decision), the Court of Appeal concluded that it did not. The Court emphasised that 'other' operations in s. 55 of the 1990 Act did not mean all other operations; and that other operations had to be '... at least of a constructive character, leading to an identifiable and positive result' or be '... similar to building operations or to engineering operations'.

Because of the wide definition given in the Act to the words building, engineering and mining, there is no recorded judicial decision of any particular activity being held to be an 'other operation'. In fact, there are only two known examples of an activity found to be an 'other operation' and those were contained in Ministerial decisions given on appeal.

When making decisions on appeal in this area, it is common for the Secretary of State (or the Inspector) to confine himself to a statement that the activity which he is considering is or is not development; or, at best, to confine himself to a reference to one of the specific operations listed in s. 55(1). In one of the decisions referred to above, however, the Inspector held that the deposit of waste materials on land for the purpose of raising the level of the land to make it suitable for agricultural use was not a building or engineering operation, but an 'other operation' for which planning permission was required [1982] JPL 741. That decision, however, was made before the Inspector had the benefit of the judgment in *Fayrewood Fish Farms Ltd* v *Secretary of State for the Environment* [1984] JPL 267. Had that been available, he might well have held that the deposit in question was an engineering operation.

In another Ministerial decision reported at [1985] JPL 129 it was held that the installation of a protective grille over a shop window and door was an 'other operation' within the meaning of s. 55(1) of the 1990 Act.

SIX

Definition of development
2: Material change of use

The term 'material change of use' is not defined in the Act. Its meaning has to be ascertained, therefore, by reference to the many cases in which the courts have had to consider its significance. In *Parkes* v *Secretary of State for the Environment* [1978] 1 WLR 1308, Lord Denning MR said that 'operations' comprised activities which resulted in some physical alteration to the land, which had some degree of permanence to the land itself; whereas 'use' comprised activities which are done in, alongside or on the land but which did not interfere with the actual physical characteristics of the land. Accordingly, he held that, for the purposes of serving a discontinuance order under what is now s. 102 of the 1990 Act, the sorting, processing and disposal of scrap materials was a 'use' of land.

6.1 Material change of use

It must be emphasised that the activity which constitutes the second limb of the term 'development' is not merely a 'change of use' but a 'material change of use'. The attitude of the courts to the question of whether or not a change of use is material is that it is largely a matter of fact and degree for the local planning authority to decide, and they will only interfere if the decision is one to which the authority could not reasonably have come. In *Bendles Motors Ltd* v *Bristol Corporation* [1963] 1 WLR 247 an application for planning permission had been made to the local planning authority for permission to erect an egg-vending machine on the forecourt of garage premises. After permission had been refused, the owners of the garage proceeded nevertheless to erect the machine on the forecourt. The machine measured some six feet in height, two feet seven inches deep and two feet seven inches wide. Since it was also free-standing and gravity-fed, it could not be considered to be operational development. The local planning authority had served an enforcement notice requiring the removal of the machine and, on appeal, the Minister had upheld the notice. The owners then appealed to the High Court against the Minister's decision on a point of law.

The Minister had upheld the enforcement notice on the ground that the stationing of the egg-vending machine on the site involved a change of use of the land on which it stood and that its introduction on the site involved a material change of use of the land, since the use of the machine was in the nature of a 'shop use', in that it attracted customers not necessarily concerned with the motoring service provided by the garage. In dismissing the appeal Lord Parker CJ quoting his own words in *East Barnet Urban District Council* v *British Transport Commission* [1962] 2 QB 484 said:

> 'It is a question of fact and degree in every case and ... the court is unable to interfere with a finding ... on such a matter unless it must be said that they could not properly have reached that conclusion.' That was dealing with a case stated from justices, but in my judgment the same is true of an appeal from the Minister himself. This court can only interfere if satisfied that it is a conclusion that he could not, properly directing himself as to the law, have reached.

Later, the Lord Chief Justice went on to say:

> I confess that at first sight, and indeed at last sight, I am somewhat surprised that it can be said that the placing of this small machine on this large forecourt can be said to change the use of these premises in a material sense from that of a garage and petrol filling station by the addition of a further use. It is surprising, and it may be, if it was a matter for my own personal judgment, that I should feel inclined to say that the egg-vending machine was *de minimis*; but it is not a question of what my opinion is on that matter, it is for the Minister to decide.

It is submitted that this was clearly a sensible decision. The court held that the Minister had not erred in law in holding that the change of use from a garage and petrol filling-station, to a garage, petrol filling-station and 'shop use' was material. Had the Lord Chief justice given precedence to his personal feelings, it would have been difficult for the local planning authority to control a later installation on the forecourt of other types of vending machines. Furthermore, if the garage and petrol filling-station use were then to be abandoned, a change to an exclusively shop use would have been achieved.

The case demonstrates that whether or not a change of use is material is a question of fact and degree in every case for decision by the local planning authority, or on appeal by the Secretary of State. It also demonstrates that a material change of use may not only occur where a change is made from, say, use A to use B, but also where a change is made from use A to use A and B by the addition of a further use.

The same approach was followed in *Hidderley* v *Warwickshire County Council* (1963) 14 P & CR 134, where the installation of an egg-vending machine on farm land adjacent to a lay-by on a public road was held to constitute a material change of use.

Apart from the approach of the courts to the word 'material', a number of propositions may be advanced with regard to the expression 'change of use':

(a) A change of use will take place where the nature or the character of the use is changed. So that to move from a residential use to a commercial use or to an industrial use, or within any permutation of those uses, will, if the change is material, fall within the definition of development.

(b) In determining whether any activity constitutes a change of use, it is the character of the use which has to be considered, not the particular purpose of a particular occupier. In *East Barnet Urban District Council* v *British Transport Commission* [1962] 2 QB 484 the Divisional Court refused to interfere with the decision of justices (who had quashed enforcement notices served on the company) that to use land as a transit depot for the handling and storage of crated motor vehicles, following upon the use of the land for the storage and distribution of coal, did not constitute development. In expressing the view that what really had to be considered was the character of the use of the land, not the particular purpose of a particular occupier, Lord Parker CJ quoted with approval a statement by Glyn-Jones J in *Marshall* v *Nottingham Corporation* [1960] 1 WLR 707 where he said:

The mere fact that a dealer in the course of his business begins to deal in goods in which he had not dealt before does not necessarily involve a change, still less a material change, in his use of the land or premises where the business is carried on. A dealer in musical instruments might 50 years ago have begun to deal in gramophones or phonographs, as I suppose they would then have been called; and then in the course of time in radio sets and later in television sets. A dealer in electrical appliances, as demand changed and fresh appliances were invented, might have successively added vacuum cleaners, refrigerators, washing machines and the like to his stock-in-trade, and he too might have begun to deal in radio and television sets. Each of them may have ceased to sell goods formerly sold for which there is no longer an adequate demand. Yet neither, in my view, has thereby altered the use he is making of his premises.

The position may be far less clear, however, where a retail business is carried on but a change takes place in the type of business, as might occur, for example, where the business of a baker is substituted for that of a butcher. Fortunately for most practical purposes the problem is dissolved by the existence of the Use Classes Order (see **6.2.3**).

6.2 Uses excluded from development

Whatever may be the meaning of the term 'material change of use', its scope is restricted by paras (d) to (f) of s. 55(2) of the 1990 Act, in which three uses are expressly stated *not* to involve the development of land. The three uses are:

(d)   A use incidental to the enjoyment of a dwellinghouse.
(e)   A use for agriculture or forestry.
(f)   A change of use within the same use class.

6.2.1   Use incidental to the enjoyment of a dwellinghouse

By s. 55(2)(d) of the 1990 Act, 'the use of any buildings or other land within the curtilage of a dwellinghouse for any purpose incidental to the enjoyment of the dwellinghouse as such' is not to be taken to involve development of the land.

Under this provision, it is not a material change of use to convert, say, a henhouse into a workshop or an outhouse to provide additional sleeping accommodation for one's family. The provision refers, however, to the *use of* buildings or other land, so that if the occupier finds it necessary to carry out operational development for the better enjoyment of that use, planning permission will be needed for that operation. The paragraph also refers to the use of any buildings or other land within the *'curtilage'* of a dwellinghouse. Precisely what constitutes the curtilage may not always be clear. The definition of the term most usually referred to is that given in a Scottish case of *Sinclair-Lockhart's Trustees* v *Central Land Board* (1950) 1 P & CR 195, as:

> ground which is used for the comfortable enjoyment of a house ... and thereby as an integral part of the same, although it has not been marked off or enclosed in any way. It is enough that it serves the purposes of the house ... in some necessary or reasonably useful way.

It has also been held in *Dyer* v *Dorset County Council* [1989] QB 346 that the definition in the *Oxford English Dictionary* is adequate for most purposes. That definition is:

> a small court, yard, garth or piece of ground attached to a dwellinghouse and forming one enclosure with it, or so regarded by the law; the area attached to and containing a dwellinghouse and its outbuildings.

It seems from *Stephens* v *Cuckfield RDC* [1959] 1 QB 516, however, that land may be a garden but not be within a curtilage. In *James* v *Secretary of State for the Environment* (1990) 61 P & CR 234, it was held that there are three criteria for determining whether land is within the curtilage of a building, namely:

(a)   physical layout,
(b)   ownership, past and present,
(c)   use or function, past and present.

In an unpublished Ministerial decision in 1993, an Inspector took the view that the cases contain a certain amount of common ground which assists in forming a view on the question of whether land lies within the curtilage of a building. From *Dyer* v *Dorset County Council* comes the notion of the curtilage of a building being essentially small in extent. From *Sinclair-Lockhart's Trustees* v *Central Land Board* comes the concept of land which serves the purpose of a house or building in some reasonably useful way being part of the building's curtilage, and from *James* v *Secretary of State for the Environment* there is the idea of the curtilage of a dwellinghouse being an area forming an enclosure with the building.

Possibly the most important part of paragraph (d) of s. 55(2), however, is the last two words. The requirement is that use must be incidental to the enjoyment of the dwellinghouse 'as such' i.e., as a dwellinghouse. Hence to use land within the curtilage of a dwellinghouse for the parking of a commercial vehicle used for business purposes is not within this provision, unless as a matter of fact and degree it is not considered to be material. This is an area of particular difficulty where a person uses outbuildings or a room in a dwellinghouse to carry on a hobby or an activity having a business or commercial element. Artists' studios and the giving of music lessons are classic examples of this problem. The use of outbuildings for mending cloth, carrying on a tailoring business or dog breeding, the use of a room for a nursing agency and the use of a kitchen to prepare sandwiches and salads for local firms, have all been held by the Secretary of State to constitute development.

In all these cases it is necessary for the authority to look at the nature and scale of the hobby or non-domestic use being carried on, and then to judge whether as a matter of fact and degree a further use has been added to the existing dwellinghouse use.

The application of the provision in s. 55(2)(d) was recently considered by the Court of Appeal in *Wallington* v *Secretary of State for Wales* [1991] JPL 942, where a challenge was made to a decision by an Inspector appointed by the Secretary of State to uphold an enforcement notice which had alleged the making of a material change in the use of a dwellinghouse by the addition of a further, wholly non-commercial use, namely the keeping within the curtilage of the dwellinghouse of some 44 dogs. It was argued on behalf of the appellant that in applying s. 55(2)(d), the Inspector had regarded the question as being whether as a matter of fact and degree it was *reasonable* to regard the relevant activity as the use of the premises for a purpose incidental to the enjoyment of the dwelling as such. It was claimed that to apply an objective test of reasonableness was erroneous, since it would place an unjustifiable restriction on an enthusiast who had an eccentric hobby of his own.

In rejecting the argument and dismissing the appeal, Slade LJ in the Court of Appeal, held that the Inspector had been entitled to have regard to what people *normally* do in dwellinghouses to decide whether, as a matter of fact and degree on the one hand, (a) the keeping of 40 or more dogs should be regarded as reasonably incidental to the enjoyment of the dwellinghouse, or on the other hand, (b) the number of dogs kept exceeded what could reasonably be so regarded.

The court also made reference to a decision of Sir Graham Eyre QC, sitting as a Deputy High Court judge, in *Emin* v *Secretary of State for the Environment* [1989] JPL 909. That decision concerned the criteria set down in Class 1.3 of the then General Development Order 1977, which dealt with development within the curtilage of a dwellinghouse 'required for a purpose incidental to the enjoyment of the dwellinghouse as such', although a distinction might be drawn between the wording of that order and of s. 55(2)(d), which does not include the word 'required'. Nevertheless, according to Slade LJ, certain observations of Sir Graham Eyre were helpful and apposite in the present case, where he had said (at p. 913):

> The fact that such a building had to be required for a purpose associated with the enjoyment of a dwellinghouse could not rest solely on the unrestrained whim of him who dwelt there but connoted some sense of reasonableness in all the circumstances of the particular case. That was not to say that the arbiter could impose some hard objective test so as to frustrate the reasonable aspirations of a particular owner or occupier so long as they were sensibly related to his enjoyment of the dwelling. The word 'incidental' connoted an element of subordination in land use terms in relation to the enjoyment of the dwellinghouse itself.

According to Farquharson LJ in the Court of Appeal in the *Wallington* case, in approaching the question of whether a use was for a purpose incidental to the enjoyment of a dwellinghouse, it was sensible to consider what would be the normal use of a dwellinghouse, although this was not determinative of the question. In his view, consideration of whether the use was subjective or objective merely complicated matters. In his judgment, the word 'incidental' meant subordinate in land use terms to the enjoyment of a dwellinghouse as a dwellinghouse. In considering whether a use came within s. 55(2)(d), one had to have regard to such things as where the dwellinghouse was situated, its size and how much ground was included in its curtilage, the nature and scale of the activity said to be incidental to enjoyment of the dwellinghouse as such and the disposition and character of the occupier.

It will be seen that the judgments in the *Wallington* case do not make clear the precise criteria to be applied in determining whether a use falls within para. (d) of s. 55(2). Slade LJ appeared to favour taking an objective view of whether an activity was incidental, whereas Farquharson LJ clearly thought little help was to be gained by considering any subjective/objective dichotomy.

Since the keeping of 44 dogs in the *Wallington* case was held to be outside the provisions of s. 55(2)(a), the question that arises is how many dogs may a person keep in order to come within the paragraph. In the *Wallington* case the Inspector had expressly accepted that to impose any specific limiting number would be 'arbitrary'; but had gone on, in order to be sure not to over-enforce, to agree with the planning authority that the requirement section of the enforcement notice should enable up to six dogs to be kept on the premises without the need for planning permission.

In a later Ministerial decision, an Inspector upheld an enforcement notice alleging a material change of use within the curtilage of a dwellinghouse by the keeping of dogs, and requiring that the number kept at the premises at any one time should be reduced to not more than three. The Inspector, who had the benefit of having seen the decision in the *Wallington* case, considered that the main issue was whether the continued keeping of the dogs (which over the years had varied between six and eight excluding puppies) would be likely to be harmful to the amenities which occupiers of neighbouring houses would reasonably be expected to enjoy. Although the Inspector considered that the figure of three dogs cited in the notice as the number which would be acceptable might be regarded as arbitrary, the number was not inappropriate to a normal domestic situation, even allowing for the fact that this figure might be exceptional when not every household had dogs.

In yet another Ministerial decision [1993] JPL 901, an Inspector again upheld an enforcement notice which had required that the number of dogs kept within the curtilage of a dwellinghouse be reduced to not more than three. The property in question was a two-bedroom mid-terrace property with a small front garden and a hard-surfaced yard area to the rear. In his decision letter, the Inspector considered it important to distinguish between the enjoyment of the dwellinghouse as such and the enjoyment of the occupier. Put another way, the occupier of a dwellinghouse might well be enjoying himself in some way which was not related to the dwellinghouse *as a dwelling*. In this particular case, for example, the evidence showed that the occupation of the dwellinghouse had been given over to a very large degree to the keeping of animals associated with an animal welfare charity.

The most recent (but unreported) Ministerial decision, involved the keeping of nine German shepherd dogs at a small semi-detached house with modest curtilage located in an urban estate of similar houses in Banbury. The Inspector's view was that the house appeared to have been given over to the dogs, to the point where the interior accommodation looked more suited to housing dogs than people; and he found that the garden was largely given over to dog runs and kennels. In his view, the scale of the dog keeping in relation to the modest size of this suburban property went well beyond that which may be considered incidental to the enjoyment of the dwelling.

In a recent judicial decision, *Croydon London Borough Council v Gladden* [1994] JPL 723, the Court of Appeal, upholding an enforcement notice served by the local planning authority, held that placing a replica Spitfire aeroplane in the garden of a dwellinghouse was not a use incidental to the enjoyment of the dwellinghouse as such. The court held that the concept of what was incidental to such enjoyment included an element of reasonableness. It could not rest solely on the unrestrained whim of the occupier, and no one could regard it as reasonable to keep a replica Spitfire as incidental to the enjoyment of the dwellinghouse. The court also considered that any pleasure, however exquisite, derived from defying the local authority was not enjoyment of the dwelling-house as such.

Another issue which is now topical is whether land within the curtilage of a dwellinghouse can be used by the owner as a private burial ground for himself and his family without the need to apply for planning permission. In a Ministerial decision [1994] JPL 305, a Scottish inquiry reporter held that it could not be so used. The reporter made no mention of the Scottish provision equivalent to s. 55(2)(d) of the 1990 Act, it being unlikely, following the decision in the *Wallington* case, to be a use incidental to the enjoyment of the dwellinghouse as such. The reporter held, however, that since the proposed project would involve the digging of only a very limited number of graves (by hand), it would not amount to an 'engineering or other operation'; and since there would be no change in the surface land use, nor any upstanding physical features resulting from the intending burials, it could not be said that the proposal amounted to a 'material change of use'.

6.2.2 Use for agriculture or forestry
The second of the three uses listed in paragraphs (d) to (f) of s. 55(2) which are expressly stated *not* to involve the development of land is:

(e) the use of any land for the purposes of agriculture or forestry (including afforestation) and the use for any of those purposes of any building occupied together with land so used.

Again the provision refers to the *use* of land for the purposes of agriculture or forestry, so operational development on land used for agriculture or forestry is not within the exclusion. Certain operational development on land used for those purposes is however, permitted development under the General Development Order.

Some disputes have arisen about whether particular activities fall within this exemption. Section 336(1) of the 1990 Act provides that 'agriculture' includes horticulture, fruit growing, seed growing, dairy farming, the breeding and keeping of livestock (including any creature kept for the production of food, wool skins or fur, or for the purpose of its use in the farming of land), the use of land as grazing land, meadow land, osier land, market gardens and nursery grounds, and the use of land for woodlands where that use is ancillary to the farming of land for other agricultural purposes. In *Crowborough Parish Council v Secretary of State for the Environment* [1981] JPL 281, it was held that the use of land for allotments was an agricultural use falling within the definition of agriculture and that in determining an appeal against what was then called a s. 64 determination, the Secretary of State had erred in law in holding otherwise.

In *Sykes* v *Secretary of State for the Environment* [1981] JPL 285, the Divisional Court had to consider whether the use of land for grazing horses was within the definition of agriculture. The Secretary of State had held that it was, and his view was supported by the court. The case raises, however, important issues with regard to the use of land for what is sometimes referred to as 'horsiculture'. This usually refers to the practice of keeping horses on land for horse-riding purposes. If the land is used intensively for that purpose the horses may need to be supplied with extra food. In such cases the question to be asked is: What use is being made of the land? Is it for the purpose of grazing? If not, then the activity may amount to a material change of use.

Donaldson LJ said:

If . . . horses are being kept on the land and are being fed wholly or primarily by other means so that such grazing as they do is completely incidental and perhaps achieved merely because there are no convenient ways of stopping them doing it, then plainly the land is not being used for grazing but merely being used for keeping the animals.

Another significant case on the definition of agriculture was *North Warwickshire BC* v *Secretary of State for the Environment* [1984] JPL 435, where Woolf held that the use of a *building* for the purposes of agriculture also fell within the paragraph. The paragraph refers to the use of land for the purposes of agriculture 'and the use for any of those purposes of any building occupied together with land so used'. The court considered that because the definition of land in s. 336(1) of the 1990 Act meant 'any corporeal hereditament, including a building', the two phrases had to be construed disjunctively. If this decision is correct, it would be possible to convert a disused building in suburbia into a chicken farm without the change amounting to development.

6.2.3   Change of use within the same use class
The third of the three uses listed in paragraphs (a) to (f) of s. 55(2) which are expressly stated *not* to involve the development of land is:

> (f)   in the case of buildings or other land which are used for a purpose of any class specified in an order made by the Secretary of State under this section, the use of the buildings or other land or, subject to the provisions of the order, of any part of the buildings or the other land, for any other purpose of the same class.

The relevant order is now the Town and Country Planning (Use Classes) Order 1987, which came into force on 1 June 1987 (see Appendix B, to which reference should be constantly made). It replaced a previous order which had remained substantially unchanged since it was first introduced in 1948. The 1987 order specifies 15 different classes of use for the purposes of paragraph (f), so that a change of use within the same use Class is not to be taken to involve the development of land. It should be noted that the effect of the Use Classes Order is to specify that a change of use which results in the old and the new uses falling within the same use Class is not development. It does not specify that a change of use involving a change from one use Class to some other use Class is necessarily development. Whether or not it is depends upon whether a material change of use has taken place. This was made clear in *Rann* v *Secretary of State for the Environment* [1980] JPL 109. The Use Classes Order is thus a liberalising measure freeing certain activities from planning control. It does not seek to restrict activities by making them subject to planning control when they would otherwise not be so.

The order is divided into four parts, which correspond broadly with (a) shopping area uses; (b) other business and industrial uses; (c) residential uses; and (d) social and community uses of a non-residential kind.

It should be noted that not all uses of buildings or other land are allocated to a particular Class in the order. Those uses not allocated to a particular Class are known as *sui generis*. Indeed, art. 3(6) of the order specifically identifies a number of uses not included in any class of the order. They are the use of buildings or other land:

(a)   as a theatre,
(b)   as an amusement arcade or centre, or a funfair,
(c)   as a launderette,
(d)   for the sale of fuel for motor vehicles,
(e)   for the sale or display for sale of motor vehicles,
(f)   for a taxi business or business for the hire of motor vehicles,
(g)   as a scrapyard, or a yard for the storage or distribution of minerals
or the breaking of motor vehicles,
(h)   for any work registrable under the Alkali, etc., Works Regulation Act
1906,
(i)   as a hostel.

Part A — Shopping Area Uses
6.2.3.1   Class A1. Shops   Under this heading, the order lists, in paragraphs
(a) to (j), the following specified uses:

(a)   for the retail sale of goods other than hot food,
(b)   as a post office,
(c)   for the sale of tickets or as a travel agency,
(d)   for the sale of sandwiches or other cold food for consumption off the
premises,
(e)   for hairdressing,
(f)   for the direction of funerals,
(g)   for the display of goods for sale,
(h)   for the hiring out of domestic or personal goods or articles,
(i)   for the washing or cleaning of clothes or fabrics on the premises,
(j)   for the reception of goods to be washed, cleaned or repaired,

where the sale, display or service is to visiting members of the public.

Hence, for example, a butcher's shop can become a travel agent or a
hair-dresser's and remain within the same use class.

Building societies are included in Class A2 (financial and professional
services); and shops for the sale of hot food in Class A3 (food and drink) (see
below).

In a recent high-profile case, *R* v *Thurrock Borough Council* (*ex parte Tesco
Stores Ltd*) [1994] JPL 328, it was necessary to consider the scope of the phrase
'visiting members of the public'. An organisation called Costco had been
granted planning permission to operate a warehouse club selling a limited
selection of products within a wide range of product categories only to
members of the club who had paid a subscription and were within categories of
person specified by Costco. Tesco argued that the development was essentially
a retail use on an industrial and commercial site which would be contrary to the
authority's development plan policy which sought to promote wholesale cash
and carry warehousing on the site but to exclude retail uses within Class A1
which would affect the vitality and viability of existing shopping centres. Tesco
argued that the warehouse club was a *sui generis* use being neither a warehouse
use nor a retail use. In dismissing Tesco's application for judicial review of the

grant of planning permission, Schiemann J held that if there was a restriction on persons who were able to enter and buy then the premises were not prima facie properly described as being used for the sale of goods to visiting members of the public. Hence, the use did not fall within Class A1.

6.2.3.2 Class A2. Financial and professional services This Class is intended to provide flexibility in the use of buildings for a sector of the economy which is rapidly expanding, particularly that part which needs to be accommodated in shop-type premises in a shopping area. It embraces use for the provision of:

(a) financial services, or
(b) professional services (other than health or medical services), or
(c) any other services (including use as a betting office) which it is appropriate to provide in a shopping area

where the services are provided principally to visiting members of the public.

This Class includes use by banks, building societies, betting shops, accountants, solicitors, architects, surveyors, mortgage and insurance brokers and law centres. Since membership of this Class depends also upon services being provided primarily to visiting members of the public, barristers' chambers do not come within it.

The requirement that the services must be provided primarily to visiting members of the public is likely to cause difficulty. Access by the public to financial institutions or professional offices may not be constant and the order does not lay down a prescribed level of access. A bank, for example, may be a building mainly for internal administration of trust accounts with little public access. It would appear not to be a use within Class A2 and any change by the bank to use for normal banking services used by the public may constitute a material change of use.

6.2.3.3 Class A3. Food and drink This Class, which embraces use for the sale of food or drink for consumption on the premises or of hot food for consumption off the premises, brings together a range of uses which were not included in any Class in the previous Use Classes Order , such as shops for the sale of hot food, restaurants, cafès, snack-bars, wine bars and public houses. This Class represents a breaking down of the traditional boundaries which used to exist in the previous order between different types of premises selling food and drink.

Part B — Other Business and Industrial Uses
6.2.3.4 Class B1. Business This Class embraces use for any of the following purposes:

(a)   as an office other than a use within Class A2 (financial and professional services),
(b)   for research and development of products or processes, or
(c)   for any industrial process,

being a use which can be carried out in any residential area without detriment to the amenity of that area by reason of noise, vibration, smell, fumes, smoke, soot, ash, dust or grit.

This Class brings together many of the uses which in the previous order were found in the office and light industry classes which now no longer exist. The Class also includes other uses broadly similar in their environmental impact, such as the use of buildings for the manufacture of computer hardware and software, computer research and development, consultancy and after-sales services, micro-engineering, biotechnology, and pharmaceutical research, development and manufacture.

An important qualification, however, is that to come within the Class, the use has to be one which can be carried out in any residential area without detriment to the amenity of that area by reason of noise, vibration, smell, fumes, smoke, soot, ash, dust or grit.

6.2.3.5   Class B2. General industrial   This Class includes any use for the carrying on of an industrial process, other than one which falls within Class B1 (the business class) or Classes B4 to B7 (the special industrial group classes).

6.2.3.6   Classes B4 to B7 (Special Industrial Groups B to E)   Uses of buildings or other land for special industrial purposes are divided, for the purposes of the order, into groups, depending upon whether they constitute alkaline works; emit heat and fumes; emit noise and dust; emit smoke; or smell and emit contaminated organic matter. The purpose is to combine together in a particular Class those uses which give rise to similar kinds of environmental pollution. The division of special industrial uses into these Classes dates from the original Use Class Order made in 1948. In practice, however, their genesis dates back to early pollution legislation of the mid 19th century. The position now is that some of these industrial uses no longer occur. There must be few buildings, one suspects, now used for the purpose of boiling blood, chitterlings, nettlings or soap; breeding maggots from putrescible animal matter; or making or scraping guts. In addition, the distribution of the uses between the special industrial classes does not adequately reflect the impact of modern pollution legislation on the control of premises which harm the environment. In 1988, research commissioned by the Department of the Environment found that there had been a decline in industrial uses falling within the Special Industrial Use Classes (B4 to B7) and that technological change combined with improved levels of environmental control, had lessened their distinctiveness from Class B2. Since then, the Environmental Protection Act 1990 has introduced a regime of integrated pollution control; air, noise and vibration control has been strengthened; and the Planning (Hazardous Substances) Act 1990 has introduced specific planning controls over the storage of hazardous substances.

Accordingly, the government announced in December 1993 that the new legislation outlined above which applies to Special Industrial Use Class processes is now sufficiently comprehensive to control potential pollution arising from changes to and from those uses. It is proposing therefore to delete Classes B4 to B7, and to include all the processes therein within Class B2.

6.2.3.7   Class B8. Storage and distribution   This Class comprises buildings and other land used for storage or as a distribution centre. Retail warehouses, where the main purpose is the sale of goods direct to members of the public visiting the premises fall within the Shops Use Class (A1), even though a limited part of the building may be used for storage.

Part C — Residential Uses
6.2.3.8   Class C1. Hotels   This Class includes boarding-houses and guest-houses, but does not include the use of a building as a hotel, boarding- or guest-house where a significant element of care is provided. Article 2 of the order provides a definition of the word 'care'. Until April 1994, 'hostels' were included in this particular use Class. Because of the threat to the amenity of tourist areas from the use made of the freedom to change the use of premises from that of a hotel to a hostel without the need to obtain planning permission, it was decided to exclude hostels from the Class; and also to provide that a hostel was not included within *any* class of the Schedule to the Order. In short, use as a hostel is made a *sui generis* use under art. 3(6) of the Order.

6.2.3.9   Class C2. Residential institutions   The uses contained in this Class relate to places where personal care or treatment is provided and to residential educational facilities.

6.2.3.10   Class C3. Dwellinghouses   This Class groups together use as a dwellinghouse by a single person, or by any number of persons living together as a family, with use as a dwellinghouse by no more than six persons living together as a single household.

The grouping together of these uses in the same Class means that it is not development when a dwellinghouse occupied by a family or a single person is used as a small community care house providing support for disabled and mentally disabled people, provided that all the residents live together as a single household and that they number no more than six including resident staff. Similarly, other groups of people, up to a maximum of six, such as students, not necessarily related to each other, may live in a dwellinghouse on a communal basis, so long as they do so as a single household. Sharing a communal living-room, toilet facilities, kitchen etc., sharing the cost of electricity, gas and telephone by the occupiers, a common doorbell, the common purchase and consumption of food, may all be evidence indicating that persons are living together as a single household. Other forms of multiple occupation, however, will generally remain outside the scope of the order.

The Housing and Planning Act 1986, amended the provisions of para. (f) of what is now s. 55(2) to make it clear that, subject to the provisions of the order, planning permission is not required where premises are subdivided; provided that both the existing and proposed use fall within the same use Class. Article 4 of the Order, however, provides that this general rule shall not apply in the case of a building used as a dwellinghouse (Class C3). The benefit of this exclusion, therefore, is not available wherever a dwellinghouse is subdivided. This accords with the special provision found in subsection (3)(a) of s. 55 of the 1990 Act.

Part D — Social and Community Uses of a Non-Residential kind
6.2.3.11 Class D1. Non-residential institutions The common element in the uses included in this Class is that the buildings are visited by members of the public on a non-residential basis. It includes use as a crèche, museum and public reading room.

6.2.3.12 Class D2. Assembly and leisure Uses in this Class include places of mass assembly such as cinemas and concert halls (but not theatres which are *sui generis*) and all indoor and outdoor sports uses except motor sports and sports involving firearms.

6.2.3.13 General points In *City of London Corporation* v *Secretary of State for the Environment* (1971) 23 P & CR 169, it was accepted that a local planning authority and the Secretary of State could grant planning permission subject to a condition that restricted the rights which would otherwise be available under the Use Classes Order. The court upheld as valid the grant of planning permission to use premises as an employment agency, but subject to a condition that the premises should be used 'as an employment agency and for no other purpose'. In Circular 13/87 the Secretary of State makes it clear that there is a presumption against conditions designed to restrict future changes of use, which, by virtue of the order, would not otherwise constitute development. Unless there is clear evidence that the uses excluded would have serious adverse effects on the environment or on amenity which was not susceptible to other control, the Secretary of State says he will consider the imposition of such conditions to be unreasonable.

It should also be noted that the General Development Order provides that certain changes made between different use Classes is permitted development. These changes are:

From	To
Sale of motor vehicles *(sui generis)*	A1 (shop)
A2 (financial and professional services) so long as the premises have a display window at ground-floor level	A1 (shop)
A3 (food and drink)	A1 (shop)
A3 (food and drink)	A2 (financial and professional services)
B1 (business) but limited to changes of use relating to not more than 235 square metres of floorspace in the building	B8 (storage and distribution)

B2 (general industrial)	B1 (business)
B2 (general industrial) but limited to changes of use relating to not more than 235 square metres of floorspace in the building	B8 (storage and distribution)
B8 (storage and distribution) but limited to changes of use relating to not more than 235 square metres of floorspace in the building	B1 (business)

The above provisions are unilateral, in the sense that they allow a change from one specified use Class to another, but not normally vice versa.

6.3 Uses included within development

Subsection (3) of s. 55 of the 1990 Act specifies two uses (in paragraphs (a) and (b)), which, for the avoidance of doubt, are declared to involve a material change of use: use of a single dwellinghouse as two and the deposit of refuse and waste material.

6.3.1 Use of a single dwellinghouse as two or more separate dwelling-houses
By s. 55(3)(a) of the 1990 Act:

... the use as two or more separate dwellinghouses of any building previously used as a single dwellinghouse involves a material change in the use of the building and of each part of it which is so used.

This provision is intended to bring under planning control the use of houses for multiple occupation. The utility of the provision, however, has been much restricted by the decision of the Divisional Court of the Queen's Bench Division in *Ealing London Borough Council* v *Ryan* [1965] 2 QB 486. Multiple occupation, it seems, is in itself not enough to fall within this provision. Here, the court had to consider the application of the provision to a dwellinghouse part of which had been let out to an old lady and to another family. An enforcement notice had been served sometime earlier requiring the respondent to discontinue the use of the house as two or more separate dwellings. On the failure to comply with the notice, the respondent had been prosecuted by the local planning authority for non-compliance with it, but acquitted by the justices. On an appeal by the authority by way of case stated, the court, in upholding the decision of the justices that there had been no breach of planning control, considered that the important phrase in the provision was the term 'separate dwellinghouses'. According to Ashworth J:

... a house may well be occupied by two or more persons, who are to all intents and purposes living separately, without that house being thereby used as separate dwellings.

In other words, people may live separately under one roof without occupying separate dwellings. His lordship then went on to say that in considering whether these were separate dwellings:

> The existence or absence of any form of physical reconstruction is a relevant factor; another is the extent to which the alleged separate dwellings can be regarded as separate in the sense of being self-contained and independent of other parts of the same property.

It should be remembered here that work for the maintenance, improvement or other alteration of a building which affects only the interior of the building, or which does not materially affect its external appearance, is itself not development by virtue of s. 55(2) of the 1990 Act.

As a result of this case, local planning authorities have sought to control multiple occupation through other means, and in particular by alleging that there has been material change of use under s. 55(1) of the 1990 Act.

6.3.2   Deposit of refuse and waste material
By s. 55(3)(b) of the 1990 Act:

> ... the deposit of refuse or waste materials on land involves a material change in its use, notwithstanding that the land is comprised in a site already used for that purpose, if

> (i)   the superficial area of the deposit is extended, or
> (ii)   the height of the deposit is extended and exceeds the level of the land adjoining the site.

It seems reasonably clear that under the first part of this provision, the deposit of refuse or waste materials on land constitutes development. But the paragraph may also be important, not for what it says, but for what it does not say. The implication of the second part of the provision is that if a hole in the ground is already being used for the deposit of refuse or waste, any further deposit of waste or refuse does not involve development of the land unless the limitations mentioned above are exceeded.

6.4   Advertising

Subsection (5) of s. 55 of the 1990 Act contains a special provision with regard to the display of certain advertisements:

> Without prejudice to any regulations made under the provisions of this Act relating to the control of advertisements, the use for the display of advertisements of any external part of a building which is not normally used for that purpose shall be treated for the purposes of this section as involving a material change in the use of that part of the building.

With reference to this provision, s. 222 of the 1990 Act provides that where the display of advertisements in accordance with the regulations relating to the control of advertisements involves the development of land, planning permission for that development shall be deemed to be granted, so that no application for planning permission is necessary. If however, the erection of an advertisement affects the character of a listed building to which it is attached, listed building consent will be required.

Under the regulations for the display of advertisements, the person responsible can be prosecuted if he displays an advertisement without 'consent'. The purpose of s. 55(5), therefore, seems to be to give a local planning authority alternative methods of proceeding in cases where an advertisement is displayed on an external part of a building not normally used for that purpose, without any 'consent' for its display having been granted. In such a case, the authority may proceed either by way of an enforcement notice for breach of planning control, or by prosecution for breach of the advertising regulations. It would be possible, though probably unnecessary, for the authority to pursue both proceedings.

6.5 Intensification

The question whether the intensification of a use constitutes a material change of use has until quite recently given rise to much uncertainty, misunderstanding and ambivalence. In one of the early cases, *Guildford Rural District Council v Penny* [1959] 2 QB 112, the Court of Appeal refused to interfere with the finding of justices that an increase in the number of caravans in a field from 8 to 27 was not development. In this case the Court was prepared to concede that intensification could be relevant to the question of whether there had been a material change of use, but thought that whether or not it was relevant depended upon the particular circumstances of the particular case. The Court gave as example the Oval cricket ground being used to provide a greater number of cricket pitches with contemporaneous playing on each pitch, or an increase of housing estate density. Later, in *Glamorgan County Council v Carter* [1963] 1 WLR 1, the court had to consider whether planning permission was needed for a caravan use commenced before 1 July 1948. The question of intensification was raised before the court and in the course of his judgment Salmon J said:

Although I do not express any concluded view on the point, I very much doubt whether intensification of use — ... confining what I say to this caravan site — could be a material change of user. Once it is established that the whole site is used as a caravan site, it does not seem to me that the use is materially changed by bringing a larger number of caravans upon the site.

The early cases in this area continued to be dominated by caravans. In *James v Secretary of State for Wales* [1966] 1 WLR 135, the Court of Appeal recognised that an intensification of an existing use could be a material change of use. In referring to this aspect, Lord Denning MR said, 'I think that a considerable increase in the number of caravans would be a material change of use'. Russell LJ said 'I would agree that ... it is possible in law for the Minister to consider that the use of land for stationing ... three other caravans is a material change of use. One swallow does not make a summer.' The latter phrase was a colourful reference to the fact that a grant of planning permission to station one caravan on land did not entitle the owner to add any more.

Yet another caravan case was *Esdell Caravan Parks Ltd* v *Hemel Hempstead Rural District Council* [1966] 1 QB 895. In dealing with the question of intensification, Lord Denning MR said:

> ... I doubt very much whether the occupier could increase from 24 to 78 without permission. An increase in intensity of that order may well amount to a material change of use — see the recent case of *James* v *Secretary of State for Wales*.

He then went on to assume that a material change of use had not taken place.

Perhaps the first important non-caravan case was *Birmingham Corporation* v *Minister of Housing & Local Government* [1964] 1 QB 178. There the local planning authority had served enforcement notices alleging the making of a material change in the use of two houses, from use as single dwellinghouses to use as houses let in lodgings, and directing that the latter use should cease. At the inquiry into the appeal the Inspector had the assistance of a legal assessor, who advised him that, because of shared facilities in one of the houses, it could not be said that there was within it separate dwellinghouses; and that as regards the other house, while it was used intensively, in the matter of residential use, intensification of use did not amount *per se* to a material change of use. Acting on this legal advice the Inspector concluded that what was alleged in the enforcement notices did not constitute development. The Minister accepted the Inspector's recommendation and quashed the enforcement notices, whereupon the local planning authority appealed to the High Court against the decision of the Minister. Allowing the appeal, Lord Parker CJ said that in his judgment the Minister had erred in law in saying that because the houses remained residential, in the sense of a dwellinghouse in which people lived, there could not be a material change of use. In his opinion, the case should go back to the Minister with the opinion of the court and it would then be for him to find whether what had taken place in each of the houses amounted to a material change in their use, despite the fact that they both remained dwellinghouses. The Minister would take into consideration the use to which they were put; that private dwellinghouses were being used for multiple paying occupation, or that houses which had been used for private families were now being used for gain by the letting out of rooms.

It will be seen, therefore, that a house may have a residential use both before and after the making of a material change of use. In considering how this can be so, it may be possible to divide up a single genus of residential use into various species of residential use, so that even though a general residential user remains, the change from a private dwellinghouse to multiple paying occupation may nevertheless constitute development. One should note that although the Inspector in his recommendation, and the Minister in his decision, both used the phrase 'intensification', the term is not used in Lord Parker's judgment. The decision did not justify, therefore, the proposition that intensification may constitute development. What happened here was that there was a change (which could be considered to be material) in the *character* of the residential use. This approach was borne out in the later case of *Clarke* v *Minister of Housing & Local Government* (1966) 18 P & CR 82. On 1 July 1948, the lodge of a large private house had been occupied by a gardener employed in connection with the commercial exploitation of the garden attached to the house. In September 1948, the lodge was sold and used as a private residence. In 1953, the house was converted into a hotel, and in 1963 the lodge was bought and used for the purpose of accommodating waiters employed by the hotel. The district council, acting as agents for the local planning authority, thereupon served an enforcement notice on the occupier alleging that there had been a material change in the use of the lodge to a use for the purpose of providing living accommodation for the hotel staff. The occupier appealed to the Minister who, in dismissing the appeal, accepted the 'conclusion' of the Inspector that a material change in the use of the lodge had taken place in 1963, from that of a use by a single family into that of multiple occupation by staff of the hotel. In dismissing an appeal to the High Court from the decision of the Minister, Lord Parker CJ said:

> I see no reason to criticise the Minister's decision... It seems to me that he was perfectly entitled to say here that there was a single family unit occupation before; that that ceased and that the change to staff accommodation was a material change of use. It is a case, as it seems to me, that does not involve a change by intensification, but by reason of totally different character of the user. I cannot see anything in law which prevented the Minister from saying that there was a change, and that that was a material change from the planning point of view.

Perhaps the only case decided on the basis that an intensification of use involved a material change of use is *Peake* v *Secretary of State for Wales* (1971) 22 P & CR 889. The case involved the part-time use of a garage in a garden for the repair by the owner of his car and occasionally his friends' cars. When the owner became redundant from his employment, he started repairing cars on a full-time basis. It was held that a change in activity from part-time to full-time could not of itself amount to a material change of use, but that the Secretary of State was entitled to conclude on the facts that there had been a change in the use of the garage for repair work by reason of the intensification of use. Clearly, the court was right to hold that there had been development. But it was not the intensification of the use that amounted to development. What had taken place was a change in the character of the use, from that of premises used as a dwellinghouse with ancillary private garage, to that of premises used as a dwellinghouse and a commercial garage.

Perhaps the greatest contribution made to the understanding of this area of law was made by Donaldson LJ in *Royal Borough of Kensington & Chelsea* v

Secretary of State for the Environment [1981] JPL 50. Here, the borough council had served an enforcement notice alleging a material change in the use of a garden adjacent to a restaurant for the purposes of a restaurant. On appeal, the Inspector had decided that the planning unit comprised the restaurant and the garden, so there was no breach of planning control in using the garden as ancillary to the restaurant. The borough council did not appeal from that part of the Inspector's decision, but they complained that the Inspector had erred by failing to consider the council's alternative argument that there had been a material change of use by intensification of the restaurant use. In dismissing the appeal, Donaldson LJ is reported to have said:

> Similarly, in *Peake's* case, the original use of the planning unit had been as a private garage. What had been objected to in the enforcement notice had been the use of the premises as a commercial garage. In a sense the vice of changing a private garage into a commercial garage was that one had far more cars coming and going. In that sense it might be said to be intensification, but half the trouble in this case (and perhaps in other cases) was that the word 'intensification' had a perfectly clear meaning in ordinary language. It had a wholly different meaning in the mouths of planners. In ordinary language, intensification meant more of the same thing or possibly a denser composition of the same thing. In planning language, intensification meant a change to something different. It was much too late no doubt to suggest that the word 'intensification' should be deleted from the language of planners, but it had to be used with very considerable circumspection, and it had to be clearly understood by all concerned that intensification which did not amount to a material change of use was merely intensification and not a breach of planning control.

> He (Donaldson LJ) hoped that, where possible, those concerned with planning would get away from the term and try to define what was the material change of use by reference to the *terminus a quo* and *terminus ad quem*. Indeed, if the planners were incapable of formulating what was the use after 'intensification' and what was the use before 'intensification', then there had been no material change of use.

The intensification of a use, therefore, may act as a catalyst of a material change. But for that to take place, there must be a change in the character of the use. For that change to take place, one must be able to give a name to the use before the change, and a name to the use after the change, and they must be of an essentially different character.

6.6   The planning unit, and dominant and ancillary uses

Problems occasionally arise as to the precise geographical area to be considered in determining whether the carrying out of a new activity on land constitutes a material change of use. The smaller the area to be considered, the greater the justification for holding that, as a matter of fact and degree, the new activity involves the development of land. The problem was demonstrated in *Bendles Motors Ltd* v *Bristol Corporation* [1963] 1 WLR 247 (the case of the freestanding, gravity-fed, egg-vending machine, see 6.1). There, counsel for the garage owners had claimed that the Minister had made a fatal error in considering only the 9 square feet upon which the egg-vending machine stood, and that in considering whether the change was material, he should have considered the premises as a whole. The evidence showed, however, that though the Minister had looked at the 9 square feet in considering whether there had been a change of use, he had in fact looked at the total area of the garage forecourt in considering whether the change was material. Hence the Minister's approach had disclosed no error of law.

An early case on the planning unit was that of *East Barnet Urban District Council* v *British Transport Commission* [1962] 2 QB 484. In that case the court had to consider whether there had been a material change of use when land previously used as a coal depot was used for the handling and storage of crated motor vehicles. The land in question had been divided into seven distinct parcels, of which only six had been used as a coal depot, whilst the seventh had remained unoccupied. It was argued on behalf of the local planning authority that because the vacant parcel had been unoccupied, it was impossible to say that no material change of use had taken place. Dismissing that argument, Lord Parker CJ said:

> Whatever unit one considers in these cases is always a matter of difficulty, but looked at as a matter of common sense in the present case it seems to me that this [i.e., the vacant parcel] was merely an unused part of the unit in question.

Almost side by side with the development of the law relating to the planning unit has been the development of the principle that land may have a dominant or primary use, to which other uses may be subservient or ancillary. Hence, in determining the use of buildings or land, it may be that regard should be had to a larger unit of which the building or land in question is merely a part. So that if land and buildings are together used for a single dominant or primary purpose, it is that purpose which determines the character of the use of the whole unit, without regard to any ancillary uses to which individual parts of the unit may be put.

One of the earliest cases to address this problem was *Vickers-Armstrong* v *Central Land Board* (1957) 9 P & CR 33, where the Court of Appeal had to consider whether a claim for loss of development value under the Town and Country Planning Act 1947 could be made in respect of a building which, although situated within the company's aviation works complex, had been used for administrative purposes. It was agreed by both parties that the highest value that could be placed on the administrative building was its value for use as a general industrial building, and that, if planning permission would have been required before it could have been used for that purpose, the loss of development value would have been £15,000. If, on the other hand, planning permission would not have been required, no loss of development value would have occurred. Crucial to the resolution of this dispute, therefore, was the nature of the use to which the administrative block had been put. If the use was that of a general industrial building, planning permission would not be required to change to that use. If, however, its use was that of general offices, planning permission would be required. The Court of Appeal, upholding the decision of the Lands Tribunal, held that the appellant's works 'as a whole' had been used for general industrial purposes and that the use of the administrative block was incidental to that main purpose. Hence, the owner had suffered no loss of development value.

It seems, from this decision, therefore, that once the planning unit has been established, the character of the dominant use which is carried on in the unit colours the character of every part of that unit, notwithstanding that some parts of it may be devoted entirely to some ancillary use. An example may be taken of a factory complex, comprising a factory where the main manufacturing processes are carried on, a car park for employees' cars, a canteen or refectory and a sports ground for recreational use by employees. The unit has a dominant (industrial) use, to which the other uses are all ancillary. It follows that the occupier of the unit may change the location of those ancillary uses without any material change of use being involved. Any operational development, of course, will need planning permission but, subject to that, planning permission will not be needed if the occupier of that unit decides that the location of the car park and sports ground should be exchanged: he might also decide that due to the additional demand for car parking spaces, the sports ground should also be used for that purpose. This too would not be development, so long as the ancillary car parking use remains a use ancillary to the dominant 'industrial' use. Should that ancillary use, however, itself become dominant (as would happen if the owner of the factory complex allowed members of the general public to use the car park), a change of use would have occurred from that of industrial use, to that of industrial use and car-parking.

It has to be said that the implications of the *Vickers-Armstrong* case were not at first generally recognised. It was, after all, a case more concerned with compensation for the loss of development rights than with the application of general principles of planning law. It was not until 1966 in *G. Percy Trentham Ltd* v *Gloucestershire County Council* [1966] 1 WLR 506 that the principle in the *Vickers-Armstrong* case was first considered to be of more general application. The facts involved a site which comprised a farmhouse, a farmyard and farm buildings. Prior to its purchase by building and civil engineering contractors, the farm buildings had been used to house tractors and livestock associated with the farm. After purchase, the farm buildings were used by the contractors for the storage of building materials. Since planning permission to use the land for that purpose had not been granted, the local planning authority sought its discontinuance by an enforcement notice served on the building contractors. The notice alleged that a material change of use had taken place from agricultural purposes (namely, the storage of farm machinery) to the storage of plant and machinery of building contractors. On appeal against the notice and in the courts, the contractors had argued that, by virtue of the then Use Classes Order, planning permission for the change was not required. They claimed that the use of the buildings and other land for the storage of tractors and for the storage of building materials, both fell within the then Class X of the Order, which spoke of 'use as a wholesale warehouse or repository for any purpose'. Accordingly, no development had taken place. Dismissing this argument, the Court of Appeal held that a repository is a place where goods are stored as part of a storage business, so that the term did not cover the use of farm buildings to store tractors where the storage was ancillary to the use of the farm. But then, after having decided the issue in narrow terms in favour of the local planning authority, the Court of Appeal went further in holding that, looked at in isolation, even if the buildings did constitute a repository or warehouse, they could not be severed from the rest of the farmhouse buildings. The court thought that, in considering the Use Classes Order, it was necessary to look at the whole of the unit being used, the whole area on which a particular activity was carried on, including uses incidental to, or included in the activity. The court gave, as an example, a baker's shop with a flour store and a dwellinghouse above in one unit, which could be changed into a butcher's shop with a meat store and dwellinghouse above without the need for planning permission. In this case, it was clear that the planning unit being considered comprised the farmhouse, farm buildings and yard, and in no sense could the unit be regarded as a warehouse or repository.

Buttressed by a further decision of the Court of Appeal in *Brazil (Concrete) Ltd* v *Amersham Rural District Council* (1967) 18 P & CR 396, where the court followed the principles it had enunciated earlier in *G. Percy Trentham Ltd* v *Gloucestershire County Council*, it became settled law that in order to see whether a change of use was permitted under the Use Classes Order, regard should be had to the whole area in which a particular activity is carried on and the primary purpose for which the whole area is used. The character of the user is then determined by that primary purpose and not by any ancillary uses.

The question that then remained to be answered was whether a similar principle applied in cases where the Use Class Order was not in issue. In *Williams* v *Minister of Housing & Local Government* (1967) 18 P & CR 514, the Queen's Bench Divisional Court decided that it did.

Williams owned a nursery garden and made his living by selling, from a timber building which was situated in one corner, fruit, vegetables and flowers grown in the garden. Then, in order to give his customers a wider choice of produce, he purchased from a market imported fruit such as bananas, oranges and lemons and placed them on sale alongside the home-grown produce. The local planning authority thereupon served an enforcement notice on Williams which, as subsequently upheld by the Minister, alleged the carrying out of development by the use of the timber building as a retail shop without planning permission and prohibiting the use of the building as a shop, except for the sale of indigenous agricultural produce grown on the land.

On appeal, the Minister took the view that the building should not be looked at in isolation and that the building and garden should be taken as a whole. He then proceeded to uphold the notice on the ground that the established use of the building was restricted to the sale of agricultural produce grown on the land and was a use incidental to the use of the premises as a nursery and market garden; and that the sale of imported fruit had effected a change in the character of the use to that of a greengrocer's shop, which constituted a material change of use.

The Divisional Court refused to interfere with the Minister's decision, taking the view that he had acted correctly in looking at the premises as a whole. The court held that the primary use of the premises was agriculture, the use of the timber building for selling produce was ancillary to that use, and that the Minister was entitled to find that although the quantitive change was small, a change which involved selling fruit not grown on the premises constituted a material change of use. In the *Williams* case it was not entirely clear what percentage of total sales was accounted for by imported fruit. A figure of 10 per cent was mentioned, however; and it seems that anything less than that order of proportion will tend to be regarded as *de minimis* and insignificant from a planning point of view.

There is now a well-established principle that the right to use land for some dominant or primary purpose includes the right to use it for any purpose which is ancillary to that dominant or primary purpose. The addition of an ancillary use, therefore cannot be a material change of use. Neither can the substitution of one ancillary use for another. But if an ancillary use becomes a dominant use, a material change of use may have taken place. This is seen not only in *Williams* v *Minister of Housing & Local Government* but also in *Jillings* v *Secretary of State for the Environment* [1984] JPL 32. There land and buildings in the Norfolk Broads had been used for boat-hire purposes, but included an ancillary use of boat manufacture. Later the manufacturing of boats increased to such an extent that it had become a primary purpose. Instead of the land being used for boat-hire purposes, it was being used for a dual purpose of boat hire and the manufacture of boats for sale. As one use had now given way to two, the Divisional Court had no qualms about upholding the validity of an enforcement notice alleging that a material change of use had taken place.

In developing the above principles, the courts have often had to consider the precise boundaries of the planning unit. Take, for example, a block of flats; or that current shopping centre phenomenon, shops located within a shop. Is the planning unit the whole building or is each individual flat or shop a planning unit? In many cases the question poses something of a conundrum. On the one hand, one is looking at the planning unit in order to determine its use. On the other, one is looking at the use in order to determine the planning unit. Fortunately, some important guidelines in resolving this problem were given by Bridge J in *Burdle* v *Secretary of State for the Environment* [1972] 1 WLR 1207. His lordship had been involved as counsel in many cases concerning disputes about the planning unit. As a judge, he used this opportunity to set out firm guidelines for its determination. According to his lordship there are three criteria for determining the correct planning unit:

(a) Whenever it is possible to recognise a single main purpose of the occupier's use of his land to which secondary activities are incidental or ancillary, the whole unit of occupation should be considered.

(b)   Even though the occupier carries on a variety of activities and it is not possible to say that one is incidental or ancillary to another, the entire unit of occupation should be considered.

(c)   Where there are two or more physically separate and distinct uses, occupied as a single unit but for substantially different and unrelated purposes, each area used for a different main purpose (together with its incidental and ancillary activities) ought to be considered a separate planning unit.

Bridge J recognised that deciding which of the three categories applied to the circumstances of a particular case at any given time might be difficult. On this he said:

> Like the question of material change of use, it must be a question of fact and degree. There may indeed be an almost imperceptible change from one category to another. Thus, for example, activities initially incidental to the main use of an area of land may grow in scale to a point where they convert the single use to a composite use and produce a material change of use of the whole. Again, activities once properly regarded as incidental to another use or as part of a composite use may be so intensified in scale and physically concentrated in a recognisably separate area that they produce a new planning unit the use of which is materially changed. It may be a useful working rule to assume that the unit of occupation is the appropriate planning unit, unless and until some smaller unit can be recognised as the site of activities which amount in substance to a separate use both physically and functionally.

In propounding the first criterion, Bridge J had in mind the commonest situation of all, where an occupier carries on a single dominant use on the land he occupies. With regard to the second criterion, Bridge J had in mind the situation that existed in *Wipperman v Barking London Borough Council* (1965) 17 P & CR 225, where an occupier of land was using it for a number of unrelated and different purposes, so that none was ancillary to any other. Furthermore, it was not possible to identify any particular part of the land as the site of any particular dominant use. In such cases, the planning unit is the entire area of occupation with the whole unit being used for a number of planning purposes.

With regard to the third criterion, Bridge J had in mind the situation where an occupier of land was using it for a number of unrelated and different purposes but it was possible to identify the particular part of the site where each purpose was carried on. In such cases it would be right to divide the unit of occupation into as many different planning units as there were different purposes carried on.

Despite the guidelines given in the Burdle case, problems continue to arise in particular cases. In *Fuller v Secretary of State for the Environment* (1987) 283 EG 847, land was being farmed by the appellant as an agricultural unit. The holding, however, comprised a widely scattered number of farms, some as much as eight miles apart. A question arose as to whether the Secretary of State in upholding an enforcement notice, was correct in holding that the agricultural unit comprised a number of separate planning units. Dismissing an appeal against the Secretary of State's decision, Stuart-Smith J held that there was clearly material evidence upon which he could come, as a question of fact and degree, to the conclusion he did. According to his lordship, the Secretary of State had been right to regard the physical separation of the farms as an important consideration, but not the only one. In so finding, he quoted with approval from the judgment of Glidewell J in *Duffy* v *Secretary of State* (1981) 259 EG 1081 where he said:

> In my judgment when buildings lie on opposite sides of a road, at some distance from each other, separated by other properties, that geographical separation must be a major, and may be the main factor in deciding whether they form one planning unit.

The concept of dominant and ancillary uses applies only to activities within the same planning unit. In *Westminster City Council* v *British Waterways Board* [1985] AC 676, Lord Bridge of Harwich said:

> The concept of a single planning unit used for one main purpose to which other uses carried on within the unit are ancillary is a familiar one in planning law. But it is a misapplication of this concept to treat the use or uses of a single planning unit as ancillary to activities carried on outside the unit altogether.

Also, in *Essex Water Co.* v *Secretary of State for the Environment* [1989] JPL 914, Sir Graham Eyre QC said 'treating the use of a single planning unit as ancillary to activities carried on outside the unit altogether is a misapplication of the concept'.

6.7 Interruption and abandonment of a use

If a use of land or buildings is temporarily discontinued, the resumption of that use is not development. If, however, a use is permanently discontinued, it would appear that the revival of that use is development.

One of the earliest cases to consider the interruption or temporary discontinuance of a use was *Fyson* v *Buckinghamshire County Council* [1958] 1 WLR 634. The facts were that from 1943 to 1949, land within the county had been used for storage purposes. From 1949 to 1956, the land was not used at all, except for a brief period of four months from the end of 1953 to March 1954. In 1956, the land was once again used for storage purposes. Subsequently, an enforcement notice was served on behalf of the local planning authority requiring the use of the land for storage purposes to be discontinued, on the ground that in 1956 a material change had been made in the use of the land without planning permission. The authority claimed that the previous storage use was discontinued in 1949, and that when the land was once again used for storage in 1956 a new use had been instituted.

On appeal to the magistrates' court, the justices found as a question of fact that no material change in the use of the land had taken place since 1948, so that no planning permission was required to carry on the storage use in 1956. On an appeal from the decision of the justices, the Divisional Court held that they were fully entitled to come to that decision. The court pointed out that since 1943 there had never been a use of the land by anyone except for a storage use; and that all that had happened was a rather long interruption of the storage use without any change having taken place.

Although *Fyson* v *Buckinghamshire County Council* shows that a use of land may survive a physical interruption of that use, the courts soon began to suggest that there might be situations where a use of land could be lost through the process of abandonment. In *Clarke* v *Minister of Housing & Local Government* (1966) 18 P & CR 82 a lodge in the garden of a large house was occupied successively by a gardener engaged in the commercial exploitation of the house, as a single family dwelling having no connection with the house, and lastly as residential accommodation for waiters employed at the house, which by now had been converted into a hotel. In upholding the validity of an enforcement notice in relation to the last of these three uses the court held that a change of occupation from that of a single family unit to staff accommodation was a change to a different character of use, and that, accordingly, there had been a material change of use. The occupier, however, had also contended that one had the right in law to go back to the use of the lodge as it existed on 1 July 1948 (the appointed day under the Town and Country Planning Act 1947), namely its use by a servant engaged in the exploitation of the garden attached to the house; and he claimed that there was no difference in use between that activity and that of waiters employed in the exploitation, not of the garden, but of the hotel. The court held that it was questionable whether there could be a right to revert back to the use of land as it existed on 1 July 1948, but that even assuming the user of the lodge on that date was that of user by a servant, that use had been wholly abandoned when it began to be used as a private residence.

The notion of abandonment was again referred to in *Webber* v *Minister of Housing & Local Government* (1967) 19 P & CR 1. Here the appellant owned and occupied a 4-acre field which since 1960 had been used for a variety of seasonal activities. Between Easter and the end of September the field was used for camping. Between September and Easter, it was used for grazing livestock, except on Saturdays when it was used as a football pitch. In addition, the field was used somewhat infrequently for local events such as flower shows. In September 1965, shortly before the campers were due to depart for the winter, the local planning authority served an enforcement notice on the appellant requiring him to remove all tents, caravans and Dormobiles from the land within 28 days. Now before 1968, if an authority had allowed four years to pass without serving an enforcement notice, it was then too late for the authority to put a stop to the contravening use. The appellant maintained that since he had been using the land in the same way since 1960, it was no longer open to the authority to take enforcement action. The local planning authority, however, maintained that a change of use was being made twice a year, from grazing to camping and then from camping back to grazing, and that since planning permission had not been obtained for the latest change of use from grazing to camping (which had taken place only six months previously), the enforcement notice could not be challenged on the ground that it had not been served within four years. The Court of Appeal held that the purpose for which land is normally used had to be ascertained by looking at its use from year to year over a considerable period of time. Here the normal use of the field was for two purposes, namely, camping in summer and grazing in winter. So long as that continued, there could not be a material change of use. Hence the seasonal change of use from grazing to camping was not a change that required planning permission. But having thus disposed of the matters in contention, Lord Denning MR, went on to suggest that if the normal use of the land were to be abandoned for a time, the resumption of it afterwards would require planning permission.

The concept of abandonment was finally recognised by the Court of Appeal in the celebrated case of *Hartley* v *Minister of Housing & Local Government* [1970] 1 QB 413. The facts were that prior to 1961, land had been used for the dual purpose of a petrol filling-station and for the display and sale of cars. In March of that year a Mr Fisher purchased the property and until his death a few months later continued to use the land for both purposes. After his death, his widow, Mrs Fisher, ran the business with the help of her 19-year-old son. Because he lacked experience in the business, however, Mrs Fisher did not allow her son to sell cars. Together, they continued to use the land for the business of a petrol filling-station only, until finally disposing of the land to Hartley in 1965. Immediately the new purchaser, in addition to continuing the petrol filling-station business, resumed the business of the display and sale of cars. Thereupon the local planning authority served an enforcement notice on Hartley, alleging a material change of use of the land without planning permission and requiring him to cease that use. On appeal to the Minister against the notice, the Minister found that by 1965 the use of the land for the purpose of car sales had been abandoned and that the present use of the site was that of a petrol filling-station only. On that ground the Minister held the enforcement notice to be valid.

Hartley then appealed to the High Court, and from there to the Court of Appeal, which held that the Minister was entitled to find that the use for car selling had been abandoned and that once a use has been abandoned, it cannot be resurrected without planning permission. Lord Denning MR said:

... when a man ceases to use a site for a particular purpose and lets it remain unused for a considerable time, then the proper inference may be that he has abandoned the former use. Once abandoned, he cannot start to use the site again, unless he gets planning permission: and this is so, even though the new use is the same as the previous one.

According to Lord Denning, whether the cessation of a use amounted to abandonment depended on the circumstances. If land remained unused for a considerable time, in such circumstances that a reasonable man might conclude that the previous use had been abandoned, it was open to the local planning authority or the Minister to do so as well. As regards the date for determining whether or not a use had been abandoned, Lord Denning thought that the material time for doing so was when the new use was started.

A number of points can be made with regard to this decision. First, although it was concerned with the abandonment of one of two dual uses and its subsequent resumption, the same reasoning would clearly apply to the abandonment and subsequent resumption of a single use of land. Secondly, the recognition that it is possible to abandon a use means that, where it does occur, land can be left with no planning use at all, other than its use for some purpose such as agriculture or forestry, which does not involve its development. Thirdly, although planning permission is required to resume an abandoned use, it is not required for the abandonment of the use. In *Hartley's* case it was unsuccessfully argued that there could be no material change of use between a 'nil' use of land (i.e., after abandonment) and the resumption of the previous use for car sales, unless there was a similar but opposite material change of use when the use of the land for car sales ceased. That point was dealt with forcibly by Widgery LJ who said:

No one can make a man continue with a branch of his business if he does not wish and no one is going to interpret this legislation as though it gave a local authority that power.

That statement echoed what his lordship (then Widgery J) had said in the Divisional Court in *Wipperman* v *Barking London Borough Council* (1965) 17 P & CR 225. In that case the planning history of the land involved the following three stages:

Stage 1   1958 to 1961   Land used for:
(a) Storage of farming materials.
(b) Storage of building materials.
(c) Residential caravan by person engaged in building and fencing work

Stage 2   1961 to 1962   Land used for:
(a) Storage of farming material.
(b) Storage of building materials.
(c) Car breaking and the storage of car parts.

Stage 3   1962 to date of Wipperman and Buckingham, trading as Five
enforcement   Star Conservatories go into occupation, give up
notice   the car-breaking use, and use the whole of the land for storage of materials used in the manufacture of conservatories and house extensions.

It will be seen that the caravan use in stage 1 had given way to a car-breaking use in stage 2; and that the car-breaking use in stage 2 had given way to a storage use in stage 3.

The court had to consider the validity of an enforcement notice which had alleged that a material change of use had taken place between stages 2 and 3.

The court said that if it had merely been a case of suspension of the car-breaking use with the storage use being maintained at its former intensity, no material change of use would have occurred. The reason for this is that merely to cease one of a number of component activities in a composite use of land did not in itself amount to a material change of use. This was the very same principle which was accepted again by the Court of Appeal in *Hartley* v *Minister of Housing & Local Government* when it expressed the view that the abandonment of a use would not amount to a material change of use.

With regard to the actual validity of the enforcement notice in *Wipperman* v *Barking London Borough Council,* the court held that although the car-breaking use had been suspended, the storage use had not been maintained at its former intensity. Instead, it had taken over the whole of the unit including that part previously used for car breaking. So, as a matter of law, it seems that where there is a site with a number of component uses, there can be a material change of use if one component is allowed to absorb the entire site to the exclusion of the other use or uses. It should, of course, be pointed out that in such cases the material change of use would result not from the intensification of that one component use but from the fact that the absorption of the entire site by that component use to the exclusion of the others has resulted in a change in the character of the use.

One further matter to be considered in relation to abandonment is the circumstances when abandonment will be held to have taken place. According to Lord Denning MR in the *Hartley* case, it is open to the local planning authority or the Minister to conclude that a use has been abandoned if land has remained unused for a considerable time in such circumstances that a reasonable man might conclude that it had been abandoned. It is submitted that in considering whether a use has been abandoned one has also to consider the intention of the party concerned, and in subsequent decisions in this area this is a factor to which much weight has been given.

In *Hall* v *Lichfield District Council,* noted at [1979] JPL 426, a woman had lived in a cottage since at least 1935. In 1961 she had entered hospital as a voluntary patient, where she remained until her death in 1974, apart from occasional visits to the cottage, the last of them in 1968. The deceased's sister and niece had been correctly advised by the council that if they removed the furniture from the cottage it would not attract rates. This they had duly done, but without informing the deceased for fear of upsetting her. Their intention at all times had been to return the furniture to the cottage if the deceased were ever to recover sufficiently to be able to live there again on her own, which had been her hope. Shortly after the deceased's death, the property was put on the market (though not sold) as a result of which doubts had been raised by the council about the lawful use of the property.

As might be envisaged, the cottage was in a dilapidated condition. It was also situated in a green belt. The view of the authority was that planning permission was necessary before residential use of the property could be resumed, and it appeared that this was not likely to be granted. The authority also took the view that because of the state of the cottage, even if residential use had not been abandoned, any works of renovation would constitute a rebuilding operation and require planning permission.

Counsel advising the personal representatives took the view that in order to prevent any confusion arising between questions relating to residential use of the property and those relating to structural alterations, it was appropriate to seek a declaration that the residential use of the cottage had not been abandoned and that there was an existing right to occupy it for that purpose. That declaration was duly granted.

That approach has also been followed in decisions made by the Secretary of State on appeal. In one such case the local planning authority had made a determination that the resumption of residential use would constitute a material change of use [1980] JPL 759. The owner of the property in question had vacated the property and, whilst empty, the property had been vandalised. The owner, however, had taken the trouble to board up the premises and had reported the vandalism to the police. Allowing the appeal against the authority's determination, the Minister held that the owner had not disclosed a firm intention to abandon the residential use of the property and he in turn granted a determination that the resumption of residential use would not constitute development.

It seems, however, that the intention of the party concerned is just one of the factors, albeit a very important factor, which has to be taken into account. In *Trustees of the Castell-y-Mynach Estate* v *Secretary of State for Wales* [1985] JPL 40 the Queen's Bench Divisional Court, in considering the validity of a determination that the resumption for residential use of a disused derelict house required planning permission, gave judicial acknowledgement to the submission of counsel that, in deciding whether a use had been abandoned, it was necessary to take into account: (a) the physical condition of the building; (b) the period of non-use; (c) whether there had been any other intervening use; and (d) the owner's intention.

The doctrine of abandonment continues to be affirmed by the courts. Recent examples include *White* v *Secretary of State for the Environment* (1989) 58 P & CR 281 and *Northavon District Council* v *Secretary of State for the Environment* [1990] JPL 579.

6.8   Subdivision of a planning unit

Except in those rare cases where a personal planning permission has been granted, planning law is concerned with the use of land, not with the identity of the person who occupies or owns it. It follows that if a large parcel of land used for a particular purpose is divided into smaller parcels, and each parcel is conveyed to a number of different purchasers, those purchasers should be able to continue to use the land for that same purpose without the need for planning permission.

This principle, however, may not apply where land which is used for both a dominant and ancillary purpose is divided into two and each part sold, so that one purchaser acquires that part of the land used for the dominant purpose and the other purchaser acquires that part used for the ancillary purpose.

In principle, it would seem that the purchaser of the part of the land previously used for the ancillary purpose cannot continue to use it for that purpose without first obtaining planning permission since he has converted what was previously an ancillary use into a dominant use. The position is less clear, however, as regards the position of the purchaser of the part of the land previously used for the dominant purpose. What was previously a dominant purpose continues to be a dominant purpose despite the change of ownership, which should suggest that no development has occurred.

It is, of course, a problem not confined to the subdivision of a planning unit consequent upon the sale of part of the unit. The problem can also arise (though less commonly so) where the owner divides up a unit without selling any part. Unfortunately the law on this issue is less than clear.

These issues have been considered by the courts on two recent occasions. In *Wakelin v Secretary of State for the Environment* [1978] JPL 769, a large house set in its own grounds had been used as a single family unit. Planning permission was then granted for the erection in the grounds of garages and additional residential accommodation subject to a condition that it should only be occupied by a close relative or member of the household staff of the main house. The additional buildings were later converted into self-contained flats, and the question then arose whether the change to separate occupancy amounted to a material change of use. The Court of Appeal thought it did. According to Lord Denning MR, the division of a large planning unit into two separate units was beyond question a material change of use. Browne LJ also considered that on the facts there had been a material change of use, but he did not think it necessary to decide whether the creation of a new planning unit out of an existing unit would *always* amount to a material change of use.

In *Winton v Secretary of State for the Environment* [1984] JPL 188, a building formerly used to make breeze-blocks had been divided into two. One part was then used for metal working; the other part for car conversions. The local planning authority then served separate enforcement notices in relation to each part alleging a material change of use without permission. The appellants then appealed to the Secretary of State against the notices and he, after an inquiry, concluded that when the new uses were instituted, there was, as a matter of fact and degree, in each case a material change of use from the permitted use. Nevertheless, he quashed the notices on the ground that planning permission should be granted for a limited period. The appellants then appealed to the High Court to quash the Secretary of State's decision. Rejecting the appeal, the High Court held that although the mere subdivision of a single planning unit into two separate planning units did not of itself amount to development, whether the subdivision amounted to a material change of use was a matter of fact and degree, which in the normal circumstances of an appeal to him was a matter exclusively for the Secretary of State to decide.

It should be noted that the appellants also argued that since the uses both before and after the subdivision fell within the same Use Class, by virtue of the then s. 22(2)(f) of the 1971 Act and art. 3(1) of the Order, no development had taken place. This argument the High Court rejected on the grounds that to hold otherwise could mean that a large factory complex with a multiplicity of separate uses but within the same Class could be subdivided into smaller units without development being involved, and that this would be inconsistent with the approach to development control indicated in the *Wakelin* case. It should be noted, however, that Parliament has now intervened in relation to uses falling within the same Use Class of the Use Classes Order. Except in the case of dwellinghouses, planning permission is not required where premises are subdivided, so long as both the old and the new use fall within the same Use Class. The provision does not, of course, affect the law as it relates to the subdivision of a planning unit outside the Use Classes Order.

SEVEN

The need for planning permission
1: Permitted development

Section 57(1) of the 1990 Act provides that, subject to the provisions of the section, planning permission is required for the carrying out of any development of land. Planning permission may be granted in three main ways, namely by development order without the need for any application to be made, by a deemed grant of planning permission, or as the result of an express application for planning permission made to the local planning authority.

A development order may be a special development order or a general development order. Section 59(3) provides that a development order may be either:

(a)   as a general order applicable, except so far as the order otherwise provides, to all land, or

(b)   as a special order applicable only to such land or descriptions of land as may be specified in the order.

Section 60(1) of the 1990 Act provides that planning permission granted by a development order may be granted either unconditionally or subject to such conditions or limitations as may be specified in the order.

Examples of the use made by the Secretary of State to grant planning permission by special development order have been given in Chapter 2.

7.1   Town and Country Planning General Development Order (the 'GDO')

In August 1992, the government announced that it proposed later in the year to consolidate and re-structure the current Town and Country Planning General Development Order 1988, as subsequently amended on numerous occasions since it was first issued. This has not yet been done.

The present Order (SI 1988 No. 1813) specifies in sch. 2, in 31 separate Parts, various classes of development which may be undertaken upon land without the permission of the local planning authority or the Secretary of State. Each Part may itself include a number of Classes of development. Development falling within the Classes is known as 'permitted development'. The Parts, which on consolidation are unlikely to be changed (either as to content or number), are as follows:

Part
1 Development within the curtilage of a dwellinghouse
2 Minor operations
3 Changes of use
4 Temporary buildings and uses
5 Caravan sites
6 Agricultural buildings and operations
7 Forestry buildings and operations
8 Industrial and warehouse development
9 Repairs to unadopted streets and private ways
10 Repairs to services
11 Development under local or private Acts or orders
12 Development by local authorities
13 Development by local highway authorities
14 Development by drainage bodies
15 Development by water authorities
16 Development by or on behalf of sewerage undertakers
17 Development by statutory undertakers
18 Aviation development
19 Development ancillary to mining operations
20 British Coal mining development
21 Waste tipping at a mine
22 Mineral exploration
23 Removal of material from mineral-working deposits
24 Development by telecommunications code system operators
25 Other telecommunications development
26 Development of the Historic Buildings and Monuments Commission for England
27 Use by members of certain recreational organisations
28 Development at amusement parks
29 Driver information systems
30 Toll road facilities
31 Demolition of buildings

7.2 Circumstances in which the General Development Order does not apply

Before considering in more detail the application of the GDO, a number of important general points should be borne in mind, all of which may have the effect of rendering the order inapplicable in Particular circumstances.

(a)   Under art. 4 of the Order, if either the Secretary of State or the local planning authority is satisfied that it is expedient that development described in any Part, Class or paragraph in sch. 2, other than Class B of Part 22 or Class C of Part 23 should not be carried out unless permission is granted for it on an application, he or they may give a direction that the planning permission granted by the GDO shall not apply. A direction so made is referred to as an 'article 4 direction'. Where such a direction has been made, its effect is to require an application for planning permission to be made for the development specified in the direction, which, if the development were to take place elsewhere, would not be required. Article 4 directions are commonly found in conservation areas. In such areas, if no directions existed, the extension of a dwellinghouse (within the prescribed limits) would be permitted development under Part 1. The owner could, therefore, build an extension which was out of character with the dwellinghouse and any surrounding buildings. If an article 4 direction has been made in relation to that development, the owner must apply for express planning permission to build the extension and the local planning authority will be able to refuse permission or otherwise secure (e.g., through conditions) that the proposed extension is in harmony with the surrounding buildings.

Where an article 4 direction is made by a local planning authority, the Secretary of State's approval is normally required. It is not required, however, where the direction relates to a listed building or to development within the curtilage of a listed building. The Secretary of State's approval is also not required for development within Parts 1 to 4 if, in the opinion of the local planning authority, the development would be prejudicial to the proper planning of their area or constitute a threat to the amenities of their area. In this latter case, however, the direction remains in force for only six months, unless before the end of that period it has been approved by the Secretary of State.

(b)   Article 3(4) of the GDO provides that nothing in the Order shall operate to permit any development which is contrary to any condition imposed by any planning permission granted or deemed to be granted under Part III of the Act.

Local planning authorities and the Secretary of State not infrequently impose conditions on the grant of planning permission to restrict the scope of development which would otherwise be permitted under the GDO. For example, a grant of planning permission for residential development may contain the following condition:

Pursuant to art. 3(4) of the Town and Country Planning General Development Order 1988, the provisions of art. 3(1) and Part 1 to the said order (relating to development within the curtilage of a dwellinghouse) shall not apply to any dwellinghouse to which this permission relates and no such development within the curtilage of any such dwellinghouse shall be carried out without the permission of the local planning authority being first obtained.

The reason for these conditions is often that the local planning authority in granting permission for the development feel that they have allowed the maximum possible development of the site and have no wish to see the landowner, having implemented the planning permission, now use his permitted development 'rights' to enlarge the size of the building. The condition is thus imposed to restrict the amount of site coverage by buildings in relation to the size of the plot.

It should be noted, however, that for permitted development rights to be withdrawn on a grant of planning permission, the condition must expressly exclude those rights *(Dunoon Developments* v *Secretary of State for the Environment* [1992] NPC 22). Note, too, should be made of an amendment made to the GDO in July 1992. Article 3(4A) now introduces a requirement that permitted development rights may only be exercised in relation to an existing use or building if the use or the construction of the building is lawful.

(c)   Some of the development which is permitted under the GDO (e.g., Part 1, Class A — the enlargement, improvement or other alteration of a dwellinghouse) has a size restriction or a tolerance related to the size of the original building. 'Original' is defined in the order as meaning, in relation to a building existing on 1 July 1948, as existing on that date; and in relation to a building built on or after 1 July 1948, as so built. The effect of this is that if, say, a dwellinghouse has been erected under a grant of planning permission in 1970, the size of the permitted development is calculated in relation to the size of the dwellinghouse as then built. An owner cannot, therefore, claim the benefit of 'permitted development rights' to extend the dwellinghouse, and then once extended claim further permitted development rights calculated on the basis of the dwellinghouse as extended. He may, however, extend a dwellinghouse on more than one occasion, so long as in total the size of all the extensions taken together, does not exceed the tolerances permitted by the order.

(d)   The extent of the permitted development which is allowed by the GDO has been modified in a number of special cases. This is particularly so in relation to what is called article 1(5) land. This is defined in the Order as land within a National Park, an area of outstanding natural beauty, a conservation area, an area specified by the Secretary of State for the purposes of s. 41(3) of the Wildlife and Countryside Act 1981, and the Broads. In Parts 1, 8, 17, 24 and 25 of sch. 2 to the Order, the development permitted where the land is article 1(5) land is more restricted than in other cases. This is because of the need to exercise greater control over minor development in highly sensitive areas.

7.3   Some further consideration of the Parts

No attempt has been made in the sections that follow to deal with every aspect of sch. 2 to the GDO, but the following are Particular points to note.

7.3.1   Part 1 — Development within the curtilage of a dwellinghouse
This is the part most frequently used in day-to-day development control, and contains eight classes of permitted development from Class A to Class H as set out below:

**Class A
Permitted
development**

A. The enlargement, improvement or other alteration of a dwellinghouse.

**Development
not permitted**

A.1   Development is not permitted by Class A if—
    (a)   the cubic content of the resulting building would exceed cubic content of the original dwellinghouse—
        (i)   in the case of a terrace house or in the case of a dwellinghouse on article 1(5) land, by more than 50 cubic metres or 10% whichever is the greater;
        (ii)   in any other case, by more than 70 cubic metres or 15%, whichever is the greater;
        (iii)   in any case, by more than 115 cubic metres;
    (b)   the part of the building enlarged, improved or altered would exceed in height the highest part of the roof of the original dwellinghouse;
    (c)   the part of the building enlarged, improved or altered would be nearer to any highway which bounds the curtilage of the dwellinghouse than—
        (i)   the part of the original dwellinghouse nearest to that highway; or
        (ii)   20 metres,
whichever is the nearest to the highway;
    (d)   the part of the building enlarged, improved or altered would be within 2 metres of the boundary of the curtilage of the dwellinghouse and would exceed 4 metres in height;
    (e)   the total area of ground covered by buildings within the curtilage (other than the original dwellinghouse) would exceed 50% of the total area of the curtilage (excluding the ground area of the original dwellinghouse);
    (f)   it would consist of or include the installation, alteration or replacement of a satellite antenna;
    (g)   it would consist of or include the erection of a building within the curtilage of a listed building; or
    (h)   it would consist of or include an alteration to any part of the roof.

A.2   In the casse of a dwellinghouse on any article 1(5) land, development is not permitted by Class A if it would consist of or include the cladding of any part of the exterior with stone, artificial stone, timber, plastic or tiles.

**Interpretation
of Class A**

A.3   For the purpose of Class A—
    (a)   the erection within the curtilage of a dwelling-house of any building with a cubic content greater than 10 cubic metres shall be treated as the enlargement of the

dwellinghouse for all purposes including calculating cubic content where—

(i)   the dwellinghouse is on article 1(5) land, or

(ii)   in any other case, any part of that building would be within 5 metres of any part of the dwellinghouse;

(b)   where any part of the dwellinghouse would be within 5 metres of an existing building within the same curtilage, that building shall be treated as forming part of the resulting building for the purpose of calculating the cubic content.

Class B
Permitted
development

B.   The enlargement of a dwellinghouse consisting of an addition or alteration to its roof.

Development
not permitted

B.1   Development is not permitted by Class B if—

(a)   any part of the dwellinghouse would as a result of the works, exceed the height of the highest part of the existing roof;

(b)   any part of the dwellinghouse would, as a result of the works, extend beyond the plane of any existing roof slope which fronts any highway;

(c)   it would increase the cubic content of the dwellinghouse by more than 40 cubic metres, in the case of a terrace house, or 50 cubic metres in any other case;

(d)   the cubic content of the resulting building would exceed the cubic content of the original dwellinghouse—

(i)   in the case of a terrace house by more than 50 cubic metres or 10%, whichever is the greater.

(ii)   in any other case, by more than 70 cubic metres or 15% whichever is the greater, or

(iii)   in any case, by more than 115 cubic metres; or

(e)   the dwellinghouse is on article 1(5) land.

Class C
Permitted
development

C. Any other alteration to the roof of a dwellinghouse.

Development
not permitted

C.1   Development is not permitted by Class C if it would result in a material alteration to the shape of the dwellinghouse.

Class D
Permitted
development

D. The erection of construction of a porch outside any external door of a dwellinghouse.

Development not permitted

D.1   Development is not permitted by Class D if—

(a)   the ground area (measured externally) of the structure would exceed 3 square metres;

(b)   any part of the structure would be more than 3 metres above ground level; or

(c)   any part of the structure would be within 2 metres of any boundary of the curtilage of the dwellinghouse with a highway.

Class E Permitted development

E. The provision within the curtilage of a dwellinghouse of any building or enclosure, swimming or other pool required for a purpose incidental to the enjoyment of the dwellinghouse as such, or the maintenance, improvement or other alteration of such a building or enclosure.

Development not permitted

E.1   Development is not permitted by Class E if—

(a)   it relates to a dwelling or a satellite antenna;

(b)   any part of the building or enclosure to be constructed or provided would be nearer to any highway which bounds the curtilage than—

(i)   the part of the original dwellinghouse nearest to that highway, or

(ii)   20 metres,

whichever is nearest to the highway;

(c)   where the building to be constructed or provided would have a cubic content greater than 10 cubic metres, any part of it would be within 5 metres of any part of the dwellinghouse;

(d)   the height of that building or enclosure would exceed—

(i)   4 metres in the case of a building with a ridged roof; or

(ii)   3 metres, in any other case;

(e)   the total area of ground covered by buildings or enclosures within the curtilage (other than the original dwellinghouse) would exceed 50% of the total area of the curtilage (excluding the ground area of the original dwellinghouse); or

(f)   in the case of any article 1(5) land or land within the curtilage of a listed building, it would consist of the provision, alteration or improvement of a building with a cubic content greater than 10 cubic metres.

Interpretation of Class E

E.2   For the purposes of Class E 'purpose incidental to the enjoyment of the dwellinghouse as such' includes the keeping of poultry, bees, pet animals, birds or other livestock for the domestic needs or personal enjoyment of the occupants of the dwellinghouse.

Class F
Permitted **F. The provision within the curtilage of a dwellinghouse**
development **of a hard surface for any purpose incidental to the**
enjoyment of the dwellinghouse as such.

Class G
Permitted **G. The erection of provision within the curtilage of a**
development **dwellinghouse of a container for the storage of oil for**
domestic heating.

Development   G.1   Development is not permitted by Class G if—
not permitted   (a)   the capacity of the container would exceed 3,500 litres;
        (b)   any part of the container would be more than 3 metres above ground level; or
        (c)   any part of the container would be nearer to any highway which bounds the curtilage than—
            (i)   the part of the original building nearest to that highway, or
            (ii)   20 metres,
whichever is nearer to the highway.

Class H
Permitted **H. The installation, alteration or replacement of a**
development **satellite antenna on a dwellinghouse or within the**
curtilage of a dwellinghouse.

Development   H.1   Development is not permitted by Class H if—
not permitted   (a)   the size of the antenna (excluding any projecting feed element, reinforcing rim, mountings and brackets) when measured in any dimension would exceed—
            (i)   45 centimetres in the case of an antenna to be installed on a chimney;
            (ii)   90 centimetres in the case of an antenna to be installed on or within the curtilage of a dwellinghouse on article 1(7) land other than on a chimney;
            (iii)   70 centimetres in any other case;
        (b)   the highest part of an antenna to be installed on a roof or a chimney would, when installed, exceed in height—
            (i)   in the case of an antenna to be installed on a roof, the highest part of the roof;
            (ii)   in the case of an antenna to be installed on a chimney, the highest part of the chimney;

(c)   there is any other satellite antenna on the dwelling-house or within its curtilage;
(d)   in the case of article 1(5) land, it would consist of the installation of an antenna—
(i)   on a chimney;
(ii)   on a building which exceeds 15 metres in height;
(iii) on a wall or roof slope which fronts a waterway in the Broads or a highway elsewhere.

Conditions   H.2   Development is permitted by Class H subject to the following conditions—
(a)   an antenna installed on a building shall, so far as practicable, be sited so as to minimise its effect on the external appearance of the building;
(b)   an antenna no longer needed for the reception or transmission of microwave radio energy shall be removed as soon as reasonably practicable.

It will be seen that Class A permits the enlargement, improvement or other alteration of a dwellinghouse, as long as the work does not infringe the limitations set out in A1 (paras. (a) to (h)), or A2.

A particular problem which sometimes arises with the application of Class A, is where an owner begins to repair or renovate a disused or dilapidated dwellinghouse in a piecemeal fashion over a prolonged period of time. The question then is whether the owner is 'improving' the dwelling and is thus within the Class, or whether he is re-erecting the dwellinghouse by stages so as to embrace its entirety and thus be outside the Class. In *Larkin* v *Basildon District Council* [1980] JPL 407, the appellant rebuilt all the four external walls of a dwellinghouse in two distinct stages. This involved first pulling down and rebuilding two walls of the dwellinghouse and then subsequently rebuilding another two walls. The appellant contended that the works were permitted development under Class I (1) of what was then sch. 1 to the General Development Order as the 'enlargement, improvement or other alteration' of a dwellinghouse. The Divisional Court considered that whether the activities with which they were concerned amounted to improvement or rebuilding depended almost entirely on matters of fact and degree. It concluded that the Secretary of State's decision that the original building had virtually ceased to exist and the operations amounted to the construction of a new dwelling and did not therefore come within the class was valid.

In *Hewlett* v *Secretary of State for the Environment* [1985] JPL 404 an enforcement notice was served by the local planning authority in respect of the works carried out to a very small building which had only three walls. This work apparently involved jacking up the roof, then undertaking certain operations to the walls in turn, and then at a later stage probably working on the roof itself. The appeal was based on the Town and Country Planning Act 1971 s. 22(2)(a) which was the forerunner to s. 55(2)(a) of the 1990 Act and it was submitted that the operations amounted to the 'maintenance, improvement or other alteration' of the building not materially affecting the external appearance. The Court of Appeal held, *inter alia*, that improvement works of rebuilding done to a building, albeit in stages, amounted to the erection of a new building and not the original building in an improved form and that this was a matter of fact and degree for the Secretary of State to decide.

Another point to note concerns the effect of the clause headed 'Interpretation of Part I' at the conclusion of that Part. Its effect is to secure that in calculating the tolerance allowed, any development carried out under an express planning permission is to be taken into account. In other words if a dwellinghouse is extended by virtue of an express planning permission, the size of the extension will eat into the tolerance allowed by the Part and may exhaust it altogether. It seems, however, that if the planning permission has not been implemented then an owner can take advantage of the full tolerance allowed by the Part and then proceed to implement the permission. This could be avoided, of course, if the local planning authority, by condition in the planning permission, excluded the operation of that part of the Order.

The remaining seven Classes of Part I cover respectively the enlargement of a dwellinghouse consisting of an addition or alteration to its roof, any other alteration to the roof of a dwellinghouse, the erection or construction of a porch outside any external door of a dwellinghouse, the provision within the curtilage of a dwellinghouse of any building or enclosure, etc., the provision within the curtilage of a dwellinghouse of a hard surface, etc., the erection within the curtilage of a dwellinghouse of a container for the storage of oil for domestic heating and the installation, alteration or replacement of a satellite antenna on a dwellinghouse or within its curtilage.

7.3.2   Part 2 — Minor Operations

Part 2 contains three classes of permitted development as set out below. It permits minor operations in relation to gates, fences, walls and other means of enclosures; means of access; and exterior painting.

Class A

Permitted development
A. The erection, construction, maintenance, improvement or alteration of a gate, fence, wall or other means of enclosure.

Development not permitted
A.1   Development is not permitted by Class A if—
    (a)   the height of any gate, fence, wall or means of enclosure erected or constructed adjacent to a highway used by vehicular traffic would, after the carrying out of the development, exceed one metre above ground level;
    (b)   the height of any other gate, fence, wall or means of enclosure erected or constructed would exceed two metres above ground level;
    (c)   the height of any gate, fence, wall or other means of enclosure maintained, improved or altered would, as a result

of the development, exceed its former height or the height referred to in sub-paragraph (a) or (b) as the height appropriate to it if erected or constructed, whichever is the greater; or

    (d)   it would involve development within the curtilage of, or to a gate, fence, wall or other means of enclosure surrounding, a listed building.

Class B
Permitted
development

B. The formation, laying out and construction of a means of access to a highway which is not a trunk road or a classified road, where that access is required in connection with development permitted by any class in this Schedule (other than by Class A of this Part).

Class C
Permitted
development

C. The painting of the exterior of any building or work.

Development
not permitted

C.1   Development is not permitted by Class C where the painting is for the purpose of advertisement, announcement or direction.

Interpretation

C.2   In Class C 'painting' includes any application of colour.

7.3.3   Part 3 — Changes of Use

Under the Town and Country Planning (Use Classes) Order 1987, a change of use within the same use class does not involve the development of land. A change of use between two use classes, however, will only constitute development if it involves a material change of use. Under Part 3 of the GDO, set out below, certain unilateral changes between different use classes is permitted development. This aspect has been mentioned earlier.

Class A
Permitted
development

A. Development consisting of a change of the use of building to a use falling within Class A1 (shops) of the Schedule to the Use Classes Order from a use falling within Class A3 (food and drink) of that Schedule or from a use for the sale, or display for sale, of motor vehicles.

Class B
Permitted
development

B. Development consisting of a change of the use of a building—
    (a)   to a use for any purpose falling within Class B1 (business) of the Schedule to the Use Classes Order from any use falling within Class B2 (general industrial) or B8 (storage and distribution) of that Schedule;

> **(b)   to a use for any purpose falling within Class B8 (storage and distribution) of that Schedule from any use falling within Class B1 (business) or B2 (general industrial).**

Development not permitted   B.1   Development is not permitted by Class B where the change is to or from a use falling within Class B8 of that Schedule, if the change of use relates to more than 235 square metres of floorspace in the building.

Class C
Permitted development   **C. Development consisting of a change of use to a use falling within Class A2 (financial and professional services) of the Schedule to the Use Classes Order from a use falling within Class A3 (food and drink) of that Schedule.**

Class D
Permitted development   **D. Development consisting of a change of use of any premises with a display window at ground floor level to use falling within Class A1 (shops) of the Schedule to the Use Classes Order from a use falling within Class A2 (financial and professional services) of that Schedule.**

Class E
Permitted development   **E. Development consisting of change in the use of any building or other land from a use permitted by a planning permission granted on an application, to another use which that permission would have specifically authorised when it was granted.**

Development not permitted   E.1   Development is not permitted by Class E if—
   (a)   the application for planning permission referred to was made before the date of coming into force of this order;
   (b)   it would be carried out more than ten years after the grant of planning permission; or
   (c)   it would result in the breach of any condition, limitation or specification contained in that planning permission in relation to the use in question.

Class E of Part 3 should also be noted. Its purpose is to encourage the use of planning permission granted in the alternative. It is possible for a local planning authority to grant more than one planning permission for the same parcel of land, e.g., for a change of use from use A to use B; also for a change of use from use A to use C. If the owner implements the first change by moving from use A to use B, he cannot subsequently move to use C without first obtaining planning permission to do so. To overcome this difficulty, Class E envisages that a local planning authority may grant planning permission for say, a change of use from use A to use B *or* C. If then, the owner implements the change to use B, he may subsequently change from use B to use C as permitted development. Two limitations on the right, however, require that the second change (to use C) must be carried out within 10 years of the grant of planning permission, and that the second change must not be in breach of any condition, limitation or specification imposed in the permission.

7.3.4 Part 4 — Temporary Buildings and Uses
This Part of sch. 2 to the Order contains the following two Classes:

Class A

Permitted development

A. The provision on land of buildings, moveable structures, works, plant or machinery required temporarily in connection with and for the duration of operations being or to be carried out on, in, under or over that land or on land adjoining that land.

Development not permitted

A.1   Development is not permitted by Class A if—
    (a)   the operations referred to are mining operations, or
    (b)   planning permission is required for those operations but is not granted or deemed to be granted.

Conditions

A.2   Development is permitted by Class A subject to the conditions that, when the operations have been carried out—
    (a)   any building, structure, works, plant or machinery permitted by this Class shall be removed, and
    (b)   any adjoining land on which development permitted by this Class has been carried out shall as soon as reasonably practicable, be reinstated to its condition before that development was carried out.

Class B

Permitted development

B. The use of any land for any purpose for not more than 28 days in total in any calendar year, of which not more than 14 days in total may be for the purposes referred to in paragraph B.2, and the provision on the land of any moveable structure for the purposes of the permitted use.

Development not permitted

B.1   Development is not permitted by Class B if—
    (a)   the land in question is a building or is within the curtilage of a building,
    (b)   the use of the land is for a caravan site, or
    (c)   the land is, or is within, an area of special scientific interest and the use of the land is for—
        (i)   a purpose referred to in paragraph B.2(b) or other motor sports;

(ii)   clay pigeon shooting;
(iii)   any war game.

Interpretation   B.2   The purposes mentioned in Class B above are—
of Class B   (a)   the holding of a market;
                         (b)   motor car and motorcycle racing including trials of
speed, and practising for these activities;

'War game' means an enacted, mock or imaginary battle conducted with weapons which are designed not to injure (including smoke bombs, or guns or grenades which fire or spray paint or are otherwise used to mark other participants), but excludes military activities or training exercises organised by or with the authority of the Secretary of State for Defence.

Under Class A of this Part, a builder's hut, used for administrative purposes on a construction site during the course of building operations, would be permitted development during the period of construction.

Class B of Part 4 permits the use of land for certain temporary purposes. The permission does not apply, however, where the land in question is a building or is within the curtilage of a building, or to the use of land as a caravan site. Some doubt exists as to whether the 28 days' grace allowed for the temporary use (or 14 in some cases) allows land to be used for that period on a permanent basis. In *Tidswell* v *Secretary of State for the Environment* [1977] JPL 104 an enforcement notice had been served requiring the discontinuance of land for use as a market. At the time of service of the notice, the contravening development had operated for a total of nine Sundays, but the use of the land for that purpose on Sundays had continued after service of the notice for at least another nine months. By the date of the appeal, the use had continued far beyond the GDO limits (every Sunday from 23 June 1974 until 15 April 1975, i.e., 37 Sundays in 1974 and 15 in 1975). The Queen's Bench Divisional Court upheld the Secretary of State's view that the benefit of the Order was not available to the appellant. In this case all the evidence suggested that the use was not a temporary use but a permanent one. The decision upheld the validity of the enforcement notice served after use of the land as a market for the first nine Sundays. It may not follow that had that use then ceased, the enforcement notice would have been upheld by the Secretary of State. Forbes J quoted Upjohn LJ in *Miller-Mead* v *Minister of Housing & Local Government* [1963] 2 QB 196 at p.231 where he said, '... a permanent user for a purpose not permitted and a temporary casual user up to 28 days in any one year are quite different things'. He went on to hold that, from the evidence available, it must have been apparent that what was there was a permanent use for a purpose not permitted and not a temporary casual user up to 14 days.

In *South Bucks District Council* v *Secretary of State for the Environment* [1989] JPL 351, the Court of Appeal held that the effect of this provision was to grant as many planning permissions as there were changes of use, so that where land was used at intervals of one week for a Sunday market, a change of use occurred every time the market was held. The significance of this decision is that it enables the local planning authority to issue an article 4 direction withdrawing the permitted development rights, even where the landowner has begun to use the 'temporary permission' but not exhausted it completely. In effect, therefore, the provision does not grant a single permission for temporary use of land for each calendar year. It allows the landowner to make up to 28 changes of use for the same activity, on each of the days permitted in any year.

In a consultation paper issued in August 1992, the government invited views on whether further control should be introduced over the temporary use of land for clay pigeon shooting, markets and car boot sales, war games and the use of land by helicopters landing and taking-off. At present, the General Development Order permits these activities to occur on land with the following specified frequencies in any one calendar year:

	On Sites of Special Scientific Interest	Elsewhere
Markets	14 days	14 days
Motor sports	nil	14 days
Clay pigeon shooting	nil	28 days
War games	nil	28 days
All others (including helicopters)	28 days	28 days

When being carried out, these activities can generate excessive traffic and noise, causing concern to local residents in the area.

After considering responses received to the consultation paper, however, the government decided not to introduce any further controls on the temporary use of land.

7.3.5   Part 6 — Agricultural Buildings and Operations
This part of sch. 2, the text of which is set out below, gives permitted development rights (where the development is, or minerals are, as the case may be, reasonably necessary for the purposes of agriculture) in relation to
— certain building works and excavation or engineering operations on agricultural units of 5 hectares or more in area (Class A);
— the extension or alteration of agricultultural buildings, the installation of certain plant and machinery, the provision of sewers etc, and certain other works, on agricultural units of not less than 0.4 but less than 5 hectares in area (Class B); and
— the winning and working of minerals on certain land (Class C).

Class A Development on units of 5 hectares or more
Permitted **A. The carrying out on agricultural land comprised in**
development **an agricultural unit of 5 hectares or more in area of—**
                       (a)   works for the erection, extension or alteration
of a building; or

(b) any excavation or engineering operations, which are reasonably necessary for the purposes of agriculture within that unit.

Development not permitted

A.1 Development is not permitted by Class A if—
(a) the development would be carried out on a separate parcel of land forming part of the unit which is less than 1 hectare in area;
(b) it would consist of, or include, the erection, extension or alteration of a dwelling;
(c) it would involve the provision of a building, structure or works not designed for agricultural purposes;
(d) the ground area which would be covered by—
(i) any works or structure (other than a fence) for accommodating livestock or any plant or machinery arising from engineering operations; or
(ii) any building erected or extended or altered by virtue of this Class, would exceed 465 square metres, calculated as described in paragraph D.2;
(e) the height of any part of any building, structure or works within 3 kilometres of the perimeter of an aerodrome would exceed 3 metres;
(f) the height of any part of any building, structure or works not within 3 kilometres of the perimeter of an aerodrome would exceed 12 metres;
(g) any part of the development would be within 25 metres of a metalled part of a trunk or classified road;
(h) it would consist of, or include, the erection or construction of, or the carrying out of any works to, a building, structure or an excavation used or to be used for the accommodation of livestock or for the storage of slurry or sewage sludge where the building, structure or excavation is, or would be, within 400 metres of the curtilage of a protected building; or
(i) it would involve excavations or engineering operations on or over article 1(6) land which are connected with fish farming.

Conditions

A.2 Development is permitted by Class A subject to the following conditions—
(a) where development is carried out within 400 metres of the curtilage of a protected building, any building, structure, excavation or works resulting from the development shall not be used for the accommodation of livestock except in the circumstances described in paragraph D.3 or for the storage of slurry or sewage sludge;
(b) where the development involves—

(i)   the extraction of any mineral from the land (including removal from any disused railway embankment); or

(ii)   the removal of any mineral from a mineral-working deposit,

the mineral shall not be moved off the unit;

(c)   waste materials shall not be brought on to the land from elsewhere for deposit except for use in works described in Class A(a) or in the creation of a hard surface and any materials so brought shall be incorporated forthwith into the building or works in question.

(2)   Subject to paragraph (3), development consisting of—

(i)   the erection, extension or alteration of a building;

(ii)   the formation or alteration of a private way;

(iii)   the carrying out of excavations or the deposit of waste material (where the relevant area, as defined in paragraph D.4 below exceeds 0.5 hectare); or

(iv)   the placing or assembly of a tank in any waters, is permitted by Class A subject to the following conditions—

(a)   the developer shall, before beginning the development, apply to the local planning authority for a determination as to whether the prior approval of the authority will be required to the siting, design and external appearance of the building, the siting and means of construction of the private way, the siting of the excavation or deposit or the siting and appearance of the tank, as the case may be;

(b)   the application shall be accompanied by a written description of the proposed development and of the materials to be used and a plan indicating the site together with any fee required to be paid;

(c)   the development shall not be begun before the occurrence of one of the following—

(i)   the receipt by the applicant from the local planning authority of a written notice of their determination that such prior approval is not required;

(ii)   where the local planning authority gives the applicant notice within 28 days following the date of receiving his application of their determination that such prior approval is required, the giving of such approval; or

(iii)   the expiry of 28 days following the date on which the application was received by the local planning authority without the local planning authority making any determination as to whether such approval is required or notifying the applicant of their determination;

(cc)   (i)   where the local planning authority gives the applicant notice but such prior approval is required the applicant shall display a site notice by site display on or near the land on which the proposed development is to be carried out, leaving the notice in position for not less than 21 days in the period of 28 days from the date on which the local planning authority gave the notice to the applicant;

(ii)   the applicant shall not be treated as not having complied with the requirements of subparagraph (i) if the site notice is, without any fault or intention of his, removed, obscured or defaced before the period of 21 days referred to in that subparagraph has elapsed, if he has taken reasonable steps for its protection and, if need be, replacement;

(d)   the development shall, except to the extent that the local planning authority otherwise agree in writing, be carried out—

(i)   where prior approval is required, in accordance with the details approved;

(ii)   where prior approval is not required, in accordance with the details submitted with the application; and

(e)   the development shall be carried out—

(i)   where approval has been given by the local planning authority, within a period of five years from the date on which approval was given;

(ii)   in any other case, within a period of five years from the date on which the local planning authority were given the information referred to in subparagraph (b).

(3)   The conditions in paragraph (2) do not apply to the extension or alteration of a building if the building is not on article 1(6) land except in the case of a significant alteration or a significant extension.

(4)   Development consisting of the significant extension or the significant alteration of a building may only be carried out once by virtue of Class A(a).

Class B Development on units of less than 5 hectares
Permitted   **B. The carrying out on agricultural land comprised in**
development **an agricultural unit of not less than 0.4 but less than 5 hectares in area of development consisting of—**
(a)   the extension or alteration of an agricultural building;
(b)   the installation of additional or replacement plant or machinery;
(c)   the provision, rearrangement or replacement of sewer, main, pipe, cable or other apparatus;
(d)   the provision, rearrangement or replacement of a private way;
(e)   the creation of a hard surface;
(f)   the deposit of waste; or
(g)   the carrying out of any of the following operations in connection with fish farming, namely, repairing

ponds and raceways; the installation of grading machinery, aeration equipment or flow meters and any associated channel; the dredging of ponds; and the replacement of tanks and nets,
where the development is reasonably necessary for the purposes of agriculture within the unit.

Development
not permitted

B.1   Development is not permitted by Class B if—
(a)   the development would be carried out on a separate parcel of land forming part of the unit which is less than 0.4 hectare in area;
(b)   the external appearance of the premises would be materially affected;
(c)   any part of the development would be within 25 metres of a metalled part of a trunk or classified road;
(d)   it would consist of, or involve, the carrying out of any works to a building or structure used or to be used for the accommodation of livestock or the storage of slurry or sewage sludge where the building or structure is within 400 metres of the curtilage of a protected building; or
(e)   it would relate to fish farming and would involve the placing or assembly of a tank on land or in any waters or the construction of a pond in which fish may be kept or an increase (otherwise than by the removal of silt) in the size of any tank or pond in which fish may be kept.

B.2   Development is not permitted by Class B(a) if—
(a)   the height of any building would be increased;
(b)   the cubic content of the original building would be increased by more than 10%;
(c)   any part of any new building would be more than 30 metres from the original building;
(d)   the development would involve the extension, alteration or provision of a dwelling;
(e)   any part of the development would be carried out within 5 metres of any boundary of the unit; or
(f)   the ground area of any building extended by virtue of this Class would exceed 465 square metres.

B.3   Development is not permitted by Class B(b) if—
(a)   the height of any additional plant or machinery within 3 kilometres of the perimeter of an aerodrome would exceed 3 metres;
(b)   the height of any additional plant or machinery not within 3 kilometres of the perimeter of an aerodrome would exceed 12 metres;
(c)   the height of any replacement plant or machinery would exceed that of the plant or machinery being replaced; or

(d)   the area to be covered by the development would exceed 465 square metres calculated as described in paragraph D.2 below.

B.4   Development is not permitted by Class B(e) if the area to be covered by the development would exceed 465 square metres calculated as described in paragraph D.2 below.

Conditions   B.5   Development permitted by Class B and carried out within 400 metres of the curtilage of a protected building is subject to the condition that any building which is extended or altered, or any works resulting from the development, shall not be used for the accommodation of livestock except in the circumstances described in paragraph D.3 or for the storage of slurry or sewage sludge.

B.6   Devlopment consisting of the extension or alteration of a building situated on article 1(6) land or the provision, rearrangement or replacement of a private way on such land is permitted subject to—
(a)   the condition that the developer shall, before beginning the development, apply to the local planning authority for a determination as to whether the prior approval of the authority will be required to the siting, design and external appearance of the building as extended or altered or the siting and means of construction of the private way; and
(b)   the conditions set out in paragraphs A.2 (2)(b) to (e) above.

B.7   Development is permitted by Class B(f) subject to the following conditions—
(a)   that waste materials are not brought on to the land from elsewhere for deposit unless they are for use in works described in Class B(a), (d) or (e) and are incorporated forthwith into the building or works in question; and
(b)   that the height of the surface of the land will not be materially increased by the deposit.

Class C Mineral working for agricultural purposes
Permitted   **C. The winning and working on land held or occupied**
development   **with land used for the purposes of agriculture of any minerals reasonably necessary for agricultural purposes within the agricultural unit of which it forms part.**

Development   C.1   Development is not permitted by Class C if any
not permitted   excavation would be made within 25 metres of a metalled part of a trunk or classified road.

Condition

C.2   Development is permitted by Class C subject to the condition that no mineral extracted during the course of the operation shall be moved to any place outside the land from which it was extracted, except to land which is held or occupied with that land and is used for the purposes of agriculture.

Interpretation
of Part 6

D.1   For the purposes of Part 6—
'agricultural land' means land which, before development permitted by this Part is carried out, is land in use for agriculture and which is so used for the purposes of a trade or business, and excludes any dwellinghouse or garden;
'agricultural unit' means agricultural land which is occupied as a unit for the purposes of agriculture, including—
    (a)   any dwelling or other building on that land occupied for the purpose of farming the land by the person who occupies the unit, or
    (b)   any dwelling on that land occupied by a farmworker;
'building' does not include anything resulting from engineering operations;
'fish farming' means the breeding, rearing or keeping of fish or shellfish (which includes any kind of crustacean and mollusc);
'livestock' includes fish or shellfish which are farmed;
'protected building' means any permanent building which is normally occupied by people or would be so occupied, if it were in use for purposes for which it is apt; but does not include—
    (i)   a building within the argicultural unit;
    (ii)   a building used for a purpose referred to in classes B3 to B7 (special industrial uses) of the Schedule to the Use Classes Order; or
    (iii)   a dwelling or other building on another agricultural unit which is used for or in connection with agriculture;
'significant extension' and 'significant alteration' mean any extension or alteration of the building where the cubic content of the original building would be exceeded by more than 10% or the height of the building as extended or altered would exceed the height of the original building; and
'tank' includes any cage and any other structure for use in fish farming.

D.2   For the purposes of this Part—
    (a)   an area calculated as described in this paragraph comprises the ground area which would be covered by the proposed development, together with the ground area of any

building (other than a dwelling), or any structure, works, plant, machinery or ponds or tanks within the same unit which are being provided or have been provided within the preceding two years and any part of which would be within 90 metres of the proposed development;

(b)   400 metres is to be measured along the ground.

D.3   The circumstances referred to in paragraphs A.2(1)(a) and B.5 are that no other suitable building or structure, 400 metres or more from the curtilage of a protected building, is available to accommodate the livestock; and

(a)   that the need to accommodate it arises from—

(i)   quarantine requirements;

(ii)   an emergency due to another building or structure in which the livestock could otherwise be accommodated being unavailable because it has been damaged or destroyed by fire, flood or storm; or

(b)   in the case of animals normally kept out of doors they require temporary accommodation in a building or other structure—

(i)   because they are sick or giving birth or newly born; or

(ii)   to provide shelter against extreme weather conditions.

D.4   For the purposes of paragraph A.2(2)(iii) the relevant area is the area of the proposed excavation or the area on which it is proposed to deposit waste together with the aggregate of the areas of all other excavations within the unit which have not been filled and of all other parts of the unit on or under which waste has been deposited and has not been removed.

D.4A In paragraph A.2(2)(cc), 'site notice' means a notice containing—

(a)   the name of the applicant,

(b)   the address or location of the proposed development,

(c)   a description of the proposed development and of the materials to be used,

(d)   a statement that the prior approval of the authority will be required to the siting, design and external appearance of the building, the siting and means of construction of the private way, the siting of the excavation or deposit or the siting and appearance of the tank, as the case may be,

(e)   the name and address of the local planning authority,

and which is signed and dated by or on behalf of the applicant.

D.5   For the purposes of Class B—
(a)   the erection of any additional building within the curtilage of another building is to be treated as the extension of that building and the additional building is not to be treated as an original building;
(b)   where two or more original buildings are within the same curtilage and are used for the same undertaking they are to be treated as a single original building in making any measurement in connection with the extension or alteration of either of them.

D.6   In Class C, 'the purposes of agriculture' includes fertilising land used for the purposes of agriculture and the maintenance, improvement or alteration of any buildings, structures or works occupied or used for such purposes on land so used.

Part 6 of sch. 2 to the GDO above, originally granted a single permission allowing certain buildings or engineering operations to be carried out on agricultural land comprised in an agricultural unit having an area of 0.4 of a hectare or more, where reasonably necessary for the purposes of agriculture within the unit. The present Part 6 was substituted for the old as from 2 January 1992. It will be seen that under the new provisions, the development allowed is divided. In particular, in Class A the permitted development is restricted to agricultural units of 5 hectares or more, subject to a minimum size of 1 hectare where the development would be carried out on a separate parcel of land within and forming part of that larger unit. Class B permitted development is restricted to agricultural land comprised in an agricultural unit with an area of 0.4 hectares or more, but less than 5 hectares in area. It should be noted that under both Class A and B it may be necessary, before exercising permitted development rights, to first apply to the local planning authority for a determination as to whether the authority's prior approval is required for certain details of the development proposed. In particular, the provisions for prior notification apply where it is proposed to erect, extend or alter an agricultural building. If the authority gives notice that prior approval is needed for such development, the applicant is required by the Schedule to display a site notice on or near the land on which the proposed development is to be carried out, leaving the notice in position for not less than 21 days in the 28 days from the date on which the local planning authority gave notice to the applicant.

The development rights permitted by Class A of Part 6 of sch. 2 apply only to building operations 'reasonably necessary for the purposes of agriculture within that unit'. In *Clarke* v *Secretary of State for the Environment* (1992) 65 P & CR 85 it was held that to qualify as permitted development, the buildings did not have to be reasonably necessary for the particular agricultural enterprise being undertaken on the unit at the time the buildings were erected; they simply have to be reasonably necessary for, and designed for, the purposes of agriculture within that unit.

One other provision should be noted. Development under Class A and B is not permitted by the Order if it involves the provision of accommodation for livestock or the storage of slurry and sewerage sludge within 400 metres of the curtilage of a 'protected building'. The purpose of the provision is to maintain a 'cordon sanitaire' between livestock and livestock slurry and nearby residential accommodation.

7.3.6   Part 7 — Forestry Buildings and Operations
This part of sch. 2 gives permitted development rights to certain operational development carried out on land used for forestry. The text is as follows:

Class A
Permitted   **A. The carrying out on land used for the purposes of**
development   **forestry, including afforestation, of development**
reasonably necessary for those purposes consisting of—
   (a)   works for the erection, extension or alteration of a building;
   (b)   the formation, alteration or maintenance of private ways;
   (c)   operations on that land, or on land held or occupied with that land, to obtain the materials required for the formation, alteration or maintenance of such ways;
   (d)   other operations (not including engineering or mining operations).

Development   A.1   Development is not permitted by this Class if—
not permitted   (a)   it would consists of or includes the provision or alteration of a dwelling;
   (b)   the height of any building or works within 3 kilometres of the perimeter of an aerodrome would exceed 3 metres in height; or
   (c)   any part of the development would be within 25 metres of the metalled portion of a trunk or classified road.

Conditions   A.2(1) Subject to paragraph (3) development consisting of the erection of a building or the extension or alteration of a building or the formation or alteration of a private way is permitted by Class A subject to the following conditions—
   (a)   the developer shall, before beginning the development, apply to the local planning authority for a determination as to whether the prior approval of the authority will be required to the siting, design and external appearance of the building or, as the case may be, the siting and means of construction of the private way;
   (b)   the application shall be accompanied by a written description of the proposed development, the materials to be

used and a plan indicating the site together with any fee required to be paid;

(c) the development shall not be begun before the occurrence of one of the following—

(i) the receipt by the applicant from the local planning authority of a written notice of their determination that such prior approval is not required;

(ii) where the local planning authority gives the applicant notice within 28 days following the date of receiving his application of their determination that such prior approval is required, the giving of such approval;

(iii) the expiry of 28 days following the date on which the application was received by the local planning authority without the local planning authority making any determination as to whether such approval is required or notifying the applicant of their determination;

(cc) (i) where the local planning authority gives the applicant notice that such prior approval is required the applicant shall display a site notice by site display on or near the land on which the proposed development is to be carried out, leaving the notice in position for not less than 21 days in the period of 28 days from the date on which the local planning authority gave the notice to the applicant;

(ii) the applicant shall not be treated as not having complied with the requirements of subparagraph (i) if the site notice is, without any fault or intention of his, removed, obscured or defaced before the period of 21 days referred to in that subparagraph has elapsed, if he has taken reasonable steps for its protection and, if need be, replacement;

(d) the development shall, except to the extent that the local planning authority otherwise agree in writing, be carried out—

(i) where prior approval is required, in accordance with the details approved;

(ii) where prior approval is not required, in accordance with the details submitted with the application;

(e) the development shall be carried out—

(i) where approval has been given by the local planning authority, within a period of five years from the date on which approval was given,

(ii) in any case, within a period of five years from the date on which the local planning authority were given the information referred to in subparagraph (b).

(2) In the case of development consisting of the significant extension or the significant alteration of the building such development may be carried out only once.

(3) Paragraph (1) does not preclude the extension or alteration of a building if the building is not on Article 1(6) land except in the case of a significant extension or a significant alteration.

Interpretation   A.3   For the purposes of this Class—
'significant extension' and 'significant alteration' mean any extension or alteration of the building where the cubic content of the original building would be exceeded by more than 10% or the height of the building as extended or altered would exceed the height of the original building;
'site notice' means a notice containing—
  (a)   the name of the applicant,
  (b)   the address or location of the proposed development,
  (c)   a description of the proposed development and of the materials to be used,
  (d)   a statement that the prior approval of the authority will be required to the siting, design and external appearance of the building or, as the case may be, siting and means of construction of the private way, and which is signed and dated by or on behalf of the applicant,
  (e)   the name and address of the local planning authority, and which is signed and dated by or on behalf of the applicant.

7.4   Proposed changes

A consultation paper issued by the government in December 1993 proposed the introduction of permitted development for minor alterations to existing commercial buildings without the need to apply for planning permission. The permitted development would be confined to the rear of shops, banks, building societies and similar high street outlets, to the conversion of space above a shop into a flat, and to ancillary development within the curtilage of schools, hospitals, colleges and universities. The permitted development would be subject to limits on size, height, proximity to curtilage boundary and in some cases external appearance of the building when viewed from the front.

EIGHT

The need for planning permission
2: Cases of doubt

Given the complexities of the definition of development and the difficulties which may arise in deciding whether in any particular case proposed development is permitted development, landowners may be in doubt about whether they need to make an express application for planning permission to the local planning authority before carrying out some activity. In such circumstances a landowner may choose from a number of options, though some of those choices will not necessarily remove his doubts.

8.1 Certificate of lawfulness of proposed use or development

Under a new s.192 of the 1990 Act, if any person wishes to ascertain whether:

(a) any proposed use of buildings or other land; or
(b) any operations proposed to be carried out in, on, over or under land,

would be lawful, he may make an application for the purpose to the local planning authority specifying the land and describing the use or operations in question. Then, if the local planning authority are satisfied on the information provided that the use or operations described in the application would be lawful if instituted or begun at the time of the application, they must issue a certificate to that effect. A certificate issued under the section must specify the land to which it relates; describe the use or operations in question (by specific use class if appropriate); give reasons for determining the use or operation to be lawful, and specify the date of the application of the certificate.

The section also provides that the lawfulness of any use or operations for which a certificate is in force shall be conclusively presumed unless there is a material change, before the use is instituted or the operations begun, in any of the matters relevant to determining such lawfulness.

In dealing with such an application the local planning authority is making a determination of law. If the applicant is aggrieved by the determination of the local planning authority, he may appeal to the Secretary of State under s. 78 of the 1990 Act, and from his determination to the High Court under s. 288.

An important limitation to the scope of a s. 192 certificate procedure is that it is not available where the proposed activity has already been carried out. In such a case the owner may either do nothing, and then if an enforcement notice is served appeal against it to the Secretary of State on the ground that the matters alleged in the notice do not constitute a breach of planning control, or alternatively bring an action in the courts for a declaratory judgment.

The s. 192 certificate procedure has now replaced the previous procedure known as a s. 64 determination, as a result of charges made by the Planning and Compensation Act 1991. The procedure is considered further in Chapter 18.

8.2   Action for a declaration

An action in the courts for a declaration is a viable but expensive alternative to making an application for a s. 192 certificate. It may also be used in circumstances where a s. 192 certificate cannot be made, namely, where the proposed activity has already been carried out.

8.3   Application for planning permission

This procedure, of course, does not resolve the question of whether an application was necessary in the first place. In addition, by making an application, the owner may be paying a fee which was in fact unnecessary. In *Wells* v *Minister of Housing and Local Government* [1967] 1 WLR 1000, it was held that an application for planning permission could be treated by the local planning authority as an application for a s. 64 determination. Now that that section has been replaced by the new s. 192, there is little doubt that an application for a s. 192 certificate may be similarly treated.

8.4   Carrying out an activity without ascertaining whether it needs permission

There may be advantages but also disadvantages in going ahead with an activity without ascertaining whether it requires planning permission, bearing in mind the power of the local planning authority to take enforcement action in respect of any breach of planning control. From a cost point of view it should be recognised that operational development is expensive to carry out and, in the event of an enforcement notice taking effect, it is expensive to have to reinstate the land to its former condition. A change of use, on the other hand, can often be carried out, and if necessary the earlier use reinstated, at much less cost.

Another difference, however, is as regards the application of the four-year rule. Enforcement action cannot be taken in respect of operational development unless served within four years of it being carried out. As regards the making of a material change of use, however, enforcement action against the contravening development may not be taken more than 10 years after it has been carried out.

Lastly, however, the unknown factor in this area is not so much whether the local planning authority would take enforcement action in respect of the contravening development, but whether if an enforcement notice were served, the notice would be upheld by the Secretary of State on appeal.

This is an aspect of planning law which affects not only those in doubt about whether they must make an application for planning permission, but also those who are in no doubt that their activity requires planning permission but who nevertheless develop without it. The position is that before serving an enforcement notice, a local planning authority will often ask the owner to submit an application for planning permission under s. 73A of the 1990 Act in respect of development carried out before the date of the application. This application enables the local planning authority to publicise the application and listen to the views of third parties on the development which has already taken place, and then to weigh up the strength of opposition to that development before deciding whether to grant or refuse permission. Where the decision taken is to refuse permission, the authority will normally also take a decision to issue an enforcement notice in respect of the development. When this procedure under s. 73A is followed, it may enable the owner to show that the environmental effects of the development are not as bad as might have been anticipated, and this may lead to the grant of planning permission and the abandonment of enforcement proposals.

Uncertainty over whether an activity constitutes development led on one occasion to a dispute between two public authorities. In *Bedfordshire County Council* v *Central Electricity Generating Board* [1985] JPL 43 the defendants were, in fact, the Nuclear Industry Radioactive Waste Executive (known otherwise as NIREX), an unincorporated association comprising four statutory bodies of which the Central Electricity Generating Board was one.

In October 1983, NIREX announced its intention to undertake investigations into the suitability of two sites for the storage of radioactive waste. One of those sites, to be used for the storage of low and intermediate-level waste was to be located at Elstow in Bedfordshire. That same month, the Secretary of State indicated in the House of Commons that an application by NIREX for planning permission to undertake investigatory drilling in order to establish the site's suitability for storage would be called in by him for his own determination. So too would any subsequent application for planning permission for the repository itself, if the earlier investigatory works showed the site to be satisfactory for that purpose.

Then in May 1984, NIREX indicated to Bedfordshire County Council, as mineral planning authority for the area, its intention to make test boreholes on the site in order to explore the soil characteristics of the clay. This was a preliminary step in advance of the investigatory drilling which was to be the subject of the application for planning permission referred to by the Secretary of State.

The preliminary work envisaged the use of a hydraulically operated machine which forced a 2-inch-diameter hollow bit into the ground. The bit was then withdrawn and the clay specimen removed. NIREX anticipated that they would need three sampling points; that the bit would be driven into the soil to a depth of between 10 and 20 metres; and that the work would be completed in two to three days. NIREX also maintained that their work was not development. The council maintained that it was, that the activity proposed would affect the character of the site if only in a very localised fashion. Furthermore, it would increase the permeability of the site and that it would be extremely difficult to back-fill the holes and pack the filling material to make it relatively impermeable.

One of the difficulties faced by the council was that the normal procedures for controlling unauthorised development would be ineffective. An enforcement notice cannot take effect until at least 28 days etc. after service, and the notice could only be served once the work had begun. Likewise, a stop notice does not become operational until three days after its service.

The council at once sought and obtained, *ex parte*, an interim injunction preventing NIREX from commencing the work. The full case was heard in chambers by Piers Ashworth QC, sitting as a Deputy High Court judge of the Queen's Bench Division. After hearing argument he dismissed the summons for an injunction, a decision the Court of Appeal refused to overturn. One of the reasons for the deputy judge so deciding was that the work did not constitute development. This, he stated, 'was only a provisional view' about which 'I may be right or wrong'. If it were not development, then clearly no case existed for the issue of the injunction. Although the Court of Appeal thought that the matter raised 'interesting issues of law', the central issue on which the application failed was whether, if the work was development, an injunction was the appropriate remedy.

In both the High Court and the Court of Appeal, NIREX questioned whether a local authority could lawfully obtain an injunction in such circumstances. NIREX based their arguments on *Stoke-on-Trent City Council* v *B & Q (Retail) Ltd* [1984] AC 754 in which it was held that a local authority was entitled to apply for an injunction if it was satisfied that a party had an intention 'flagrantly to breach the criminal law'. The county council argued that this was not in fact the test to be applied, but rather that their lordships should base their decision on the rule in *American Cyanamid Co.* v *Ethicon Ltd* [1975] 1 AC 396 that a court could grant an interlocutory injunction if the balance of convenience favoured the continuance of an injunction until the trial of the substantive matter.

Their lordships, however, considered that even if they were to look at the case from the *American Cyanamid Co.* point of view, they could only consider the balance of convenience if they were satisfied that, first, if an injunction were not granted, the county council would suffer injury which could not fairly be compensated by an award of damages, and, secondly, irreparable damage would be caused to the site if the drillings were permitted. This was, of course, a point of dispute between the parties.

Their lordships were clearly not satisfied on either ground. According to Griffiths LJ,

Looking at this matter with a little common sense, all that was wanted was to bore three — true deep but tiny — holes in a 400-acre site. There was some evidence it is true, that that might cause some damage to the clay beneath, but there was equally evidence to the effect that those holes, of such small diameter, would be very quickly self-sealing and cause no damage.

Their lordships held, therefore, that they could not grant an injunction under the *American Cyanamid* principle and at the same time were not prepared to accept that NIREX were attempting flagrantly to breach the criminal law as had happened in the *Stoke-on-Trent City Council* v *B & Q (Retail) Ltd* case.

NINE

Applications for planning permission 1: Pre-submission requirements

In the year ended 31 March 1994, district planning authorities in England received 478,000 applications for planning permission and related consents. About 87 per cent were approved, most of them subject to conditions.

The Town and Country Planning (Applications) Regulations 1988 (SI No. 1812) provide that an application for planning permission shall:

(a) be made on a form provided by the local planning authority;

(b) include the particulars specified in the form and be accompanied by a plan which identifies the land to which it relates and any other plans and drawings and information necessary to describe the development which is the subject of the application; and

(c) except where the authority indicate that a lesser number is required, be accompanied by three copies of the form and the plans and drawings submitted with it.

Under the above regulations, the local planning authority may direct an applicant to supply further information or require him to verify particulars of information given before determining an application.

9.1 Outline planning permission

Where the permission sought is for the erection of a building, and the applicant so desires, an application may be made for 'outline planning permission'. The purpose in allowing such an application to be made is that it gives a prospective developer the opportunity to find out at an early stage, and before he has incurred substantial cost, whether or not a proposal is likely to be approved by the local planning authority. When such an application is made the applicant need not submit details of any proposed 'reserved matters'.

An *application* for outline planning permission may result in the *grant* of outline planning permission (as opposed to what is often referred to as 'full' planning permission). An outline planning permission is defined in art. 2 of the Town and Country Planning (Applications) Regulations to mean:

... planning permission for the erection of a building, subject to a condition requiring the subsequent approval of the local planning authority with respect to one or more reserved matters ...

'Reserved matters' are then defined to mean:

(a)   siting, (b) design, (c) external appearance, (d) means of access, (e) the landscaping of the site.

It is well-settled case law that the grant of outline permission constitutes a commitment by the local planning authority to the principle of the development, thus preventing the authority from refusing to approve any reserved matter on grounds which go to the principle of the development (*Lewis Thirkwell* v *Secretary of State for the Environment* [1978] JPL 844). In granting outline planning permission, therefore, the local planning authority have committed themselves to the form of development which is comprised in the permission subject only to the subsequent approval of any or all of those specified reserved matters. A local planning authority, however, may consider that they are unable to determine an application for outline planning permission independently of any reserved matters. This view is frequently taken with regard to applications for the erection of buildings in conservation areas. In such cases, the local planning authority can require the applicant to submit further details with regard to all the reserved matters or any of them before proceeding to consider the development proposal.

It is not uncommon for appellants to submit with an application for outline planning permission details of the proposed development 'for illustrative purposes only'. There is no doubt that such details can be a material consideration in determining whether or not to grant the outline permission being sought. If, however, the applicant has not indicated that details are submitted for illustrative purposes only or has not otherwise indicated that they are not formally part of the application, the local planning authority should treat the detail as part of the proposed development; and cannot reserve the matter by condition for subsequent approval unless the application is amended by the withdrawal of the details.

Although outline planning permission is a permission granted subject to a condition requiring approval of reserved matters, it was held in *R* v *Newbury District Council (ex parte Stevens)* (1992) 65 P & CR 438 that, contrary to previous doubts, the authority had the power under s. 78 of the 1990 Act to impose a condition on the grant of approval of a reserved matter, even though that aspect had not been mentioned in the outline permission, so long as the condition did not derogate from the outline permission already granted.

Apart from completing the appropriate application form, the following further requirements are imposed on the applicant.

9.2 Notification of owners

It is sometimes said that anyone can make an application for planning permission. If this be so, the prospect that a beggar might apply for planning permission for the redevelopment of land in Bermondsey or Belgravia (if he can afford the fee) is unlikely to raise much enthusiasm with the local planning authority for the area. The consideration of applications for planning permission is a costly and time consuming business for local planning authorities. Nevertheless, applications for planning permission have been made by persons with little capacity to implement the permission should it be granted. In 1980, the British Airports Authority, which is responsible for airport development in the country, made an application for outline planning permission to extend the airport capacity of Stansted Airport. The Town and Country Planning Association's view was that the expansion of airport capacity in the South-east would be better accommodated by building a new airport at Maplin Sands in Essex. In order that consideration should be given to this at the same time as the proposed development at Stansted, the Association applied for planning permission (which was subsequently withdrawn) for that development. Furthermore, the local authority within whose area Stansted was located, the Uttlesford District Council, thought that a better solution to the expansion of Stansted was an expansion of the terminal facilities at London Heathrow Airport. Accordingly, the district council submitted an application to the local planning authority for the Heathrow area for the building of a fifth passenger terminal complex at the airport. Both that application and the application submitted by the British Airports Authority were then called in by the Secretary of State for his own decision and treated for all practical purposes as one.

Although it is probably incorrect to say that anyone can apply for planning permission, it is not necessary that the applicant should have any present interest in the land that is the subject of the application. In *Hanily* v *Minister of Local Government & Planning* [1952] 2 QB 444, where a third party had applied for and been granted planning permission to develop land without the knowledge of the owner of the land, the High Court thought that anybody who genuinely hoped to acquire an interest in the land could properly apply for planning permission.

Whatever the applicant's position, however, if he is not the owner of an interest in every part of the land to which the application relates, he has been required since 1962 to give notice of the application to the holders of certain interests in the land. Prior to the Planning and Compensation Act 1991, the matter was dealt with by s. 66 of the 1990 Act. The section provided that a local planning authority should not entertain any application for planning permission unless it was accompanied by one of four prescribed certificates signed by or on behalf of the applicants, which indicated that no person other than the applicant was the owner of any of the land to which the application related, or that the applicant had given notice to those who were the owners, or that he had tried but had been unable to do so.

The position before the 1991 Act was that whilst the 1990 Act described in some detail the procedures to be followed for giving notice to owners not themselves the applicants, other detailed requirements, including the form of each of the four different forms of certificate, were prescribed by the General Development Order.

The 1991 Act sought to rationalise the position and provide for greater flexibility in the statutory provisions by transferring those provisions previously found in the body of the primary legislation to subordinate legislation made under it. Accordingly, a new s. 65 inserted into the 1990 Act by the Planning and Compensation Act 1991 empowers the Secretary of State to prescribe by development order the detailed arrangements and procedures for dealing with the notice to be given to owners of interests in land when they are not parties to the application.

Pursuant to that new provision, article 12 of the General Development Order now provides:

(1) ... an applicant for planning permission shall give requisite notice of the application to any person (other than the applicant) who on the prescribed date is an owner of the land to which the application relates, or a tenant,—

(a) by serving the notice on every such person whose name and address is known to him; and

(b) where he has taken reasonable steps to ascertain the names and addresses of every such person, but has been unable to do so, by local advertisement after the prescribed date.

The 'prescribed date' under the article is defined as being 'the day 21 days before the date of the application'. 'Tenant' is defined as 'the tenant of an agricultural holding any part of which is comprised in the land to which an application relates', and the 'requisite notice' means 'notice in the appropriate form which is set out in Part 1 of sch. 4 to the Order.

Under the Order, the applicant or the person applying on his behalf is required to serve on an owner or tenant of any land to which the application relates, notice that he is applying to the local planning authority for planning permission for development, details of which must be specified. The notice must also inform the owner of the land or tenant, that if he wishes to do so he may make representations about the application to the local planning authority within 21 days of service of the notice.

For the purpose of these provisions the term 'owner' means any person having a freehold interest or a leasehold interest the unexpired term of which is not less than seven years. Where a leasehold interest exists in land, therefore, an applicant who owns the freehold interest in the land to which the application relates will not be required to give specific notice to the owner of any leasehold interests with less than seven years to run. If, on the other hand, the applicant is himself the owner of a leasehold interest, he must give specific notice to the freeholder whatever the length of his term.

If, however, any of the land to which the application relates is or forms part of an agricultural holding, specific notice must be given to the tenant thereof, irrespective of the length of his interest. The purpose in giving notice of an application to the tenant of an agricultural holding, whatever his interest, is that the tenant may lose his security of tenure if the landlord can show that he wishes to put the land to some non-agricultural use.

The effect of the Order is to require applicants not only to notify owners and agricultural tenants of a planning application they intend to submit in relation to the owner's or tenant's land, but also requires the applicant to certify, in the appropriate form prescribed in sch. 4 to the Order, that the notification requirements have been satisfied. The Schedule also lists the certificates which must be completed in order to inform the local planning authority, and on appeal the Secretary of State, that the notification requirements have been fulfilled. The four certificates, only one of which is required to be submitted with the application for planning permission are as follows:

Certificate A   This certificate states that on the day 21 days before the date of the accompanying application nobody, except the applicant, was the owner (as earlier defined) of any part of the land to which the application relates.

Certificate B   This certificate states that the applicant has given the requisite notice to everyone else who, on the day 21 days before the date of the accompanying application, was the owner (as earlier defined) of any part of the land to which the application relates. The certificate further requires the applicant to list the owners to whom notice has been given, the address at which notice was served and the date of service.

Certificate C   This certificate applies where the applicant is able to discover and give notice to some but not *all* persons owning an interest in the land. It states that the applicant is unable to issue certificate A or B; also that the applicant has given the requisite notice to persons (who must be specified) who on the day 21 days before the date of the application were owners (as earlier defined) to which the application relates.

As well as listing the names of owners notified, along with their addresses at which they were served and the date notice was served, the certificate must also state that the applicant has taken all reasonable steps open to him (which must be specified) to find out the names and addresses of the *other* owners of the land or of a part of it, but that he has been unable to do so. The steps taken must include publication in a newspaper circulating in the locality in which the land is situated.

Certificate D   This certificate applies where the applicant is unable to discover the names of *any* of the persons owning an interest in the land. It states that the owner is unable to give certificate A; also that he has taken the reasonable steps open to him (which must be specified and include publication of notice of the application in a newspaper circulating in the locality), to find out the names and addresses of everyone else who on the day 21 days before the date of the application was the owner (as earlier defined) of any part of the land to which the application relates, but that he has been unable to do so.

It should be noted that, under the Order, each of the above certificates must also state either that none of the land to which the application relates is, or is part of an agricultural holding or that the applicant has given the requisite notice to every person who on the day 21 days before the date of the application was a tenant of an agricultural holding on all or part of the land to which the application relates.

The above procedures also apply to any appeal made to the Secretary of State under s. 78 of the 1990 Act. Furthermore, under the Order, the above procedures apply to applications for planning permission for development consisting of the winning and working of minerals, but with some variations.

There is no point in giving an owner notice of an application to develop land in which he has an interest, unless he is also given the opportunity to make representations with regard to the development proposed. Hence, the Order provides that where a certificate contains a statement that notice of the application has been given to another, the local planning authority shall not determine the application before the end of a period of 21 days beginning with the date when the notice was served on that person. In addition, the Order provides that, in determining the application, the local planning authority must take into account any representations made to them during that period by such persons.

It should be noted that, other than for certificate A, the procedure merely requires the applicant to state in a certificate that notice of the application has been given to the appropriate persons. Under the Order, authorities are required to notify their decisions to the applicants, but apart from notifying owners and agricultural tenants who have made representations on any application for planning permission affecting their land, there is no statutory requirement for authorities to notify their decision to other parties. The system does not guarantee that the applicant has actually given notice and, because acknowledgement of the authority's decision is restricted, the owner of an interest in the land may remain unaware that an application has been made. In practice it is known that the certificate procedure does not work particularly well, particularly where applications are submitted by an agent on behalf of the applicant.

It seems that non-compliance with these provisions may have a variable effect. Section 65(6) provides that if a person issues a certificate which purports to comply with any requirements imposed by virtue of the section and contains a statement which he knows to be false or misleading in a material particular; or recklessly issues a certificate which purports to comply with any such requirement and contains a statement which is false or misleading in a material particular, he shall have committed an offence and be liable on summary conviction to a fine not exceeding level 5 on the standard scale. Of more importance than any criminal sanction, however, is the effect of a certificate containing a false, misleading or inaccurate statement on any planning permission which has been granted. In R v *Bradford-on-Avon Urban District Council (ex parte Boulton)* [1964] 1 WLR 1136, an application was made for an order of certiorari to quash a grant of planning permission for residential development. A certificate which had been signed on behalf of the applicant, stated that he was the owner of the fee simple in the land. In fact the applicant was not the owner of the fee simple. He had been negotiating for the purchase of the land from the owner, who was in fact privy to the application. Refusing to grant the order sought, the Divisional Court held that, on the true construction of the statutory provisions, a planning authority had jurisdiction to entertain an application for planning permission if it was accompanied by a genuine certificate in the approved terms signed by the applicant, and that a factual error in the certificates did not deprive the authority of that jurisdiction.

One factor which seemed to influence the decision was that a grant of planning permission runs with the land and is relied on by subsequent purchasers. If a purchaser was to be required to investigate whether the certificate submitted with the application was correct in its factual averments before being able to rely on the grant, the conveyancing difficulties would be formidable.

Following the *Bradford-on-Avon* case it was generally recognised, though with some reluctance, that the grant of planning permission would survive any factual error in the content of a certificate, at least as long as there was no actual dishonesty. The more recent case of *Main* v *Swansea City Council* [1985] JPL 558, however, has done much to clarify the position. In this case outline planning permission had been granted for residential development. The certificate which had accompanied the application stated that notice of the application had been given to all other owners of land, namely, the city council. It transpired that the land the subject of the application also included land owned by a person whose identity was unknown, and that the certificate did not specify that notice of the development had been published in a local newspaper circulating in the locality as was required. The appropriate certificate was thus certificate C, not B which had been submitted. The applicant had applied for judicial review to quash the grant of planning permission. The Court of Appeal held that in considering the failure of the applicant to comply with the statutory requirements, one had to look not only at the nature of the failure, but also at such matters as the identity of the applicant for relief, the lapse of time before proceedings were taken and the effect on other parties and on the public. In this case the court had no doubt that the defect in the certificates was sufficient to enable it to strike down the subsequent grant of planning permission in certain circumstances, as where, for example, a prompt application had been made by the owner of the non-council land. Although the defects were not such as to render the grant a nullity, the court held that it had discretion whether to grant the relief sought. In refusing to exercise that discretion in favour of the applicant, the court took into account the fact that, throughout the period between the grant of the outline permission and the approval of reserved matters (over three years), the applicant had not objected; that the scheme which had been approved did not involve the development of the land not owned by the city council; and that the Secretary of State in full knowledge of the position had not sought relief. It was too late, therefore, for the applicant to obtain the necessary relief to quash the permission and with it the subsequent approval of reserved matters.

Although the courts are now able, in the exercise of their discretion, to give relief to a petitioner where there is an error in the certificate submitted, in an appropriate case a remedy in private law may be available.

In *English* v *Dedham Vale Properties Ltd* [1978] 1 WLR 93, the prospective purchaser of a parcel of land submitted an application for planning permission to develop the land in the vendors' names and without their authority. The application, which was subsequently granted, was signed by an employee of the prospective purchaser stating himself to be the vendors' agent. The accompanying certificate described the applicants (i.e., the vendors) as the estate owners in fee simple of the land to which the application related. The certificate would in fact have been accurate had it been made with the vendors' authority. Without that authority, however, the application should have been accompanied by a certificate stating that the vendors had received notice of the making of the application.

In making the application, the purchaser's employee had asked that the decision notice be sent to him at the purchaser's address. Hence the vendors remained ignorant of the application for planning permission and of its subsequent grant and, whilst still unaware, conveyed the land in question to the purchaser for a price lower than they would have done had they known the true position. As a result, the surviving vendor (one having died) brought an action against the purchaser claiming, *inter alia,* damages for fraudulent misrepresentation in regard to the prospects of obtaining planning permission, and an account of the profits which had accrued to the purchasers as a result of the grant. In the Chancery Division it was held by Slade J that whilst there had not been any misrepresentation by the purchaser as to the prospect of obtaining planning permission and he was therefore absolved from any charge of fraud, he was accountable to the vendors for the profit he had received as a result of making the planning application. This was because, in relation to the application, he had assumed the character of self-appointed agent of the vendors, thereby placing himself in a fiduciary relationship with them; and he had failed to disclose to them the fact that the application had been made. Slade J also held that where, during the course of negotiations for a contract for the sale and purchase of a property, the proposed purchaser, in the name of and purportedly as agent for the vendor but without the vendor's consent or authority, took some action in regard to the property such as making a planning application, which, if it had been disclosed to the vendor might reasonably have been likely to influence him in deciding whether or not to conclude a contract, a fiduciary relationship arose between the two parties which gave rise to a duty on the purchaser to disclose to the vendor before the conclusion of the contract what he had done as the vendor's purported agent; and, in the event of non-disclosure, the purchaser was liable to account to the vendor for any profit he made in the course of the purported agency, unless the vendor had consented to his retaining the profit.

9.3   Bad neighbour development

For certain classes of development designated by the General Development Order, the old, s. 65 of the 1990 Act provided (before being replaced under the Planning and Compensation Act 1991 with a new provision) for the publication of notices of applications for planning permission for 'designated development'. The General Development Order then designated the development subject to these provisions.

Such development was of a very limited kind and was more usually referred to as 'bad neighbour development'. It included development of the 'Clochemerle' kind as well as other places of public resort. Following the decision in 1991 to provide for compulsory publicity for *all* planning applications (see Chapter 10), these provisions have now been repealed.

9.4 Fees for planning applications

Under s. 303 of the 1990 Act, the Secretary of State may make regulations for the payment of a fee to local planning authorities in respect of applications made to them for any permission, consent, approval, determination or certificate.

The Town and Country Planning (Fees for Applications and Deemed Applications) Regulations 1989 (SI No. 193), as amended, now provide for fees to be payable where an application is made for planning permission, for a certificate of lawful use or development, for the approval of reserved matters, for consent to the display of advertisements and on a deemed application for planning permission which arises when an appeal is made against an enforcement notice.

The fees charged are based on broad categories of development and are designed to relate the fee to the approximate cost of processing the application. Initially, fees were intended to cover 50 per cent of costs, but in July 1990, it was announced that in future fees would recover 100 per cent. Successive increases since then have made progress towards that goal, so that following the increase in fees due to take place on 3 January 1995, the rate of recovery of local authorities' costs in processing and determining planning applications will be 80 per cent nationally.

It will be seen that, at present, fee rates are fixed nationally and local authorities have no discretion on what fee to charge. In June 1994, the government issued a consultation paper in which it was proposed that legislation be introduced to allow local planning authorities to set their own fees from 1996, subject only to the authority having an accounting system adequate to ensure that fees are set at the appropriate rate; an up-to-date development plan for their area; and, in the preceding 12 months, to have determined a target number of applications within a period of eight weeks.

When the Fee Regulations were amended in 1991, the opportunity was taken to eliminate the 75 per cent concession which had previously applied to a duplicate planning application (associated with twin-tracking).

A more recent change is to remove, from 3 January 1995, an earlier concession, which provided for a 50 per cent reduction in fees where applications are made to convert an established use certificate issued under s. 194 of the 1990 Act, as originally enacted, into a certificate of lawful use.

9.5 Twin-tracking

With some of the more important development proposals, it is not uncommon for a developer to submit two identical applications for planning permission for the same development. The purpose of this appears to be two-fold. First, if the local planning authority has not determined either of the applications for planning permission within the prescribed period of eight weeks for doing so, the developer may exercise his right to appeal to the Secretary of State against non-determination of one of the applications. The authority cannot then determine that application and the developer knows that he has a place in the appeal queue. It allows the authority and developer to continue to negotiate over the second application. If the authority subsequently grants planning permission for the development on the second application, the developer will then withdraw his appeal against non-determination of the other.

The second, but less important reason for twin-tracking is that if the authority grants planning permission subject to conditions on both applications, the developer may appeal to the Secretary of State against only one decision. Since in determining appeals, the Secretary of State is acting *de novo* with regard to the application, he may decide to refuse planning permission entirely. In which case, the developer still has another planning permission, but one subject to conditions.

9.6   Consultations with the local planning authority

It is common practice to hold discussions with the local planning authority before formally submitting an application for planning permission. Circular 28/83 advises applicants to do this so that guidance can be given on how the authority's planning policies should influence the applicant's proposals before a formal application is made; that information required by the authority for proper consideration of the application can be agreed and provided with the formal application; and that applications are submitted in the correct form and accompanied by the correct fee. It may also be that, after informed discussions with the local planning authority, applicants may decide to adjust their proposals in order to meet the authority's objections to their original scheme.

The House of Lords has held that where pre-planning application discussions are held with the local planning authority, the authority have no power to make a charge for so doing (*R* v *Richmond upon Thames London Borough Council, ex parte McCarthy & Stone (Developments) Ltd* [1992] 2 AC 48).

9.7   The planning register

Under s. 69 of the 1990 Act, every local planning authority must keep in such manner as may be prescribed by development order, a register containing such information as may be prescribed with respect to applications for planning permission made to the authority. The register must be kept available for inspection by members of the public at all reasonable hours.

Under the General Development Order, the register of applications for planning permission is to be kept in two parts. Part I must contain a copy of every application for planning permission and of any application for approval of reserved matters submitted to the authority and not finally disposed of, together with copies of plans and drawings submitted with them. Part II must contain in respect of every application for planning permission,

(a)   a copy (which may be photographic) of the application and of plans and drawings submitted in relation thereto;

(b)   particulars of any direction given under the Act or the Order in respect of the application;

(c)   the decision (if any) of the local planning authority in respect of the application, including details of any conditions subject to which permission was granted, the date of such decision and the name of the local planning authority;

(d)   the reference number, the date and effect of any decision of the Secretary of State in respect of the application, whether on appeal or on a reference under section 35 [now section 77 of the 1990 Act] of the Act;

(e)   the date of any subsequent approval (whether approval of reserved matters or any other approval required) given in relation to the application.

It should also be mentioned that elsewhere in the 1990 legislation, local planning authorities are required to keep registers open for public inspection for other matters such as environmental impact statements accompanying applications, simplified planning zone schemes, enforcement notices and stop notices.

TEN

Applications for planning permission 2: Procedure on receipt of application by the local planning authority

10.1 Acknowledgement

An application for planning permission is made to the authority with responsibility for determining the application. In the case of a non-metropolitan area, most applications fall to be determined by the district planning authority for the area in which the land is situated. If the application relates to a county matter, application must be made to the county planning authority for the area.

On receipt of the application, the local planning authority is required to send an acknowledgement to the applicant in the terms (or substantially in the terms) set out in Schedule 3 to the General Development Order. A requirement of the Order is that the authority shall notify the applicant of their decision on the application within eight weeks from the date on which the application was received, or such extended period as may be agreed upon in writing between the applicant and the local planning authority. Accordingly, the acknowledgement states that if notice of the decision has not been given by the appropriate date, the applicant may appeal to the Secretary of State in accordance with s. 78 of the 1990 Act within a further period of six months.

The precise effect of the provision that the authority shall give notice of their decision within the prescribed period was considered by the Court of Appeal in *James* v *Secretary of State for Wales* [1966] 1 WLR 135. Under the special provisions of the Caravan Sites and Control of Development Act 1960, where express planning permission for the use of land as a caravan site had not previously been given, an application for a site licence under the Act also operated as an application for planning permission. Then if, within six months of the application having been made, express planning permission had not been given, permission for the use of the land as a caravan site was deemed to have been given.

James claimed that by virtue of these provisions he had deemed permission for the use of his land as a caravan site without restriction. The authority maintained, however, than an express planning permission for a restricted number of caravans had previously been granted, so that James could not claim the benefit for any larger number. James thereupon contended, but unsuccessfully, that since the express planning permission had not been given within two months of the application, the permission was, therefore, null and void. In his judgment, which examined the effect of the requirement to give notice of the decision within the prescribed period, Lord Denning MR said:

> The grant or refusal of permission after two months is not void, but at most voidable. If a planning authority allow more than two months to go by, and then *give* permission, with or without conditions, the permission is good. At any rate it is good, if it is accepted and acted upon. Or if an appeal is made against it, for it is then too late to avoid it. If a planning authority allow more than two months to go by, and then *refuse* permission, the party aggrieved can appeal against the refusal. Alternatively he can treat the failure to determine within two months as a refusal and appeal on that ground. If he does not appeal, he cannot afterwards say that the grant or refusal was bad because it was made after the two months.

The two-month period mentioned by Lord Denning in the *James* case has now been reduced to the eight weeks mentioned earlier. It is a decision of the utmost importance. Unless the applicant has appealed against non-determination of the planning application, it enables the local planning authority to grant a valid planning permission after the eight-week period has expired; but it also gives the applicant the option of either implementing the permission or appealing against any conditions which it might contain. If planning permission is refused after the eight-week period, the applicant may appeal against the refusal. If no decision has been given by the end of the period of eight weeks, the applicant can appeal against non-determination of his application under s. 78 of the 1990 Act. If he does so, this deprives the authority of the power to take a decision upon it.

Local planning authorities are now determining only about 65 per cent of applications for planning permission within the statutory eight-week period. One of many reasons why they fail to determine more within that period is the obligation placed upon them to consult with or notify others with regard to different kinds of application.

10.2   Power to decline to determine applications

Before the Planning and Compensation Act 1991, a local planning authority could not refuse to determine an application for planning permission. Every application had to be considered on its merits, despite the fact that the merits may have already been considered and rejected on a previous application made for the same or similar development. It was thought that by making repeat applications for the same development, developers were sometimes able to wear down the resistance of local planning authorities and neighbours to the development, so that planning permission for it would eventually be granted.

Now under s. 17 of the 1991 Act, a new s. 70A has been inserted into the 1990 Act to provide that a local planning authority may decline to determine an application for planning permission for the development of any land if:

(a)   within a period of two years ending with the date on which the application is received by the authority, the Secretary of State has refused a similar application referred to him under s. 77; or has dismissed an appeal against the refusal of a similar application; and

(b)   in the opinion of the authority there has been no significant change since the refusal or, as the case may be, dismissal mentioned in paragraph (a) in the development plan, so far as material to the application, or in any other material considerations.

For the purposes of this new provision, an application for planning permission for the development of land is only to be taken to be similar to a later application if the development and the land to which the application relates are, in the opinion of the local planning authority, the same or substantially the same.

Under the new s. 70A no appeal may be made to the Secretary of State if the local planning authority has given notice to the applicant that it has declined to determine an application under the provisions of this section. Judicial review would appear to be the only method of challenge.

A decision of the Scottish Court of Session in *Noble Organisation Ltd* v *Falkirk District Council* 1994 SLT 100 is the first to consider the power now given to local planning authorities to decline to determine an application for planning permission. Although the case was concerned with the Town and Country Planning (Scotland) Act 1992, s. 26A, the provisions of s. 70A of the 1990 Act are identical.

In the Scottish case an application had been made to change the use of vacant shop premises to an amusement centre with ancillary retail sales. Following the refusal of permission by the local planning authority and on appeal by the Secretary of State, the petitioners submitted a second application for change of use to an amusement centre/snack bar with exclusive retail sales area, claiming that it went a substantial way to meet some of the objections made to the first application. In judicial review proceedings the petitioners sought to have the decision by the authority to decline to determine the second application quashed on the ground that the authority had acted unreasonably, or *ultra vires*. Rejecting the petition, the Court of Session held that on the facts and having regard to all relevant considerations, including a ministerial circular on the operation of the new provision, the second application was similar to the first and that the amendments made to the second were merely cosmetic.

The Court emphasised that the application of the section might involve a two-stage process. First, the local planning authority had to make a judgment on a matter of fact as to whether or not the second application was the same or substantially the same as the first application. Then, if the answer to that was that the second application was the same or substantially the same, the authority had a discretion to decide whether they should decline to determine the application at all, or alternatively, deal with it on its merits as an application for planning permission.

10.3 Publicity for planning applications

Prior to the Planning and Compensation Act 1991, publicity for planning applications was limited to a number of special situations, such as applications for 'bad neighbour' development referred to in 9.3. There was no general duty placed on local planning authorities to give publicity to an application for planning permission, the matter being regarded as being purely a matter between the applicant and the local planning authority as guardian of the public interest. Some local planning authorities, however, adopted a policy of consulting with third parties such as neighbours where, in the opinion of the authority, the proposed development would be likely to affect them adversely. There was no statutory requirement that this should be done, but was regarded by many a local planning authority as a feature of good administration.

If a local planning authority had a policy of notifying third parties of an application, the failure to do so did not give rise to any legal consequence. A complaint might be made, however, to a Local Commissioner (the Local Ombudsman), who in the past has held that an authority's failure to comply with their own policy in this regard amounted to maladministration. If it could be shown that the complainant had suffered injustice as a result of that maladministration, the report of the Local Ombudsman could result in a remedy being provided by the local planning authority. Occasionally this led to an authority making a payment to the complainant which reflected the depreciation in the value of his property caused by the development carried out.

In Scotland there has been for many years a formal system of neighbour notification of all planning applications. The responsibility for notification rests with the applicant, who must serve, on any party holding a notifiable interest in neighbouring land, a copy of the application, together with a notice stating that the plans or drawings relating thereto may be inspected in the planning register or other specified place.

The position in England and Wales is now radically altered as a result of the Planning and Compensation Act 1991. By the 1991 Act, the Secretary of State was given power in a new s. 65 of the 1990 Act to make provision by development order requiring notice to be given of any application for planning permission. At the same time, the government expressed a wish to extend publicity requirements to cover all types of application. This has now been done by amendments made to the General Development Order, which came into force on 17 July 1992. Under the Order, responsibility for publicising planning applications is imposed on the local planning authority.

At the time of writing, the relevant provisions are to be found in art. 12B of the Order. As indicated in Chapter 7, however, this reference is likely to be changed when the Order is next restructured and consolidated. Article 12B now provides:

An application for planning permission shall be publicised by the local planning authority to which the application is made in the manner prescribed by this article.

The article requires three different levels of publicity according to the nature of the development applied for, namely, development of a kind specified in art. 12B(2) (called para. 2 applications), major development, and other development not falling under either of these two heads.

10.3.1 Development specified in article 12B(2) (paragraph 2 applications)

Article 12B of the General Development Order provides that in the case of an application for planning permission for development which:

(a)   is the subject of an application falling within Schedule 1 or 2 to the Town and Country Planning (Assessment of Environmental Effects) Regulations 1988,

(b)   does not accord with the provisions of the development plan in force in the area in which the land to which the application relates is situated, or

(c)   would affect a right of way to which Part III of the Wildlife and Countryside Act 1981 applies,

the publicity given to the application shall be by giving notice (in the form set out in Schedule 5 to the Order) by posting a site notice in at least one place on or near the land to which the application relates for not less than 21 days, *and* by publishing the notice in a newspaper circulating in the locality in which the land to which the application relates is situated.

10.3.2 Major development

Under art. 12B(4) of the Order, in the case of an application for planning permission which is not a para. 2 application (see 10.3.1), if the development proposed is major development the application shall be publicised by giving notice (in the form set out in Schedule 5 to the Order) by posting a site notice in at least one place on or near the land to which the application relates for not less than 21 days, *or* serving the notice on any owner or occupier of any land adjoining the land to which the application relates. In addition to the above alternatives, a notice must also be published in a newspaper circulating in the locality in which the land to which the application relates is situated.

Article 12B defines 'major' development as development involving any one or more of the following:

(a)   the winning and working of minerals or the use of land for mineral working deposits;

(b)   waste development;

(c)   the provision of dwellinghouses where—

    (i)   the number of dwellinghouses to be provided is 10 or more; or

(ii)   the development is to be carried out on site having an area of 0.5 hectare or more and it is not known whether the development falls within paragraph (c)(i);
(d)   the provision of a building or buildings where the floor space to be created by the development is 1,000 square metres or more; or
(e)   development carried out on a site having an area of 1 hectare or more.

As indicated earlier, the General Development Order no longer contains a list of developments classified as 'bad neighbour'. It is considered, however, that applications for certain types of development may warrant the wider publicity now accorded to 'major development' as described above.

In Circular 15/92, 'Publicity for Planning Applications', the Secretary of State expressed the view that it is the responsibility of local planning authorities to decide, on a case-by-case basis, whether developments falling outside the categories of major development listed above, were likely to create wider concern and require publicity beyond the minima set out in the Order (see 10.3.3). The Circular then listed the following types of development which might require a newspaper advertisement in addition to either a site notice or neighbour notification:

(a)   those affecting nearby property by causing noise, smell, vibration, dust or other nuisance;
(b)   attracting crowds, traffic and noise into a generally quiet area;
(c)   causing activity and noise during unsocial hours;
(d)   introducing significant change, for example, particularly tall buildings;
(e)   resulting in serious reduction or loss of light or privacy beyond adjacent properties;
(f)   those affecting the setting of an ancient monument or archaeological site;
(g)   proposals affecting trees subject to tree preservation orders.

10.3.3   Other development
In the case of development not falling within 10.2.1 or 10.2.2 above, art. 12B(5) of the Order provides that the application for planning permission shall be published by giving notice (in the form set out in Schedule 5 to the Order) by posting a site notice in at least one place on or near the land to which the application relates for not less than 21 days, or serving the notice on any owner or occupier of any land adjoining the land to which the application relates.

10.3.4   Summary
The following is a summary of the above publicity requirements for planning applications under the provisions of art. 12B.

Nature of development	Publicity required
Development where application accompanied by environmental statement Development involving a departure from development plan Development affecting public right of way	Advertisement in a local newspaper *and* site notice
Major development	Advertisement in local newspaper *and* either site notice *or* neighbour notification
Minor development	Site notice or neighbour notification

It should be noted that in all cases where a site notice is required or given, art. 12B provides that the local planning authority are not to be treated as having failed to comply with that requirement if the notice is, without fault or intention of the authority, removed, obscured or defaced before the period of 21 days has elapsed, if the authority have taken reasonable steps for its protection and, if need be, replacement.

Furthermore, art. 12B is applied by the Order to any appeal made to the Secretary of State under s. 78 of the 1990 Act as it applies to any application for planning permission. The Order also provides that the local planning authority should take into account any representations made within 21 days from the date notice of the application is given or 14 days from the date any advertisement appeared in a local newspaper, and that the local planning authority shall not determine an application for planning permission until the expiration of those periods.

One criticism of the provisions relating to publicity for applications for planning permission is that no obligation is placed on a local planning authority to publicise:

(a)   changes to applications made after they have been submitted and accepted by the authority;

(b)   applications required by a condition imposed in a previous planning permission (e.g., a time-limited permission); or

(c)   applications made for the approval of reserved matters following the grant of outline planning permission.

Circular 15/92 recognises that in such cases the local planning authority has discretion to decide whether further publicity is desirable, and they should take into account the following considerations:

(a)   Were objections or reservations raised at an earlier stage substantial and, in the view of the local authority enough to justify further publicity?

(b)   Are the proposed changes significant?

(c)   Did earlier views cover the matters now under consideration?

(d) Are the matters now under consideration likely to be of concern to parties not previously notified?

10.4 Notification requirements

10.4.1 Development affecting highways
Under the General Development Order, the local planning authority is required to notify the Secretary of State of applications for planning permission for development which consists of or includes the formation, laying out or alteration or a means of access to certain trunk roads or special roads or the development of land within 67 metres of certain roads. The procedure enables the Secretary of State to consider whether to give a direction under the Order restricting the power of the local planning authority to grant planning permission for the development.

10.4.2 Parish and community councils
Under para. 8 of Schedule 1 to the 1990 Act, a local planning authority must, if requested to do so by the council of any parish or community situated in their area, notify the council of any relevant planning application and any alteration to that application which has been accepted by the authority. For this purpose a relevant planning application includes not only an application for planning permission, but an application for approval of any reserved matter under an outline planning permission.

Under these provisions a parish or community council may ask the local planning authority to notify it of all applications for planning permission or for a particular category, such as applications for industrial development. In practice, however, it is not uncommon for local planning authorities to whom a request has been made to be notified of a particular category of application, to notify the parish or community council without restriction to any particular category of development. This is no doubt done to avoid the possibility that a mistake might otherwise be made.

10.4.3 Development affecting the character or appearance of a conservation area
Under s. 73(1) of the Planning (Listed Buildings and Conservation Areas) Act 1990, where an application for planning permission is made to a local planning authority and the development would, in the opinion of the authority, affect the character or appearance of a conservation area, the authority must publish in a local newspaper circulating in the locality in which the land is situated, and display on or near the land for not less than seven days, a notice indicating the nature of the development in question and naming a place where a copy of the application can be seen.

Here, the local planning authority may have to take two independent decisions. First, to decide if the proposed development would, if granted, affect the character or appearance of a conservation area. If so, the application must be given publicity. Secondly, and after publicity has been given to the application and any representations received taken into account, to decide whether planning permission should be granted.

10.4.4   Development affecting the setting of a listed building

Under s. 66(1) of the Planning (Listed Buildings and Conservation Areas) Act 1990, the local planning authority, in considering whether to grant planning permission for development which affects a listed building or its setting, are required to have regard to the desirability of preserving the building or its setting or any features of special architectural or historic interest which it possesses.

Under s. 67 of that Act, if the local planning authority are of the opinion that the development would affect the setting of a listed building, they must publish in a local newspaper circulating in the locality in which the land is situated and for not less than seven days display on or near the land, a notice indicating the nature of the development in question and naming a place where a copy of the application can be seen.

10.4.5   Applications relating to county matters

Under the General Development Order, a county planning authority must, in relation to a county matter, give the district planning authority an opportunity to make recommendations as to how the county should determine applications for planning permission, applications for certificates of lawfulness of existing use or development, certificates of lawfulness of proposed use or development and the approval of reserved matters.

10.4.6   Duplication of publicity and notice requirements

The provisions of art. 12B of the General Development Order, referred to earlier, may result in a degree of overlapping or duplication with other statutory requirements, or indeed within the article itself. For example, 'major' development may also require an environmental assessment, and the article applies different publicity requirements to each. Again, the publicity for development which is not specified within art. 12B(2) (para. 2 applications) and is not major development may be different from the publicity required under the Planning (Listed Buildings and Conservation Areas) Act 1990 in respect of applications for development affecting the character or appearance of a conservation area or the setting of a listed building. Clearly, in order to be within the law, the more demanding of the publicity requirements should be followed. Conversely, in the case of 'twin-tracking', it is not necessary to advertise the two applications separately, so long as they are made simultaneously, and the publicity should make it clear that there are two applications. If not made simultaneously, both applications will need to be separately published.

10.5   Consultation

The provisions of the General Development Order allow for the views of specialist bodies to be obtained on particular types of development. The Order provides that, before granting planning permission for certain specified types of development, a local planning authority should consult with named authorities or persons. For example, where the development would involve the manufacture, processing, keeping or use of a hazardous substance likely to lead to a notifiable quantity of such substance, the authority are required to consult with the Health and Safety Executive. Of more general application is the requirement to consult with the local highway authority where the development involves the formation, laying out or alteration of any means of access to a highway; with the British Coal Corporation where the development consists of a building or pipeline in an area of coal working notified by the corporation to the local planning authority; and with the Minister of Agriculture, Fisheries and Food where the development is not development for agricultural purposes and is not in accordance with the provisions of the development plan and would involve the loss of not less than 20 hectares of grades 1, 2 or 3a agricultural land. According to a written answer to a Parliamentary question in the House of Commons in January 1992, the Ministry of Agriculture, Fisheries and Food objected to only 26 planning applications in 1990, as opposed to 489 in 1981. It should also be noted that under these provisions, the Secretary of State may give a direction to a local planning authority requiring them to consult with any person or body named in the direction. Where consultation is required, the consultee must be given at least 14 days' notice to make representations, which must be taken into account by the local planning authority before they determine the application.

10.6 Development not in accordance with the provisions of the development plan

Section 74(1)(b) of the 1990 Act authorises the local planning authority, in such cases and subject to such conditions as may be prescribed by a development order, or by directions given by the Secretary of State thereunder, to grant planning permission which does not accord with the provisions of the development plan. In addition the General Development Order authorises local planning authorities to grant permission for development not in accordance with the development plan in such cases and subject to such conditions as may be prescribed by directions given by the Secretary of State. The relevant directions for England are the Town and Country Planning (Development Plans and Consultation) Directions 1992, which were issued as Annex 3 to Circular 19/92. These Directions, which came into force on 17 July 1992, replace the Town and Country Planning (Development Plans) (England) Direction 1992.

The new Directions apply to 'departure applications', that is an application for planning permission for development which does not accord with the provisions of the development plan in force in the area in which the application site is situated.

Where a departure application which a local planning authority do not propose to refuse is for—

(a) development which consists of or includes the provision of—
   (i) more than 150 houses or flats; or
   (ii) more than 10,000 square metres of retail floor space;

(b) development of land of an interested planning authority, or for the development of any land by such an authority, whether alone or jointly with any other person; or

(c) any other development which, by reason of its scale or nature or the location of the land, would significantly prejudice the implementation of the development plan's policies and proposals,

the authority are required by the Directions to send to the Secretary of State—

(i)   a copy of the application (including copies of any accompanying plans and drawings);

(ii)   a copy of the requisite notice (that is, a copy of the notice required by art. 12B of the General Development Order in the form set out in Schedule 5 to the Order (see 10.3.1 to 10.3.4);

(iii) a copy of any representations made to the authority in respect of the application;

(iv)   a statement of the issues involved in the decision and of any views expressed on the application by a government department or another local planning authority.

Thereafter, subject only to the Secretary of State's call-in power, the local planning authority are free to grant planning permission after the expiration of a period of 21 days, beginning with the date notified to the local planning authority by the Secretary of State as the date of receipt of the documents which are required to be sent to him by the authority ((i)-(iv) above) and after considering any objections received.

It should, of course, be noted that departure applications are subject (like all applications) to the statutory publicity required under art. 12B of the General Development Order (see 10.3).

An important question raised in the past is the precise consequences that flow from a failure to comply with the Directions. Does a failure to do so render the subsequent grant of planning permission void? In an old case, *Gregory* v *Camden London Borough Council* [1966] 1 WLR 899, it was held that a neighbour did not possess the necessary standing to challenge a grant of planning permission for development which involved a departure from the development plan, but had been granted without compliance with the procedure required by the Direction. In a more recent case, *R* v *St Edmundsbury Borough Council (ex parte Investors in Industry Commercial Properties Ltd)* [1985] 1 WLR 1168, an application was made to the High Court for judicial review to quash outline planning permission granted to J. Sainsbury plc for the erection of a supermarket on land in Bury St Edmunds town centre. One of the many grounds for challenge alleged that there had been a defect in the statutory advertisement required by the then Town and Country Planning (Development Plans) (England) Direction 1981, in that it had not included any reference to the fact that the application conflicted with the development plan. It was contended by the applicants for judicial review, that the requirements of the Direction were mandatory and a condition precedent to the grant of a valid planning permission. Rejecting that contention, Stocker J thought that to construe the Direction as mandatory would involve difficulties likely to lead to practical and commercial problems. He had no doubt that the words 'in the opinion of the local planning authority' did require that proper consideration be given to the problem, but it seemed to him inappropriate for a Direction, the breach of which involved the proposition that planning permission granted was void, should be regarded as mandatory since this might involve investigating the committee's opinion and whether such opinion was based upon full and proper consideration. The words themselves suggest that a directive and procedural order, rather than a mandatory one, arose.

After expressing the view that the absence of information in the statutory advertisement had had no effect because a wide section of the public were aware that the development would involve a departure from the town map, Stocker J went on to say that if he was wrong in his conclusion that the direction was a procedural one, and not mandatory involving a condition precedent, he would, in the exercise of discretion, not have made an order for judicial review on this ground.

The approach of Stocker J in *R v St Edmundsbury Borough Council* was followed later by Macpherson J in *R v Carlisle City Council (ex parte Cumbrian Co-operative Society Ltd)* [1986] JPL 206, where it was held that a failure to comply with the Direction did not invalidate the grant of a deemed planning permission by the local planning authority for development of a superstore on a site owned by the authority.

ELEVEN
Determinations of applications for planning permission

11.1 Delegation

Under s. 101 of the Local Government Act 1972, a local authority may arrange for the discharge of any of their functions by a committee, a subcommittee, an officer of the authority, or by any other local authority.

Every local planning authority has made arrangements for their planning functions to be delegated to a committee. Many local planning authorities have also made arrangements for the delegation of functions to subcommittees. Delegation to subcommittees may be a useful exercise where it is desired to divide the geographical area of an authority into sub-areas, with planning functions in respect of each sub-area being exercised by a separate subcommittee.

Most local planning authorities have also made arrangements for the discharge of many of their functions by an officer of the authority. The actual scope of the officer's delegated power will, like all delegation arrangements, depend upon the terms of the particular scheme of delegation. It will frequently be the case that where power is given to an officer of an authority to determine planning applications, the power will be restricted to a limited range of development proposals. In cases where planning functions are not delegated to an officer but are exercised by a committee or a subcommittee of the authority, the role of officers will be to ensure that all considerations material to the decision to be made are brought to the attention of the committee or subcommittee together with (in most cases) a recommendation as to how the application should be dealt with. The Local Government Ombudsman has rightly advised local authorities that any report to a committee should provide all the material that members need to make an informed decision. The report should be in clear terms and should cover as necessary the relevant law and policy; sufficient and accurate information to enable members to understand the issues to be considered or determined; a summary of the outcome of any consultation or seeking of advice; a reference to all the considerations which have to be taken into account; the identification of possible approaches which could be adopted; the reasons for any recommendations; and an analysis of any financial or other significant implications which are relevant. Although there is also a power under s. 101 for a local planning authority to delegate the power to discharge their functions to another authority, the power is rarely exercised in relation to planning functions.

As with the exercise of all delegated power, the actions of the delegatee, acting within the four corners of his power, will bind the delegator. Furthermore, where power to discharge functions has been delegated to another, the donor of the power is usually free to withdraw that power before it has been exercised. Under s. 101(4), however, where a power to discharge a function has been delegated to a committee, a subcommittee or an officer, this does not prevent the authority or the committee (as the case may be) discharging the function themselves. In *R v Yeovil Borough Council (ex parte Trustees of Elim Pentecostal Church, Yeovil)* (1971) 23 P & CR 39 the Church had made two applications for planning permission. The minutes of the planning committee of the council recorded its decision that 'the town clerk be authorised to approve the application subject to [certain] conditions when evidence of an agreement about the car-parking facilities has been received'. At a subsequent meeting the planning committee, after having heard evidence that the development would be detrimental to the amenities of the area, changed its mind and decided to refuse the application. The applicants thereupon applied for an order of mandamus requiring the authority to issue conditional planning consent for the development, contending that the committee had already committed themselves, and that as all that remained was for the town clerk to issue notices of approval, the council were in no position to change their mind.

The Queen's Bench Divisional Court held that, on the facts, there was no question of planning permission having been granted at any time before the town clerk had expressed a view with regard to the adequacy of any evidence presented to him. Moreover, the council had delegated the final determination of the application to the town clerk, and unless and until he had made such determination within the authority granted to him, no question of planning permission having been granted arose; and the clerk not having finally determined the matter before the later committee meeting, it was open to the council to change their mind and to withdraw their provisional approval and refuse the application.

Officers of the local planning authorities also exercise many functions of a magisterial nature, as where they transmit to the applicant the decision made by the local planning authority. In *Norfolk County Council v Secretary of State for the Environment* [1973] 1 WLR 1400, a company made an application for planning permission to build an extension to a factory. The planning committee refused the application. Then, by mistake, the planning officer sent a notice to the applicant saying planning permission had been granted. As soon as the mistake was discovered the council sent a letter to the applicant apologising, together with a proper notice of refusal. The company immediately cancelled, without penalty, an order for new machinery. But it continued to maintain that it had the benefit of a valid planning permission. In order to bring matters to a head, the company commenced development. This enabled the council to serve an enforcement notice against which the company appealed to the Secretary of State. He duly proceeded to quash the notice, so the council appealed to the High Court under what was then s. 246 of the 1971 Act against that decision. Allowing the appeal, the court held that the council were entitled to serve the enforcement notice because the officer concerned only had authority to transmit to the applicant the decision of the planning committee. He had no authority himself to make a decision on the planning application so that the notice given by him could not be regarded as a grant of planning permission.

A similar approach was taken in *Attorney-General* v *Taff-Ely Borough Council* (1981) 42 P & CR 1. The facts were that in 1975, Cooperative Retail Services Ltd (CRS) applied for planning permission to develop land as a superstore. A few months later, Sir Robert McAlpine Ltd (with Tesco stores in mind) applied for planning permission to develop other land for the same purpose just half a mile away from the CRS site. It was clear that only one of the two applications could be granted and that it was the Tesco site that was favoured by the local planning authority. Accordingly they refused planning permission for the CRS site. On the very same day, the authority considered and adopted a recommendation of a subcommittee of their planning committee that planning permission be granted for the development of the Tesco site. A dispute then arose as to the exact status of the subcommittee's decision. CRS took the view that it had merely expressed the authority's preliminary views on the application, prior to discussions taking place between the authority and the Mid-Glamorgan County Council who were the county planning authority for the area. Tesco's agents, however, took the view that the action of the subcommittee constituted a grant of planning permission for the development, and threatened the authority that if they did not issue the grant they would bring an action for mandamus to compel them to do so and for damages for the loss they had suffered. The town clerk then duly issued the grant of planning permission that Tesco had sought. Once this had been done, Tesco proceeded to buy the land for which the permission had been granted. CRS now threatened the authority that it would sue for a declaration that Tesco had not been granted a valid planning permission; whereupon the authority resolved to ratify the earlier action of the town clerk. CRS then did what it had threatened and brought an action for a declaration. The Court of Appeal (1979) 39 P & CR 223 held that on the true construction of the relevant minutes of the planning subcommittee, the local planning authority had not resolved to grant planning permission for the development of the Tesco site. Furthermore, since the town clerk could only transmit to the applicant the decision of the local planning authority, the authority could not ratify what was in fact a nullity. On appeal to the House of Lords, the decision of the Court of Appeal was upheld.

There was then a rather surprising aftermath. The decision of the House of Lords had left the application for the Tesco site still to be determined. At that stage, the Secretary of State intervened and called in the application for his own decision. Also outstanding was an appeal to the Secretary of State by CRS against the decision of the authority to refuse planning permission for its site. In October 1982, following a local inquiry into both applications, the Secretary of State granted planning permission for the Tesco site, but refused to grant it for the CRS site.

That, however, was not the end of the matter. Even before the decision of the Secretary of State was known, Tesco maintained it had suffered loss through the negligence of the clerk in purporting to issue notice of a grant of planning permission when no grant had in fact been made. Tesco maintained that it had bought the land on the strength of what it thought to be a grant of planning permission. If the company were eventually to lose on the planning merits, its loss of development value would be considerable. If it were eventually to win (as it did) it would still suffer loss as land purchased with planning permission is plainly more valuable than land with only the chance of permission at some later date. In the ensuing action for damages in the Queen's Bench Division, Beldam J in an unreported decision, held that the clerk had been negligent in issuing the notice, despite the fact that he had been stampeded into doing so by threats that if he did not his ratepayers would be faced with a very large claim for damages.

The court went on to hold, however, that the plaintiff could not recover damages for the clerk's negligence, because it had, by its agents, been aware of the circumstances in which the notice had been issued and could not, therefore, be said to be bona fide purchasers of the land for value without notice of the particular circumstances in which the notice to grant planning permission had been issued.

11.2 Estoppel

Another but a related matter which has led to much litigation is the question of promissory estoppel, or the extent to which a statement made by an officer of a local planning authority may bind the authority.

One of the earliest cases concerning estoppel in the planning field was *Southend-on-Sea Corporation* v *Hodgson (Wickford) Ltd* [1962] 1 QB 416. There, a prospective purchaser of premises had written and asked the borough engineer and surveyor whether the premises could be used as a builders' yard. The borough engineer had replied that there was an existing user right for that purpose and that no planning permission was necessary. Relying on that statement the purchase went ahead and the land was used as a builders' yard. The local planning authority then served an enforcement notice on the purchasing company requiring the use of the land for the purpose to be discontinued. The company appealed successfully against the notice to the magistrates' court, whereupon the authority appealed against the magistrates' ruling to the Queen's Bench Divisional Court. The company argued that having represented that the premises had an existing use as a builders' yard, the authority were estopped from later contending that planning permission to use it for that purpose was required. Rejecting the argument, the Divisional Court held that a public authority could not be estopped from exercising its statutory powers by the representations of its officers.

This decision may have been no more than a restatement of conventional wisdom on the doctrine of estoppel, but it came to be treated with some reservation following decisions in two later cases.

In *Wells v Minister of Housing & Local Government* [1967] 1 WLR 1000, the appellants were builders' merchants, carrying on business on land in accordance with existing use rights. They wished to erect on the land a concrete batching plant, but were not sure whether the development was permitted under the provisions of the General Development Order. In an attempt to resolve that difficulty the appellants decided to apply for planning permission. After considering the application, an officer of the authority replied that no application was necessary as the development was permitted development under the General Development Order.

The appellants then decided to build a taller batching plant than the one they had originally intended to build, but one which exceeded the tolerance allowed under the General Development Order. They proceeded to apply to the authority under the Public Health Act 1936 for building by-law consent for the taller plant. An officer of the authority in granting that consent and believing the application to be for the smaller plant, struck out (but not illegibly so) the words in the consent that warned applicants not to take action on the consent until the approval of the planning authority had been obtained. On receipt of this consent, the applicants considered the striking out of the phrase to be confirmation that no planning permission was required for the taller plant. After the plant had been erected, the local planning authority served an enforcement notice requiring it to be removed. The appellants appealed against the notice to the Minister, who dismissed the appeal. They then appealed to the Queen's Bench Divisional Court, and from that court to the Court of Appeal, which upheld the validity of the notice.

As regards the application for planning permission made for the smaller of the two batching plants (which was never erected), the court held that, although no express application had been made to the authority for a determination as to whether an express application for planning permission was required (then known as a s. 53 determination), the officer's letter that the proposed development was permitted development under the General Development Order constituted a valid determination and was not reversible by the authority.

With regard to the taller batching plant against which the enforcement proceedings had been taken, the court held that the building by-law consent could not be regarded as a valid s. 53 determination because in order for it to be that there had to be a positive statement in writing that planning permission was not required, and this had not been given.

The case was followed a few years later in *Lever Finance Ltd v Westminster (City) London Borough Council* [1971] 1 QB 222. There, the plaintiff had applied for and was granted planning permission to erect 14 houses in accordance with detailed plans submitted with the application. A month later the plaintiffs' architect prepared a larger site plan showing a number of small variations from the original plan. The architect sent the revised plan to the authority's planning officer who, in response, telephoned the architect to tell him that the variations were not material. Believing that no further permission was required, the plaintiff started to build in accordance with the later plan. Local residents then complained, so at the suggestion of the planning officer the plaintiff applied for planning permission for the variations. Although that application was supported by the planning officer it was refused by the authority's planning committee, which also resolved to serve an enforcement notice to prevent any further building taking place. Within two days the plaintiff had applied to the High Court for a declaration that there existed a valid planning permission for the building under construction. This was duly granted by the High Court and, on appeal, affirmed by the Court of Appeal. The court held that the subsequent variation was in fact material and that planning permission for the variation should have been obtained. But the proven practice of the local planning authority had been to delegate to their planning officer the authority to say whether or not a variation was material, and since the plaintiff had acted on the decision that the variations were not material, no further planning permission was required. During the course of his judgment, Lord Denning MR cast doubts on the authority of *Southend-on-Sea Corporation* v *Hodgson (Wickford) Ltd.* Referring to it, Lord Denning said:

> I know that there are authorities which say a public authority cannot be estopped . . . from doing its public duty. . . . But those statements must now be taken with considerable reserve. There are many matters which public authorities can now delegate to their officers. If an officer, acting within the scope of his ostensible authority, makes a representation on which another acts, then a public authority may be bound by it, just as much as a private concern would be.

The judgment of Lord Denning was thereafter taken at its face value, particularly by the Secretary of State in dealing with appeals against enforcement notices. *Any* representation made by an officer within the scope of his ostensible authority was regarded as capable of binding the authority. The doctrine of estoppel was poised to run wild and duly did so. That in turn led to extreme caution by the officers of local planning authorities in giving advice and guidance to prospective applicants for planning permission. Eventually, sanity was restored by the judgment of a strong Court of Appeal in *Western Fish Products Ltd* v *Penwith District Council* [1978] JPL 623.

There a dispute had arisen between the plaintiff company and the local planning authority over whether land previously used for the production of fertiliser from fish could be used by the company for the production of fishmeal as animal food and fresh fish for human consumption without planning permission. The company contended it could; the authority contented otherwise.

The company claimed that a letter received from an officer of the authority amounted to a statement that planning permission was not required. To resolve the dispute, which had culminated in the refusal of the local planning authority to grant applications for planning permission and for an established use certificate, and the service of an enforcement notice and a stop notice by the authority, the company sought a declaration in the High Court claiming, *inter alia*, that the representations made by the officer estopped the authority from denying that planning permission was not necessary for the company's project.

The Court of Appeal held:

(a) that planning permission was required for the company's intended use;
(b) that the statement made by the officer was merely a statement of the purposes for which the site had previously been used, so no estoppel could be founded on any representations contained in the officer's letter.

This effectively disposed of the plaintiff company's case, but the Court of Appeal then went on to deal (*obiter*) with the estoppel issue in the following terms:

(c) Even if the officer's statement did operate as a representation as to the new use, it would not operate as an estoppel because the company had not acted upon the statement to its detriment.
(d) Even if the company had acted on the statement to its detriment, the statement would not bind the authority because:

(i) promissory estoppel could only be used as a shield (e.g., as a defence to enforcement proceedings) and not as a sword; and
(ii) a local planning authority could not be estopped from performing their statutory duties under planning legislation through the representations of an officer.

In holding that a representation by an officer did not create an estoppel to prevent the performance of statutory duties, the Court of Appeal was reestablishing the authority of *Southend-on-Sea Corporation* v *Hodgson (Wickford) Ltd*. In doing so, the Court of Appeal referred to the many statutory obligations that were placed upon local planning authorities in performing their duties under the planning Acts, such as the need for them to consider the development plan and any other material considerations before exercising their development control functions. If representations made by officers were to dictate the way in which those functions were to be exercised, the local planning authority would be dispensing with those statutory obligations.

The Court of Appeal recognised, however, that there were two exceptions to this general principle. First, if the local planning authority delegated to officers the power to determine specific questions, such as whether an application for planning permission was necessary, any decisions they made could not be revoked. The principle, however, did not, as may have been suggested, extend to every representation made by an officer within his ostensible authority. For estoppel to arise there had to be some evidence which justified the person dealing with the planning officer thinking that what the officer said would bind the authority. Here, each case must depend upon the circumstances.

The second exception to general principle was where a local planning authority waived some procedural requirement relating to any application (as in *Wells* v *Minister of Housing & Local Government* [1967] 1 WLR 1000). Then the authority might be estopped from relying on the lack of formality.

A recent case which fits four-square with *Lever Finance Ltd* v *Westminster (City) London Borough Council* [1971] 1 QB 222 is *Camden London Borough Council* v *Secretary of State for the Environment* (1993) 67 P & CR 59, in which the owners of a dwellinghouse had been granted planning permission for a mansard roof extension and roof terrace. Their architect then wrote to the authority's planning officer seeking approval for minor variations of the approved plans. The reply stated: '... in my view, the variations as shown on the drawing are minor and would not constitute development requiring planning permission'. The work was then completed in accordance with the varied plans. A subsequent letter from the authority stated that the works were in fact materially different from those approved, and an enforcement notice was issued. On appeal, an Inspector quashed the notice on the ground of estoppel, holding that the writer of the first letter had ostensible authority to approve the variations. The Inspector's decision was upheld by the High Court on appeal.

Although the Court of Appeal in *Western Fish Products Ltd* v *Penwith District Council* re-established the general principle that estoppel cannot be raised to prevent a local authority performing its statutory duties, the giving of misleading advice may nevertheless be a ground for making a complaint to the Local Ombudsman. In one report (No. 627/H/80) the planning officer of a local planning authority had told a prospective purchaser of land during discussions that he could see no objection to the erection of a two-storey building on the land. The prospective purchaser acted on that advice and completed the purchase. Then, the planning officer, contrary to his earlier advice, recommended to the authority that planning permission be granted only for a bungalow. After a finding by the Local Ombudsman of injustice suffered as a result of maladministration, the local planning authority made an *ex gratia* payment of £2,000 to the complainant to compensate him for his loss.

11.3 Determination of a planning application

Section 70(2) of the 1990 Act provides that the local planning authority, in dealing with an application for planning permission, 'shall have regard to the provisions of the development plan, so far as material to the application, and to any other material considerations'.

As stated earlier, the courts have held that the expression 'shall have regard to the provisions of the development plan', does not require that the plan should be slavishly adhered to. As long as the development plan was considered, an authority have been able to base their decision on 'other material considerations'. Indeed, this is recognised in s. 74(1) of the 1990 Act, which gives the Secretary of State power to regulate the manner in which applications for planning permission are dealt with by local planning authorities, and in particular applications for planning permission for developments which do not accord with the provisions of the plan. When the term 'material considerations' was first introduced into the law by the Town and Country Planning Act 1947, the intention may have been to allow local planning authorities, when determining applications for planning permission, to have regard to any amendments the authority were proposing to make to the approved development plan. In other words, the term was seen mainly as an adjunct to the preceding phrase, 'the provisions of the development plan'. The position has now been altered as a result of a new provision inserted into the 1990 Act by the Planning and Compensation Act 1991, which appears to give the development plan a place of primacy over other material considerations in the exercise by local planning authorities of their development control functions.

Section 26 of the 1991 Act provided that the following provision should be added at the end of Part II of the 1990 Act:

54A. Where, in making any determination under the planning Acts, regard is to be had to the development plan, the determination shall be made in accordance with the plan unless material considerations indicate otherwise.

The effect of this new provision may not be entirely clear. It plainly increases the emphasis to be given to the provisions of the development plan in the exercise of development control functions, and emphasises that decisions should be 'plan-led', rather than, as in the past, regarding the development plan as just another material consideration carrying no special weight. This interpretation would accord with the obligation now placed on all local planning authorities to prepare district-wide local plans for their areas. The effect of the new provision appears to be to raise a legal presumption that if proposed development accords with the provisions of the current development plan, planning permission should be granted; unless, that is, material consider-ations indicate otherwise. Contrariwise, it would seem that if the development proposal does not accord with the development plan, planning permission may still be granted if material considerations indicate otherwise.

The Secretary of State's view of this new provision is now expressed in Planning Policy Guidance Note PPG1 (Revised in March 1992), 'General Policy and Principles'. The guidance note says (at paras. 25-8):

25   The approach that decision-makers should take to the consideration of planning applications is set out in sections 70(2) and 54A of the 1990 Act (the latter inserted by section 26 of the 1991 Act). Section 70(2) requires the decision-maker to have regard to the development plan, so far as it is material to the application, and to any other material considerations. Where the development plan is material to the development proposal, and must therefore be taken into account, section 54A requires the application or appeal to be determined in accordance with the plan, unless material considerations indicate otherwise. In effect, this introduces a presumption in favour of development proposals which are in accordance with the develop-ment plan. An applicant who proposes a development which is clearly in conflict with the development plan would need to produce convincing reasons to demonstrate why the plan should not prevail. . . .

26   Those deciding planning applications or appeals should therefore look to see whether the development plan contains policies or proposals which are relevant to the particular development proposal. Such material policies and proposals may either give support to a development proposal in a particular location or indicate that it is not appropriate. If the development plan does contain material policies or proposals and there are no other material considerations, the application or appeal should be determined in accordance with the development plan.

27   Where there are other material considerations, the development plan should be taken as a starting-point, and the other material considerations should be weighed in reaching a decision. One such consideration will be whether the development plan policies are up to date and apply to current circumstances, or whether they have been overtaken by events (the age of the plan is not in itself material). For example, policies and proposals in the plan may have been superseded by more recent planning guidance issued by the government, or developments since the plan became operative may have rendered certain policies or proposals in the plan incapable of implementation or out of date.

28   In those cases where the development plan is not relevant, for example because the plan does not contain a policy relating to a particular development proposal, or there are material policies in the plan which pull in opposite directions so that the plan does not provide a clear guide for a particular proposal, the planning application or appeal should be determined on its merits in the light of all the material considerations.

The new provision has been considered by the courts on a number of occasions including *St Albans District Council* v *Secretary of State for the Environment* [1993] JPL 374. In considering the effect s. 54A, the Deputy Judge, Mr David Widdicombe QC, after accepting as common ground that the section had no relevance to applications for consent to the demolition of a listed building under the Planning (Listed Buildings and Conservation Areas) Act 1990, felt it was clear that s. 54A did set up a presumption in favour of the development plan, but for its rebuttal it was sufficient if there were 'material considerations which indicate otherwise'. One question to arise is how easily can the presumption be rebutted? The use of the words 'indicate otherwise' suggests that the presumption may not be a strong one. Furthermore, it may be that the presumption in favour of allowing applications for development, 'having regard to all material considerations, unless the development would cause demonstrable harm to interests of acknowledged importance', could be a material consideration which indicates otherwise. Whether or not it does so, the presumption in favour of development sits uncomfortably with the new s. 54A.

The *St Albans District Council* case also demonstrates that although there is no need for an Inspector to refer expressly to the new section in arriving at a decision, it should be clear from the decision letter that he has correctly applied the section. Indeed, Inspectors as a matter of course now expressly identify in decision letters the development plan and its relevant policies for the purpose of s. 54A, and then go on to identify other material considerations.

In a later case, *R* v *Canterbury City Council (ex parte Spring Image Ltd)* [1994] JPL 427, the High Court declared a resolution of the local planning authority *ultra vires* (but exercised its discretion not to grant judicial review) where the Director of Planning had misinterpreted the section in giving technical advice to the relevant committee of the authority. In his report, the Director had said:

> Section 54A of the 1990 Planning Act requires local authorities to have regard to the provisions of the development plan . . . in determining planning applications, unless material considerations indicate otherwise. I consider that this is a situation where 'material considerations' do indeed indicate otherwise.

Mr David Keene QC, sitting as a deputy High Court judge, found that this had misstated the approach embodied in s. 54A. He pointed out that there were two obligations placed on a local planning authority under the 1990 Act. First, under s. 70(2), to have regard to all material considerations; secondly, by virtue of s. 54A, to make a determination in accordance with the plan unless material considerations indicated otherwise. The deficiency in the Director of Planning's report was that he had conflated the two statutory requirements and, in doing so, had distorted both of them. To say that s. 54A required local authorities to have regard to the provisions of the development plan unless material considerations indicated otherwise misstated both obligations.

In determining applications for planning permission, it is also necessary to consider the term 'other material considerations'. Whatever the genesis of the term may have been, it is now recognised to have a much wider connotation.

In *Stringer* v *Minister of Housing & Local Government* [1970] 1 WLR 1281, Cooke J, in upholding a decision to refuse planning permission for development which would have interfered with the working of the Jodrell Bank telescope said,

> It may be conceded at once that the material considerations to which the Minister is entitled and bound to have regard in deciding the appeal must be considerations of a planning nature. I find it impossible, however, to accept the view that such considerations are limited to matters relating to amenity. . . it seems to me that any consideration which relates to the use and development of land is capable of being a planning consideration.

Among the matters commonly regarded as relating to the use and development of land are the siting of buildings, their number, area, height, mass, design and external appearance; means of access; landscaping; impact on neighbouring land; availability of infrastructure; traffic considerations and communications.

The following are other examples of considerations held by the courts to be material:

(a)   The safeguarding of land required for a road-widening scheme (*Westminster Bank Ltd* v *Minister of Housing & Local Government* [1971] AC 508).

(b)   The protection of an ancient monument (*Hoveringham Gravels Ltd* v *Secretary of State for the Environment* [1975] QB 754).

(c)   The likelihood of the proposed development being carried out (*Sovmots Investments Ltd* v *Secretary of State for the Environment* [1979] AC 144).

(d)   The risk of flooding to neighbouring landowners (*George Wimpey & Co. Ltd* v *Secretary of State for the Environment* [1978] JPL 776).

(e)   Disturbance or annoyance to neighbouring occupiers from a casino (*Ladbroke (Rentals) Ltd* v *Secretary of State for the Environment* [1981] JPL 427).

The following are some examples of considerations held by the courts to be immaterial:

(a)   The question of whether development was economically worthwhile (*Walters* v *Secretary of State for Wales* [1979] JPL 171).

(b)   The absence in a proposal for development of any provision for planning gain (*Westminster Renslade Ltd* v *Secretary of State for the Environment* [1983] JPL 454).

Note that the Race Relations Act 1976, s. 19A, makes it unlawful for a planning authority to discriminate against a person in carrying out their planning functions. This provision was inserted into the 1976 Act by the Housing and Planning Act 1986 following concern that the 1976 Act might permit such discrimination.

Given the language used in s. 70(2) of the 1990 Act and the original intent behind the use of the words 'other material considerations' it is not surprising that government policy should lie fairly and squarely within that term. The main vehicle for the articulation of government policy is planning Policy Guidance Notes, and these will always be a material consideration in making development control decisions. It must be borne in mind, however, that a Guidance Note cannot remove from the local planning authority or Secretary of State the obligation to consider the development plan for the area, which must always be pre-eminent. In *E.C. Gransden & Co. Ltd* v *Secretary of State for the Environment* (1982) 54 P & CR 86, Woolf J (as he then was) made it clear that a policy statement in a Guidance Note or Circular cannot turn what would otherwise be a material planning consideration into an irrelevant consideration. But it seems from that case that a Note or Circular can decide that more weight should be given to one or to some material considerations than to others, though the authority would not act *ultra vires* if it preferred some other weighting.

In *E.C. Gransden & Co. Ltd* v *Secretary of State for the Environment*, Woolf J set out *in extenso* the proper approach to policy considerations embodied in Circulars. He said (at pp. 93–4):

. . . it seems to me, first of all, that any policy, if it is to be a policy which is a proper policy for planning purposes, must envisage that in exceptional circumstances the Minister has the right to depart from that policy. If the situation was otherwise ... it would be an improper attempt to curtail the discretion which is provided by the Act, which indicates that in determining planning applications regard is not only to be had to the provisions of the development plan so far as material, but also to any other material considerations.

What then is the significance of the inspector having failed to follow the policy? Does that mean that this court has to quash his decision? The situation, as I see it, is as follows: first, section 29 [now s. 70] lays down what matters are to be regarded as material, and the policy cannot make a matter which is otherwise a material consideration an irrelevant consideration. Secondly, if the policy is a lawful policy, that is to say if it is not a policy which is defective because it goes beyond the proper role of a policy by seeking to do more than indicate the weight which should be given to relevant considerations, then the body determining an application must have regard to the policy. Thirdly, the fact that a body has to have regard to the policy does not mean that it needs necessarily to follow the policy. However, if it is going to depart from the policy, it must give clear reasons for ... doing so in order that the recipient of its decision will know why the decision is being made as an exception to the policy and the grounds upon which the decision is taken.

Fourthly, in order to give effect to the approach which I have just indicated it is essential that the policy is properly understood by the determining body. If the body making the decision fails to properly understand the policy, then the decision will be as defective as it would be if no regard had been paid to the policy.

Fifthly, if proper regard, in the manner in which I have indicated, is not given to the policy, then this court will quash its decision unless the situation is one of those exceptional cases where the court can be quite satisfied that the failure to have proper regard to the policy has not affected the outcome in that the decision would in any event have been the same.

The materiality of Circulars and Planning Policy Guidance Notes was also considered in *Carpets of Worth Ltd* v *Wyre Forest District Council* (1991) 62 P & CR 334, where Purchas LJ said:

I must consider the status of these documents. They are not issued under statutory authority. 'Prescribed' considerations involve regulations made by the Secretary of State under section 287 of the 1971 Act and are therefore subject to resolution of each House of Parliament. Ministerial circulars as published or as summarised in PPGs have therefore no formal statutory force and should therefore not be treated as such for any purpose. This includes in my judgment the manner in which they should be construed and/or applied. They constitute announcements of the current ministerial planning policy. The only statutory obligation upon the local planning authority is 'to have regard to them'. They are in no way bound by them.

Then later he said:

Although the local authority is not bound by the policy circulars, it should observe them and depart from them only if there are clear reasons, which should be stated, for so doing.

11.3.1   Previous appeal decisions

In *North Wiltshire District Council* v *Secretary of State for the Environment* (1992) 65 P & CR 137, the Court of Appeal held that it was indisputable that a previous appeal decision concerning the same application site was a material consideration in determining a subsequent application for the development of the same site. The reason is the need for like cases to be decided in a like manner so that there is consistency in the appellate process. In his judgment Mann LJ said:

Consistency is self-evidently important to both developers and development control authorities. But it is also important for the purpose of securing public confidence in the operation of the development control system. I do not suggest and it would be wrong to do so, that like cases *must* be decided alike. An Inspector must always exercise his own judgment. He is therefore free upon consideration to disagree with the judgment of another but before doing so he ought to have regard to the importance of consistency and to give his reasons for departure from the previous decision.

It is also proper that in determining an application for planning permission, regard should be had to the previous planning history of the application site. This may be particularly important where the land has the benefit of a previous planning permission which has not been implemented and a new development proposal has to be considered. This gives rise to what has been called the fall-back principle, and it requires the decision maker in determining the second application for planning permission to have regard to the merits of the previous decision and the reasons for it. A recent example of the operation of this rule occurred in *Postwood Developments Ltd* v *Secretary of State for the Environment* [1992] JPL 823.

Although the term 'material considerations' has come to be construed liberally and widely, the following areas have caused particular difficulty.

11.3.2   Protection of private interests

It is constantly said that the object of planning control is to restrict private development in the public interest and not in the private interest.

Although it is not the proper function of planning law to protect private interests, in the course of protecting the public interest a landowner may obtain a benefit which he would not otherwise enjoy. In *Stringer* v *Minister of Housing & Local Government* [1970] 1 WLR 1281, the director of the Nuffield Radio Astronomy Laboratories, which operated the Jodrell Bank radio telescope, sought to persuade the local planning authority that in considering applications for planning permission in the surrounding area, they should have regard to the efficient operation of the telescope. It appeared that the efficiency of the telescope was affected by electrical sparks and other forms of disturbance which emanated from terrestrial sources in the neighbourhood, since those sources produced signals similar to the signals the telescope received from outer space. The danger of interference from such things as radios, televisions and motor vehicles, however, diminished the more distant they were from the telescope. So the local planning authority, the rural district council and the University of Manchester (which owned the telescope) entered into an agreement whereby the local planning authority undertook to discourage development within a certain radius of the station. Stringer became a victim of this agreement. His application for planning permission was refused on the ground that, if granted, the development would interfere with the efficient running of the telescope. His appeal against the refusal to the Minister was dismissed. Stringer then appealed to the High Court under what is now s. 288 of the 1990 Act for an order quashing the Minister's decision.

The court held that the agreement between the local planning authority and the University was null and void because its intention was to bind the local planning authority to disregard considerations which it was required to have regard to under what is now s. 70(2) of the 1990 Act. The agreement breached the basic principle that a public authority cannot by contract bind itself to disregard its statutory duties. The court went on, however, to consider that the Minister's decision was valid. The Minister had not been party to the improper agreement and had not bound himself to follow any particular course of action. In determining the appeal, which included the determination of the planning application as if it were made to him de novo, the Minister was entitled to have a policy with regard to the proposed development and here that policy was to discourage development in the vicinity of the telescope. As long as that policy was not followed blindly so as to exclude the consideration by him of all material considerations, his decision could not be faulted.

Faced with the likely success of that argument, however, Stringer also argued that the Minister had taken into account a consideration which was not material, namely the private interests of Jodrell Bank radio telescope. Dismissing that argument, Cooke J held that the term 'material considerations' was not limited to considerations of amenity and that in a proper case might take into account private interests as well as public interests. The fact that the proposed development would interfere with the operation of the telescope was a material consideration in determining the application.

The decision was followed shortly after in *RMC Management Services Ltd* v *Secretary of State for the Environment* (1972) 222 EG 1593. The company had applied to the High Court to quash a decision of the Secretary of State dismissing an appeal from a refusal by the local planning authority to grant planning permission for the erection of a ready-mixed concrete batching plant. The reason given for the dismissal of the appeal was that the development would generate an abnormal level of airborne abrasive dust which would affect the operations of four neighbouring establishments. The four establishments had been attracted to that area by the relatively clean air needed to carry on their high-precision engineering work. The company alleged that in so deciding the Secretary of State was seeking to protect the extraordinary requirements of adjacent occupiers in the use and enjoyment of their land at the expense of and to the detriment of the company in the use and enjoyment of its land. It was not disputed that the proposed use would have been normal for an industrial estate and that it would not have given rise to an actionable nuisance by escape of dust, even if carried out in a residential area. In dismissing the application Bristow J adopted the language of Cooke J in *Stringer v Minister of Housing & Local Government* where he said:

In principle, it seems to me that any consideration which relates to the use and development of land is capable of being a planning consideration. Whether a particular consideration falling within that broad class is material in any given case will depend upon the circumstances.

In dealing with the application before him, Bristow J thought that the Secretary of State was entitled to ask himself whether the proposed development was compatible with the proper and desirable use of other land in the area. In his view the risks to the four special clean-air neighbours was a planning consideration which the Secretary of State was entitled to consider and right to consider material.

So the fact that the special interests of adjoining occupiers of land in clean air was protected, gave them (as a side-effect), a benefit under planning law they would not have enjoyed at common law.

11.3.3 Creation of a precedent

The courts have accepted the principle that although land may be suitable for the development proposed, the local planning authority may refuse planning permission for that development if to grant it would be likely to lead to a proliferation of applications for similar development, which the authority would then find it difficult to refuse.

In *Collis Radio Ltd v Secretary of State for the Environment* [1975] JPL 221, the owners of a warehouse, who had used it for storing electrical goods, began to use it to carry on a cash and carry business. The local planning authority had served an enforcement notice on the owners requiring them to cease and to restore the land to its former user. The Secretary of State dismissed the owners' appeal against the notice on the ground, *inter alia,* that while the development on the appeal site was unlikely to have a particularly harmful effect on the existing shopping centres, a proliferation of such developments might. The owners appealed to the Secretary of State against the notice solely on the ground that 'planning permission ought to be granted' for the development. Their appeal to the court against the Secretary of State's decision to uphold the enforcement notice was based on the ground that the effect, if planning permission were to be granted, of possible future developments of the type enforced against, was not a material consideration. In dismissing the appeal, Lord Widgery CJ said that it was of great importance when considering a single planning application to ask what the consequences in the locality would be and what side-effects would flow if permission were granted. In so far as planning permission for the one site was judged by the Secretary of State in the light of the consequences for other sites, no error of law had been disclosed.

The decision of the Divisional Court in *Collis Radio Ltd* v *Secretary of State for the Environment* was followed by Woolf J in *Anglia Building Society* v *Secretary of State for the Environment* [1984] JPL 175, where planning permission for a change of use from retailing to that of a building society branch office was refused on the ground that to grant the permission would create a precedent that might adversely affect the authority's planning policy for the area, which was to preserve primary shopping areas and to resist non-retail uses except in exceptional cases. Here, although the presence of building society offices in the area was not in itself objectionable, other building societies might use the grant of permission as a lever to establish offices in the area, and this would have led to a dilution of the predominantly retailing character of the area.

11.3.4 Existence of alternative sites

The operation of the planning control system relies heavily on the local planning authority responding to development proposals made by individual landowners or developers for individual sites. Hence, as a matter of principle, it would seem that the question of alternative sites ought not to be a material consideration in determining whether planning permission should be given for the development of the land the subject of the application. The courts, however, have not followed that approach. In *R* v *Royal County of Berkshire (ex parte Mangnall)* [1985] JPL 258, the applicant sought judicial review to quash a grant of planning permission for the extraction of sand given in favour of a neighbouring landowner on the ground that the authority had failed to have proper regard to the existence of an alternative site. It was alleged that before granting planning permission, the authority should have made a comparative evaluation of both sites. According to Nolan J, there was no hard-and-fast rule governing the evaluation of alternative sites, but the statutory duty to have regard to material considerations would, in certain cases, more easily recognised than defined, require the consideration of another possible site than that for which permission was sought. In his judgment, there were serious environmental disadvantages in allowing the development of the neighbouring land. He thought that here the requirement to 'have regard to the provisions of the development plan ... and to any other material considerations', could not be complied with unless the authority had regard to the merits or demerits of the other site, but that it was reading too much into the section to say that an equal evaluation of that site was required. Since it was shown that the authority had in fact considered the merits of the alternative site, the application for judicial review failed.

It seems, therefore, that the merits or demerits of an alternative site *can* be a material consideration, but that the authority is under no duty to evaluate the alternative site in the same way as it must do with the application site. This seems reasonable, since there would be no practical way of securing that without the submission of a planning application for the development of the alternative site.

In *R* v *Carlisle City Council (ex parte Cumbrian Cooperative Society Ltd)* [1986] JPL 206 Macpherson J held that on an application to consider the use of land as a superstore there was no need for the authority to consider *in detail* the merits of alternative sites. Precisely when the merits or demerits of an alternative site can be material was not exhaustively spelt out in the *Mangnall* case. Some help in this area, however, has been given in *Greater London Council* v *Secretary of State for the Environment* [1986] JPL 193. Here, Cable Cross Projects Ltd had applied to the London Docklands Development Corporation for planning permission for office development. The Secretary of State had called in the application and an Inspector, after holding an inquiry, had recommended that permission be refused. The Secretary of State, however, after considering the Inspector's report, had decided to grant permission. The local council then appealed unsuccessfully to the High Court under what is now s. 288 of the 1990 Act for an order to quash the Secretary of State's decision. One of the grounds of challenge was that the Secretary of State had failed to have regard to a material consideration by not examining other comparable sites. In the Court of Appeal, Oliver LJ thought that there were cases where a comparable site had to be a material consideration; an obvious example was an airport. Without seeking to lay down a test for every case, because definition was always dangerous in these circumstances, he thought it might be that comparability was appropriate generally to cases having the following characteristics: first of all, the presence of a clear public convenience, or advantage, in the proposal under consideration; secondly, the existence of inevitable adverse effects or disadvantages to the public or to some section of the public in the proposal; thirdly, the existence of an alternative site for the same project which would not have those effects, or would not have them to the same extent; and fourthly, a situation in which there could only be one permission granted for such development, or at least only a very limited number of permissions.

The question of alternative sites was considered by the High Court in *Edwards* v *Secretary of State for the Environment* (1993) 66 P & CR 393. A number of applications had been made for planning permission for the construction of roadside service areas on different sites along an improved trunk road. All had been refused by the local planning authority and appeals were pending. In one case the appeal was by the written representation procedure but another applicant had elected for a planning inquiry and requested that all the appeals be considered at the same inquiry. The Secretary of State had refused this request and the appeal by written representation went ahead before an Inspector and succeeded. However, the High Court quashed the Inspector's decision because he should have taken account of the alternative proposals: the case had the four characteristics set out in *Greater London Council* v *Secretary of State for the Environment*. An appeal by the Secretary of State from the decision of the High Court was subsequently dismissed by the Court of Appeal. That decision has now been reported at [1994] JPL B110.

11.3.5 Risk of piecemeal development

It seems that if a landowner makes an application for planning permission to develop only part of his land, there may be circumstances where the authority would be justified in refusing permission until such time as the landowner has indicated to the authority his proposals for the remainder of his land.

In *Rugby School Governors* v *Secretary of State for the Environment* [1975] JPL 97, the school had applied for planning permission to develop part of the school estate. The local planning authority had decided to deal with it on the ground that piecemeal development of the estate was bad planning practice and that individual applications should await a master plan, the preparation of which had been agreed earlier with the applicants. The school then appealed to the Secretary of State, who directed that it be determined by an Inspector. He dismissed the appeal. The school then applied to quash his decision on the ground that the Inspector had, while purporting to give a considered refusal, failed to determine the appeal or that he had taken into account irrelevant considerations. Refusing the application, Willis J held that by his endorsement of the authority's policy, the Secretary of State could not be said to have failed to comply with his statutory obligation to determine the appeal. He also held that given the background, it would require special circumstances to justify permitting an individual application to proceed in advance of agreement on a master plan. It should be noted that here the authority should have decided, like the Inspector on behalf of the Secretary of State, to refuse the application instead of deciding not to determine it.

11.3.6 Preservation of existing uses

One of the first cases to consider the relevance of the existing use of land as a material consideration in determining an application for planning permission for the development of the land was *Granada Theatres Ltd* v *Secretary of State for the Environment* [1976] JPL 96. There, the owners of a cinema applied for planning permission to change its use to that of a bingo and social club. Following the refusal of the application, the owners appealed to the Secretary of State who, mainly as a result of a petition by children for the retention of the cinema, dismissed the appeal. The application to quash that decision was based on the grounds that the Secretary of State had taken a mistaken view that the refusal of the permission would ensure the continued use of the building as a cinema and that he had acted contrary to the rules of natural justice in that he had taken into account the petition without giving the applicants an opportunity to comment on it. On both those grounds the Secretary of State consented to the decision being quashed by the court.

In *Clyde & Co.* v *Secretary of State for the Environment* [1977] JPL 521 planning permission had been granted to erect a building, the western half of which was to be used for offices, the eastern half to be used as dwellings. The applicants proceeded to build and occupy the western half, but the eastern half was not completed. The applicants then made a further application to change the permitted use of the eastern half from residential to office use. The application was refused, and an appeal to the Secretary of State against the refusal was not upheld. The applicants then applied to the High Court for the decision to be quashed on the ground that the Secretary of State had erred in law in basing his decision on the ground that the loss of residential accommodation ought to be resisted. The Divisional Court granted the application, but this was reversed by the Court of Appeal which restored the Secretary of State's decision. The Court of Appeal held that the Secretary of State's ground for refusal was not wrong in law. Housing need was a material consideration, and if permission for office use was refused, there was at least a fair chance that the building would be used for housing rather than be allowed to stand empty.

The next important case to be considered by the courts was *Granada Theatres Ltd* v *Secretary of State for the Environment* [1981] JPL 278. Here the applicants owned a cinema in Chichester where trade had declined to such an extent that it had become the second most unprofitable cinema in the Granada group. The company had applied for planning permission to change the use of the cinema to another bingo and social club. On refusal of the application, the applicants had appealed to the Secretary of State, but without any success. In his decision letter the Secretary of State had said that he did not regard as material the alleged demerits such as they might be of bingo as an activity, and he had not been influenced by unfavourable comments made about it in connection with the appeal. He did, however, consider public demand for the retention of a cinema facility in Chichester on the one hand and for the introduction of commercial bingo on the other as well as the availability of alternative suitable premises and ways and means of providing these facilities. He accepted that, notwithstanding the expression of public opinion in favour of retaining the cinema, the appellant company faced difficulties in running the cinema as it stood, but the company had already given some thought to the possibility of finding an alternative use which would still incorporate a cinema element. He also accepted that the proposed change of use to bingo was likely to be much more profitable than the present use. However, he concluded that it might well be that a cinema and bingo operation or a multiunit cinema were not the only possibilities, and despite the appellant's declared intention of closing the present cinema soon, the Secretary of State could not rule out the hope that, as the Inspector had suggested, an increased interest in the cinema or further examination of alternative ways of using the building could yet result in the retention of a viable cinema facility. He therefore rejected the appeal.

In an action to quash the Secretary of State's decision, Forbes J, referring to the decision in *Clyde & Co.* v *Secretary of State for the Environment,* confessed to be surprised that it should have been necessary for there to be an authority for the proposition that in a change of use case the desirability of preserving the existing use was a material consideration, because it seemed to him so self-evident a proposition. According to his lordship, however, there could be situations where the question of desirability of retaining the existing use was not material. If all the parties agreed that the continuation of an existing use was undesirable, one need not consider the question of desirability further. It was a concluded question. But where there was a dispute between the parties about whether an existing use should be retained or not, it seemed to him inevitable that the desirability of retaining it was a material question. Here, the sole issue for the Secretary of State to decide was whether there was a possibility, a reasonable possibility perhaps, that the existing use would be preserved if planning permission was refused. His lordship decided that it was reasonable for the Secretary of State to come to that conclusion and so refused to interfere with his decision.

The test so far applied by the courts in considering the relevance of an existing use in determining planning applications has been whether, if permission were refused, there would be a 'fair chance' or 'a possibility' or 'a reasonable possibility' that the existing use would continue.

In *Westminster City Council* v *British Waterways Board* [1985] AC 676 however, the House of Lords held that the preservation of an existing use which had been temporarily suspended could not afford a ground of refusal of planning permission for an otherwise acceptable change of use, unless it could be shown that the refusal might lead to a resumption of the suspended use. In dealing with the question of resumption, Lord Bridge of Harwich thought that the 'fair chance' test was, on the facts, an unnecessarily lax criterion. In his view, in a contest between the planning merits of two competing uses, to justify the refusal of permission for use B on the sole ground that use A ought to be preserved, it must be necessary at least to show 'a balance of probabilities' that if permission is refused for use B, the land in dispute will be effectively put to use A.

More recently, in *Vikoma International Ltd* v *Secretary of State for the Environment* [1987] JPL 38, a house had been used for offices for a number of years without planning permission. The occupiers then applied for planning permission for a limited period of five years. The authority refused to grant permission and proceeded to serve an enforcement notice alleging a material change of use from residential to office use and requiring the latter's discontinuance. The occupiers appealed to the Secretary of State, who upheld the enforcement notice and dismissed the appeal against the refusal of planning permission. The occupiers then challenged his decision on the enforcement notice solely on the question of planning permission. It was contended that the Inspector, who had made the decision standing in the shoes of the Secretary of State, had not gone far enough in merely asking the question, 'Does the property provide a reasonable standard of accommodation?' He should also have asked whether there was a fair chance that the residential use would be resumed, and this would have required an examination into the economics of repairing the house for residential use. Quashing the decision, David Widdicombe QC (acting as a Deputy High Court Judge) held that the Inspector should have posed the 'fair chance' test or some equivalent of it. It is interesting to note that, although the failure to do so did not affect the result, the learned Deputy judge was not referred to the judgment of Lord Bridge of Harwich *in Westminster City Council* v *British Waterways Board*.

More recently still, in *London Residuary Body* v *Lambeth London Borough Council* [1990] 1 WLR 744, the House of Lords in allowing an appeal from a decision of the Court of Appeal, held that in exercising powers under s. 29 of the 1971 Act, (s. 70 of the 1990 Act) a local planning authority was not bound to apply a competing needs test of whether in planning terms the desirability of preserving the existing use outweighs the merits of the proposed new use. After considering the cases of *Clyde & Co.* v *Secretary of State* [1977] JPL 521 and *Westminster City Council* v *British Waterways Board* [1985] AC 676, Lord Keith of Kinkel said:

In my opinion nothing in either the *Clyde* case or in the *Westminster Council* case is properly to be interpreted as laying down that the competing needs test exists as a matter of law. Such a proposition would involve putting an unwarranted gloss on the language of s. 29(1) of the 1971 Act. The most that can be extracted from the two cases is that the desirability of preserving an existing use of land is a material consideration to be taken into account under that subsection, provided there is a reasonable probability that such use will be preserved if permission for the new use is refused. If the Court of Appeal is right, it must follow that the presumption in favour of development can in law only receive effect where other planning considerations for or against a proposed use are evenly balanced. Such a straitjacket cannot properly be imposed on the Secretary of State. It must be left to him, in the exercise of a reasonable discretion, to form his own judgment whether any planning objections are of sufficient importance to overcome the presumption. This was the view taken, in my opinion correctly, by Simon Brown J. It should be kept in mind that in the case of many individual planning applications, for example to build a single house somewhere in the country, there is no question of it being possible to prove a need for the development. There may, however, be some planning objection to it which is not of very great weight. In such a situation it must surely be open to the determining authority to decide that the presumption may properly receive effect and to grant planning permission.

Whether or not there is a reasonable probability that an existing use will be preserved will depend on the individual facts of each case. Factors like the institution of a new use in breach of planning control, the demolition of a building in which an old use took place, a sustained period of disuse and evidence that the old use ceased because it was not economically viable to carry it on, remain of great evidential value in determining the future use of a parcel of land.

11.3.7   Personal circumstances of the applicant

Although in practice the personal circumstances of an applicant do occasionally result in his obtaining a favourable decision from the local planning authority, the legal authority for this practice is not of long standing.

In *New Forest District Council* v *Secretary of State for the Environment* [1984] JPL 178, a Mr Clarke was the owner of a bungalow built with an occupancy condition restricting its use to past or present employees of an adjacent hotel, or to agricultural or forestry workers. He had made a number of applications for planning permission to use the bungalow without the occupancy condition and, save for the last, all had been refused. Finally, the Secretary of State had granted planning permission on appeal. The local planning authority claimed in the Queen's Bench Division that the Secretary of State had wrongly taken into account Mr Clarke's financial circumstances and that this was not a material consideration. Rejecting that argument, Taylor J held that it was proper to take into account personal circumstances and personal hardship where matters might be very evenly balanced, and to consider the effect the decision might have on the individual applicant. Obviously such a consideration could only be peripheral to the main planning issues which had to be taken into account.

In *Tameside Metropolitan Borough Council* v *Secretary of State for the Environment* [1984] JPL 180 it again was held that the Secretary of State was entitled to take personal hardship into account.

The consideration of personal circumstances, but only on a marginal basis, was given the seal of the highest judicial authority in *Westminster City Council* v *Great Portland Estates plc* [1985] AC 661. In that case the respondent company had challenged both the industrial and the office policies contained in the Westminster City local plan. With regard to industrial development, the general policy was that applications for planning permission for new industrial floor space and the creation of new industrial employment were to be encouraged. That general policy was modified in the case of applications for planning permission to rehabilitate or redevelop existing industrial premises. In these cases the authority's general policy was supplanted where considered necessary to maintain the continuation of industrial uses important to the diverse character, vitality and functioning of Westminster. There the policy was to be to protect 'specific industrial activities' from redevelopment. The respondent company challenged this latter aspect as being outside the purposes of planning law. The essence of the company's argument was that the protection of specified industrial activities was not a policy concerned with the development and use of land, but one concerned with the protection of particular users of land. It was irrelevant, it was claimed, to have regard in this way to the interests of individual occupiers.

In rejecting the challenge to the authority's industrial policy, Lord Scarman, giving the only speech, but one concurred in by all the other Law Lords, adopted the general principle enunciated by Lord Parker CJ in *East Barnet Urban District Council* v *British Transport Commission* [1962] 2 QB 484 that in considering whether there had been a change of use, 'what is really to be considered is the character of the use of the land, not the particular purposes of a particular occupier'. It was a logical process, Lord Scarman thought, to extend the ambit of that statement to the formulation of planning policies and proposals. However, like all generalisations, he said, the statement of Lord Parker had its own limitations. Personal circumstances of the occupier, personal hardship, and the difficulties of business which are of value to the community were not to be ignored in the administration of planning control.

A good example of the application of *Westminster City Council* v *Great Portland Estates plc* with somewhat unusual consequences is seen in recent decisions involving listed buildings in the Lake District. In December 1987, the South Lakeland District Council became aware that original windows in a row of listed terrace houses at Nos. 1, 3 and 4 Eastside, The Square, Burton-in-Kendal, had been replaced by modern casement windows without listed building consent. Following a decision by the authority to take enforcment action to remedy the breaches of control, the owner of No. 3 submitted an application for listed building consent to retain the new windows. On appeal to the Secretary of State, an Inspector allowed the appeal and granted the retrospective listed building consent applied for.

In *South Lakeland District Council* v *Secretary of State for the Environment and Rowbotham* [1991] JPL 440, the local planning authority then sought unsuccessfully to challenge that decision in the High Court, which held, *inter alia*, that the Inspector had not erred in regarding the personal circumstances of the elderly applicant, namely the costs and disruption which would be caused by having to replace the original windows and the loss of the comfort an aged resident would derive from double glazing, as material factors to be taken into account in applying planning legislation. The High Court also made it clear (as had the Inspector in his decision letter) that the granting of the consent afforded no precedent in relation to other pending cases.

Accordingly, the local planning authority then proceeded to take listed building enforcement action against the owners of Nos. 1 and 4 Eastside. Both owners appealed against the notice to the Secretary of State. The same Inspector in both cases concluded that the replacement windows were inappropriate and upheld the notices. In one of them, personal circumstances were advanced by the appellant but discounted by the Inspector. In both cases reference was made to replacement windows installed at No. 3 Eastside with now listed building consent. On this aspect the Inspector said:

> ... the fact that inappropriate windows have been granted consent at No. 3 makes it more, and not less, important to ensure that appropriate windows are installed elsewhere in the front façade. Consequently, I find no merit in the suggestion that, for uniformity, inappropriate windows should be installed in all the windows of the front elevation of Nos. 1-4.

Following the decision the elderly occupant of No. 3, whose personal circumstances were crucial to the decision to grant listed building consent vacated the premises, which were then put up for sale.

11.3.8 Affordable housing

One issue on which there is an absence of a clear and authoritative statement of the law is the extent to which a local planning authority can use its powers to promote the provision of 'affordable housing', that is, housing accessible to people who cannot afford to buy in the open market. Government policy has been that if there was a demonstrable need then planning permission might be granted exceptionally for affordable housing on sites which would not normally receive permission and which would be additional to those provided for in development plans. It was recognised that where this took place secure arrangements would have to be made to ensure that subsequent occupants complied with the objectives of the policy.

The difficulty is that the policy may conflict with the principle that planning seeks to control the character of the use of land not the particular purpose of a particular occupier, though personal circumstances may also be a material consideration.

Some new light may have been shone on this conflict by *Mitchell* v *Secretary of State for the Environment* [1994] EGCS 111. The local planning authority had a policy 'to resist proposals for the conversion into self-contained accommodation of houses in multiple occupation meeting a known and established need'. The authority had failed to determine an application for permission to change the use of a house in multiple occupation into self-contained flats and there was an appeal to the Secretary of State, who applied the authority's policy and dismissed the appeal. The High Court had then quashed the Secretary of State's decision on the ground that the authority's policy was not a material consideration which could be taken into account. An appeal by the Secretary of State against that decision, however, was upheld by the Court of Appeal. The Court held that 'material considerations' were not confined to questions of amenity and environmental impact. The need for housing in a particular area could be a material consideration. No sensible distinction could be drawn between a need for housing generally and a need for a particular type of housing, whether defined in terms of cost, tenure or otherwise. The fact that the need might be dictated by considerations of cost or type was irrelevant.

In the *Mitchell* case the local planning authority's policy had been contained in its draft Unitary Development Plan. In *ECC Construction Ltd v Secretary of State for the Environment* [1994] EGCS 143, the High Court followed that decision, but went further in holding that it was not necessary for the need for affordable housing to be included in formulated policies; it could arise by implication.

11.3.9 Enabling development

In *R v Westminster City Council, ex parte Monahan* [1988] JPL 107, the Court of Appeal made clear that 'any other material considerations' could properly include 'financial considerations'. In this case an application had been made to the High Court for judicial review to quash a grant of planning permission and various consents for the demolition of a number of listed and unlisted buildings as part of a development scheme to improve the facilities at the Royal Opera House, Covent Garden. The main purpose of the scheme had been the redevelopment of the Opera House, but this could only proceed if permission were also granted for adjacent commercial development which would provide the funds needed to improve the Opera House. But for this essential link, planning policy would have dictated that planning permission would not have been granted for the commercial development alone. In the courts the appellants claimed unsuccessfully that the local planning authority had taken into account a consideration that was not material, namely the generation of finance from part of the proposed development to be used for the benefit of the Opera House; and had failed to consider a material consideration, namely that if finance was a material consideration, they had not considered other sources of finance available to the Opera House not involving the commercial development.

Upholding the decision of the High Court, the Court of Appeal held that financial constraints on the economic viability of a desirable planning development are unavoidable facts of life in an imperfect world and virtually all planning decisions involve some kind of balancing exercise. Provided that the ultimate determination of a planning decision is based on planning grounds and not on some ulterior motive, and that it is not irrational, there is no basis for holding it invalid in law solely on the ground that it has taken account of, and adjusted itself to, the financial realities of the overall situation. The meaning of 'material consideration' in the Town and Country Planning Act has been circumscribed in wide terms and these do not exclude financial considerations from being treated as material in appropriate cases. Hence, the financing of the development scheme was capable of being a material consideration, as it related to the use and development of land.

It may be that the *Covent Garden* case will lead to an increase in the number of cases where it is claimed that any detriment suffered by a grant of permission for part of a development scheme contrary to established policy, would be more than offset by the benefit to be gained from other aspects of the scheme if the whole were to be allowed to proceed.

In two recent Ministerial decisions the *'Covent Garden* influence' can be seen. The first decision granted planning permission for the erection of eight houses in the walled kitchen garden of Croome Court, Worcester, a Grade 1 listed building, the construction of which was begun in 1751 by 'Capability' Brown, and was now unoccupied and in need of restoration. The Inspector found that the proposed development would be contrary to the policies of the approved structure plan for the area. Also, that having regard to s. 56(3) of the 1971 Act, the proposal should normally fail. However, he accepted the applicant's contention that if the development were permitted the profit realised from the sale of eight building plots would generate enough cash to enable restoration of the house to proceed. At the inquiry, the parties had favoured a planning agreement to achieve this. In the event, this did not prove possible, so the Inspector dealt with it by conditions.

In the second decision, the Secretary of State had to consider whether to grant planning permission to Wates Homes Ltd for the erection, *inter alia,* of a superstore at Broadlands, Hampshire. The applicants argued that by permitting the development, sufficient funds would be generated to secure the restoration and future maintenance of Broadlands House and surrounding estate, which included no less than 50 listed buildings.

In dismissing the appeal, the Secretary of State considered that whilst it was reasonable to take that into account, he could not agree with the Inspector's judgment that the needs of this historic house could justify the introduction of an inappropriate and intensive form of development, with all its attendant disturbance into a countryside area contrary to structure plan policies.

This decision raises the question of whether, if one is to take advantage of the *Covent Garden* approach, there has to be a functional link between the proposed development and the land to be benefited by it, or for both to be on the same site. In this instance, the site of the proposed development was approximately two miles from Broadlands House itself.

Another example of enabling development is a 1994 ministerial decision, where planning permission was given for a 36-hole golf-course with clubhouse and car parking on land at Mapledurham Estate, Mapledurham, near Reading, in an Area of Outstanding Natural Beauty. A significant reason for so doing was that some of the listed buildings in the estate's ownerhsip were in need of urgent repair, and the income from the proposed golf-course would enable a 20-year programme of repairs to be undertaken.

11.3.10 Planning and pollution control

Pollution controls in the United Kingdom are exercised through a range of organisations and a variety of mechanisms, including licensing and authorisation procedures which are applied to processes and substances which can have potentially harmful effects on the environment. In the past few years, a sustantial body of new legislation such as the Control of Pollution Act 1974, the Environmental Protection Act 1990 and the Water Resources Act 1991 have considerably extended the scope and effectiveness of pollution controls. The relation between planning and pollution control, however, is not particularly clear. An early case, *Ladbroke (Rentals) Ltd* v *Secretary of State for the Environment* [1981] JPL 427, established that disturbance or annoyances caused to other occupiers of land is a relevant planning consideration regardless of powers to control the source under other legislation. It should also be noted that under the Town and Country Planning (Assessment of Environmental Effects) Regulations 1988, a local planning authority must not grant planning permission for any development of land to which the regulations apply, unless they first take into account environmental information.

The government takes the view, expressed in a consultation paper on planning and pollution control issued in May 1992, that 'it is not the job of the planning system to duplicate controls which are the statutory responsibility of other bodies', though it admitted that the dividing line between the two forms of control was not always 'clear-cut'. The problem has been discussed in the recent case of *Gateshead Metropolitan Borough Council* v *Secretary of State for the Environment* (1993) 67 P & CR 179. The Northern Regional Hospital Authority had applied to the local planning authority for outline planning permission for a clinical waste incinerator which had been refused. On appeal to the Secretary of State by the health authority, an Inspector had concluded that whilst an appropriate plant could be built to meet the various standards relating to emission limits laid down by HM Inspectorate of Pollution under the Environmental Protection Act 1990, the effect on air quality and agriculture in the locality was insufficiently defined, and that public disquite about environmental pollution could not be sufficiently allayed to make the proposed development acceptable. Accordingly, he recommended to the Secretary of State that planning permission for the incinerator should be refused. The Secretary of State, however, declined to accept the recommendation and granted permission for the development on the grounds first, that the Secretary of State could not lawfully abdicate his planning responsibilities to the Environmental Protection Act 1990 regime; secondly, that there was no evidence on which he could be satisfied that controls under that regime would be adequate and thirdly, that if he could not properly be satisfied that these concerns could be dealt with under that regime, it followed that the proposal would not comply with structure plan requirements for the consequences in terms of environmental impact to be acceptable.

In an unsuccessful application to the High Court to quash the Secretary of State's decision, it was held that the environmental impact of emissions into the atmosphere was a material consideration in determining planning applications, but so too was the existence of pollution controls. After remarking that any attempt to draw a demarcation line between the two forms of control was not helpful, the learned deputy judge went on to say:

> At one extreme there will be cases where the evidence at the planning stage demonstrates that potential pollution problems have been substantially overcome, so that any reasonable person will accept that the remaining details can sensibly be left to the EPA authorisation process.
>
> At the other extreme, there may be cases where the evidence of environmental problems is so damning at the planning stage that any reasonable person would refuse planning permission, saying, in effect, there is no point in trying to resolve these very grave problems through the EPA process. Between these two extremes there will be a whole spectrum of cases disclosing pollution problems of different types and differing degree of complexity and gravity.

This judgment was subsequently upheld by the Court of Appeal, but has not, as yet, been reported.

It seems, therefore, that the weight to be given to environmental issues and the power to control them under pollution legislation in determining applications for planning permission is a matter for the particular decision-maker, be it local planning authority or Secretary of State. It should also be borne in mind that Her Majesty's Inspector of Pollution is not likely to pay regard to the effect of noxious emissions on the development potential of any area, nor to the question of whether in any particular case the location of a particular process would make the area less attractive for securing the regeneration of the area.

11.3.11 Environmental information
Under the Town and Country Planning (Assessment of Environmental Effects) Regulations 1988 (SI No. 1199), a local planning authority or the Secretary of State must not grant planning permission for any development to which the regulations apply, unless they have first taken into consideration any environmental information. This area of law is dealt with in the next chapter.

TWELVE

Environmental assessment

A requirement for the environmental assessment of certain major development projects, represents the first direct impact of European Community law on domestic town and country planning law. The terms of EC Directive No. 85/337, *The Assessment of the Effect of Certain Public and Private Projects on the Environment,* have been implemented in the UK as far as possible within normal town and country planning procedures. There are in fact 18 sets of statutory provisions which implement the Directive, dealing with such matters as afforestation projects, highways, harbour works, land drainage, pipelines and Salmon farming. The main vehicle for the implementation of the Directive in England and Wales, however, has been the Town and Country Planning (Assessment of Environmental Effects) Regulations 1988 (SI No. 1199) (the Regulations). Similar regulations apply to Scotland. The Regulations came into force on 15 July 1988. At the same time the Secretary of State issued a Circular No. 15/88 giving guidance on the new procedures. Where the procedure for the approval of projects requiring environmental assessment under the Directive is dealt with under other legislation (e.g. highways under the Highways Acts), separate subordinate legislation has been introduced. Hence, separate regulations exist dealing with land drainage improvement works, salmon farming in marine waters, highways, harbour works and electricity and pipeline works. All of these, however, fall outside the scope of this chapter.

Most of the regulations governing environmental assessment have been introduced under powers given to Ministers by the European Communities Act 1972. During the passage of the Planning and Compensation Act 1991 through Parliament, however, the government accepted the view that as regards planning legislation there should be some direct statutory authority for the implementation of the European Community Directive. In addition, it considered that there was an argument for extending environmental assessment to types of project beyond those specifically required by the Directive. Accordingly, s. 15 of the 1991 Act inserted a new s. 71A into the 1990 Act to give the Secretary of State power to make regulations about the consideration to be given, before planning permission for development is granted, of the likely environmental effects of the proposed development. He can thus at any time enlarge the classes of development for which environmental assessment may be required. Under this new provision, the government amended the Assessment of Environmental Effects Regulations in April 1994 by adding privately financed toll roads to sch. 1 to the Regulations, thus making environmental assessment of such projects mandatory in every case. They also amended the Regulations to add wind generators, motorway service areas and coast protection works to sch. 2, the effect of which is to require environmental assessment where a particular development proposal would be likely to have significant effects on the environment.

According to para. 7 of Circular No. 15/88, 'environmental assessment' is 'a technique for the systematic compilation of expert quantitative analysis and qualitative assessment of a project's environmental effects, and the presentation of results in a way which enables the importance of the predicted results, and the scope for modifying or mitigating them, to be properly evaluated by the relevant decision-making body before a planning application decision is rendered'.

In order to understand the procedures that have to be followed, it is important to understand the following terminology:

(a) *Environmental assessment* is essentially a process. It is the whole process required to reach a decision on whether or not to allow the project to proceed. Environmental assessment involves the presentation, collection and assessment of information on the environmental effects of a project, and also the final judgment upon it. An important part of that process is the submission of an environmental statement.

(b) *Environmental statement* is the information which is put forward by the developer in conjunction with his application for planning permission for the project.

(c) *Environmental information* is the information provided by the developer via the environmental statement; but also includes the information and responses given by or received from various statutory consultees and third parties. As such it is a material consideration in determining the application for planning permission.

12.1 Projects requiring environmental assessment

The Regulations apply to two separate lists of projects:

(a) 'schedule 1 projects', for which environmental assessment is mandatory;

(b) 'schedule 2 projects', for which environmental assessment is required only if the particular project is considered likely to give rise to significant effects on the environment by virtue of factors such as its nature, size or location.

12.1.1 Schedule 1 projects
The following types of development ('schedule 1 projects') require environmental assessment in every case:

(1)   The carrying out of building or other operations, or the change of use of buildings or other land (where a material change) to provide any of the following—

1.   A crude-oil refinery (excluding an undertaking manufacturing only lubricants from crude oil) or an installation for the gasification and liquefaction of 500 tonnes or more of coal or bituminous shale per day.
2.   (a)   A thermal power station or other combustion installation with a heat output of 300 megawatts or more (not being an installation falling within paragraph (b)); and

(b)   A nuclear power station or other nuclear reactor (excluding a research installation for the production and conversion of fissionable and fertile materials, the maximum power of which does not exceed 1 kilowatt continuous thermal load).

3.   An installation designed solely for the permanent storage or final disposal of radioactive waste.
4.   An integrated works for the initial melting of cast-iron and steel.
5.   An installation for the extraction of asbestos or for the processing and transformation of asbestos or products containing asbestos—

(a)   where the installation produces asbestos-cement products, with an annual production of more than 20,000 tonnes of finished products; or
(b)   where the installation produces friction material, with an annual production of more than 50 tonnes of finished products; or
(c)   in other cases, where the installation will utilise more than 200 tonnes of asbestos per year.

6.   An integrated chemical installation, that is to say an industrial installation or group of installations where two or more linked chemical or physical processes are employed for the manufacture of olefins from petroleum products, or of sulphuric acid, nitric acid, hydrofluoric acid, chlorine or fluorine.
7.   A special road; a line for long-distance railway traffic; or an aerodrome with a basic runway length of 2,100 m or more.
8.   A trading port, an inland waterway which permits the passage of vessels of over 1,350 tonnes or a port for inland waterway traffic capable of handling such vessels.
9.   A waste-disposal installation for the incineration or chemical treatment of special waste.

(2)   The carrying out of operations whereby land is filled with special waste, or the change of use of land (where a material change) to use for the deposit of such waste.

12.1.2   Schedule 2 projects
The following types of development ('schedule 2 projects') require environmental assessment only if they are likely to have significant effects on the environment by virtue of factors such as their nature, size or location.

1. Agriculture

    (a)   water-management for agriculture
    (b)   poultry-rearing
    (c)   pig-rearing
    (d)   a salmon hatchery
    (e)   an installation for the rearing of salmon
    (f)   the reclamation of land from the sea

2. Extractive industry

    (a)   Extracting peat
    (b)   deep drilling, including in particular—

        (i)   geothermal drilling;
        (ii)   drilling for the storage of nuclear waste material;
        (iii)   drilling for water supplies;

but excluding drilling to investigate the stability of the soil.
    (c)   extracting minerals (other than metalliferous and energy-producing minerals) such as marble, sand, gravel, shale, salt, phosphates and potash
    (d)   extracting coal or lignite by underground or open-cast mining
    (e)   extracting petroleum
    (f)   extracting natural gas
    (g)   extracting ores
    (h)   extracting bituminous shale
    (i)   extracting minerals (other than metalliferous and energy-producing minerals) by open-cast mining
    (j)   a surface industrial installation for the extraction of coal, petroleum, natural gas or ores or bituminous shale
    (k)   a coke oven (dry distillation of coal)
    (l)   an installation for the manufacture of cement

3. Energy industry

    (a)   a non-nuclear thermal power station, not being an installation falling within schedule 1, or an installation for the production of electricity, steam and hot water

(b)   an industrial installation for carrying gas, steam or hot water; or the transmission of electrical energy by overhead cables
(c)   the surface storage of natural gas
(d)   the underground storage of combustible gases
(e)   the surface storage of fossil fuels
(f)   the industrial briquetting of coal or lignite
(g)   an installation for the production or enrichment of nuclear fuels
(h)   an installation for the reprocessing of irradiated nuclear fuels
(i)   an installation for the collection or processing of radioactive waste, not being an installation falling within schedule 1
(j)   an installation for hydroelectric energy production
(k)   a wind generator

4. Processing of metals

(a)   an ironworks or steelworks including a foundry, forge, drawing plant or rolling mill (not being a works falling within schedule 1)
(b)   an installation for the production (including smelting, refining, drawing and rolling) of non-ferrous metals, other than precious metals
(c)   the pressing, drawing or stamping of large castings
(d)   the surface treatment and coating of metals
(e)   boilermaking or manufacturing reservoirs, tanks and other sheet-metal containers
(f)   manufacturing or assembling motor vehicles or manufacturing motorvehicle engines
(g)   a shipyard
(h)   an installation for the construction or repair of aircraft
(i)   the manufacture of railway equipment
(j)   swaging by explosives
(k)   an installation for the roasting or sintering of metallic ores

5. Glass making   the manufacture of glass

6. Chemical industry

(a)   the treatment of intermediate products and production of chemicals, other than development falling within schedule 1
(b)   the production of pesticides or pharmaceutical products, paints or varnishes, elastomers or peroxides
(c)   the storage of petroleum or petrochemical or chemical products

7. Food industry

(a)   the manufacture of vegetable or animal oils or fats
(b)   the packing or canning of animal or vegetable products
(c)   the manufacture of dairy products
(d)   brewing or malting

(e) confectionery or syrup manufacture
(f) an installation for the slaughter of animals
(g) an industrial starch manufacturing installation
(h) a fish-meal or fish-oil factory
(i) a sugar factory

8. Textile, leather, wood and paper industries

(a) a wool scouring, degreasing and bleaching factory
(b) the manufacture of fibre board, particle board or plywood
(c) the manufacture of pulp, paper or board
(d) a fibre-dyeing factory
(e) a cellulose-processing and production installation
(f) a tannery or a leather dressing factory

9. Rubber industry the manufacture and treatment of elastomer-based products

10. Infrastructure projects

(a) an industrial estate development project
(b) an urban development project
(c) a ski-lift or cable-car
(d) the construction of a road, or a harbour, including a fishing harbour, or an aerodrome, not being development falling within schedule 1
(e) canalisation or flood-relief works
(f) a dam or other installation designed to hold water or store it on a longterm basis
(g) a tramway, elevated or underground railway, suspended line or similar line, exclusively or mainly for passenger transport
(h) an oil or gas pipeline installation
(i) a long-distance aqueduct
(j) a yacht marina
(k) a mortorway service area
(l) coast protection works

11. Other projects

(a) a holiday village or hotel complex
(b) a permanent racing or test track for cars or motor cycles
(c) an installation for the disposal of controlled waste or waste from mines
and quarries, not being an installation falling within schedule 1
(d) a waste-water treatment plant
(e) a site for depositing sludge
(f) the storage of scrap iron
(g) a test bench for engines, turbines or reactors

(h)   the manufacture of artificial mineral fibres

(i)   the manufacture, packing, loading or placing in cartridges of gunpowder or other explosives

(j)   a knackers' yard

12.   The modification of a development which has been carried out, where that development is within a description mentioned in schedule 1.

13.   Development within a description mentioned in schedule 1, where it is exclusively or mainly for the development and testing of new methods or products and will not be permitted for longer than one year.

12.1.3   Identifying relevant schedule 2 projects

The criteria for determining whether a sch. 2 project requires environmental assessment is whether or not it is likely to give rise to significant effects on the environment by virtue of factors such as its nature, size or location. In Circular No. 15/88, the Secretary of State expresses the view that environmental assessment will be needed for sch. 2 projects in three main types of case, namely:

(a)   for projects which are of more than local importance;

(b)   occasionally for projects on a smaller scale which are proposed for particularly sensitive or vulnerable locations; and

(c)   in a smaller number of cases, for projects with unusually complex and potentially adverse environmental effects.

As regards projects on a smaller scale which are proposed for particularly sensitive or vulnerable locations ((b) above), the Circular says that consideration should be given to the need for environmental assessment where a project is likely to have significant effects on the special character of a protected site, such as a national park, area of outstanding natural beauty, a site of special scientific interest, a nature reserve or an area or monument of major archaeological importance. The Secretary of State, however, does not consider that there should be an automatic presumption that assessment will be needed simply because the proposal is located in such an area.

Given the range of sch. 2 projects and the importance of locational factors, it is (as the Circular emphasises) not possible to formulate criteria or thresholds to provide a simple test of whether or not environmental assessment is required. The most that such criteria can offer is a broad indication of the type or scale of project which may be a candidate for assessment — and, conversely, an indication of the sort of project for which assessment is not likely to be required. In Appendix A to the Circular No. 15/88, the Secretary of State has listed for certain of the categories of project in sch. 2, criteria and thresholds, which are intended to indicate the types of case which in the Secretary of State's view, will require environmental assessment under the Regulations.

In addition to the advice given in Circular No. 15/88, a further Circular No. 7/94 sets out indicative criteria and thresholds, where appropriate, for the two new categories of project added to sch. 2 by the amendments to the Regulations made in April 1994.

12.1.4 Who decides whether environmental assessment is required?

Given the lack of a simple test for deciding whether or not environmental assessment is required for sch. 2 projects, on whom does the decision depend? In the first instance, under reg. 5, it is open to a developer at any time prior to submitting an application for planning permission to ask the local planning authority to state whether in their opinion the proposed development would be a sch. 1 or 2 application requiring preparation of an environmental statement. Where this is done, the authority must notify its opinion to the developer within three weeks of receiving the request, unless that period has been extended by agreement made with the developer in writing. If the authority gives an opinion that an environmental statement is required, they must give reasons for that opinion. It is then open to the developer to apply to the Secretary of State for a direction on the matter. If the Secretary of State then directs that an environmental statement is required, he too must give reasons for the direction.

Secondly, it is open to a developer to volunteer an environmental statement when submitting an application for planning permission. Where this is done, the applicant may expressly state that the documents submitted with the application constitute an environmental statement for the purposes of the Regulations. In that case the application must be treated as an application to which environmental assessment applies.

Thirdly, a developer may submit an application for planning permission for development which the local planning authority consider to be development within sch. 1 or 2 without an accompanying environmental statement. In such a case the authority must within three weeks notify the developer that in their opinion submission of an environmental statement is required and the reason therefor. The developer may then have regard to the authority's opinion and within three weeks notify the authority of his intention to supply an environmental statement or ask the Secretary of State for his direction on the matter. If he does neither, the application is deemed to have been refused at the end of that three-week period. The procedure for asking the Secretary of State for a direction is similar to that described above with regard to the pre-application procedure.

Fourthly, where an application for planning permission is called in by the Secretary of State for his own decision and is not accompanied by an environmental statement, and the Secretary of State considers the development to be within sch. 1 or 2, he must notify the parties concerned. The developer will then have three weeks to notify the Secretary of State that he will provide an environmental statement. If he does not so notify, the Secretary of State cannot determine the application and will inform the developer accordingly.

12.2 The environmental statement

There is no provision in the Regulations as to the form the environmental statement should take. Schedule 3 of the Regulations, however, specifies what it should contain.

SCHEDULE 3

1. An environmental statement comprises a document or series of documents providing for the purpose of assessing the likely impact upon the environment of the development proposed to be carried out, the information specified in paragraph 2 (referred to in this schedule as 'the specified information').

2. The specified information is—

(a) a description of the development proposed, comprising information about the site and the design and size or scale of the development;

(b) the data necessary to identify and assess the main effects which that development is likely to have on the environment;

(c) a description of the likely significant effects, direct and indirect, on the environment of the development, explained by reference to its possible impact on—

human beings;
flora;
fauna;
soil;
water;
air;
climate;
the landscape;
the inter-action between any of the foregoing;
material assets;
the cultural heritage;

(d) where significant adverse effects are identified with respect to any of the foregoing, a description of the measures envisaged in order to avoid, reduce or remedy those effects; and

(e) a summary in non-technical language of the information specified above.

3. An environmental statement may include, by way of explanation or amplification of any specified information, further information on any of the following matters—

(a) the physical characteristics of the proposed development, and the land use requirements during the construction and operational phases;

(b) the main characteristics of the production processes proposed, including the nature and quantity of the materials to be used;

(c) the estimated type and quantity of expected residues and emissions (including pollutants of water, air or soil, noise, vibration, light, heat and radiation) resulting from the proposed development when in operation;

(d) (in outline) the main alternatives (if any) studied by the applicant, appellant or authority and an indication of the main reasons for choosing the development proposed, taking into account the environmental effects;

(e) the likely significant direct and indirect effects on the environment of the development proposed which may result from—

(i)   the use of natural resources;
(ii) the emission of pollutants, the creation of nuisances, and the elimination of waste;

(f) the forecasting methods used to assess any effects on the environment about which information is given under subparagraph (e); and
(g) any difficulties, such as technical deficiencies or lack of know-how, encountered in compiling any specified information.

In paragraph (e), 'effects' includes secondary, cumulative, short, medium and long term, permanent, temporary, positive and negative effects.

4. Where further information is included in an environmental statement pursuant to paragraph 3, a non-technical summary of that information shall also be provided.

In order to help a developer prepare an environmental statement, reg. 8 provides that a developer may give the local planning authority notice in writing that he intends to make a sch. 1 or 2 application and to submit an environmental statement with his application. On receipt of the notice, the authority must then inform a number of specified bodies of that fact. The bodies specified are those who would be statutory consultees under the General Development Order in relation to the application, any principal council for the area in which the land is situated, the National Conservancy Council, the Countryside Commission, and where the development would in the opinion of the authority be likely to involve radioactive wastes, or controlled or special waste likely to require the consent of a water authority, with HM Inspectorate of Pollution. When such bodies have been notified, they are required to make information which is in their possession available to the developer on request.

On receipt of an application for planning permission accompanied by an environmental statement, the local planning authority is required by art. 12B of the General Development Order (see Chapter 10) to publicise the application (and the environmental statement). This requires the authority not only to display a site notice and advertise in a local newspaper, but to indicate in them that a copy of the environmental statement is included in the documents open to public inspection. If, however, the environmental statement is submitted after the planning application, reg. 13 places the responsibility for publicising the statement on the applicant. Under reg. 14, the local planning authority is required to send a copy of the application and of the environmental statement (provided by the developer) to the Secretary of State, placing a copy of the statement in Part I of the planning register and advising statutory consultees that the statement will be taken into account in determining the application, asking whether they wish to receive a copy of the statement and informing them that they may make representations.

Under reg. 16, the local planning authority is given 16 weeks from the date of receipt of the environmental statement to determine the application for planning permission, as opposed to the normal period of eight weeks.

A recent amendment to the Regulations has inserted a new reg. 25A, which makes provision for the application of the Regulations to planning applications where the local authority is also the applicant.

12.3   Environmental information

Regulation 2 defines 'environmental information' as meaning 'the environmental statement prepared by the applicant or appellant ... , any representations made by any body required by those Regulations to be invited to make representations or to be consulted and any representations duly made by any other person about the likely effects of the proposed development.'

Under reg. 4, planning permission is not to be granted for any development requiring environmental assessment unless the local planning authority and the Secretary of State or an Inspector, have first taken environmental information into account. In short, in the consideration of applications for planning permission involving sch. 1 or 2 development, environmental information is a material consideration.

It should be emphasised that neither United Kingdom law nor Community law requires a local planning authority or the Secretary of State to refuse planning permission for any project in respect of which there has been an environmental assessment. Environmental information is merely one of many considerations that an authority must take into account in determining an application. Furthermore, there is no direct provision in the law that ensures that the environmental impact of development requiring environmental assessment is properly considered though, since April 1994, the regulations have been amended to require a local planning authority, when notifying their decision to grant planning permission pursuant to a sch. 1 or sch. 2 application, to state in writing that they have taken into account 'environmental information'; and reg. 4(2) has always precluded any grant of planning permission unless the environmental information has been taken into account. In particular, it should be noted that a local planning authority is under no duty to provide any statement as to the weight it has given to environmental information; neither is it under any duty to give reasons for a decision to grant planning permission for development.

To improve the system it has been suggested that environmental assessment should take place at an earlier stage in the development process than at the application for planning permission stage and that the environmental effects of development subject to environmental assessment should be monitored against the results predicted by the assessment once the development has taken place.

12.4   Judicial challenge

The question of whether there has been compliance with the Environmental Assessment Regulations has been considered by the courts on a number of occasions, mostly in relation to the question of whether proposals 'in the pipeline' (that is, development proposals made before 15 July 1988 but approved thereafter) were subject to the Environmental Assessment Regulations. The most relevant decision on the application of the Regulations is *R v Swale Borough Council, ex parte the Royal Society for the Protection of Birds* [1991] JPL 39. The Royal Society had applied for judicial review of a grant of planning permission which had been issued by the Borough Council without any environmental assessment having been carried out. In rejecting the Royal Society's argument that the Town and Country Planning (Assessment of Environmental Effects) Regulations 1988 applied, Simon Brown J held that the decision whether any particular development was or was not within the scheduled descriptions was a matter exclusively for the planning authority, subject only to *Wednesbury* challenge. He considered that questions of classification were essentially questions of fact and degree, not of law; and that the court was not entitled upon judicial review to act effectively as an appeal court and to reach its own decision so as to ensure that EEC obligations were properly discharged. This subjective approach to the implementation of the regulations in the United Kingdom could well mean the European Community Directive being interpreted differently in different member States of the European Community.

Simon Brown J also concluded that the question of whether or not development was of a category described in either Schedule had to be answered strictly in relation to the development applied for, not for any development beyond that. But the further question arising in respect of Schedule 2 development, namely the question whether it 'would be likely to have significant effects on the environment by virtue of factors such as its nature, size or location', should be answered differently. He thought the proposed development should not then be considered in isolation if in reality it was properly to be regarded as an integral part of an inevitably substantial development. If this were otherwise, developers would be able to defeat the object of the regulations by piecemeal development proposals.

12.5 Statistics

Since environmental assessment was introduced in 1988, about 200 Environmental Statements a year have been submitted for projects requiring planning permission.

THIRTEEN
Conditions

Almost all planning permissions that are granted are granted subject to conditions. It often happens that the problem with decisions relating to land use is not over the question of whether the development should be permitted at all, but on what terms it should be permitted. Conditions may be imposed, therefore, not only to enhance the quality of the development but to ameliorate any adverse effects that might otherwise flow from the development. It is not uncommon, for example, for the grant of planning permission for mineral working to contain more than 50 conditions in order to achieve that purpose. Local planning authorities are often criticised for imposing unnecessary conditions, and it may be that a reported grant of a permission subject to a condition that 'before any of the dwellings are occupied a rear wheelbarrow access shall be provided for each dwelling without going through the dwelling', lends some credibility to that view. But this is a matter of administrative discretion, not of law. Section 70(1) of the 1990 Act provides that in dealing with an application for planning permission, a local planning authority:

(a) ... may grant planning permission, either unconditionally or subject to such conditions as they think fit; or

(b) ... may refuse planning permission.

In addition to the power to impose such conditions as the authority think fit and without prejudice to the generality of that power, the Act gives the authority power to impose a number of specific conditions on the grant of planning permission.

13.1 The general power

Although couched in the widest of all possible terms, the power to impose conditions is not unlimited.

In *Pyx Granite Co. Ltd* v *Ministry of Housing & Local Government* [1958] 1 QB 554 Lord Denning said at p. 572:

Although the planning authorities are given very wide powers to impose 'such conditions as they think fit', nevertheless the law says that those conditions, to be valid, must fairly and reasonably relate to the permitted development. The planning authority are not at liberty to use their powers for an ulterior object, however desirable that object may seem to them to be in the public interest.

The law was later restated in this form by the House of Lords in *Fawcett Properties Ltd* v *Buckingham County Council* [1961] AC 636.

In *Newbury District Council* v *Secretary of State for the Environment* [1981] AC 578, the House of Lords were required to consider again the validity of a condition imposed under the general power now given by s. 70(1) of the 1990 Act. According to their lordships, conditions must comply with the following tests:

(a)   They must be imposed for a planning purpose and not for an ulterior one.

(b)   They must fairly and reasonably relate to the development permitted.

(c)   They must not be so unreasonable that no reasonable authority could have imposed them.

13.1.1   Imposed for a planning purpose

Like all statutory powers, a power can only be exercised for the purpose for which it is given. Conditions which are imposed for some ulterior purpose, therefore, are not exercised within that power. One of the leading cases in this area is *R* v *Hillingdon London Borough Council (ex parte Royco Homes Ltd)* [1974] QB 720. Here the applicant was able to obtain an order of certiorari to quash a grant of planning permission which had been made subject to *ultra vires* conditions.

The planning permission in question had permitted the development of land for residential purposes. It had been granted subject to two conditions which had required that the dwellings approved by the permission be designed to conform to space and heating standards laid down by the Department of the Environment for local authority housing, and that they be constructed at a cost which did not exceed the relevant cost yardstick for such housing. A further two conditions required the dwellings be first occupied by persons on the housing waiting list of the authority, and that for a period of 10 years from the date of first occupation they be occupied as the residence of a person who occupied by virtue of a tenure which would not be excluded from the protection of the Rent Act 1968 by any provision of s. 2 of the Act. In the Queen's Bench Divisional Court, Lord Widgery CJ was in no doubt that the latter two conditions were *ultra vires* the authority and, although he considered that the first two conditions did not have a clear badge of *ultra vires* upon them, was unable to sever one set of conditions from the other because they had all been designed for a single purpose. Furthermore, he held that since the conditions were fundamental to the planning permission, the planning permission fell with the invalid conditions. Although the Lord Chief justice considered the conditions to be *ultra vires* because they were unreasonable, Bridge J based his finding of *ultra vires* upon improper motive, namely, the attempt by the authority to transfer on to the shoulders of the applicant a duty (of housing people in need) which Parliament had placed upon the authority as a housing authority.

In 1987, the London Borough of Brent sought to impose a condition in a planning permission for residential development which provided that '25 per cent of the units the construction of which is hereby permitted shall not, without the written consent of the council, be occupied for a period of 10 years from the date that they were first occupied, otherwise than by a tenant or tenants on a periodic tenancy'. The reason for the condition was expressed to be 'To ensure that new residential developments contribute to meeting the needs of the borough's residents for low-cost housing and to offset the decline in the level of rental housing in the borough'. In discharging the condition the Secretary of State considered that it did not serve a planning purpose, did not fairly relate to the permitted development and was an unreasonable interference with a landowner's normal rights. He also had serious doubts about its legality ([1988] JPL 222).

13.1.2   Fairly and reasonably relate to the permitted development

This test was first approved in *Pyx Granite Co. Ltd* v *Ministry of Housing & Local Government* [1958] 1 QB 554, where the courts had to consider the validity of conditions attached to grant of planning permission for quarrying for a limited period. The conditions in question limited the hours each day between which quarrying should be carried on, and required that all plant and machinery be removed from the site when no longer required and that the site be left in a tidy condition. The Court of Appeal, upholding the legality of the conditions, made it clear that they would have been quashed if they had not fairly and reasonably related to the development permitted. Although the case eventually reached the House of Lords, their Lordships held for the company on another ground, which relieved them of having to express an opinion on the validity of the conditions.

The principle was accepted by the House of Lords, however, in *Fawcett Properties Ltd* v *Buckingham County Council* [1961] AC 636. There, the local planning authority had granted planning permission for the erection of cottages in the green belt subject to a condition that 'the occupation of the houses shall be limited to persons whose employment or latest employment is or was employment in agriculture ... or in forestry, or in an industry mainly dependent upon agriculture and including also the dependants of such persons'. Fawcett Properties Ltd then purchased the properties and asked for a declaration that the condition was *ultra vires*. The House of Lords refused to grant the declaration, holding that the condition fairly and reasonably related to the permitted development.

In granting permission, the authority had recognised that agricultural workers need to live close to their place of work. The purpose of the authority in imposing the condition (now known as an agricultural occupancy condition) was to prevent the cottages being occupied by commuters, which would have infringed their policy of preserving green-belt land from development.

In *British Airports Authority* v *Secretary of State for Scotland* [1980] JPL 260, the Scottish Court of Session took the view that a condition attached to a grant of planning permission for development at Aberdeen Airport which restricted the hours between which aircraft might take off or land, fairly and reasonably related to the development permitted. A clear case where there was no connection between the condition and the development permitted was seen in *Newbury District Council* v *Secretary of State for the Environment* [1981] AC 578. There, planning permission had been granted for a period of 10 years for a change in the use of hangars previously used for the storage of civil defence vehicles, to use for the storage of synthetic rubber. The permission was subject to a condition that at the end of the 10 year period the hangars should be demolished. The House of Lords held the condition to be *ultra vires* as it did not fairly and reasonably relate to the development permitted. It is difficult to see how their lordships could have arrived at any other conclusion. The planning permission which was given related to the use of the property for a 10-year period. The requirement to demolish the hangars at the end of the period in no way restricted the quality or the nature of that use. The essential nexus between the permission without the condition and the condition was not just tenuous but non-existent.

13.1.3 Not be unreasonable
It will be recalled that in *R* v *Hillingdon London Borough Council (ex parte Royco Homes Ltd)* [1974] QB 720, the Lord Chief Justice considered that the imposition of conditions which gave to the occupiers of houses erected under a planning permission rights to security of tenure were *ultra vires* because they were unreasonable. A further example of a condition held to be void because it was unreasonable occurred in *Hall & Co. Ltd* v *Shoreham-by-Sea Urban District Council* [1964] 1 WLR 240. There, the company had been granted planning permission for industrial development subject to a condition requiring it to construct an ancillary road over the entire frontage of the site at its own expense and to give a right of passage over it to persons proceeding to and from adjoining properties. The Court of Appeal held the condition to be unreasonable because its effect was to require the company to construct and dedicate a public road at its own expense. A similar view was taken in *City of Bradford Metropolitan Council* v *Secretary of State for the Environment* [1986] JPL 598 where it was held that a condition which required a highway maintainable at public expense to be widened by the applicant was manifestly unreasonable and *ultra vires*.

It is now quite clear that a condition in a planning permission which requires the developer to carry out or fund a public function of a local planning authority as a price for getting that permission is unlawful. This is so, irrespective of whether the initiative for the imposition of the condition comes from the local planning authority or, as it did in *City of Bradford Metropolitan Council* v *Secretary of State for the Environment* from the applicant himself. In such circumstances, however, it may be possible for the applicant to fund that function by the parties entering into what is now known as a s. 106 obligation.

Another case which fell four-square within the situation considered in *Hall & Co. Ltd* v *Shoreham-by-Sea Urban District Council* was *M.J. Shanley Ltd* v

Secretary of State for the Environment [1982] JPL 380. Here, the company had proposed to the local planning authority that if it was granted planning permission for residential development for 10 acres of land in the green belt, it would lay out a further 40 acres of land for recreational purposes and then, having done so, would donate the 40 acres to the public as public open space. The proposal having met with a favourable response from the authority, the company proceeded to buy additional land, but was then surprised when the authority refused to grant the planning permission. The company appealed to the Secretary of State who, in upholding the authority's refusal, held that a condition requiring the provision of 40 acres of open space would be invalid and unenforceable. On a subsequent application by the company to quash the decision of the Secretary of State, Woolf J supported the view taken by the Secretary of State of the invalidity of the condition.

13.1.4 Other tests of the validity of conditions
Apart from the three tests laid down in *Newbury District Council* v *Secretary of State for the Environment* [1981] AC 578 for the validity of a condition, it seems that a condition may also be void because it is either uncertain or unenforceable. In addition, it was thought at one time that a condition could not take away existing use rights.

13.1.4.1 Uncertain conditions   A condition may be void for uncertainty if it can be given no meaning at all, or no sensible or ascertainable meaning. A condition which is merely ambiguous will not fail for uncertainty, though the courts may be required to resolve the ambiguity. In *Fawcett Properties Ltd* v *Buckingham County Council* [1961] AC 636, it was agreed that the condition limiting occupation of houses to workers (or the dependants of workers) in agriculture or forestry, or industries mainly dependant upon agriculture or forestry, could mean that a retired sheep farmer from New Zealand or a retired furrier from London would qualify, but not a telephone operator from Chalfont St Giles. The House of Lords held that in the context agriculture meant agriculture in the locality and so on, so that the condition was not void for uncertainty.

In *Alderson* v *Secretary of State for the Environment* [1984] JPL 429 the Court of Appeal applied *Fawcett Properties Ltd* v *Buckingham County Council* in reversing a decision of the High Court that a condition attached to a planning permission which limited the occupation of premises to persons employed locally in agriculture was void, because the word 'locally' had no ascertainable meaning. Although it was said on behalf of the respondents that some authorities preferred to spell out a precise boundary to the area in which the agriculture was being carried on, the court held that the word locally had a perfectly intelligible meaning even though some doubtful cases might arise.

In *David Lowe & Sons Ltd* v *Musselburgh Corporation* 1974 SLT 5, the Scottish Court of Session was required to construe a grant of planning permission for residential development of three agricultural sites subject to a condition that:

The sites are approved for the burgh's estimated future local authority and private housing needs over the next 20 years which cannot be accommodated within the existing burgh boundaries, in the proportion of one private house to four local authority houses.

Although one judge thought that it was a statement of the reason why planning permission was granted rather than a condition, the condition was held to be void on the ground that it was not capable of any certain or intelligible interpretation.

13.1.4.2 Unenforceable conditions There are a number of instances where the Secretary of State has discharged a condition in a planning permission on the ground that it is unenforceable. It seems that such a condition may also be invalid. In *British Airports Authority* v *Secretary of State for Scotland* [1980] JPL 260, a condition was imposed in the grant of permission for development at Aberdeen Airport concerning the flight path of aircraft taking off and landing at the airport. The condition was concerned with matters over which the applicants had no control, since statutory authority to prescribe the direction of flight or aircraft lies with the Civil Aviation Authority. Since there were no steps the applicants could take to secure the result required by the condition, the authority was held to have no power to impose it under the relevant statutory provisions.

13.1.4.3 Existing use rights At one time it was thought that a condition in a planning permission could not take away existing use rights. In *Allnatt London Properties Ltd* v *Middlesex County Council* (1964) 15 P & CR 288, planning permission had been granted for the demolition and replacement of industrial buildings forming part of a factory complex. The permission was granted subject to a condition that the replacement buildings were to be used only in conjunction with the main factory and, for the first 10 years, only by persons or firms who at the date of the permission occupied industrial premises in Middlesex. The purpose of the condition was to restrain any further influx of industrial development into the county without inhibiting the rebuilding of existing industrial premises. The effect of the condition, however, was to restrict for 10 years the number of potential purchasers of the company's property. Glyn-Jones J held that the condition was void. The company had a right to continue with the existing use of the factory complex and that right could not be taken away without compensation.

It was perhaps unfortunate that no appeal was made from this decision. A planning permission granted without conditions would also, if implemented, take away existing use rights without compensation. The owner would have the option not to implement the permission and to retain existing use rights, or to do so and lose them. Logically, it should make no difference where the planning permission has a condition attached to it.

The authority of *Allnatt London Properties Ltd* v *Middlesex County Council* was not to last too long. In *Kingston-upon-Thames Royal London Borough Council* v *Secretary of State for the Environment* [1973] 1 WLR 1549, planning permission had been granted to rebuild a station subject to a condition that land to the south of the station should be used for car-parking. When the condition was not complied with the authority served an enforcement notice. On appeal, the Secretary of State discharged the condition, because the land was being used to carry the electric traction cable and, on the authority of *Allnatt London Properties Ltd* v *Middlesex County Council,* that right could not be taken away without compensation. The local planning authority then sought to challenge the Secretary of State's decision. The Divisional Court allowed the appeal and returned the case to the Secretary of State for reconsideration. In considering *Allnatt London Properties Ltd* v *Middlesex County Council,* Lord Widgery CJ considered it correctly decided but for the wrong reason. The defect in the condition was that it did not reasonably relate to the development permitted. Bridge J, on the other hand, considered the decision to be wrong. He referred to the power of the local planning authority to regulate the use of land other than land in respect of that for which planning permission is granted, the exercise of which must encroach on the existing use rights of that other land. So long as a condition in a planning permission fairly and reasonably relates to the development permitted, the effect on existing use rights in no way affects its validity.

Reaffirmation of the principle was given in *Peak Park Joint Planning Board* v *Secretary of State for the Environment* [1980] JPL 114 where, after calling in an application for development for his own decision, the Secretary of State granted planning permission for the development but refused to impose certain conditions (as sought by the authority) on the ground that they would have affected existing use rights and were *ultra vires.* On a challenge to that decision, Sir Douglas Frank QC, sitting as a Deputy High Court judge, held that the Secretary of State was wrong to hold that the conditions would be *ultra vires* because they derogated from existing use rights and remitted the matter back to him for further consideration.

13.2 Specific powers to impose conditions

Although specific powers to impose conditions are also given to local planning authorities, it seems that their use should be subject to the same limitations as is the use of the general power, namely, that they must be imposed for a planning purpose, be fairly and reasonably related to the permitted development and not be manifestly unreasonable. The following specific powers are given to authorities.

13.2.1 Regulating other land

Section 72(1)(a) of the 1990 Act provides that a condition may be imposed on the grant of planning permission:

> for regulating the development or use of any land under the control of the applicant (whether or not it is land in respect of which the application was made) or requiring the carrying out of works on any such land, so far as appears to the local planning authority to be expedient for the purposes of or in connection with the development authorised by the permission.

An example of its use would be where an owner of land applies for planning permission to erect a dwellinghouse with cesspit arrangements for the disposal of sewage. The authority may grant permission subject to a condition that the owner lays a sewer under adjoining land in his control to connect the dwellinghouse to the public sewer system. For the condition to be imposed, the land must be under the 'control' of the applicant. This requirement does not necessarily require the applicant to own an estate or interest in the land. In *George Wimpey & Co. Ltd* v *New Forest District Council* [1979] JPL 313, Sir Douglas Frank QC held that the question of whether land was in the applicant's control became a question of fact and degree for the Secretary of State and depended upon whether the control was of a degree and kind sufficient to satisfy him that the condition could be complied with.

If the land over which the condition is to be imposed is not under the control of the applicant, it may be possible to impose the same conditions under the general power in s. 70(1). In *Atkinson* v *Secretary of State for the Environment* [1983] JPL 599, planning permission had been granted for the erection of dwellinghouses on agricultural land subject to a condition that outbuildings should be demolished and that the road access to the site be widened. The appellants agreed that the condition could not properly be imposed under what is now s. 72(l)(a), because at that time the relevant land was not under the control of the developer. The Secretary of State, on the other hand, argued that the general power to impose conditions provided the authority with the power to do what they had done. In the Queen's Bench Division, Woolf J held that the authority did have that power. Some concern was expressed, however, that if the condition was not complied with it would be unreasonable to enforce the condition against a wholly innocent neighbouring landowner. Prudence required, therefore, that where there was a danger of a developer not being in control of all the land subject to the planning permission, the condition should make it clear that, before the benefit of the planning permission could be obtained, the developer must have actually secured his ability to comply with the condition himself. So, for example, where planning permission is granted for residential development subject to a condition that access be provided over land which is owned by a neighbour, the condition should specify that the construction of the houses should not commence until after the access has been constructed.

In a Ministerial decision in 1988, the Secretary of State in an appeal against an enforcement notice, considered *ultra vires* on the grounds of unreasonableness a condition in a grant of planning permission for a change of use of three floors of the old Derry and Toms building in Kensington High Street, London, from 'retail use' to 'use for exhibition purposes and ancillary restaurant'. The condition required that 'The loading or unloading of vehicles visiting the premises, including those delivering fuel, shall not be carried out otherwise than from within the curtilage of the building'. The Secretary of State considered that the condition was dependant upon the action of others, such as the police or the highways authority, and since it purported to regulate use of the public highway, was unreasonable.

13.2.2   *Grampian*-type conditions

The ability of a local planning authority to impose conditions under the general power to do so, over land not under the control of the applicant was again raised in *Grampian Regional Council* v *City of Aberdeen District Council* (1984) 47 P & CR 633. In this case planning permission had been made for a change of use of land from agricultural use to industrial use. The applicants had appealed to the Secretary of State for Scotland against non-determination of the application within the statutory time-limit, and he had delegated the determination of the appeals to a reporter (Inspector) who took the view that traffic to and from the site would constitute such a hazard as to justify the refusal of planning permission. He considered that the hazard would be removed if an existing road could be closed, but concluded that it would not be competent to grant planning permission subject to a condition requiring the closure of the road since it did not lie wholly within the power of the first respondents to secure the closure, any closure order that they might make requiring confir-mation by the Secretary of State under s. 198(1) of the Town and Country Planning (Scotland) Act 1972, which would not necessarily be granted. He accordingly dismissed the appeals. The First Division of the Inner House of the Court of Session allowed an appeal by the first respondents, holding that, while a condition requiring something to be done that was not within the control of the first respondents would be incompetent, a condition requiring that no development be commenced until the road had been closed would be competent. The appellants appealed, contending that the imposition on the grant of planning permission of any negative condition related to the occurrence of an uncertain event was unreasonable and, therefore, invalid and that in any event it was undesirable that there should be prolonged uncertainty as to whether the development would be able to go forward or not.

In dismissing the appeal the House of Lords held that there was a crucial difference between a positive and a negative type of condition in that the latter was enforceable while the former was not; that the reasonableness of any condition had to be considered in the light of the circumstances of the case and that in the present case, where the proposals for development had been found by the reporter to be generally desirable in the public interest, it would have been not only not unreasonable but highly appropriate to grant planning permission subject to the condition in question; that, moreover, it was impossible to view such a condition as unreasonable and not within the scope of s. 26(1) of the Town and Country Planning (Scotland) Act 1972 if regard was had to s. 198(1), from which it was reasonable to infer that it was precisely that type of condition that had been envisaged by the legislature when enacting s. 26(1). (Note that ss. 26(1) and 198(1) of the Scottish Act are identical to ss. 29(1) and 209(1) of the Town and Country Planning Act 1971, now ss. 70(1) and 247(1) of the 1990 Act.)

Since the *Grampian* case, the imposition of negative conditions (known colloquially as *Grampian*-type conditions) has risen in popularity, particularly with regard to highway works necessary on other land before any development on the application land can begin. Their utility, however, is restricted by the advice contained in Appendix A to PPG 13: *Highways Considerations in Development Control* that such conditions should not be imposed where such

works are unlikely to be done within a reasonable period, usually five years —
the normal lifetime of a planning permission.

In *Jones* v *Secretary of State for Wales* (1990) 88 LGR 942, the Court of Appeal
upheld the advice in PPG 13, holding that it was unlawful for a local planning
authority to grant planning permission subject to a condition which prevented
development until some obstacle had been removed, unless there was a
reasonable prospect of that obstacle being removed. The decision was
purportedly based on the *Grampian* case, where it was said that the question
whether a condition was unreasonable depended upon the circumstances of the
case.

In *British Railways Board* v *Secretary of State for the Environment* [1994] JPL 32,
however, the House of Lords held that the mere fact that a desirable condition
appeared to have no reasonable prospects of fulfilment did not mean that
planning permission ought necessarily to be refused. Their lordships went on to
hold that *Jones* v *Secretary of State for Wales* was wrongly decided. According to
their Lordships the owner of the land to which the application relates may object
to the grant of planning permission for reasons which may or may not be sound
on planning grounds. If the owner's reasons are sound on planning grounds
then no doubt the application will be refused. But if they are unsound, the mere
fact that the owner objects and is unwilling that the development should go
ahead cannot in itself necessarily lead to a refusal. The function of the planning
authority is to decide whether or not the proposed development is desirable in
the public interest. The answer to that question is not to be affected by the
consideration that the owner of the land is determined not to allow the
development so that permission for it, if granted, would not have reasonable
prospects of being implemented. That does not mean that the planning
authority, if it decides that the proposed development is in the public interest, is
absolutely disentitled from taking into account the improbability of permission
for it, if granted, being implemented. For example, if there were a competition
between two alternative sites for a desirable development, difficulties of bringing
about implementation on one site which were not present in relation to the other
might very properly lead to the refusal of planning permission for the site
affected by the difficulties and the grant of it for the other. But there is no
absolute rule that the existence of difficulties, even if apparently insuperable,
must necessarily lead to refusal of planning permission for a desirable
development. A would-be developer may be faced with difficulties of many
different kinds in the way of site assembly or securing the discharge of restrictive
covenants. If he considers that it is in his interests to secure planning permission
notwithstanding the existence of such difficulties, it is not for the planning
authority to refuse it simply on their view of how serious the difficulties are.

13.2.3   Limiting the life of the permission
Section 72(1)(b) of the 1990 Act provides that a condition may be imposed
on the grant of planning permission:

> for requiring the removal of any buildings or works authorised by the
> permission, or the discontinuance of any use of land so authorised, at the end

of a specified period, and the carrying out of any works required for the reinstatement of land at the end of that period.

This kind of planning permission is called a 'term consent' or 'a permission granted for a limited period'. It was this kind of condition that was successfully challenged in *Newbury District Council* v *Secretary of State for the Environment* [1981] AC 578. It has several advantages in practice. First, where land is awaiting redevelopment, planning permission can be granted for a limited period for development which would not otherwise be allowed, such as for a charity shop in an area zoned for residential development. In such cases, the temporary permission is normally sought by the applicant himself. Secondly, where there have been strong objections to proposed development, the term consent enables the parties to 'have a trial run', so that it becomes clear during the currency of the term whether or not the objections made were well founded. If not, at the end of the term, another planning permission without a similar condition can be granted.

A somewhat unusual example of such a condition being imposed occurred in 1994, when consent (for three years) was granted for the retention of a fibreglass fish attached to the side extension of a dwellinghouse on land in Norbury, London SW16. The local planning authority had served an enforce-ment notice requiring its removal on the ground that its presence was detrimental to the amenities of nearby residents. It appeared that the fibreglass fish was a reproduction of a marlin caught by the appellant in the Pacific Ocean, and he wished to retain it as a work of art commemorating this achievement. The appellant had earlier attracted some notoriety by placing at various times on or near the appeal site, a military tank, a self-propelled gun, a large replica Spitfire and an assortment of smaller items, some lit up at night. All had attracted traffic and activity and media attention to the site.

In dealing with the planning merits of the case, the Inspector concluded that the presence of unauthorised developments at the appeal site, including the fish, had caused demonstrable harm to residential amenity and traffic safety in the area. He felt, however, that there was insufficient evidence available for him to come to a proper view of the extent to which that harm was attributable to the presence of the fish and to assess the future impact of the fish alone. In the circumstances, he decided to grant planning permission for the fish on a temporary basis, thus giving a proper opportunity for the impact of the fish alone to be tested.

Subsequently the local planning authority were to seek a 'planning injunc-tion' against the occupier requiring him, *inter alia*, to remove the replica Spitfire. This was the subject of further proceedings in *Croydon London Borough Council* v *Gladden* [1994] JPL 723 (see Chapter 18).

Where a term consent has been granted, planning permission is not normally required to revert to the previous use. Section 57(2) of the 1990 Act deals with the right to revert in these terms.

Where planning permission to develop land has been granted for a limited period, planning permission is not required for the resumption, at the end of that period, of its use for the purpose for which it was normally used before the permission was granted.

The effect of these provisions was considered in *Smith v Secretary of State for the Environment* [1983] JPL 462. It is clear that if a landowner has been granted a term consent no planning permission is required to return to the last normal use of the land. If the landowner has been granted a succession of term consents (as sometimes happens when redevelopment of land is delayed), the right is to return to the last normal use of the land before the first term consent was implemented. But the provision requires no account to be taken of any use of land begun in contravention of planning control. So if a term consent has been granted to change from a use of land which was begun in contravention of planning control, the owner cannot under the section revert to that use at the end of the term, nor can he revert to any earlier use of the land, without a grant of planning permission.

13.2.4 Requiring the development to be commenced
Section 72(3) of the 1990 Act provides that where:

(a) planning permission is granted for development consisting of or including the carrying out of building or other operations subject to a condition that the operations shall be commenced not later than a time specified in the condition; and

(b) any building or other operations are commenced after the time so specified,

the commencement and carrying out of those operations do not constitute development for which that permission was granted.

It should be noted that the provision only applies to building or other operations. Furthermore, the provision is concerned with the commencement of such development, not its completion.

In practice little use has ever been made of this statutory power. Since 1968 its purpose has been met by new mandatory conditions relating to the commencement and completion of development which have been imposed in most planning permissions granted since April 1969. These provisions are now to be found in ss. 91 to 95 of the 1990 Act, to which reference is made later.

13.2.5 Limiting the benefit to a particular person
It may sometimes be appropriate to confine the benefit of a planning permission to a particular person. The power to do so derives from the wording of s. 75(1) of the 1990 Act which provides:

Without prejudice to the provisions of this Part [of the 1990 Act] as to the duration, revocation or modification of planning permission, any grant of planning permission to develop land shall (except in so far as the permission otherwise provides) enure for the benefit of the land and of all persons for the time being interested in it.

Personal planning permissions are comparatively rare, because if it is thought desirable to avoid a perpetuation of a use of land, a term consent can best achieve that purpose. The power is a statutory recognition, however, that planning permission may be granted in circumstances where permission would otherwise be refused. A personal planning permission may sometimes be granted on hardship grounds, and may sometimes be linked to a term consent.

Sometimes a personal planning permission may result from service of an enforcement notice issued by the local planning authority. A recent case concerned contravening development of an industrial nature located in a rural area. In quashing the enforcement notice the Secretary of State granted a temporary and personal planning permission for a period of two years for the contravening development in order to allow the owner to search for an alternative location for his business during that period.

13.2.6 Specifying the use to which a building may be put

Mention has previously been made of s. 75(2) and (3) of the 1990 Act which provides that:

(2) Where planning permission is granted for the erection of a building, the grant of permission may specify the purposes for which the building may be used.

(3) If no purpose is so specified, the permission shall be construed as including permission to use the building for the purpose for which it is designed.

13.3 Effect of an invalid condition

Where a condition is held to be invalid, the question arises whether the condition can be severed from the planning permission so that the permission survives shorn of its invalidity, or whether the condition cannot be severed so that the whole planning permission is void *ab initio*.

In *Hall & Co. Ltd* v *Shoreham-by-Sea Urban District Council* [1964] 1 WLR 240, a condition which required the company effectively to dedicate a road to the public at the company's expense was held to be invalid. The local planning authority had argued that if the condition was void, then the whole planning permission was a nullity. The Court of Appeal was persuaded by that argument because the invalid condition was fundamental to the whole of the planning permission. The suggestion in this and later cases was that if the invalid condition was incidental or trivial then it could be severed from the permission; if it were fundamental then the whole permission fell.

In *Allnatt London Properties Ltd* v *Middlesex County Council* (1964) 15 P & CR 288, a condition was held to be void because it took away existing use rights. In argument, the local planning authority were unable to give any grounds on which a reasonable planning authority could have refused planning permission assuming the condition to be void. Not surprisingly, therefore, the court held that the permission could stand free of the condition. The condition impugned was clearly not one which was fundamental to the permission.

The trivial/fundamental dichotomy was eventually supported by the House of Lords in *Kent County Council* v *Kingsway Investments (Kent) Ltd* [1971] AC 72. Here the House of Lords held that conditions in an outline planning permission requiring details of proposals to be submitted to and approved by the authority before any work began and that the permission should cease to have effect after the expiration of three years unless within that time notice of approval of the detailed proposals had been given were valid. Their lordships went on, however, to consider the position if they had found otherwise. According to their lordships, if the invalid conditions are unimportant, incidental or merely superimposed on the permission, then the permission might endure. If the conditions are part of the structure of the permission, then the permission falls with it.

In *R* v *St Edmundsbury Borough Council (ex parte Investors in Industry Commercial Properties Ltd)* [1985] 1 WLR 1168 it was said *(obiter)* that if a condition requiring the developer of a superstore to provide three independent retail units was invalid, it could be severed from the permission.

One of the difficulties faced by landowners in the past seeking to challenge a condition is uncertainty whether the courts would hold the condition to be trivial or fundamental. The risk in challenging was that success might lead to loss of the whole planning permission. Now, due to a provision introduced originally by the Housing and Planning Act 1986, it may be possible to avoid that risk. Under what is now s. 73 of the 1990 Act an application may be made to the local planning authority for the development of land without complying with conditions subject to which a planning permission was granted. On an application the authority must only consider the question of the conditions, and they may decide that the permission shall be subject to the same conditions as were previously imposed, that the permission should be granted subject to different conditions, or that permission should be granted unconditionally. There is a right of appeal to the Secretary of State and a right of challenge in the normal way to the courts on a point of law. Jurisdiction in all cases is limited to the conditions and decisions relating to those conditions. The new provisions may mean that if the procedure is used to appeal against a condition on the ground that it is invalid and that ground finds favour with the courts then, however fundamental the condition, only the condition will be struck down, leaving the permission to survive shorn of the invalidity.

It should also be noted that s. 73A of the 1990 Act provides for an application to be made to a local planning authority for planning permission for development which has already been carried out. This procedure applies not only to development carried out without planning permission, but to development carried out without complying with some condition subject to which planning permission was granted. It would seem that a developer must implement the permission and breach the condition before making an application under the section.

13.4 Duration of planning permissions

Prior to 1969, one of the risks a local planning authority faced in granting planning permission was that the permission might never be implemented.

This could be important in practice where development had to be restricted because of inadequate infrastructure. For example, a planning permission given to A (but not implemented) might prevent planning permission being given later to B because the existing infrastructure might not support both developments. In 1968, power was given to local planning authorities to impose conditions which it was thought would alleviate that problem. The statutory provisions are now to be found in the 1990 Act.

13.4.1 Full planning permissions

Section 91 of the 1990 Act provides that every planning permission granted, or deemed to be granted, shall be subject to the condition that the development to which it relates must be begun not later than the expiration of:

(a)   five years beginning with the date on which the permission is granted or ... deemed to be granted; or

(b)   such other period (whether longer or shorter) beginning with that date as the authority concerned with the terms of planning permission may direct.

The period mentioned in (b) above is to be the period which the authority consider appropriate having regard to the provisions of the development plan and to any other material considerations.

The section further provides that if planning permission is granted without such a condition, it shall be deemed to have been granted subject to the condition in paragraph (a) above. The above provisions do not, for reasons which are in most cases self-evident, apply to:

(a)   any planning permission granted by a development order;

(b)   any planning permission granted under s. 73A for development carried out before the making of an application;

(c)   any planning permission granted for a limited period;

(d)   any planning permission granted for the winning and working of minerals (which is subject to special provisions relating to the commencement of the development);

(e)   any planning permission granted by an enterprise zone scheme;

(f)   any planning permission granted by a simplified planning zone scheme;

(g)   any outline planning permission (which is subject to special rules).

It should be noted that the standard five-year period may be varied at the discretion of the local planning authority or on appeal by the Secretary of State. This power to vary may be useful where it is desired to phase the commencement of large-scale development over a prolonged period of time.

The existence of time-limits with which development must be begun imposes pressure on the developer to do so, since s. 93(4) provides that development carried out after the date by which the condition requires it to be carried out shall be treated as not authorised by the permission. In other words, if the condition is not complied with, the benefit of the permission will be lost.

This may be of little consequence to the landowner, who may reapply for planning permission which, if granted, will contain a like condition. The problem arises, however, where there has been a change in planning policy by the local planning authority since the first grant of permission, which results in the renewal application being refused. In such a case land which had a value which reflected the right to develop will no longer have that value. It will often be important, therefore, to ensure that development is begun by the date specified in the condition. If it is, then the planning permission will be kept alive. If not, then the permission will be lost.

Section 56 of the 1990 Act prescribes the activities that constitute compliance with the requirement that the development should be begun. It provides that development shall be taken to be begun on the earliest date on which any 'material operation' (previously called a 'specified operation') comprised in the development begins to be carried out. 'Material operation' is defined in s. 56(4) to mean:

(a) any work of construction in the course of the erection of a building;

(b) the digging of a trench which is to contain the foundations, or part of the foundations, of a building;

(c) the laying of any underground main or pipe to the foundations, or part of the foundations, of a building or to any such trench as is mentioned in paragraph (b);

(d) any operation in the course of laying out or constructing a road or part of a road;

(e) any change in the use of any land which constitutes material development.

In the context of paragraph (e), material development means any development other than:

(a) development for which planning permission is granted by a general development order for the time being in force and which is carried out so as to comply with any condition or limitation subject to which planning permission is so granted;

(b) development falling within any of paragraphs 1, 2, 3 and 5 to 8 of schedule 3 . . .; and

(c) development of any class prescribed for the purposes of this subsection.

It is clear that great care must be taken to ensure compliance with the section.

In *High Peak Borough Council* v *Secretary of State for the Environment* [1981] JPL 366, Courtdale Developments Ltd wished to exploit a planning permission with a five-year time-limit, and so, within that time, the company arranged for a mechanical digger to dig a trench of the requisite width and depth to contain foundations. It had then proceeded to fill in the trench with the earth which had been excavated. The trench had been dug in order to keep the planning permission alive but back-filled to prevent animals and children falling into it. The Queen's Bench Divisional Court held that the company's action in digging the trench was an operation under what is now s. 56(4) of the 1990 Act so that the permission had not expired.

In *South Oxfordshire District Council* v *Secretary of State for the Environment* [1981] JPL 359 trenches had been dug which appeared to fulfill the requirements of what is now s. 56(4), but they had not been dug for the development to which the planning permission related. Accordingly, the Secretary of State did not consider that that was sufficient to comply with the provisions, a conclusion which Woolf J was prepared to accept.

In *Malvern Hills District Council* v *Secretary of State for the Environment* [1982] JPL 439, an enforcement notice had been served by the local planning authority on a company alleging a breach of planning control. The Court of Appeal was required to decide whether or not marking out with pegs the line of part of a proposed road constituted a 'specified operation'. If it did do so, the planning permission was still alive and there would be no breach. A divided court held that the work was a specified operation and found that, contrary to the view of the authority, the Secretary of State had not erred in law in so finding.

In this case the company had always believed that the condition which required the development to be begun by a set date had been complied with and so proposed to continue with the development despite its dispute with the authority. The local planning authority, who thought otherwise, had not only served an enforcement notice on the company requiring the cessation of all construction work on the site, but also a related stop notice. Now, under s. 186 of the 1990 Act, compensation is payable for loss suffered due to the service of a stop notice if it is quashed on the ground that the matters alleged in the enforcement notice do not constitute a breach of planning control. Following a dispute over the amount of the company's loss, compensation was eventually determined by the Lands Tribunal, which awarded the company £42,562.

In *Hillingdon London Borough Council* v *Secretary of State for the Environment* [1990] JPL 575, the High Court held that in considering whether a planning permission had been kept alive by the carrying out of what is now called a 'material operation', the test to be applied was not simply whether the developer had intended to keep the planning permission alive, but whether he had intended to carry on with the development. An earnest of intention to develop is what is required.

The facts were that in 1982 the second respondents were granted outline planning permission to construct an hotel in West Drayton. By reason of the approval of the reserved matters in July 1985, the development had to commence before 19 July 1987, the date when the planning permission expired. Prior to that date the second respondents caused top soil to be removed from the site and an area to be laid with hardcore. The appellant council issued an enforcement notice alleging a breach of planning control and, following an appeal against that notice, the Secretary of State for the Environment, by a decision of an Inspector, allowed the appeal, deciding that the works carried out were 'material operations'.

The council appealed, contending that the second respondents carried out the works merely to keep the planning permission alive and had no genuine intention of carrying through the development; that the works were not works that were part of the development permitted by the planning permission; and as there was no genuine intention to carry through the development, the works carried out were a 'colourable' operation and there was no unequivocal intention to carry through the development to completion.

Macpherson J held that on the evidence the Inspector was entitled to find that the works carried out were 'material operations.' There was also no flaw in the Inspector's conclusions that whilst the second respondents were not fully committed to the development for which planning permission had been granted, it could nevertheless not be said that development would not go ahead. The work, therefore, was not colourable in the manner claimed by the authority.

Unhappiness with the state of the law once led the government to propose amending the law to re-define 'commencement of development'. Under the proposal it was to become necessary for developers to have completed work to the value of 10 per cent of the total cost of the development as at the expiry of the time limit for commencement in order to keep a planning permission alive. This proposal has now been abandoned

13.4.2 Outline planning permissions
The provisions relating to the duration of planning permission are slightly modified with regard to outline planning permission. Section 92 of the 1990 Act provides that where outline planning permission is granted for development consisting in or including the carrying out of building, or other operations, it shall be granted subject to conditions:

(a) that, in the case of any reserved matter, application for approval must be made not later than the expiration of three years beginning with the date of the grant of outline planning permission; and
(b) that the development to which the permission relates must be begun not later than —

(i) the expiration of five years from the date of the grant of outline planning permission; or
(ii) if later, the expiration of two years from the final approval of the reserved matters or, in the case of approval on different dates, the final approval of the last such matter to be approved.

Once again, the standard periods of three, five and two years mentioned in the section may be varied at the discretion of the local planning authority or, on appeal, by the Secretary of State.

It is important to remember that in order to keep the planning permission alive, the final approval of reserved matters, whether given by the local planning authority or by the Secretary of State on appeal, must result from an application for approval made to the authority within three years from the date of the grant of outline planning permission. If a landowner applies within the three year period for approval of reserved matters and approval is not given, he cannot submit a further application for approval of reserved matters, unless that too is submitted within three years of the date of the grant of the outline permission. A landowner can submit more than one application for approval of reserved matters within that three-year period, and as long as one of those applications is approved (even if after the three years has expired) the planning permission will survive to the next stage. Then, so long as the landowner carries out a material operation within five years of the grant of outline permission or two years from final approval of reserved matters, whichever is the later, the planning permission will have been kept alive once again.

It should be noted too, that a landowner may wish to submit a series of applications, each for the approval of specific reserved matters. For example, he may wish to obtain approval of matters relating to layout, siting, design and external appearance before he is able to apply for the approval of matters relating to landscaping. All such applications, however, should be made within the specified three-year period.

It seems, however, as a result of a decision of the High Court in *R* v *Secretary of State for the Environment (ex parte Corby Borough Council)* [1994] JPL B86, that a developer can apply to the local planning authority under s. 73 of the 1990 Act for an amendment to the conditions imposed on the grant of outline planning permission with regard to time-limits for the submission of details of reserved matters and for the commencement of the development even after the date for submission of an application for approval of reserved matters has passed. The only limitation on this is imposed by s. 73(4), the effect of which is that s. 73 does not apply where planning permission was granted subject to a condition relating to the commencement of the development and the development has been begun.

13.4.3   Completion notices

The provisions considered so far operate to secure that, as far as possible, development is begun within the period stipulated in the permission. The provisions do not secure that the development once begun will actually be completed. Accordingly, s. 94 of the 1990 Act provides that if the local planning authority are of opinion that the development will not be completed within a reasonable period, they may serve a completion notice on the owner and occupier of the land and any other person who in the opinion of the local planning authority will be affected by the notice, stating that the planning permission will cease to have effect at the expiration of a further period (being not less than 12 months) after the notice takes effect. A completion notice will only take effect after confirmation by the Secretary of State who, before confirming the notice, must give a person on whom the completion notice was served and the authority, an opportunity of appearing before, and being heard by, an Inspector appointed for that purpose.

Section 94(4) provides that if a completion notice takes effect, the planning permission referred to in it shall become invalid at the expiration of the period specified in the notice. Section 95(5) then goes on to provide that the previous sub-section shall not affect any permission so far as development carried out under it before the end of the period mentioned in that subsection is concerned.

Now, since planning permission is granted for development and not for a series of stages in the development process, that provision appears to mean that once a completion notice has taken effect, any act of development which has taken place in the process of partially implementing the permission will be development undertaken without planning permission, and thus be liable to enforcement notice procedure. So if, for example, planning permission has been granted for the erection of a two-storey building and only the ground floor has been built by the time a completion notice takes effect, no planning permission would exist for the single-storey building. It would be otherwise, however, if, as happened in another context in the case of *F. Lucas & Sons Ltd v Dorking & Horley Rural District Council* (1964) 62 LGR 491, a grant of planning permission for the erection of a number of houses could be constructed as a grant of a number of mini-planning permissions, each of which authorised the construction of an individual house.

This view of the law appears to be supported by the Ministerial Decision quoted at [1985] JPL 496, where the Secretary of State upheld an enforcement notice requiring the removal of an uncompleted building erected pursuant to a planning permission for the building which had ceased to have effect as a result of the coming into effect of a completion notice.

FOURTEEN

The construction, scope, effect and life of a planning permission

14.1 Construction of a planning permission

Doubts sometimes arise about the precise construction of a grant of planning permission. The construction will occasionally involve looking not only at the notification of the decision but also behind the notification at the application for planning permission.

The rule established by the courts is that if the planning permission is on the face of it a complete and self-contained document, not incorporating by reference any other document, the planning permission will stand on its own. If, on the other hand, the planning permission incorporates other documents such as the application for planning permission, then those documents must be taken into account in construing the permission.

In *Miller-Mead* v *Minister of Housing & Local Government* [1963] 2 QB 196, the Court of Appeal held that a planning permission runs with the land and cannot be cut down by reference to the application pursuant to which it was granted. The reason for the court taking that view was that the permission may come into the hands of people who have never seen the application and who must, therefore, rely on the actual words used in the grant. The decision ignored the fact that applications for planning permission (and also the grant) must be entered by the local planning authority in a planning register which is available for public inspection at all reasonable times.

Although ideally an applicant for planning permission should be able to see the precise terms of the permission from the permission itself (i.e. the notification of the decision to grant), the decision in *Miller-Mead* v *Minister of Housing & Local Government* created difficulties for the many local planning authorities who expressly link the grant of permission to the application to which it relates. Indeed, six weeks later, in *Wilson* v *West Sussex County Council* [1963] 2 QB 764, the Court of Appeal had to consider a grant of planning permission which said: 'The council hereby permit the following development, that is to say . . . in accordance with the plan and application No. . . . submitted to the council on . . .'.

Although the court thought that the incorporation of the 'relevant correspondence' into the permission was a very unfortunate practice, it held that where the permission specifically incorporates the terms of the application for planning permission, it was proper, and indeed necessary, to refer to the terms of the application in construing the permission.

A few years later, in *Slough Estates Ltd v Slough Borough Council (No. 2)* [1971] AC 958, the House of Lords confirmed the later view of the Court of Appeal that it was proper to look at the application if it were incorporated in the permission itself.

In *Manning v Secretary of State for the Environment* [1976] JPL 634, planning permission had been granted for a limited period for the erection of a riding school, to be used by a private riding school together with disabled riders. The reason for the grant of the permission was that it would enable facilities for disabled riders to be provided. Later, towards the end of that period, an application was made for the renewal of the permission. The permission, when granted, referred to 'continued use of indoor riding school'. A dispute then arose over whether the later permission was to be construed as widely as the first and include the use, not only for the disabled but for the general riding school as well, or whether (as the local planning authority had maintained) the use was limited to disabled persons only. The plaintiff, contending that it was not so limited, obtained a declaration to that effect in the High Court. The Court of Appeal, upholding the decision of the High Court, held that in this case it was relevant not only to look at the planning permission, but also at the previous history, the previous application and the previous permission.

Although it is better to restrict the scope of this decision to the interpretation of 'renewal applications', it is significant that Stephenson LJ thought that because documents such as applications for and grants of permission were rarely drafted by lawyers, they should in his view 'be given a tolerant view'.

It also seems that, unless incorporated in the permission, it is not permissible to look at the resolution of the authority, or of the appropriate committee of the authority, in order to construe the permission. In *R v West Oxfordshire District Council (ex parte Pearce Homes Ltd)* [1986] JPL 523 the planning committee of the authority adopted a resolution that planning permission be granted subject to the execution of an agreement under what is now s. 106 of the 1990 Act. Details of the resolution were then notified to the applicants by letter. Subsequently, the applicants were refused permission for the development on the ground that the site had now been scheduled by the Secretary of State under the Ancient Monuments and Archaeological Areas Act 1979. In an application for judicial review of the authority's decision to refuse planning permission, the company alleged that the resolution had the effect of granting the planning permission it was seeking, or alternatively that if it did not then permission had been granted by the subsequent letter.

Refusing the application, Woolf J held that, ordinarily, to decide what planning permission had been granted, all it was necessary to do was to look at the actual notification of the decision. Normally one could not look at the resolution except to determine other issues, such as whether or not an officer had authority to notify the grant of planning permission. His lordship went on to hold that the letter subsequent to the resolution did not amount to a grant of planning permission. It had simply anticipated that a grant would be made once an agreement had been completed.

In *Wivenhoe Port Ltd* v *Colchester Borough Council* [1985] JPL 396, the Court of Appeal favoured the view that, if it were necessary to do so, it was appropriate to look at the application *as an aid* to the construction of a planning permission. The reason for this approach was the recognition that a grant of planning permission is made in response to an application, and that the permission granted cannot purport to grant something outside the terms of the application.

In later cases, *Oakimber Ltd* v *Elmbridge Borough Council* (1991) 62 P & CR 594 and *Staffordshire Moorlands District Council* v *Cartwright* (1991) 63 P & CR 285, the Court of Appeal held that the terms of a planning permission had to be construed in the factual context of the application on which it was based. More recently, in *R* v *Secretary of State for the Environment (ex parte Slough Borough Council)* [1994] EGCS 67, Schiemann J considered that there was a strong public interest in the court taking a grant of planning permission as granting what it purported to grant, though where the permission was not prima facie clear, or where an application was expressly incorporated in the permission, different considerations arose. The mere recital of the application number at the top of the permission did not incorporate the application into the planning permission.

14.2 Scope of a planning permission

Although, as stated, the grant of planning permission cannot purport to grant something outside the terms of the application, this does not mean that the grant must replicate precisely what has been applied for.

In *Bernard Wheatcroft Ltd* v *Secretary of State for the Environment* [1982] JPL 37 an application for planning permission had been made for 'approximately 420 dwellings on 35 acres of land'. Permission was refused. On appeal the Inspector recommended the appeal be refused, but indicated that if it were possible to restrict the area to 25 acres and for the number of dwellings to be reduced to 250, then such development would not be objectionable. In accepting his Inspector's recommendation that the appeal be dismissed, the Secretary of State considered he had no power to grant planning permission for development on a smaller site and with houses at a lower density than that which was indicated on the original application form. In granting an application made to the High Court to quash the Secretary of State's decision, Forbes J held that it was permissible to grant planning permission subject to a condition that only a reduced development was to be carried out, provided that the result did not differ substantially from the development proposed in the original application. This was an aspect to which the Secretary of State had failed to have regard. What clearly cannot be done is to consider an amendment to an application which would have the effect of altering its whole character.

The reason for such a principle is that members of the public and others may have a right to be consulted on an application for planning permission which would then be denied to them if an authority could grant planning permission for development substantially different from that which was applied for. In a later case, *Wessex Regional Health Authority* v *Salisbury District Council* [1984] JPL 344, Glidewell J upheld the decision of an Inspector to refuse planning permission for residential development. The appellants had invited the Inspector, during an appeal against a refusal of planning permission by the local planning authority, to consider the argument that if 48 houses were too many, but 37 were acceptable, he could grant planning permission subject to a condition limiting the number to 37. The Inspector decided that 48 houses were too many and dismissed the appeal. He also took the view that in the circumstances a reduction in number from 48 to 37 differed substantially from the development proposal and should rightly form the basis of a fresh application.

In *R* v *St Edmundsbury Borough Council (ex parte Investors in Industry Commercial Properties Ltd)* [1985] 1 WLR 1168 an application had been made for development of 'a supermarket with ancillary accommodation including storage, preparation plant, office-staff/customer areas, surface-level car-park, loading and unloading areas and appropriate landscaping with access'. Stocker J reached perhaps a surprising conclusion that a condition in the grant of planning permission for the development which stated, 'At least three small independent retail units shall be provided in addition to the proposed supermarket', was within the general ambit of the permission sought.

The principle here stated has had ramifications in other situations which have not led to litigation. In the aftermath of the decision in *Bernard Wheatcroft Ltd* v *Secretary of State for the Environment,* the Secretary of State had to consider an application by the National Coal Board to exploit what became known as the Vale of Belvoir coalfield.

The National Coal Board had applied for planning permission to construct and work three mines at Hose, Saltby and Ashfordby, and to tip spoil adjacent to those three sites. The Inspector had recommended the grant of permission for all three mines, but that permission be refused for the proposed spoil tips at Hose and Saltby.

After considering the report the Secretary of State concluded that the development of the mine at Hose was environmentally unacceptable. In addition, before tipping at any of the sites could be contemplated, the possibility of other methods of spoil disposal should be further examined. So had there been acceptable proposals for the disposal of spoil, the Secretary of State would have been prepared to grant planning permission for the development of the mines at Ashfordby and Saltby.

The National Coal Board had submitted, however, one application for planning permission covering all the underground coal extraction in Leicester-shire, together with the three mine complexes and three spoil tips, thus opting to stand or fall by a strategy of developing the whole coalfield as one project. In his decision letter the Secretary of State said:

in those circumstances the granting of planning permission for only part of the development would be in effect granting a permission for development which is significantly different in kind from the proposal which was the subject of the application. This may be a point which the Board would wish to bear in mind in future.

In a more recent case, *Breckland District Council* v *Secretary of State for the Environment* (1992) 65 P & CR 34, the local planning authority sought to quash the decision of an Inspector whereby he had allowed an appeal for a 16-pitch gypsy caravan site in Norfolk. The case is believed to be the first to come before the courts where an amendment of a planning application by an Inspector involved the enlargement of the application site. The effect of the amendment was to increase the application site by 50 per cent, bringing it nearer to three nearby residences and increasing the number of pitches. In quashing the Inspector's decision Mr David Widdicombe QC, sitting as a deputy judge, considered that the legal validity of an enlargement might be harder to justify than a reduction. He thought the test of validity of the action was derived from *Bernard Wheatcroft Ltd* v *Secretary of State for the Environment* but it was an exercise of discretion which could only be challenged within the *Wednesbury* rules. He held that the parish council and local residents were deprived of the opportunity to be consulted on the proposed amendment, and it was *Wednesbury* unreasonable of the Inspector to hold that the amendment did not substantially alter the proposal. The decision to allow the amendment was unreasonable and therefore invalid.

14.2.1 Split decisions

A variant of the principle in *Bernard Wheatcroft Ltd* v *Secretary of State for the Environment* [1982] JPL 37 is the development of what may be called the 'split decision', whereby planning permission is granted not for reduced development as in *Wheatcroft,* but for only part of the land the subject of the application, whilst being refused for the remaining part.

A recent example is a Ministerial decision involving the North Wiltshire District Council, where an application had been made for the erection of 11 detached houses on land at Tetbury Hill, Malmesbury. In default of the decision within the prescribed period, the applicants had appealed to the Secretary of State. About half of the site was included within the 'limits of development' for the town of Malmesbury as identified on the proposals map in the Malmesbury local plan. The remainder of the site lay outside the limits. The Inspector took the view that that part of the development which lay within the limits-of-development boundary would be acceptable, but not that which lay outside. Although the applicants had objected at the inquiry to the making of a split decision, the Inspector dismissed the appeal and refused planning permission for development of that part of the site which lay outside the limit-of-development boundary, but at the same time allowed the appeal and granted planning permission for the erection of dwellinghouses in respect of that part of the application site which lay inside the boundary. For obvious reasons, the grant of planning permission was a grant of outline planning permission, with approval of details relating to siting, design, external appearance, means of access and landscaping being reserved for the approval of the local planning authority.

The legality of the practice of giving a split decision on an application for planning permission has not yet been tested in the courts, but it is thought that the principle to be applied is the same as that in the *Wheatcroft* case, namely, that any permission granted should not be substantially different from the development applied for.

14.3   Effect of planning permission

Until the decision of the Divisional Court in *Petticoat Lane Rentals Ltd* v *Secretary of State for the Environment* [1971] 1 WLR 1112, it had always been assumed, but with only slender authority for so doing, that the implementation of a planning permission destroyed the old use to which the land had previously been put. The case concerned a site which had been cleared after having been bombed during the Second World War. It had been leased to a company, which used it to let out stalls to street traders every day of the week. In 1963, planning permission had been granted for a new commercial building on the site supported on pillars. The open ground floor was to be used as a carparking and loading area ancillary to the commercial use of the building. Under the terms of the permission that area could continue to be used for market trading on Sundays, when the ground floor would not be needed for that ancillary purpose. Almost immediately after the building had been constructed, market traders began to use the ground floor not only on Sundays but also on every other day of the week.

Almost inevitably the local planning authority served an enforcement notice on the company alleging the making of a material change of use without permission and requiring the discontinuance of weekday trading. The company appealed. After a public inquiry, the Secretary of State upheld the notice on the grounds that any existing use rights had been extinguished with the implementation of the permission. The Divisional Court held, dismissing an appeal by the company, that, where an area of open land was developed by the erection of a new building over the whole site, the land as such was merged into the new building and a new planning unit was created with a new use; and that any use to which the new building was put thereafter was a change of use which, if not authorised by the planning permission, could be restrained by planning control.

In so holding, the court relied heavily on one of its earlier decisions, namely *Prossor* v *Minister of Housing & Local Government* (1968) 67 LGR 109. This was a case of a petrol service station on a main road where the occupier sought and obtained planning permission to rebuild the petrol station. He was given such permission and an express condition was attached to the permission to the effect that no retail sales other than the sale of motor accessories should be carried on on the site. In fact, having let the establishment, the occupier began to exhibit second-hand cars for sale on the site, which was clearly a breach of the condition if the condition was effective. It was argued in favour of the occupier that he was enabled to do that because there was a continuing and unbroken use of the land for the sale of second-hand cars, and in his contention the fact that he had had a new and inconsistent planning permission and had implemented it did not destroy that right. Lord Parker CJ, having dealt with a number of arguments not relevant to the present appeal, put the matter thus:

> Assuming . . . that there was at all material times prior to April 1964 [the date of the rebuilding] an existing use right running on this land for the display and sale of motor cars, yet by adopting the permission granted in April 1964, the appellant's predecessor, as it seems to me, gave up any possible existing use rights in that regard which he may have had. The planning history of this site, as it were, seems to me to begin afresh on 4 April 1964, with the grant of this permission, a permission which was taken up and used, and the sole question here is: has there been a breach of that condition?

Although in the *Prossor* case the use of the land for the display of second-hand cars had been expressly prohibited by a condition of the planning permission, the court in *Petticoat Lane Rentals Ltd v Secretary of State for the Environment* thought that to be irrelevant. According to Widgery LJ, the fact that there was an express prohibition was no more than an indication of the fact that the draftsman of the permission had found it easier to express his wishes in that way.

Although the court in the *Petticoat Lane Rentals Ltd* case was unanimous in holding that the existing use of the land had been extinguished by the erection upon it of a new building, both Bridge J and Lord Parker CJ drew a distinction between, on the one hand, a case where land formerly open and not built upon had been used for a certain purpose and subsequently the land itself had been built upon; and on the other hand, a case where open land had been used, that land had subsequently been embodied in the curtilage of a site developed by building for other purposes but the building had not extended over all the land used for the former purpose. It is quite clear that in the latter situation, the local planning authority can, by express condition, exclude the right to continue the former use of the land not built upon. Without such a condition being imposed, however, the position is far from clear.

The decision in *Prossor v Minister of Housing & Local Government* was considered by the House of Lords in *Newbury District Council v Secretary of State for the Environment* [1981] AC 578. One of the three main issues to be determined in that case was whether the company concerned, having been granted planning permission to change the use of hangars from the storage of civil defence vehicles to use for the storage of synthetic rubber, could subsequently contend that no permission was necessary on account of existing use rights. In deciding that there was no bar to the right of the company to do so, their lordships referred to the *Prossor* case. Relating that case to the facts before him, Viscount Dilhorne felt that *Prossor's* case was not sustainable on the basis that obtaining and taking up planning permission in itself prevents reliance on existing use rights. He went on:

If, however, the grant of planning permission, whether it be permission to build or for a change of use, is of such a character that the implementation of the permission leads to the creation of a new planning unit, then I think that it is right to say that existing use rights attaching to the former planning unit are extinguished. It may be that in the *Prossor* case the erection of the new building created a new planning unit. If it did, and it is not very clear from the report, then in my view that case was rightly decided.

It is clear that in this case the grant of the planning permission in May 1962 did not create a new planning unit and so, in my opinion, [the company] were not precluded from relying on the existing use rights attaching to the site.

The idea that the implementation of a planning permission may lead to the creation of a new planning unit was echoed by Lord Fraser of Tullybelton in the *Newbury* case when he said:

> The only circumstances in which existing use rights are lost by accepting and implementing a later planning permission are, in my opinion, when a new planning unit comes into existence.

The relevance of a new planning unit was again considered, this time by the Court of Appeal, in *Jennings Motors Ltd* v *Secretary of State for the Environment* [1980] JPL 521. There, land had been used for many years for the repair and maintenance of vehicles and the sale and hire of cars. In 1975, a new single-storey building was erected without planning permission on a small part of the site to replace an existing building. The new building was used for vehicle repair and servicing. Eventually the local planning authority served an enforcement notice which required not the demolition of the building, but the discontinuance of the use to which the building had been put. The occupiers appealed against the notice and, after an inquiry, the Inspector concluded that the planning unit was the site as a whole, and that the use could be carried on anywhere within the site, thus the appeal should be allowed. The Secretary of State, however, upheld the enforcement notice on the ground that when the new building was erected a new planning history was commenced in respect of it for which there had been a material change of use from 'no use'. The Divisional Court upheld the Secretary of State's decision, but on appeal by the occupiers the Court of Appeal allowed the appeal, holding that the erection of a new building on part of a whole site does not in itself constitute a new planning unit or a new chapter in the planning history and, accordingly, the Secretary of State had erred in law in holding that development had taken place.

The decision in the *Jennings* case was concerned with the question of whether an established use survived within the new building. It did not determine the question of whether the implementation of a planning permission on part of a site created a new planning unit or introduced a new chapter in planning history as regards the rest of the site.

This latter aspect was considered subsequently by the Divisional Court of the Queen's Bench Division in *South Staffordshire District Council* v *Secretary of State for the Environment* [1987] JPL 635. Apart from preferring the term 'new chapter in planning history' to that of 'new planning unit', the court considered that established use rights on the rest of a site would survive implementation of planning permission to erect a building on another part of the site, unless the development which took place was inconsistent with the established use.

Unfortunately, the cases subsequent to the *Petticoat Lane Rentals Ltd* case have not succeeded in resolving the problem there identified of the effect of implementing a planning permission which affects only part of the original planning unit, on the existing use rights of the part of the unit not affected by the development. Until this problem is resolved, a person applying for planning permission to develop part of his land should consider restricting his application to that part only, leaving the authority to restrict the existing use rights of the other part by condition, if they should consider this to be necessary. Otherwise, it might be harder to maintain that the grant of permission and its implementation for the part has led to the creation of a smaller planning unit carved out of the old so that the existing use rights in what is left of the old still remain.

14.4   Public rights of way and development

Under s. 247 of the 1990 Act the Secretary of State may, by order, authorise the stepping up or diversion of any highway, if satisfied that it is necessary to do so in order to enable development for which planning permission has been granted to be carried out. A more limited power (not requiring the authorisation of the Secretary of State) is given to local planning authorities to make orders authorising the stopping up or diversion of any footpath or bridleway in order to enable development for which planning permission has been granted to be carried out. The grant of planning permission does not in itself authorise the stopping up or diversion of rights of way and if those rights are obstructed before any order has been made, the development cannot proceed until the obstruction has been removed. It should be emphasised that the grant of planning permission does not guarantee that any order will be made under these provisions. No assumption should be made that merely because planning permission has been granted, an order will invariably be made or confirmed under these provisions.

14.5   Planning permission and actions in nuisance

Where planning permission is given for the development of land and sub-sequently implemented, the question whether the use of the land amounts to an actionable nuisance is decided by reference to the neighbourhood as it is following implementation of the permission and not as it was previously. In *Gillingham Borough Council* v *Medway (Chatham) Dock Co. Ltd* [1993] QB 343, a local authority unsuccessfully brought proceedings for a declaration that the defendants' operation of their premises around the clock as a commercial port amounted to a public nuisance because of noise and vibration from heavy vehicular traffic using residential roads leading to the port. The court held that the grant of planning permission for the use of the premises as a commercial port operating 24 hours a day changed the character of the surrounding residential area, so that it could no longer claim protection in nuisance from what would previously have been restrained.

14.6 Life of a planning permission

Once granted, planning permission will continue in force until one of the following events deprive it of its effectiveness:

(a) Where the development authorised by the permission has been carried out and completed. Here the permission is spent. The benefit of the permission has been accepted and the development which has been carried out in accordance with the terms of the permission becomes part of the existing use rights in the land. Where a personal planning permission has been granted, the permission will cease on the death of the person concerned.

(b) Where planning permission has been granted subject to a condition imposed under ss. 91 and 92 of the 1990 Act requiring development to be begun within a specified period, and the development has not been begun within that period.

(c) Where planning permission is revoked under s. 97 of the 1990 Act. This provision empowers a local planning authority to revoke or modify any planning permission to develop land granted on an application under Part III of the Act at any time in the case of permission for the carrying out of building or other operations, before the operations are completed and, in the case of permission for a change of use, before the change of use has taken place. The revocation or modification, however, will not affect any building or other operations carried out before the coming into force of the revocation or modification order. Unless an order is unopposed it will not come into effect until confirmed by the Secretary of State. The revocation or modification of a planning permission entitles any person interested in the land to claim compensation from the local planning authority under s. 107 of the 1990 Act for any expenditure, loss or damage incurred in carrying out work rendered abortive by the revocation or modification, and any other loss or damage sustained which is directly attributable to the revocation or modification. In calculating the latter head of claim, the value of any other planning permission granted or likely to be granted for the development of the land must be taken into account. The willingness of the local planning authority, therefore, to grant an alternative permission to the one to be revoked or modified will reduce the compensation payable and may, at the same time, lead to the order being unopposed.

Where the development permitted by a planning permission has been carried out and completed, the local planning authority cannot serve a revocation or modification order. Under s. 100 of the 1990 Act, however, the authority can require that any use of land should be discontinued, or that conditions should be imposed on the continuance of a use of land or that any buildings or works should be altered or removed. Any such discontinuance order is required to be confirmed by the Secretary of State. As with revocation or modification orders, compensation must be paid to any person who has suffered damage in consequence of the order under s. 115 of the 1990 Act.

(d)　Where more than one planning permission has been granted in respect of land, and the carrying out the development authorised by one permission makes it impossible to carry out the development authorised by another. This may extend beyond cases where the implementation of the planning permission makes it physically impossible to implement another. In *Pilkington v Secretary of State for the Environment* [1973] 1 WLR 1527 the owner of land was granted planning permission to build a bungalow on part of the land, site B. It was a condition of the permission that the bungalow should be the only house to be built on the land. He built the bungalow. Later the owner discovered the existence of an earlier permission to build a bungalow and garage on another part of the same land, site A. That permission contemplated the use of the rest of the land as a smallholding. He began to build the second bungalow and was then served with an enforcement notice alleging a breach of planning control. The Divisional Court held that the two permissions could not stand in respect of the same land, once the development sanctioned by the second permission had been carried out. The effect of building on site B was to make the development authorised in the earlier permission incapable of implementation. The bungalow built on site B had destroyed the smallholding: and the erection of two bungalows on the site had never been sanctioned.

In *Pioneer Aggregates (UK) Ltd v Secretary of State for the Environment* [1985] AC 132, Lord Scarman thought the *Pilkington* decision was a common-sense decision and correct in law.

It appears, however, that mere incompatibility of the planning permission with another planning permission already implemented is not in itself enough to invalidate it. In *Prestige Homes (Southern) Ltd v Secretary of State for the Environment* [1992] JPL 842, Mr Malcolm Spence QC, sitting as a deputy judge, thought (in accordance with the *Pilkington* decision) that in a case where the permission is, on its facts, incapable of being implemented, any development carried out on that site cannot be in pursuance of that permission. But where, as in the instant case, it was a question of the mere incompatibility of a planning permission with another planning permission already implemented, that alone was not enough to invalidate the planning permission. The deputy judge considered that the *Pilkington* doctrine should not be extended, and allowed an appeal against the decision of an Inspector to dismiss an appeal against an enforcement notice which had required the appellants to cease the construction of a dwellinghouse.

It should be noted that although existing use rights may be abandoned, it is not possible to abandon a planning permission. In *Pioneer Aggregates (UK) Ltd v Secretary of State for the Environment* [1985] AC 132, the respondent company, after a long period of non-user, had resumed the use of land for mining operations. The local planning authority alleged that the resumption constituted development and served an enforcement notice on the company requiring the use to be discontinued. The issue reached the House of Lords which held that there was no general rule of law that a planning permission which is capable of being implemented according to its terms can be abandoned. Their lordships thought that the clear implication of what is now s. 75(1) of the 1990 Act was that only the statute or the terms of the permission itself could stop the permission enduring for the benefit of the land and for all persons for the time being interested therein.

The principle that a valid permission capable of implementation could not be abandoned by the conduct of the owner or occupier was followed in *Camden London Borough Council* v *McDonald's Restaurants Ltd* (1992) 65 P & CR 423. The case concerned property used as a restaurant between 1972 and 1987. In December 1987 the Secretary of State had granted planning permission for a single storey rear extension which had never been implemented. Between 1987 and 1991 when McDonald's had taken a lease of the premises, the property had either remained vacant or been used as a bookshop. When McDonald's sought to implement the permission to build the extension, the local planning authority maintained that the permission had lapsed. In granting declarations that the planning permission for the extension was valid and subsisting and that the ground floor of the premises could lawfully be used for restaurant purposes, the Court of Appeal held that one had to 'look back at the permission . . . and see whether in fact the development there contemplated can now be carried out'. Here the premises were still in existence and it remained physically possible to build the extension.

The authority had also claimed that the use of the premises as a bookshop fell within Class A1 of the Use Classes Order and that it would not be lawful to change the use of the premises back from A1 to A3 without planning permission. The court held, however, that the permission for the extension was for operational development, not a grant of permission for a material change of use.

FIFTEEN

Development by the Crown, statutory undertakers and local authorities

15.1 The Crown

The 1990 Act does not bind the Crown. This is an application of a fundamental principle of the constitution that the Crown is not bound by statute unless expressly named or bound by necessary implication. Government departments, however, that propose to carry out development (of a kind other than that permitted by the General Development Order) are required (as a matter of good administration) to consult the local planning authority in accordance with the arrangements set out in Circular No. 18/84.

The arrangements provide for the department concerned to send to the local planning authority copies of a statement of its proposal, marked 'notice of proposed development', sufficient to enable the authority to appreciate its nature and extent. The statement should be accompanied by a location plan showing the relationship of the proposed development to adjoining property and, in the case of operational development, plans of the proposed development. If the Crown does not hold all the interests in the land, the department concerned should notify the owner, any agricultural tenant and any other tenant with an interest having at least seven years to run of the notice of proposed development.

On receipt of the notice of proposed development, the local planning authority should treat it in the same way as they would treat an ordinary planning application, so giving to it the same publicity as they would if the development proposed were the subject of an application for planning permission made by a private person.

This advice has been re-emphasised with recent amendments made to the General Development Order for compulsory publicity for all planning applications. Paragraph 30 of Circular No. 15/92, 'Publicity for Planning Applications', says:

> Developments by the Crown not requiring planning permission should receive the same publicity as if permission were needed. Where Crown

development proposals involve matters of national security, it may not be possible fully to comply with normal publicity requirements. In such cases, the local authority should discuss the appropriate level of publicity with the Government department involved. Any unresolved disputes should be referred to the Department of the Environment.

The local planning authority, having considered any objections made to the proposed development, must then decide whether or not to support the proposal. Where the authority object to the proposed development, the department concerned, if it decides to proceed with it, should notify the Department of the Environment, which must then determine the dispute between the department and the authority.

The procedure ensures that development proposals by government departments receive the same publicity as development proposals made by private individuals. Although it is true that the local planning authority have no power to prevent the development taking place, the power of the Secretary of State to determine the matter if the authority should object to the proposed development accords with his power to grant planning permission to a private person on appeal, where the local planning authority have decided to refuse it.

Although the Crown is not bound by the 1990 Act, the statute recognises that interests in the same parcel of land may be owned by both the Crown and private persons. This makes it necessary for the Act to contain specific provisions relating not to the Crown but to Crown land.

Section 293(1) of the 1990 Act defines Crown land as 'land in which there is a Crown interest or a Duchy interest'. 'Crown interest' means an interest belonging to Her Majesty in right of the Crown or belonging to a government department or held in trust for Her Majesty for the purposes of a government department. 'Duchy interest' means an interest belonging to Her Majesty in right of the Duchy of Lancaster or Duchy of Cornwall.

The 1990 Act applies to Crown land in the following ways:

(a)   The owner of an interest in Crown land (e.g., the owner of a leasehold interest) may apply for planning permission in the normal way. He can only be served with an enforcement notice, however, if the appropriate authority agree.

(b)   A development plan may include proposals relating to the use of Crown land, and any power to compulsorily acquire land under Part IX of the Act may, with the agreement of the appropriate authority, be exercised in relation to any interest in the land which is held otherwise than by the Crown.

(c)   A building which for the time being is Crown land may be included in a list compiled or approved by the Secretary of State under s. 1 of the Planning (Listed Buildings and Conservation Areas) Act 1990. The effect of this is that although the Crown does not require listed building consent to carry out works to a listed building which are likely to affect the character of the building as a listed building (and cannot be served with a listed building enforcement notice if it does), any other person having an interest in the land and carrying out such works must obtain listed building consent. If listed building consent has not been obtained, that other person may, if the appropriate authority agree, be served with a listed building enforcement notice.

(d) The owner of an interest in Crown land may, if the appropriate authority agree, serve a purchase notice under Part VI of the Act requiring the district council to purchase its interest.

(e) The appropriate authority in relation to any Crown interest or Duchy interest may enter into a planning obligation under s. 106 of the 1990 Act. However, a planning obligation entered into in relation to Crown land cannot be enforced by injunction, nor can the power to enter land and carry out operations to which the obligation relates be exercised without the consent of the appropriate authority.

The 'appropriate authority' for the purpose of the above provisions means the Crown Estates Commissioners, the Chancellor of the Duchy of Lancaster, the Duke of Cornwall or the appropriate government department, as the case may be.

The rules relating to the Crown and Crown land created a special problem when the Crown sought to dispose of land surplus to requirements. This was particularly acute in the case of surplus National Health Service land. Although the Crown does not require planning permission for its own development, and there is no restriction placed on a private person owning an interest in Crown land applying for planning permission, it was not possible before 1984 for a third party (i.e., a person not owning an interest in Crown land) to apply for planning permission for the development of Crown land. These provisions prohibited prospective purchasers from applying for permission for the development of land prior to its purchase. This meant that the purchase price paid for the land reflected the absence of any clear statement of what development was permitted, thus reducing its market value and resulting in a loss to the Exchequer.

In anticipation of this problem, Circular No. 49/63 had recommended that where a government department sought to dispose of land, it could obtain an 'opinion' from the local planning authority as to whether planning permission would be forthcoming in the event of a formal application being made. In face of an adverse decision from the authority, the department could then apply to the Secretary of State for his opinion as to whether, if an application came before him on appeal, he would grant permission for the development.

In R v Worthing Borough Council (ex parte Burch) [1984] JPL 261, Mann J held the procedure to be ultra vires, on the ground that the practical effect of such an opinion would be to deny to local objectors the rights and advantages conferred on them by the normal appeal procedures and constrain the local planning authority in considering a subsequent application for planning permission.

The problem was rectified by the Town and Country Planning Act 1984, the provisions of which have now been incorporated in the 1990 Act. The Act now enables the 'appropriate authority' or a person authorised in writing by that authority to apply for planning permission, or a determination of the lawfulness of an existing use or development in respect of any Crown land. Any permission or consent granted is to apply only to development or works carried out after the land has ceased to be Crown land, or to development or works carried out by virtue of a private interest in the land (s. 299).

The 1984 Act also enabled enforcement action to be taken against development carried out on Crown land otherwise than by or on behalf of the Crown at a time when no person is entitled to occupy it by virtue of a private interest. The power is now contained in s. 295 of the 1990 Act. This power is particularly useful to enable local planning authorities to control trespass by gypsies on Crown land, and mobile snack-bars or refreshment vans located on the laybys of trunk roads. The enforcement notice is called a 'special enforcement notice' and can be served by the authority only with the consent of the appropriate authority.

In June 1992 the government decided, as part of a policy outlined in the Citizen's Charter to progressively remove any immunities which sheltered departments and Crown bodies from regulations, inspection and enforcement requirements placed on others and to bring to an end the exemptions now granted to the Crown under planning legislation. In a subsequent consultation paper issue in November 1992, the government proposed that when a suitable legislative opportunity occurred, Crown bodies would be required to apply to the local planning authority for planning permission, listed building consent, conservation area consent and scheduled monument consent in the same way as a private individual. Crown bodies would also be subject to the statutory regimes pertaining to the protection of trees and the control of outdoor advertisements. Limited exceptions to these proposed changes would be necessary where national or prison security was involved, or for trunk road proposals which were already subject to statutory procedures equivalent to those found in town and country planning legislation.

The government considered, however, that it would be inappropriate for the enforcement provisions of planning legislation, particularly criminal sanctions and powers of entry, to apply to the Crown. It therefore proposed that an authority that wished to enforce planning controls against the Crown should be able to apply to the High Court for a declaration. It was expected that the Crown would then act to correct any breach of planning control found by the court.

It is likely that any new arrangements will also provide an informal appeal mechanism to deal with disputes between local planning authorities and the Crown with regard to enforcement. This would be in addition to the right of the authority to apply for a declaration.

15.2 Statutory undertakers

The expression 'statutory undertakers' is defined in s. 262(1) of the 1990 Act to mean:

> persons authorised by any enactment to carry on any railway, light railway, tramway, road transport, water transport, canal, inland navigation, dock, harbour, pier or lighthouse undertaking or any undertaking for the supply of hydraulic power and a relevant airport operator. . . .

In addition, for the purposes of many of the Act's provisions, any gas supplier, water or sewerage undertaking, the National Rivers Authority, the

Post Office and the Civil Aviation Authority are deemed to be statutory undertakers.

Statutory undertakers wishing to develop land must normally apply for planning permission to do so to the local planning authority. Modifications to the normal procedures are made in relation to applications for the development of 'operational land' of such bodies.

Where an application for planning permission for the development of operational land comes before the Secretary of State, as with an appeal against an adverse decision by the local planning authority or because the application has been called in under s. 77 of the 1990 Act, the Secretary of State is required to act in relation to the appeal or called-in decision jointly with the appropriate Minister; that is, the Minister responsible for the operations of the particular statutory undertaker.

Apart from the above modification, planning permission for certain development of statutory undertakers is granted under various classes of the General Development Order. Much of that permitted development is extensive in character. In addition, other legislation may require development by statutory undertakers to be authorised by a government department. In such cases, s. 90(1) of the 1990 Act provides that the department concerned may, in granting that authorisation, direct that planning permission for the development shall be deemed to be granted, subject to such conditions as may be specified. The value of this procedure is that it enables the authorising department to consider all matters relating to the proposed development at the same time, many of which may not be related to the land use matters, such as the significance of the proposed development to the strategic functions and responsibilities of the industry concerned.

15.3 Local authorities

Local authorities, like statutory undertakers, must obtain planning permission for any development they propose to carry out. As with statutory undertakers, certain development by local authorities is permitted development under the various classes of the General Development Order. Furthermore, where other legislation requires development by a local authority to be authorised by a government department, s. 90(1) of the 1990 Act provides that the department concerned may, in granting the authorisation, direct that planning permission for the development be deemed to be granted.

There are other special provisions, however, which apply to other development. Section 316 of the 1990 Act empowers the Secretary of State to make regulations governing development of local planning authorities' land and development of any land by local planning authorities jointly with another person. The current regulations are the Town and Country Planning General Regulations 1992 (SI No. 1492). The new regulations revoke and replace regulations made in 1976 which had been subject to much criticism.

In essence those old regulations gave a local planning authority the power, by passing two resolutions, to grant themselves planning permission for development carried out by them or by others on their land. It was alleged that local planning authorities were not able to act impartially in such matters when they were plaintiff and jury in their own cause. Moreover, because a local planning authority might gain financially when disposing of land with the benefit of planning permission, it was claimed that planning permission might be granted which would be refused if the 'applicant' were not the authority.

The requirements of the Town and Country Planning General Regulations have always been regarded as fundamental and strict, and a failure to comply with them has been regarded by the courts as fatal. Many of the cases, whilst still relevant to the new statutory provisions, turn on the interpretation of the old 1976 Regulations and the provisions of the 1990 Act, before amendments were made to that Act by the Planning and Compensation Act 1991. In *Steeples* v *Derbyshire County Council* [1985] 1 WLR 256, Webster J held that the failure to place notices in the planning register as required by the regulations rendered the deemed grant of planning permission *ultra vires* and void.

In *R* v *Lambeth London Borough Council (ex parte Sharp)* [1987] JPL 440, the authority proposed to construct a floodlit synthetic athletics track with seats for 1,100 spectators in some 6 acres of parkland. Among a number of irregularities committed by the authority in the process of obtaining deemed planning permission for the development was a failure in a newspaper advertisement required by the regulations to specify the period within which objections to the proposed development should be made to the authority. Croom-Johnson LJ granted *certiorari* to quash the deemed grant of permission. Unanimously upholding that decision, the Court of Appeal held that the breach of the regulations had been fundamental. In the course of his judgment, Stephen Brown LJ had this to say about the regulations:

It must be borne in mind that this is a special form of procedure to be operated where the authority is in effect seeking to grant permission to itself. It is nominally acting on behalf of the Secretary of State inasmuch as the second resolution, if properly passed, operates as a deemed permission of the Secretary of State. It seems to me that it is not necessary to consider whether these requirements are 'mandatory' or 'directory', or whether they go to powers or duties. One has to look at the terms of the regulations, and a breach of them, in my judgment, clearly provides a basis upon which the court can be seised of an application for judicial review. It is of course material to consider the nature of such a breach — that is to say, its gravity and relevance — when considering whether relief shall be granted. For my part, I am satisfied that the breach in question, which I find the judge was right to hold established, was fundamental, bearing in mind that it is a provision which requires notification of proposed development to members of the public. This was in a conservation area and is obviously a matter of general local public interest. Public notification of the proposed grant of planning permission must accordingly be of fundamental public importance. I would hold that this is not a mere procedural technicality but rather it is a requirement fundamental to the operation of this particular planning procedure.

A few months later in the High Court in *R* v *Doncaster Metropolitan District Council (ex parte British Railways Board)* [1987] JPL 444, Schiemann J followed the approach of the Court of Appeal in the *Lambeth* case and quashed a resolution of the authority to carry out development involving the building of a superstore in the town centre, in the light of a host of irregularities in the procedures followed by the authority.

The process by which authorities are able in effect to grant planning permission to themselves has been subject in recent years to much criticism. In this area local planning authorities are seen by many to be partial to their own development proposals. The stakes are high, since the value of a grant of planning permission may be considerable. This used to be particularly so where development proposals were made for under-used, county-council owned playing fields. Until the law was changed by the Planning and Compensation Act 1991, such development proposals were determined not by the district council as local planning authority for their area but by the county council.

The problem however was best seen with regard to the growth in the desire for superstores and hypermarkets. Although it is no part of the planning system to protect commercial interests from competition, the effect of such development on shopping outlets in existing town centres is something which must be taken into account in deciding whether they should be allowed. The problem becomes acute in cases where there are a number of proposals for superstore development in the same area, since the greater the number, the greater the impact on the existing centre.

Frequently because of this impact, there is general agreement between authorities and developers that the number of superstores in any area should be limited. When this is followed by a number of applications for such development by different developers, the question of which one is to be preferred can often pose a difficult decision for the authority. To meet this difficulty, a local planning authority may fail to issue a decision within the prescribed period for doing so, in the hope that at least one of the applicants will appeal to the Secretary of State against the non-determination of the application, and that other applications not determined will be called in by the Secretary of State. It is he who will then make the decision, after holding a composite local inquiry into all the applications.

A further difficulty arises, however, when one of the proposed sites for such development is on land in which the local planning authority has an interest. As regards local authority proposals for such development, the statistics show that only the most controversial applications are called in by the Secretary of State for his own determination. In the year 1984/85 a little over 12,300 deemed permissions were granted. Of those 1,400 were in respect of land vested in local authorities but where the development was carried out by others. In 1985 only 18 applications for development of local-authority land were called in by the Secretary of State. Inevitably if an authority deals with an application in which it has an interest and grants planning permission, it is difficult for the authority to avoid suggestions of bias. The problem in this area first reached the courts in a non-superstore context.

In *Steeples* v *Derbyshire County Council* [1985] 1 WLR 256, the county council, who were the local planning authority, wished to develop an amusement park and construct a car-park and public conveniences on land which they owned which formed part of Shipley Park. The plaintiff owned the adjacent land. The council entered into an agreement with a development company whereby the company undertook to manage the proposed development and the council agreed to take all reasonable steps to obtain a grant of planning permission and to pay the company a substantial sum by way of damages if they failed to take all reasonable steps. The council passed a resolution granting the planning permission sought. The plaintiff contended that the authority had failed to comply with the requirements of natural justice in that, although the decision to grant planning permission may have been fairly made, it was not seen to be fairly made. He claimed that because of the authority's undertaking to the developers to use their best endeavours to obtain planning permission and their acceptance of a liability in damages if they failed to use their best endeavours, the decision to grant permission would be seen by members of the public to have been prejudged.

In the High Court, Webster J considered it probable that a reasonable man, not having been present at the meeting of the authority's planning committee when the decision was made, and not knowing that the decision was, in fact, fairly made, but knowing of the existence of the contract and all its terms, would think there was a real likelihood that the provisions in the contract which required the county council to use their best endeavours to obtain planning permission had had a material and significant effect on the committee's decision to grant the permission. Accordingly he held that the decision was either voidable or void.

The application to a local planning authority's actions of the test of whether a reasonable man would consider that there was a real likelihood of bias, as opposed to the existence of actual bias, would create considerable difficulties for authorities given that the statutory procedures impose an obligation on the authority alone to determine the planning status of the land in which it has an interest. Unless the Secretary of State were to intervene, it is difficult to see how a local planning authority could ever be seen to exercise its statutory powers properly.

The issue of planning permission for the leisure park in Shipley Park was raised again before Woolf J in R v Amber Valley District Council (ex parte Jackson) [1985] 1 WLR 298. The facts were that the development company had issued a writ against the Derbyshire County Council arising out of the failure to obtain planning permission. The company also applied for permission on its own account to the Amber Valley District Council. There had been a meeting of the predominant political party of the district council which had decided, in principle, to support the application for a leisure park and members of the same dominant political group on the county council had decided to withdraw their opposition based on transport grounds. In these circumstances, the applicant, a representative of the Friends of Shipley Park, applied for an order prohibiting the Amber Valley District Council from considering an application for planning permission on the grounds that the matter had been predetermined by the decision of the predominant political party on the council. Dismissing Mr Jackson's application, Woolf J cited from the judgment of Lord Denning MR in *Metropolitan Properties Co. (FGC) Ltd* v *Lannon* [1969] 1 QB 577 at p. 599, on which Webster J had relied in the *Steeples* case, that the appropriate test was a 'real likelihood of bias', and observed that that case related to allegations of bias on the part of a rent assessment committee. Woolf J said, at p. 304:

> Standing by itself, I would have difficulty in applying that well-known statement of principle to an administrative decision of a planning committee. Lord Denning MR was dealing with a person or body who sits at least in a quasi-judicial capacity, and this case could be readily distinguished on its facts.

The correct test to be applied in judging an authority's actions was first considered in the context of superstore development in *R* v *Sevenoaks District Council (ex parte Terry)* [1985] 3 All ER 226. In that case, the council as local planning authority had granted planning permission to a company called Fraser Wood Properties in respect of a site known as the Old Post Office Yard for the purpose, *inter alia*, of erecting a supermarket. The council had, on an earlier date, approved a recommendation that an offer by Fraser Wood to purchase a lease of the site should be accepted and the officers were authorised to take all necessary action. The formal agreement between the council and Fraser Wood was not entered into until after the date on which planning permission was granted. In an application for judicial review of the council's decision, the applicant contended that the planning permission was void on the grounds that the council had fettered the discretion of the planning committee and further, or alternatively, that the council gave to reasonable people the appearance that they regarded themselves as committed.

Dismissing the application, Glidewell J said in relation to these situations:

> ... but it is not uncommon for a local authority to be obliged to make a decision relating to land or other property in which it had an interest. In such a situation, the application of the rule designed to ensure that a judicial officer does not appear to be biased would, in my view, often produce an administrative impasse. In my judgment, the correct test to be applied in the present case is for the court to pose to itself the question: had the district council before 5 January 1982 acted in such a way that it is clear that, when the committee came to consider Fraser Wood's application for planning permission, it could not exercise proper discretion? ... if the answer to the question is No, it is in my judgment neither necessary nor desirable for the court to go further and consider what the opinion of a reasonable man would be. In so far this formulation differs from that adopted by Webster J in *Steeples* v *Derbyshire County Council*, I respectfully disagree with him.

The issue again arose for determination in the Queen's Bench Division in *R* v *St Edmundsbury Borough Council (ex parte Investors in Industry Commercial Properties Ltd)* [1985] 1 WLR 1168. There the council's planning committee had granted outline planning permission to J. Sainsbury plc for the erection of a supermarket on land owned by the council. The applicants for relief had applied for judicial review to quash the council's decision. The circumstances which gave rise to their application were that at the meeting at which the committee had considered the matter, the committee had before it seven applications for supermarkets in respect of six sites, one of which was made on the applicants' behalf. Each of the applications was refused, save for that made by Sainsbury's for a supermarket on land owned by the council, who had entered into a contract to sell a 125-year lease of the site to Sainsbury's in the event of planning permission being obtained. The applicants contended that the council had thereby fettered themselves from proper exercise of their discretion and that the decision in favour of Sainsbury's had given rise to the inference of bias.

Dismissing the application and applying the dictum of Glidewell J in *R v Sevenoaks District Council (ex parte Terry)* Stocker J held that the test of what a hypothetical reasonable man would apprehend had no application in determining the validity of an administrative decision such as the grant of planning permission. The sole test was whether, despite its interests or its previous actions, the planning authority genuinely and impartially exercised its discretion, since there were many cases in which a local authority's own interests and land were likely to be affected by a favourable planning decision made by it. Accordingly, once a planning authority's decision was found or conceded to be fair there was no requirement to pose some further test by which the decision might be impugned as unlawful or void, either by reference to what the reasonable man would suspect or by reference to whether viewed through some other eyes, such as those of the judge, there was a real likelihood of bias.

A recent decision of the High Court has again drawn attention to the problem of development of local authority owned land. In *R v London Borough of Merton and Speyhawk Land and Estates Ltd, ex parte Burnett* [1990] JPL 354, Pill J dismissed an application for judicial review seeking declarations that grants of planning permission, listed building consent and conservation area consent, given in connection with the redevelopment of land in Wimbledon town centre were *ultra vires*. In addition, an application for *certiorari* to quash the grants was also refused.

The Wimbledon town centre redevelopment proposals had had a long history, with rival proposals being made by the Greycoat Group and Speyhawk Land and Estates Ltd. The rival proposals had indeed been a factor which influenced the Secretary of State to call in the Wimbledon town centre local plan, the plan being approved by him in July 1988, along with the applications for planning permission and listed building consent submitted by the Greycoat Group (see Chapter 4). At the same time, the Secretary of State refused planning permission for the Speyhawk scheme.

At an earlier date the council and Speyhawk Land and Estates Ltd had entered into a development agreement, subsequently varied, whereby the council were to assemble the land ownership on the site for comprehensive development, and if the necessary consents were obtained, to sell the land to the company for the development. The initial purchase price for the land was to be £23,200,000.

In April 1989, on further applications made by the company the council proceeded, in the absence of any direction by the Secretary of State to refer the relevant decisions to him, to grant the planning permission and listed building and conservation area consents which were to be the subject of the judicial challenge.

The challenge was made on two grounds. First, that because most of the land was owned by the council, the applications, although made by the company, were subject to the Town and Country Planning General Regulations 1976 (which were in force at that time); and that reg. 7 obliged the council to lodge the applications with the Secretary of State for decision. Secondly, that even if the council had power to entertain the applications, the council's discretion had been improperly fettered by virtue of the development agreement entered into with the company. Actual bias, or alternatively the appearance of bias, it was claimed, required that the decisions should be quashed.

Dismissing the application for judicial review, Pill J held that notwithstanding the interest the council had in the grant of planning permission which had been sought for their land, the regulations did not operate as a prohibition on the application for permission being made by the company, nor were the council obliged to lodge the application with the Secretary of State.

With regard to the allegation that the council had fettered their discretion and been biased in their consideration of the various applications, Pill J concluded that the reports submitted to the various committees of the council were not so unfair, so tendentious or placed so much emphasis on the financial aspects of the proposals that members could not approach their planning duties in a proper manner. Furthermore, having considered the development agreements and considered them in the context of the other evidence, he could not hold that in granting planning permission, the planning sub-committee had been fettered in exercising its planning responsibilities.

It seemed that in bringing the action the applicant had hoped to stop what she considered to be the widespread practice of local authorities getting their development company partners to apply for planning permission in respect of the authorities' own land. According to Pill J, it was perhaps strange that the operation of reg. 7 of the 1976 Regulations could be avoided by the application for planning permission being made by 'development partners.' But safeguards for the public existed in the Secretary of State's power to call in the application and additionally, in this instant case, in the obligation to refer the application for listed building consent to English Heritage.

With regard to bias and the fettering of discretion, it seems clear that the courts will readily recognise that where a local planning authority acts as both developer and the regulator of the development, the separation of functions within the authority by means of the construction of a 'Chinese Wall,' is wholly unrealistic. On the other hand, an arrangement whereby nothing is said in reports to planning committees of the council's financial rights and duties in relation to development proposals for its own land, will not necessarily exclude all inference of bias.

As a result of continued disquiet over the procedures by which local planning authorities obtain planning permission for development on their own land, in February 1990 the Secretary of State issued a consultation paper seeking views on proposals to amend the law relating to development by local authorities. This has now been done.

The main features of new regulations, the Town and Country Planning General Regulations 1992, are as follows:

(a)   a local planning authority must make an application to itself for planning permission to develop land within its area. Local planning authorities therefore, can continue to grant themselves planning permission for development carried out by them, such as schools or local authority housing, and will also be able to grant themselves permission for development undertaken jointly with another person, such as a joint venture with a housing association where the authority's interest is significant;

(b)   for all other development proposals to be carried out on local-authority-owned land by other parties, planning permission now has to be sought from the responsible development control authority (thus a county council which is, for example, seeking to dispose of land with planning permission has to apply to the district council, unless the development is a 'county matter'; and the district council has to apply to the county council for development which is a 'county matter';

(c)   local planning authorities which now have to make a planning application to themselves or to another local planning authority will be subject to broadly the same statutory procedures as other applicants;

(d)   applications are required to be publicised as prescribed by a development order in the same way as applications from the public;

(e)   to avoid a conflict of interest, applications must not be determined by a committee, subcommittee or officer responsible for the management of the land or buildings concerned;

(f)   planning permission granted to local planning authorities for development by them or jointly will not pass to subsequent owners of the land; for example, an authority will not be able to grant itself planning permission for council housing then change its mind and sell the land with planning permission to a developer.

SIXTEEN
Planning agreements and planning obligations

16.1 Introduction and enabling powers

Planning obligations are a development from the power first given to local planning authorities by s. 34 of the Town and Country Planning Act 1932 to enter into planning agreements with landowners for regulating the development or use of their land. From that Act, the power found its way into the Town and Country Planning Act 1947; and thence into the Town and Country Planning Act 1971 as s. 52. On the consolidation of planning legislation in 1990, s. 52 of the 1971 Act was replaced by s. 106 of the Town and Country Planning Act 1990 as the new statutory authority for the power to enter into planning agreements. Now, following the passing of the Planning and Compensation Act 1991, the original s. 106 of the 1990 Act has been replaced in its entirety by new ss. 106, 106A and 106B which have been inserted into the 1990 Act in its place. The replacement sections also introduced new arrangements and new terminology. From 25 October 1991, the power to enter into a 'planning agreement' under the 1990 Act has been repealed and replaced by the power to enter into a 'planning obligation'.

It should be emphasised that the new provisions relating to planning obligations do not affect planning agreements entered into under either s. 52 of the Town and Country Planning Act 1971, or the original s. 106 of the 1990 Act (now repealed). Such agreements will continue to play an important part in regulating the use and development of land and the provisions still need to be considered in some detail.

Section 52 of the 1971 Act and the old s. 106 of the 1990 Act provided:

(1) A local planning authority may enter into an agreement with any person interested in land in their area for the purpose of restricting or regulating the development or use of the land, either permanently or during such period as may be prescribed by the agreement.

(2)   Any such agreement may contain such incidental and consequential provisions (provisions of a financial character) as appear to the local planning authority to be necessary or expedient for the purposes of the agreement.

(3)   An agreement made under this section with any person interested in land may be enforced by the local planning authority against persons deriving title under that person in respect of that land as if the local planning authority were possessed of adjacent land and as if the agreement had been expressed to be made for the benefit of such land.

It should be emphasised that the ability of a local planning authority to enter into an agreement with a landowner to restrict the use and development of land represented a significant relaxation in the normal rules governing the ability of a party to enforce covenants of a restrictive nature against a successor in title of the person who had originally entered into the covenant. In ordinary law, successors in title to the covenantee (the person owning the land benefiting from a covenant), can only enforce a covenant against the covenantor and his successors in title if he owns adjacent land capable of being benefited. So that through a planning agreement entered into under s. 52 of the 1971 Act or the old s. 106 of the 1990 Act, a local planning authority could take a restrictive covenant from a landowner and enforce it against subsequent owners, notwithstanding that the authority itself owned no land in the vicinity.

An early problem, however, was that although a planning agreement allowed local planning authorities to enforce *restrictive* covenants against later pur-chasers of land without the need for the authority to own any adjacent land, the section did not extend to allowing a local planning authority to enforce *positive* covenants against such owners. Thus, an authority had no power to require owners other than the original contracting party to do something; merely not to do something, such as not to develop. This particular defect was cured by s. 126 of the Housing Act 1974, so that thereafter a local planning authority could, via an agreement made under both statutory provisions, require a landowner or his successors in title not only to refrain from carrying out development on the affected land but also actually to carry out works, such as erecting a building and maintaining it. The power in s. 126 of the Housing Act 1974 was later incorporated via s. 33 of the Local Government (Miscellaneous Provisions) Act 1982 within the old s. 106 of the 1990 Act.

In addition to the powers available under s. 52, some local planning authorities took powers under local Acts of Parliament to enter into similar forms of agreement. Furthermore, local authorities were able to make use of a general power available under s. 111 of the Local Government Act 1972 to make agreements with developers. This provision gives local authorities power:

to do any thing (whether or not involving the expenditure, borrowing or lending of money or the acquisition or disposal of any property or rights) which is calculated to facilitate, or is conducive or incidental to, the discharge of any of their functions.

As regards the powers available to authorities under planning legislation to enter into planning agreements, there is some evidence that, at first, they provided a useful mechanism for controlling development in advance of the preparation by a local planning authority of a development plan for its area. Once that point had passed, however, the need for such agreements disappeared. Indeed, it has been estimated that in the 25 years up until 1968, no more than 500 agreements were made. In the 1970s, however, the position began to change dramatically, and there was evidence that the statutory provision was being used in a way quite unconnected with its original purpose. Local planning authorities saw the statutory provision as an opportunity for obtaining a 'planning gain' for their community. In some cases, the grant of planning permission was made conditional upon the applicant entering into a planning agreement. So no agreement, no planning permission. In return for the grant of planning permission, the developer would be expected to enter into an agreement to provide some public benefit, which might or might not be related to the development for which planning permission was to be granted. He might, for example, be required to contribute towards the provision of infrastructure or the restoration of a listed building or a church, or to provide public amenities such as open spaces or community centres. For the most part planning agreements were sought and obtained for a proper and legitimate planning purpose. For example, it might take the form of a requirement that the applicant should pay for improvements to a nearby (off-site) road junction to accommodate traffic to be generated by the development; or that he should pay for a new sewer which would be needed if the development was to take place; or that after the building authorised by the planning permission has been erected, existing buildings on the site should be demolished; all constitute examples of planning agreements entered into for a legitimate planning purpose.

Occasionally however, planning agreements were sought for purposes which could be considered of doubtful legality. Examples might include a requirement that the applicant provide new roads or sewers in excess of that required to serve the additional demand generated by the particular development in question; or that he provide at his own expense local authority housing; or that he be allowed an increase in the density or plot ratio normally permitted in return for the dedication of land as open space or as a footpath.

It will be seen that the use of planning agreements linked to the grant of planning permission can raise both moral and legal issues. It raises a moral issue when used by a local planning authority to circumvent the general principle that landowners are entitled to planning permission for the development of their land unless there is a substantial planning objection to the development, by the addition of a requirement that they should contribute something in return for that entitlement. It raises a legal issue in the sense that there is vagueness and uncertainty over the extent of authorities' power to require a planning agreement to be entered into as part of a 'planning permission package'. It is not surprising, therefore, that during the late 1970s, commentaries on the use of s. 52 agreements were sometimes characterised by such terms as 'the sale of planning permissions' or 'cheque-book planning'; and in severe cases, their use was regarded by developers as little short of blackmail.

On the other hand the system was not universally disliked by developers. The giving of a public benefit was often seen as a small price to pay in return for a grant of planning permission, and often enabled development which would otherwise have been controversial to be more readily accepted by the community. This may explain why so few attempts have been made to challenge such agreements in the courts. The question of planning gain was raised in *Westminster Renslade Ltd* v *Secretary of State for the Environment* [1983] JPL 454. The appellant developer had sought planning permission for comprehensive development involving offices, car-parks, a bridge, a new station and a transport interchange at Feltham railway station in Hounslow. On appeal, the Inspector upheld the decision of the local authority to refuse permission, on the ground, *inter alia,* that the plans did not show sufficient provision for car-parking that would be under public control. In the High Court, Forbes J, quashing the decision, held that the Inspector was not entitled to treat the provision of publicly controlled car-parks as a valid material consideration in determining the appeal. According to Forbes J, if a developer freely chose to give away his rights because he considered it more likely he would be granted planning permission if he did so, it might be legitimate to take into account what the developer was providing as planning gain. But it was not right to say that planning permission could be refused unless a landowner took on a burden which should more properly be shouldered by the local planning authority. The decision seems to suggest that if there is a genuine planning objection to proposed development, but that objection can be overcome by some action taken by the developer, then that is a legitimate consideration to be taken into account by the authority. For example, if lack of infrastructure is the sole reason for refusing planning permission for development, but the developer agrees to provide it himself or to meet the cost of providing it, that is a proper consideration to be taken into account. If, on the other hand, the authority is seeking a contribution from the developer towards the provision of public facilities (as by requiring the dedication of open space), which the authority is required to provide, that is not a proper consideration to be taken into account.

So prolific is the use now made of planning agreements to obtain planning gain from a developer, that provisions covering the matter are often contained in development plans.

In *London Borough of Richmond upon Thames* v *Secretary of State for the Environment* [1984] JPL 24, an application was made for planning permission for the addition of an entrance hall and offices to an existing building in Richmond. The local planning authority had refused planning permission, because, *inter alia,* the development proposed did not provide adequate planning advantages as required by the development plan for the area. The relevant policy in the plan stated that 'all office developments will normally be required to provide planning advantage which is considered most appropriate to the site'.

On appeal, the Inspector felt unable to regard the development-plan policy requirement of planning gain as a prerequisite for the grant of planning permission as being a valid reason for its refusal. It seems that the Inspector took the view that in the light of a then recently published report by the Property Advisory Group on the subject of planning gain, the development plan policy might not be a valid policy. In the High Court, Glidewell J held that if that were the case it was a view the Inspector was not entitled to take. In the exercise of the court's discretion, however, he decided not to quash the decision.

Whatever the limits of the power to enter into a planning agreement, they cannot be used to fetter the exercise by a local planning authority of their statutory powers.

In *Windsor & Maidenhead Royal Borough Council* v *Brandrose Investments Ltd* [1983] 1 WLR 509, a developer and the local planning authority entered into a s. 52 agreement under the Town and Country Planning Act 1971, whereby the developer undertook to demolish existing buildings and redevelop the site on which the buildings stood. The authority then granted the developer outline planning permission to develop its property along the lines contemplated in the agreement. But then later, the authority designated land as a conservation area pursuant to what is now s. 69 of the Planning (Listed Buildings and Conservation Areas) Act 1990, which included the developer's land. This meant that buildings in the conservation area could not be demolished without the authority's consent. When the developer started to demolish in accordance with the permission and the agreement, the authority sought an injunction restraining it from proceeding with the demolition. The Court of Appeal held that a s. 52 agreement could not fetter an authority's discretion in the exercise of their statutory powers and the agreement could not bind the authority not to exercise their powers to designate a conservation area, even though the effect of so doing might be to frustrate the purposes of the agreement.

Nevertheless, the legal contours within which planning agreements operate are far from certain. In *R* v *Gillingham Borough Council, ex parte Parham Ltd* [1988] JPL 336, a comparison was made between the powers of a local planning authority to impose conditions in a grant of planning permission, and the power of an authority to enter into statutory planning agreements. In the view of the court, an agreement had to satisfy two of the three requirements for the imposition of a valid condition as set out in the decision of the House of Lords in *Newbury District Council* v *Secretary of State for the Environment* [1981] AC 578. First, since the power to enter into a statutory agreement was given by planning legislation, an agreement can only be entered into for a planning purpose, not an extraneous one. Secondly, as with the exercise of all public law powers, the power has to be exercised reasonably in accordance with *Wednesbury* principles *(Associated Provincial Picture Houses Ltd* v *Wednesbury Corporation* [1948] 1 KB 223). In the view of the court, however, it was not necessary that the purposes of a statutory planning agreement should 'fairly and reasonably be related to the permitted development'.

In *R* v *Wealden District Council, ex parte Charles Church (South East) Ltd* [1989] JPL 837, it was again held that the test of a fair and reasonable relationship to the development proposed did not apply to the making of statutory planning agreements. If this is correct, then there is no legal fetter on the power of the local planning authority to extract planning gain, other than the test of reasonableness and the knowledge that if the authority attempts to extract too much in the way of gain, the Secretary of State on appeal may grant planning permission without any planning agreement at all. If, on the other hand, the courts were to decide that a planning agreement must fairly and reasonably relate to the permitted development, the advantages of a planning agreement as opposed to the imposition of conditions in the planning permission becomes otiose, apart from the fact that a condition cannot require monetary payments to be made by a developer whereas a developer may agree to do so via a planning agreement, and the fact that it was easier for an authority to enforce the terms of a planning agreement (by an injunction) than it is to enforce compliance with a condition (by an enforcement notice).

More recently, in *Safeway Properties Ltd* v *Secretary of State for the Environment* [1991] JPL 966, the Court of Appeal allowed an appeal from the refusal of the High Court to quash a decision by the Secretary of State to refuse outline planning permission for a superstore, petrol filling station and ancillary development, on the ground that the Inspector who had conducted the inquiry into the appeal had wrongly excluded from consideration an offer by the developers to provide financial assistance for the implementation of traffic management measures which, it was claimed, would go some way to alleviate the effects of increased traffic in the vicinity of the site and would benefit the already overcrowded traffic system in the locality generally. The Court of Appeal held that there were insufficient reasons for the Inspector to conclude that the measures to be financed by Safeways were not so directly related to the proposed development of the site that the superstore ought not to be permitted without them. Unfortunately, because the court was concerned merely with the correctness of the interpretation given by an Inspector to the ministerial Circular on Planning Agreements, No. 22/83, it did not have an opportunity to clarify the legal uncertainty over the precise relationships between the determination of applications for planning permission and planning gain.

The position is still not free from doubt. In *R* v *Plymouth City Council (ex parte Plymouth and South Devon Co-operative Society)* [1993] JPL 1099 (a case concerned with planning obligations and referred to later), the Court of Appeal held that the test of materiality for the purpose of s. 70(2) of the 1990 Act was, as with a condition imposed in a grant of planning permission, that (a) it had to serve a planning purpose, (b) it had to relate fairly and reasonably to the development permitted, and (c) it had to be not *Wednesbury* unreasonable. Yet in *Good* v *Epping Forest District Council* [1994] JPL 372 (a case concerned with planning agreements) the Court of Appeal accepted that planning agreements could be valid even though they went beyond what could be required by condition. Indeed Ralph Gibson LJ, who gave the leading judgment, said:

> ... it is not surprising that section 52 agreements might go to matters beyond those that fairly and reasonably relate to the development ... because there would be little point in enacting section 52 ... if section 52 agreements were confined to those matters which could be dealt with by way of conditions.

In 1980, the growing use of planning agreements together with uncertainty about the legal and administrative contours within which they should operate, persuaded the government to ask a body called the Property Advisory Group to consider and report on the arrangements whereby local planning authorities, in granting planning permission, achieve planning or amenity gains at the expense of developers.

Following the Group's report, *Planning Gain,* the government issued Circular No. 22/83 giving guidance and advice on how far it was proper for a local planning authority to seek from a developer benefits which went beyond the development for which planning permission was being sought. The Circular said that authorities were not entitled to treat an applicant's need for planning permission as an opportunity to obtain wholly extraneous benefits from the developer. According to the Circular, the reasonableness of asking the developer to accept an obligation over and above his development proposals depended substantially on whether what was required:

(a)   was needed to enable the development to go ahead, e.g., provision of adequate access, water supply, sewerage and sewage disposal facilities;

(b)   in the case of financial payments, would contribute to meeting the cost of providing such facilities in the near future;

(c)   was otherwise so directly related to the proposed development and to the use of land after its completion that the development ought not to be permitted without it, e.g., the provision, whether by the developer or by the authority at the developer's expense, of car-parking in or near the development or of reasonable amounts of open space related to the development; or

(d)   was designed in the case of mixed development to secure an acceptable balance of uses.

Where those tests were met two others were to be applied. They were whether:

(a)   the extent of what was required was fairly and reasonably related in scale and kind to the proposed development;

(b)   what the developer was being asked to provide or help to finance represented in itself a reasonable charge on the developer as distinct from being financed by national or local taxation or other means (e.g., as a charge on those using the facility provided).

The Circular reminded authorities that sought to impose unreasonable obligations in connection with a grant of planning permission that the developer was entitled to refuse to accept the demands being made and to appeal to the Secretary of State against any subsequent refusal of permission or imposition of a condition or the non-determination of the application.

16.2   Proposals for change

One of the many problems with planning agreements was that only the developer and local planning authorities could be parties to it. A developer was not obliged to enter into an agreement and if a local planning authority decided to hold out for one, he could only appeal against non-determination of the application or its refusal, whichever was the case. The Inspector or the Secretary of State could then conclude, however, that permission could be given if there was an agreement to meet some requirement that could not be met by the imposition of a condition. In such cases, the only action the Inspector could take, apart from refusal, was to suggest that an agreement might be entered into. This was unsatisfactory, however, since on the one hand the Inspector or Secretary of State could not specify the terms of such an agreement which was a matter for negotiation between the parties; and, on the other, the developer might be unable to reach agreement on its terms with the local planning authority.

Accordingly, the government proposed that there should be statutory provision to enable a developer to give a unilateral undertaking (which would be binding on him and on successors in title) to carry out certain works or to do whatever the undertaking may specify. The advantage of such an undertaking, which would be enforceable by the local authority, was that it would not be necessary for the local planning authority to agree its terms. In considering the related planning application or appeal, the authority or the Secretary of State respectively would be required to have regard to the terms of any unilateral undertaking offered by the developer (or any agreement into which he was willing to enter), and the developer would be able to give further undertakings (or offer to enter into further agreements) during the course of appeal proceedings.

Another difficulty with planning agreements related to the power given by s. 299 of the 1990 Act for an application for planning permission to be made for the development of Crown land prior to its disposal. The provision did not, however, enable a government department to enter into a planning agreement with the local planning authority under the old s. 106 of the 1990 Act. Difficulties had arisen in cases where the local planning authority considered that such an agreement was needed before planning permission could be granted. The government proposed, therefore, an amendment to s. 299 to enable government departments to enter into s. 106 agreements in appropriate circumstances and to give unilateral undertakings as proposed above.

The government's other proposal was to amend the law concerning the extent to which s. 52 or s. 106 agreements could be discharged or modified. A party to such an agreement could apply to the Lands Tribunal for the agreement (or part of it) to be discharged if it was obsolete, but there was no provision for appeal against an agreement which, while not obsolete in legal terms, no longer had utility or validity for planning purposes. For example, an individual might have bought land which enjoyed planning permission for residential development but was subject to a s. 52 or s. 106 agreement to maintain access to a community building beyond the site. If in the time elapsed since the permission was granted and the agreement was made, a different access to the community building has been provided across other land, the need for the planning agreement in connection with the residential permission will have disappeared. Furthermore, the Lands Tribunal had no jurisdiction either to modify or discharge a *positive* covenant contained in a planning agreement.

Accordingly, the government decided to legislate to enable a party entering into or giving the new planning obligation to apply to the local planning authority for the obligation (or part of it) to be discharged on the ground that its planning purpose has ended or was no longer relevant, so that the permission would become (to that extent) unencumbered.

Research carried out for the Department of the Environment prior to the Planning and Compensation Act 1991 on the use of planning agreements indicated that the average proportion of planning decisions accompanied by planning agreements within the sample authorities over the survey period April 1987 to March 1990 was just over 0.5 per cent. The application of those findings to all local planning authorities in England suggests that the number of planning agreements entered into by them is likely to have been between 6,500 and 8,000 annually. The report also reveals, however, that just over 10 per cent of planning agreements had conditions imposed in the grant of planning permission replicated in the agreement, and that almost 20 per cent of agreements cited particular stages in the development process (such as subsequent approval of plans or materials) as matters for agreement. This practice, however, was quite contrary to Ministerial guidance, expressed in Circular No. 16/91, that the terms of a condition imposed on a planning permission should not be restated in a planning obligation.

16.3   Planning obligations (the new regime)

Section 12 of the 1991 Act replaced s. 106 of the 1990 Act with a new ss. 106, 106A and 106B. The new section 106, amended the law relating to 'planning agreements' by enabling a developer to enter into a 'planning obligation', which may be done *either* by agreement with the authority, or by the developer giving a unilateral undertaking. In addition, the new s. 106 provides for planning obligations to include positive obligations. The new provisions, however, do not affect planning agreements entered into on or before 25 October 1991. These agreements will continue to be governed by the old law.

The new s. 106A of the 1990 Act enables a person bound by a planning obligation to apply to the local planning authority for its modification or discharge, and the new s. 106B enables a person bound by an obligation to appeal to the Secretary of State where the local planning authority refuse or fail to determine an application for its modification or discharge.

16.4   Creation of planning obligations

The new s. 106 of the 1990 Act provides that any person interested in land in the area of a local planning authority may, by agreement or otherwise, enter into an obligation (defined as 'a planning obligation'). The section provides that such obligation may restrict the development or use of land in some specified way; require specified operations or activities to be carried out in, on, under or over land; require the land to be used in some specified way; or require a sum or sums to be paid to the authority on a specified date or dates or periodically. It is interesting to note that the new section sets out in rather more detail than did the old the purpose of a planning obligation. The obligation may provide for money payments to be made, either of a specific amount or by reference to a formula, and require periodical payments to be paid indefinitely or for a specific period. There is no specific requirement, however, that the payments relate to the land itself or to the development which is to be carried out.

It will be apparent that (as with the old provision) it is still open to a developer to agree with a local planning authority to enter into a planning obligation. Such agreement, however, is no longer essential. It may be, therefore, that after negotiation with a developer the local planning authority declines to accept a planning obligation offered by the developer. Now, under the new provisions, on an appeal to the Secretary of State against the refusal of planning permission (or perhaps an appeal against non-determination of an application), the Secretary of State is able, at the same time as granting planning permission, to accept under the new s. 106 an undertaking by the developer to which the local planning authority are not a party but which, when accepted by the Secretary of State, is enforceable by the authority against the party giving it and any of their successors in title.

As with agreements under the old s. 106, a planning obligation runs with the land and may be enforced not only against the person entering into the obligation but also persons deriving title from that person. Although under the old s. 106, it was possible for an obligation entered into by the local planning authority to be enforced by means of an injunction, the new s. 106 now specifically provides for enforcement by this means. In addition, however, the new section provides that in the event of a breach of any requirement in a planning obligation to carry out any operations, the local planning authority may enter the land and carry out the operations and recover the cost of doing so from the person against whom the obligation is enforceable. The new s. 106 provides that a planning obligation may not be entered into except by way of a deed (presumably to ensure enforceability should there be an absence of consideration from the authority); that the deed should state that the obligation is a planning obligation for the purposes of the section; that it identifies the land concerned; that it identifies the person entering into the obligation and states his interest; and that it identifies the authority by whom the obligation is enforceable. Under the section a planning obligation may be unconditional or subject to conditions. It may also impose restrictions or requirements for an indefinite or specified period, thus enabling, for example, an obligation to end when a planning permission expires.

The new s. 106 also provides that a planning obligation shall be a local land charge for the purposes of the Local Land Charges Act 1975. If, therefore, it is not registered as a local land charge, it remains binding upon a bona fide purchaser of the land for value, but such purchaser will be entitled under the Act to compensation for non-registration.

16.5 Modification and discharge of planning obligations

Under the old law, any person wishing to secure the modification or discharge of a restrictive covenant entered into as part of a s. 52 or s. 106 agreement, could apply to the Lands Tribunal under s. 84 of the Law of Property Act 1925. This procedure was considered to be unsatisfactory, since, as previously stated, the discharge or modification of positive covenants in an agreement was outwith the jurisdiction of the Lands Tribunal; and in determining whether or not to allow discharge or modification of restrictive covenants, the courts have taken the view that a restrictive covenant such as one not to build on land is not necessarily obsolete because planning permission has since been granted for the development of that land.

Accordingly, it has been decided that, since covenants are entered into exclusively for a planning purpose, the jurisdiction of the Lands Tribunal should not apply to planning obligations. The new s. 106A of the 1990 Act, therefore, provides that any person against whom a *planning obligation* is enforceable at any time after the 'relevant period', may apply to the local planning authority for the obligation to be modified in some specified way or to be discharged. The 'relevant period' means such period as may be prescribed by the Secretary of State, or a period of five years from the date the obligation is entered into.

Where an application is made to a local planning authority to modify or discharge a planning obligation, the authority may determine that the obligation should continue to have effect without modification; or if the obligation no longer serves a useful purpose, that it shall be discharged; or if the obligation continues to serve a useful purpose but would serve that purpose equally well if it had effect subject to the modifications specified in the application, that it shall have effect subject to those modifications.

16.6 Appeals

The new s. 106B of the 1990 Act provides for a right of appeal to the Secretary of State when a local planning authority fails to determine an application for the discharge or modification of a planning obligation within the prescribed period for so doing, or determines that a planning obligation shall continue to have effect without modification. On an appeal, the Secretary of State has the same powers in relation to the application as has the local planning authority. Where an appeal is made under these provisions, the applicant or the authority must be given an opportunity of appearing before and being heard by a person appointed by the Secretary of State for that purpose.

The new statutory provisions enable the Secretary of State to make regulations governing applications to a local planning authority to modify or discharge a planning obligation and appeals to the Secretary of State when such applications are refused or not determined. The regulations now made, the Town and Country Planning (Modification and Discharge of Planning Obligations) Regulation 1992 (SI 1992 No. 2832), make provision with regard to the form and content of applications and appeals, notification of and publicity for applications, determination of applications and determination of appeals by persons appointed by the Secretary of State.

It should be noted that the 1991 Act also inserts a new s. 299A into the 1990 Act. The provision enables a planning obligation to be entered into (by the appropriate authority) with regard to Crown land. Once entered into, the obligation can be enforced against any person with a private interest in the land. In any other case, however, enforcement of the obligation, whether by injunction or by entering land, requires the consent of the appropriate authority.

16.7 Conclusion

In advance of the commencement of the amendments made to the 1990 Act, the Secretary of State issued a new Circular No. 16/91, 'Planning Obligations'. This Circular cancels the old Circular No. 22/83 on Planning Gain which gave advice on the use of planning agreements. The new Circular not only describes the legal effect of the new s. 106 but gives policy guidance on the use of planning obligations. Although there are some differences between the two Circulars, the essential guidance remains the same. Paras B7 to B9 as follows:

B7   As with conditions (see DOE Circular 1/85, Welsh Office Circular 1/85), planning obligations should only be sought where they are necessary to the granting of permission, relevant to planning, and relevant to the development to be permitted. Unacceptable development should never be permitted because of unrelated benefits offered by the applicant, nor should an acceptable development be refused permission simply because the applicant is unable or unwilling to offer such unrelated benefits.
B8   The test of the reasonableness of seeking a planning obligation from an applicant for planning permission depends on whether what is required:

(a)   is needed to enable the development to go ahead, for example the provision of adequate access or car parking; or
(b)   in the case of financial payment will contribute to meeting the cost of providing such facilities in the near future; or
(c)   is otherwise so directly related to the proposed development and to the use of the land after its completion, that the development ought not to be permitted without it, e.g., the provision, whether by the applicant or by the authority at the applicant's expense, of car parking in or near the development, of reasonable amounts of open space related to the development, or of social, education, recreational, sporting or other community provision the need for which arises from the development; or
(d)   is designed in the case of mixed development to secure an acceptable balance of uses; or to secure the implementation of local plan policies for a particular area or type of development (e.g., the inclusion of an element of affordable housing in a larger residential development); or
(e)   is intended to offset the loss of or impact on any amenity or resource present on the site prior to development, for example in the interests of nature conservation. The Department welcomes the initiatives taken by some developers in creating nature reserves, planting trees, establishing wildlife ponds and providing other nature conservation benefits. This echoes the Government's view in *This Common Inheritance* (Cm. 1200) that local

authorities and developers should work together in the interest of preserving the natural environment.

Planning obligations can therefore relate to land, roads or buildings other than those covered by the planning permission, provided that there is a direct relationship between the two. But they should not be sought where this connection does not exist or is too remote to be considered reasonable.

B9 If what is required passes one of the tests set out in the preceding paragraph, a further test has to be applied. This is whether the extent of what is required is fairly and reasonably related in scale and kind to the proposed development. Thus a developer may reasonably be expected to pay for or contribute to the cost of infrastructure which would not have been necessary but for his development, but his payments should be directly related in scale to the benefit which the proposed development will derive from the facilities to be provided. So, for example, a developer may reach agreement with an infrastructure undertaker to bring forward in time a project which is already programmed but is some years from implementation.

For the first time, Ministerial policy guidance has accepted that the provision of social infrastructure by a developer may be a legitimate requirement of any decision to grant planning permission for development.

The Circular, however, also introduces two new criteria to the test of reasonableness, namely whether what is required from the developer is designed to secure the implementation of local plan policies for a particular area or type of development (e.g., affordable housing), or whether what is required is intended to offset the loss of or impact on amenities or resource present on the site prior to development (e.g., in the interests of nature conservation).

It can be seen that the real importance of the amendments made to the 1990 Act by the Planning and Compensation Act 1991 is twofold. First, the amendments enable a landowner to offer to the authority or Secretary of State a unilateral undertaking to be bound by an obligation. As stated earlier, if, under the old provisions, planning permission was refused because an applicant was unable to agree the terms of an agreement with an authority, the Secretary of State had to decide any appeal on the basis of that non-agreement. Now he can usurp the role of the authority, accept the undertaking and grant planning permission. Secondly, the new provisions provide a simplified system for the modification or discharge of planning obligations entered into after 25 October 1991, whether of a restrictive or positive kind, where the planning merits alone dictate that they should be modified or discharged.

The changes themselves, however, do not appear to have clarified the extent to which a local planning authority can require a developer to provide — or take into account an offer from a developer to provide — community benefits beyond those demanded by the development itself. The problem has been considered by the Court of Appeal in three recent cases.

(a) *R v Plymouth City Council (ex parte Plymouth and South Devon Co-operative Society)* [1993] JPL 1099

In 1992, the market leaders in the food retailing business J. Sainsbury plc and Tesco Stores Ltd were each granted planning permission by Plymouth City Council, the local planning authority for the city, for the erection of a superstore on the city's outskirts. Both permissions were dependent upon the companies entering into an agreement under s. 106 of the 1990 Act as amended whereby each company covenanted to provide, or provide funding for, various projects which formed no part of the development itself. In particular, J. Sainsbury plc agreed to provide the city with a tourist information centre, an art gallery display and a bird-watching hide. The company also agreed to make contributions towards the development of the city's park-and-ride facilities and a much-needed increase in the city's crèche provision for working mothers. The total cost to the company of meeting these and other covenants was to be in excess of £3.6 million. Tesco Stores Ltd too agreed to provide, following the grant of planning permission, a variety of benefits not directly related to the development for which the company had applied.

Not surprisingly, a third major food retailer present in the area, the Plymouth and South Devon Co-operative Society, sought (albeit unsuccessfully) both in the High Court and the Court of Appeal to challenge the Council's decision. The society had found itself faced with two competitors, whereas previously it had expected that there would, at most, be only one.

It will be recalled that s. 70(2) of the 1990 Act provides that in determining an application for planning permission, the local planning authority 'shall have regard to the provision of the development plan, so far as material to the application, and to any other material consideration'. The Society's case was that the City Council had acted unlawfully by taking into account immaterial considerations, namely, the offers by the other two food retailers to provide some or all of the community benefits. The Society argued that in order for a benefit to be taken into account it had to be 'necessary', that is, needed in order to overcome what would otherwise be a planning objection to the development or some harm which would flow from it. Both the High Court and the Court of Appeal rejected the Society's argument. A unanimous Court of Appeal [1993] JPL 1099 held that the test of materiality was (as with a condition imposed in a grant of planning permission by the *Newbury* case) threefold, namely, it had to serve a planning purpose; it had to fairly and reasonably relate to the development permitted; and it had to be not *Wednesbury* unreasonable. The Court of Appeal held that all the benefits offered by Sainsbury's and Tesco met that threefold test.

The decision of the Court of Appeal was thought by some to have far-reaching consequences. It would seem that in determining applications for planning permission, a local planning authority can now take into account any benefit (including those not necessary for the development to proceed) provided that it fairly and reasonably relates to the permitted development). The benefit no longer has to be one whose absence would justify the refusal of planning permission. The decision suggested that the advice contained in para. B8 of Circular No. 16/91 is, at best, inaccurate. At worst, it indicates an avenue whereby the test currently laid down in the Circular can be circumvented by a developer anxious to secure planning permission from a local planning authority who are themselves anxious to obtain a contribution from developers to meet the cost of other socially desirable benefits. Above all, despite judicial statement in the case that planning permission cannot be bought or sold, it raises the spectre that this indeed may happen, particularly in those cases where the scales between a grant or refusal of planning permission are evenly balanced.

(b) *Tesco Stores Ltd v Secretary of State for the Environment and West Oxfordshire District Council and Tarmac Provincial Properties Ltd* [1994] JPL 919
Tesco Stores Ltd and Tarmac Properties Ltd both sought planning permission to build a retail store on the outskirts of Witney in Oxfordshire. Following a public inquiry into both proposals, the Inspector recommended permission for Tesco but not for Tarmac. Contrary to those recommendations the Secretary of State refused Tesco's application but granted Tarmac permission.

At the public inquiry, the county council had argued that full private funding for a new road to the west of the town (the West End Link Road) had to be provided if a superstore was to be built on either of the proposed sites. Tesco was willing to provide such funding if it was permitted to develop its site.

The Secretary of State considered that, given the distance between the link road and the proposed store, the relationship between them was tenuous. Using the tests of reasonableness set out in para. B8 of Annex B to Circular 16/91, the Secretary of State did not consider that the link road was necessary to enable any of the superstore proposals to go ahead, or was otherwise so directly related in scale to any of the proposed developments that they might not be permitted without it. Full funding of the link road was not, according to the Secretary of State, fairly and reasonably related in scale to any of the proposed developments. Furthermore, given that the increase in traffic using the link road as a result of building the superstore might be less than 10 per cent, it would be unreasonable to seek even a partial contribution from developers towards the cost.

Tesco applied under s. 228 of the 1990 Act for the Secretary of State's decisions to be quashed. It argued that its offer to fund the link road was a material consideration which the Secretary of State should have taken into account and that he had erred in applying the tests in Annex B of Circular 16/91, in particular, that he had applied an inappropriate test of necessity. This challenge was upheld in the High Court but rejected by the Court of Appeal.

In the High Court the learned deputy judge, following the *Plymouth* case, held that although the offer of full funding went beyond what was 'necessary', it was a material consideration because it was fairly and reasonably related to the proposed development. Although the tests is *Newbury District Council v Secretary of State for the Environment* [1981] AC 578 (which had been applied to planning obligations in the *Plymouth* case) were silent on the question of scale, the Secretary of State should have had regard to the Tesco offer. The Court of Appeal, however, held that he had done so, but because the Secretary of State had found that there was only a tenuous connection between the link road and the proposed development, he must have concluded that the offer of full funding was material but had given it no weight (which he was entitled to do). Steyn LJ said that it was not open to the Secretary of State to dilute the *Newbury* requirements but, in the exercise of his wide statutory discretion, he could adopt a more stringent policy. Steyn LJ, however, thought that his reasoning could not easily be reconciled with the decision in the *Plymouth* case, which he considered 'obliquely destroyed the core of the Circular' and 'became perilously close to emasculating the principle that planning permission may not be sold and bought'.

(c) *Good* v *Epping Forest District Council* [1994] JPL 372

In *Good* v *Epping Forest District Council* the plaintiff sought unsuccessfully sought to challenge the legality of a s. 52 agreement concerning an agricultural occupancy requirement on the ground that its provisions could not have been imposed as planning conditions, and therefore could not have been imposed under a planning agreement. It was argued that as a local planning authority can decide applications only on the basis of material considerations, a planning agreement should not stray beyond what was material.

Rejecting the argument, the Court of Appeal held that a s. 52 agreement could go beyond what could be required by the use of conditions in a grant of planning permission. In other words, an agreement could go beyond what was necessary to allow the development to proceed, or beyond what was fairly and reasonably related to the development. Although the case concerned a s. 52 agreement, there is no reason to suppose that it would not apply equally to a planning obligation entered into under the new s. 106 of the 1990 Act.

In the *Tesco* case, Steyn LJ suggested that the *Plymouth* case may require reconsideration. Furthermore, the decision in *Good* v *Epping Forest District Council* sits unhappily with both the *Plymouth* and *Tesco* decisions. So three Court of Appeal decisions in different cases, by nine different Lord Justices of Appeal, have failed to lay down the precise limits on the ability of a local planning authority to require or receive community benefits in excess of what is necessary for a development to proceed. For this to be achieved a ruling from the House of Lords is needed.

The legal conflict is that if the test for the receipt of community benefits is to be no more than whether the provision of them is material to the decision in the sense that they comply with the *Newbury* test, the criteria set out in the Circular becomes of little consequence. If, however, the criteria to be applied is that stated in the Circular, the Secretary of State may be open to an allegation that he is misdirecting himself as to the scope of his discretion.

SEVENTEEN
Appeals

17.1 Introduction

From most decisions of local planning authorities there is an appeal to the Secretary of State and from him to the courts on a point of law.

The main right of appeal is that given by s. 78 of the 1990 Act, which provides for an appeal against the refusal of planning permission or a conditional grant of planning permission.

The s. 78 machinery is also available where the local planning authority have failed to give a decision on an application for planning permission within the period prescribed for so doing, and appeals against the refusal of any approval required under the General Development Order or an outline planning permission.

Other appeal machinery exists in relation to enforcement notices, listed buildings and conservation area consents, listed building enforcement notices, certificates of lawfulness of existing or proposed use or development, tree preservation orders and advertising consent.

Unless an application for planning permission is granted unconditionally, the applicant is told in addition to the decision the reasons for the decision, and that he may give notice of appeal to the Secretary of State within a period of six months or such longer period as the Secretary of State may allow.

A notice of appeal, made by completing a form obtainable from the Secretary of State, should be accompanied by a copy of such of the following documents as are relevant to the appeal:

(a) the application made to the local planning authority which has occasioned the appeal;

(b) all plans, drawings and documents sent to the authority in connection with the application;

(c) all correspondence with the authority relating to the application;

(d) any notices or any certificates provided to the authority in accordance with the provisions of a development order made under s. 65 of the Act;

(e)   any other plans or drawings relating to the application which were not sent to the authority;

(f)   the notice of the decision if any;

(g)   if the appeal relates to an application for approval of reserved matters, the application for outline planning permission, the plans submitted with that application and the outline planning permission granted.

An applicant must also send a copy of the notice of appeal, and of any such plans or drawings mentioned in para. 2(e) as accompany it, to the local planning authority on the same date as he gives notice to the Secretary of State.

The Secretary of State is not bound to entertain the appeal, though the occasions on which he has not done so are thought to be rare. Under s. 79(6) of the 1990 Act, if the Secretary of State is of the opinion that, having regard to the provisions of ss. 70 and 72(1) of the Act and the development order, planning permission could not have been granted by the local planning authority or could not have been granted by the authority otherwise than subject to the conditions imposed, he may decline to determine the appeal. This might occur, for example, where the local planning authority has been directed by the Secretary of State to refuse planning permission or to impose conditions on any permission granted.

Before determining an appeal under s. 78, the Secretary of State is required by s. 79(2), if either the applicant or the local planning authority so desire, to afford to each of them an opportunity of appearing before and being heard by, a person appointed by the Secretary of State for that purpose. In most cases where use is made of this facility, a public local inquiry takes place before a person appointed for that purpose, known as an 'Inspector'.

Although in law the decision made on appeal is that of the Secretary of State, in the majority of cases appeal decisions are made by Inspectors, that is, by members of the Department's Planning Inspectorate, standing in the shoes of the Secretary of State. In 1968 it was established that more than 90 per cent of the recommendations made by Inspectors to the Minister following a public local inquiry were accepted by him. It was decided, therefore, to give Inspectors the power to make decisions on behalf of the Minister. These cases are sometimes referred to as 'transferred cases'. Given originally for a limited class of development and a limited range of appeals, the power has now been extended by the Town and Country Planning (Determination of Appeals by Appointed Persons) (Prescribed Classes) Regulations 1981 (SI No. 804) to all planning appeals (with the exception of appeals by statutory undertakers relating to the development of operational land), to all enforcement notice appeals and to some appeals made against the refusal of listed building consent and listed building enforcement notices. Under the 1990 Act, however, the Secretary of State has power to recover jurisdiction from an Inspector in any particular case. These cases are known as 'recovered' cases.

Among the criteria for recovering jurisdiction are the following:

(a)   Residential development of 150 or more houses.

(b)   Proposals for development of major importance having more than local significance.

(c)   Proposals giving rise to significant public controversy.

(d)   Proposals which raise important or novel issues of development control.

(e)   Retail development over 100,000 square feet.

(f)   Proposals for significant development in the green belt.

(g)   Major proposals involving the winning and working of minerals.

(h)   Proposals which raise significant legal difficulties.

(i)   Proposals against which another government department has raised major objections.

(j)   Cases which can only be decided in conjunction with a case over which Inspectors have no jurisdiction (so-called 'linked' cases).

In the year 1993/94, of 14,113 appeals decided in England, 13,868 were decided by Inspectors on behalf of the Secretary of State, whilst only 245 were recovered and decided by the Secretary of State.

Not every case recovered by the Secretary of State for his own decision necessarily involves the Secretary of State personally making the decision. It will often be made by a senior official in the decision branch of the department, acting for the Secretary of State. Recovered cases which are likely to be referred personally to the Secretary of State include:

(a)   Cases in which the decision branch propose to go against the Inspector's recommendation on the planning merits.

(b)   Cases involving significant development in the green belt.

(c)   Where the proposed decision is to refuse permission for a development involving more than 150 dwellings, or covering more than 6 hectares.

(d)   Where it appears that there is considerable political interest because of representations received from a Member of Parliament.

(e)   Sensitive or major appeals.

17.2   Dismissal of appeals in cases of undue delay

Section 18 of the 1991 Act has introduced a new provision in the 1990 Act to deal with delay by developers in the determination of appeals. In the past this has occurred with twin-tracking, the tactical device whereby developers submit two identical applications for planning permission to the local planning authority. The intention in doing so is to allow negotiations with the authority to continue on one application after the expiry of the eight-week period for the authority to determine the application, whilst at the same time lodging an appeal to the Secretary of State against non-determination of the other application. Once an appeal is lodged, the developer may do little to pursue the appeal until the authority have either granted planning permission, in which case the appeal is withdrawn; or refuse planning permission, in which case the appeal is reactivated. Such action may impose considerable additional costs on both the authority and the Planning Inspectorate. In order to deal with this problem, the 1991 Act introduces a new subsection (6A) in s. 79 of the 1990

Act. It provides that if at any time before or during the determination of an appeal it appears to the Secretary of State that the appellant is responsible for undue delay in the progress of the appeal, he may give the appellant notice that the appeal will be dismissed unless the appellant takes within the period specified in the notice such steps as are specified in the notice for the expedition of the appeal. Then, if the appellant fails to take those steps within that period, the Secretary of State may dismiss the appeal without any consideration of its merits.

17.3 Natural justice

It is a long-established principle that in the interval between the decision of the local planning authority and the decision of the Secretary of State (or Inspector), the Secretary of State should not 'listen to one party behind the back of the other'. In short, the decision-maker is required by the rules of natural justice 'to hear both sides'.

One of the earliest cases to establish this was *Errington* v *Minister of Health* [1935] 1 KB 249, where the local authority had made a draft clearance order under housing legislation. Objections had been made to the order and a local inquiry held. After receiving the Inspector's report, the Minister had entered into correspondence with the authority and the Inspector, and an official of the Ministry and officers of the local authority had visited and conferred on the site. Subsequently, the Minister had confirmed the order. The objectors then successfully claimed that in hearing further evidence of one party (the local authority) behind the backs of the others (the objectors) the Minister had been guilty of a breach of natural justice and that his decision should not be allowed to stand.

A more recent example is *Fairmount Investments Ltd* v *Secretary of State for the Environment* [1976] 1 WLR 1255. In this case the applicants owned a number of houses within an area declared to be a clearance area under the Housing Act 1957. The local planning authority had subsequently made a compulsory purchase order for the purpose of demolishing the houses which it considered to be unfit for human habitation. The applicants, who contended that the houses could be rehabilitated without demolition, objected to the order and an inquiry was duly held. At the inquiry the authority published documents showing the reasons for the order and a summary of the principal grounds of unfitness. This emphasised settlement but did not suggest that it was a continuing problem. The summary did not refer to the foundations of the applicants' property nor did it suggest that they were defective and at the inquiry no reference was made to the foundations. Following the inquiry, the Inspector had visited the houses in question. In his report he had stated that the settlement in all the houses appeared to be due to the foundations 'not having been taken deeply enough into the clay'. He concluded that because of that it was his opinion that 'satisfactory rehabilitation would not be financially viable'. Following his report, the Secretary of State had confirmed the order.

In quashing the Secretary of State's decision, the House of Lords held that the decision had been made in breach of the rules of natural justice. It had been based on an opinion formed by the Inspector about the adequacy of the foundations which had not formed part of the authority's case and which the applicants had not been given an opportunity to refute. In the words of Lord Russell of Killowen, the applicants had not had 'a fair crack of the whip'.

Unfortunately, the application of the rules of natural justice to administrative decisions must remain uncertain both as regards their extent and scope. With thousands of appeal decisions to be made each year, administrators require something more concrete on which to base the conduct of the inquiry process than sporadic judicial decisions. Accordingly, the Lord Chancellor, after consultation with the Secretary of State, has exercised a power under what was s. 11 of the Tribunals and Inquiries Act 1971 (now the Tribunals and Inquiries Act 1992) to make rules (Inquiry Procedure Rules) for the conduct of the most popular type of inquiry. In the field of s. 78 appeals, the existence of statutory Inquiry Procedure Rules now means that inquiries have to be conducted within the discipline of both the common law rules of natural justice and the statutory Inquiry Procedure Rules. Administrators know that if they comply with the Inquiry Procedure Rules, they are not likely to infringe the rules of natural justice. But unfortunately, it does occasionally happen.

In *Hambledon & Chiddingfold Parish Councils* v *Secretary of State for the Environment* [1976] JPL 502, it was said that although compliance with the Inquiry Procedure Rules did not mean *ipso facto* that there must have been compliance with the rules of natural justice, a complainant attempting to show otherwise faced a heavy burden of proof.

In *Granada Theatres Ltd* v *Secretary of State for the Environment* [1976] JPL 96, it was held that taking into account petitions and letters not disclosed to the applicants was a breach of the rules of natural justice.

In *Hudson* v *Secretary of State for the Environment* [1984] JPL 258, it was held that the Inspector had erred in not giving the parties an opportunity to deal with a matter of substance which had influenced his decision.

In *Simmons* v *Secretary of State for the Environment* [1985] JPL 253, the Inspector was seen by the appellant in discussion with the chairman of the planning committee of the local planning authority after the close of the inquiry. Although the Inspector was totally absolved from any bias, the decision was quashed as being contrary to natural justice.

In *Furmston* v *Secretary of State for the Environment* [1983] JPL 49, the Secretary of State submitted to judgment and paid the applicants' costs where it was alleged the Inspector had discussed the applicants' development proposal with a representative of the district council before the site meeting and with a representative of the county council after the site meeting, without any representative of the applicant being present. Although in later correspondence with the applicant the Secretary of State had said that the discussion with the county council representative had been about the district council's lack of cooperation in forwarding documentation to them, the applicant pursued his challenge because he considered that justice must not only be done but seen to be done. In fact, the Secretary of State had nothing to lose by submitting to judgment; an identical planning application to the district planning authority having by then been granted.

In *Second City (South West) Ltd* v *Secretary of State for the Environment* (1990) 61 P & CR 498, the Secretary of State had dismissed an appeal against a refusal of planning permission for residential development. In his decision letter, the Secretary of State had referred to the site as being 'outside the village fence of Backwell as identified on the Woodspring Rural Areas Local Plan' which was on deposit, and where development would not be allowed. Because the applicants had not been given an opportunity to deal with this aspect, the High Court quashed the Secretary of State's decision.

In *Cadbury Schweppes Pension Trust Ltd* v *Secretary of State for the Environment* [1990] EGCS 86, an Inspector refused to relax a condition in a planning permission granted for mixed industrial and office use in adherence to a local policy statement for the provision of on-site car-parking. Because the applicant had not been given an opportunity to comment on the point or to show that it was fallacious the High Court quashed the decision.

A somewhat unusual case is *Rockhold Ltd* v *Secretary of State for the Environment* [1986] JPL 130, where three applications for planning permission had been made for the same site. Each had gone to appeal and different Inspectors had rejected the appeals for different reasons. The applicants had challenged the decision made by the last Inspector on a number of grounds, but in particular that the decision of an Inspector ought to be consistent with earlier decisions. Forbes J held that although Inspectors ought generally to be consistent in their decisions, each Inspector was free to exercise his own judgment on matters of planning merit. After the decision had been given, however, the appellants learnt that the Inspector who had determined the appeal had also acted as a field officer (planning) for a local amenity group, the Chiltern Society. His responsibilities there included the vetting of planning applications within the area covered by the Society. Although an appeal to the Court of Appeal from the decision of Forbes J was pending, the appellants sought and obtained leave to apply for judicial review of the Inspector's decision. One reason for so doing was that if an appeal under what is now s. 288 of the 1990 Act were to succeed, it would not automatically follow that a fresh inquiry would be held. Another reason was that the additional ground of attack on the decision (namely the *appointment* of the Inspector) might not fall within the ambit of that section. The judicial review proceedings were subsequently abandoned, but only after the Court of Appeal had agreed (contrary to its normal practice) to quash the Inspector's decision by a consent order.

In another case, resolved without resort to the courts, the Inspector, accompanied by his architectural assessor, had, prior to the opening of a local inquiry into the applications for planning permission for the redevelopment of Limehouse Basin in London's East End, visited the site both on foot and by helicopter. The helicopter was, however, provided by the local planning authority and a representative of the authority had been present on the visit.

At the opening of the inquiry objectors to the application asked the Inspector to withdraw on the ground that there had been a breach of natural justice. The Inspector refused their request, but in turn offered them an opportunity to accompany him on a site visit by helicopter. This offer was accepted by some objectors but without prejudice to their rights, which they then pursued by asking the Secretary of State to intervene and remove the Inspector. This the Secretary of State duly did.

In a letter to the parties, the Secretary of State said he was satisfied that the Inspector did not in fact do anything on his original site visits which could in any way have resulted in unfairness to any of the parties at the inquiry; but he concluded that, in all the circumstances, the best course would be for him to close the inquiry and begin proceedings afresh, with a new Inspector and assessor.

The law does not require that Inspectors should deny themselves all social intercourse with the parties involved. In *Cotterell* v *Secretary of State for the Environment* [1991] JPL 1155, after a site visit, the Inspector had gone to a public house in the company of representatives of both sides. Before leaving the assembled company, the appellants' representative had offered to buy another round of drinks but this had been refused. In the event the Inspector remained in the pub with the other side for a further 20 minutes whilst they consumed another round of drinks bought by the Inspector. Dismissing an application to quash the Secretary of State's decision to uphold the local planning authority's refusal to grant planning permission for development, the learned deputy judge held that, bearing in mind the occasion started with everyone together and that the appellants' representative left the others alone, it fell on 'the right side of the line'.

In *Fox* v *Secretary of State* [1993] JPL 448, the High Court refused to quash a decision of the Secretary of State upholding the local planning authority's decision to refuse the appellant planning permission for residential development. The Inspector who conducted the inquiry had travelled to the appeal site in the company of the authority's planning officer and another witness. It appears that before doing so the Inspector had given the appellant assurances that he would not discuss the case during the journey; assurances which had been accepted by the appellant, who had travelled to the site on his own.

The court took the view that in all the circumstances, a reasonable man would not have thought that anything might have taken place during the car journey which might have affected the Inspector's impartiality. Hence, there had been no breach of natural justice. The judge added, however, that he doubted the wisdom of the Inspector asking an unrepresented appellant whether he objected to him travelling without the appellant in a car with the council's witnesses.

17.4 Written representation procedure

In many cases the Secretary of State invites the appellant and the local planning authority to dispense with a local inquiry if he considers that he can obtain the information he needs to determine the appeal from written statements submitted by the parties. The advantage of this procedure is that it is often quicker, simpler and cheaper than proceeding by way of local inquiry. It is also advantageous if the matter in dispute is one of law rather than policy, since legal argument can be presented in written form at the outset, rather than presented orally before the Inspector. The disadvantage is that publicity and openness associated with the local inquiry are absent. Nevertheless, written representation procedure (as it is called) is extremely popular. Although either the appellant or the local planning authority can demand to be heard by an Inspector, in the year 1993/94 of 14,113 appeals decided under these provisions, 11,237 (nearly 80 per cent) were decided by way of written representation procedure, as against 1,176 decided following a local inquiry and 1,700 following a hearing.

Until the Housing and Planning Act 1986, the procedure depended upon informal agreement, subject only to compliance with the rules of natural justice. There were no procedural rules applicable as with local inquiries. The 1986 Act introduced a provision (now found in s. 323 of the 1990 Act) under which the Secretary of State may make regulations prescribing the procedure to be followed where an appeal is dealt with by this method. Under this power, the Secretary of State has made the Town and Country Planning (Appeals) (Written Representations Procedure) Regulations 1987 (SI No. 701). Circular 11/87 gives guidance on the operation of the regulations. Under the regulations:

(a)   The Secretary of State is required to give immediate notice of receipt of the appeal to the local planning authority.

(b)   The authority must give specified information to interested third parties. It must also complete and submit to the Secretary of State, together with related documents, an appeals questionnaire including any representations already made by third parties. The authority may elect to treat the appeals questionnaire and the documents submitted with it as their representations in relation to the appeal. If they do not so elect, they must submit their representations to the Secretary of State.

(c)   The applicant's notice of appeal and the documents which accompany the appeal are to comprise the appellant's representations in relation to the appeal. The appellant may, however, within 17 days, make further representations by way of reply to the local planning authority.

(d)   The Secretary of State may proceed to a decision on the appeal. As all the stages required to be taken by the regulations must be taken within a prescribed timetable, the regulations allow the Secretary of State to decide the appeal taking into account only such written representations and supporting documents as have been submitted within the relevant time-limits.

The purpose of the regulations is to set a strict timetable for the operation of the appeal procedure. The timetable assumes a single exchange of statements by the parties to the appeal, though both have the opportunity to comment on each other's submission. Although not covered by the regulations (because they are intended only to provide a discipline for the parties), the Inspector will visit the site which is the subject of the appeal. Two weeks' notice of a site visit is normally given to the parties to enable them to attend should they wish to do so.

17.5 Informal hearings

As an alternative to written representation procedure or the formal local inquiry, the parties may be invited by the Secretary of State to agree to the appeal being dealt with by informal hearing. Where both parties agree, the Inspector takes a more active role in the proceedings by leading a discussion rather than by following the more formal procedures of the local inquiry. The proceedings are intended to be more relaxed than those of a local inquiry, and the parties waive their rights to cross-examine each other's witnesses.

17.6 Local inquiries

The procedure followed at a local inquiry held under s. 78 is regulated substantially by the common law rules of natural justice and by the Town and Country Planning (Inquiries Procedure) Rules 1992 (SI No. 2038) or the Town and Country Planning Appeals (Determination by Inspectors) (Inquiries Procedure) Rules 1992 (SI No. 2039). Both sets of Inquiry Procedure Rules deal with the procedure to be followed before, during and after an inquiry. Both sets also apply to local inquiries held by the Secretary of State in connection with appeals relating to tree preservation orders, listed buildings, and conservation area consents. The former set of rules apply when the Secretary of State is to make the decision after considering a recommendation of the Inspector (recovered cases), the latter set when the Inspector is making the decision on behalf of the Secretary of State (transferred cases).

Because most appeals where a local inquiry is held are determined by Inspectors, the latter set of rules (SI 1992 No. 2039) are dealt with below in some detail.

It should be noted that the Inquiries Procedure Rules have a dual purpose. As mentioned earlier, the parties involved know that by following the rules they are not likely to infringe the rules of natural justice. The second purpose of the rules, however, is to impose a discipline on the parties so that the inquiry process is conducted as efficiently and effectively as possible, which in turn should lead to speedier decisions. The rules, which came into effect on 30 September 1992, were accompanied by an explanatory Circular No. 24/92.

The 1992 rules replaced rules made in 1988. The 1988 rules had made a number of important changes to the procedures to be followed before, during and after a local inquiry. Under the pre-1988 rules, once an appeal had been accepted by the Secretary of State, the parties needed to take little formal action until 42 days before the opening of the inquiry, when the local planning authority's statement of case became due. Under the rules made in 1988 and now the 1992 rules, this is no longer possible, since all the major stages in the appeal process are programmed to take place from what is called the 'relevant date'. This is the date of the Secretary of State's written notice to the applicant and the local planning authority that it is his intention to cause a local inquiry to be held. In short, the relevant date is a trigger for all subsequent stages of the inquiry process, so that the period between acceptance of the appeal and the inquiry itself is used to greater advantage. In addition, however, the new rules provide for an early exchange of statements of case and a requirement for the pre-inquiry exchange of proofs of evidence.

17.6.1 Transferred cases (SI 1992 No. 2039)

17.6.1.1 Procedure before the inquiry

(a)   On receiving the relevant notice from the Secretary of State that an inquiry is to be held, the local planning authority must inform the Secretary of State and the appellant in writing of the name and address of any statutory party who made representations to them. Statutory parties are the owners of the land or a tenant of an agricultural holding to which the application relates, who made representations to the local planning authority within 21 days of being served with a notice of the application as required by the General Development Order (r.4(1)).

(b)   The Secretary of State must notify the name of the Inspector to every person entitled to appear at the inquiry (r. 5(1)).

(c)   No later than six weeks after the relevant date, the local planning authority must serve a statement of case on the Secretary of State, the appellant and any statutory party (r. 6(1)). Under the rules a statement of case means a 'written statement which contains full particulars of the case which a person proposes to put forward at an inquiry and a list of any documents which that person intends to refer to or put in evidence'. According to the Ministerial guidance it would be helpful if the parties provided with their statement, the data, methodology and assumptions used to support their submission. In addition, the rules provide that if the Secretary of State or any local authority has previously given to the local planning authority a direction restricting the grant of planning permission for which application was made, or the Secretary of State or any other Minister of the Crown or government department or local authority has expressed, in writing, to the local planning authority, the view that the application should not be granted either wholly or in part, or should be granted only subject to conditions, the local planning authority must include the terms of any direction; and any views expressed or representations made on which they intend to rely in their submission at the inquiry, in their statement of case.

(d)   No later than nine weeks after the relevant date, the appellant must serve a statement of case on the Secretary of State, the local planning authority and any statutory party (r. 6(3)). In addition, the Secretary of State may require *any other person* who wishes to appear at an inquiry to serve a statement of case within four weeks of being required to do so (r. 6(6)).

It will be seen that by giving the authority six weeks, but the appellant nine weeks after the relevant date to serve a statement of case, the rules give the appellant a period of three weeks for assessing the authority's statement before he is required to serve his own. Statements of case prepared under this rule are referred to colloquially as 'rule 6 statements'. It is also provided in r. 6(5) that the appellant and local planning authority may each require the other to send them a copy of any document, or of the relevant part of any document referred to in the list of documents comprised in that party's statement of case.

(e)   Where the Inspector considers it desirable to do so, he may hold a pre-inquiry meeting at not less than two weeks' written notice to the appellant, the local planning authority, any statutory party and any other person entitled to appear or whose presence at the inquiry appears to the Inspector to be desirable. Pre-inquiry meetings are normally held only when the inquiry is likely to last several weeks, either because of the 'highly technical evidence' which is likely to be submitted or because the inquiry is to deal with several proposals involving more than one applicant or appellant. Its purpose is to encourage the parties to prepare for the inquiry and avoid wasting time at the inquiry with matters which are not relevant nor in dispute. Pre-inquiry meetings may deal with such matters as: the identification of issues, nature of evidence to be submitted, exchange of proofs of evidence, presentation and numbering of plans and documents, normal sitting hours of the inquiry, its likely duration, order of presentation of cases or issues and facilities available (telex, photography, etc.).

It should be noted too, that the Inspector may not later than 12 weeks after the relevant date serve on the appellant, the local planning authority and any statutory party a written statement of the matters which appear to him to be likely to be relevant to his consideration of the appeal. Such a statement is usually served in advance of any pre-inquiry meeting (r. 7).

(f)   Unless a lesser period of notice is agreed, the Secretary of State must give not less than four weeks' written notice of the date, time and place for the holding of the inquiry to every person entitled to appear.

The rules also provide that the date fixed by the Secretary of State shall be, unless he considers it impractical — not later than 20 weeks after the relevant date. At present this '20 week' limit is not being met in all cases, but the position should improve as more and more appeals are dealt with under this new procedure. It should also be noted that the Secretary of State may require the local planning authority to serve notice of the inquiry on specified persons or classes of persons; publish notice of the inquiry in one or more newspapers circulating in the locality; and post a notice in a conspicuous place or places near to the land (r. 10).

17.6.1.2   Procedure during the inquiry

(g)   The appellant, the local planning authority, and if not the local planning authority the county or district council in whose area the land is situated, statutory parties and any other person who has served a statement of case, are among those entitled to appear at the inquiry (r. 11(1)). In addition the rule also provides that nothing in r. 11(1) 'shall prevent the Inspector from permitting any other person to appear at an inquiry, and such permission shall not be unreasonably withheld' (r. 11(2)). The latter part of this rule allows the Inspector to permit any person who can make a contribution to the determination of the appeal to appear at the inquiry.

(h)   Where the Secretary of State or any local authority has given the local planning authority a direction restricting the grant of planning permission or the Secretary of State or any other Minister or any government department or local authority has expressed in writing to the local planning authority the view that the application should not be granted, the appellant may, not later than two weeks before the date of the inquiry, apply to the Secretary of State for a representative of the Secretary of State, Minister, department or local authority to be made available at the inquiry. The rules provide that the representative shall give evidence and be subject to cross-examination to the same extent as any other witness, but that the representative of a Minister or government department shall not be required to answer any question which in the opinion of the Inspector is directed to the merits of government policy (r. 12).

(i)   A person entitled to appear at an inquiry who proposes to give, or to call another person to give, evidence at the inquiry by reading a proof of evidence must send a copy of the proof to the Inspector together with a written summary. No written summary, however, is required where the proof of evidence proposed to be read contains no more than 1,500 words. Where a copy of a proof of evidence is sent to the Inspector in accordance with the rule (with or without a summary) this must normally be done no later than three weeks before the date fixed for the holding of an inquiry; and copies of that proof and any summary must be sent at the same time to the other party and to any statutory party. Where a written summary is so provided, only the summary is to be read at the inquiry, unless the Inspector permits or requires otherwise (r. 14).

(j)   Except as is otherwise provided in the rules, the procedure at an inquiry is at the discretion of the Inspector.

The rules provide that the appellant shall normally begin and have the right of final reply; and that other persons entitled or permitted to appear shall be heard in such order as the Inspector may determine. The appellant, the local planning authority and statutory parties are entitled to call evidence and to cross-examine persons giving evidence, but any other person appearing may do so only to the extent permitted by the Inspector. Where a person gives evidence at an inquiry by reading a summary of his evidence, his statement of evidence may be tendered in evidence and the person cross-examined on it as if the statement were given orally. The Inspector may allow the local planning authority (or the appellant or both of them) to alter or add to any submissions made in their r. 6 statement, but must give (if necessary by adjourning the inquiry) the other party and any statutory parties, an adequate opportunity of considering the fresh submission. If any person appearing or present at an inquiry, behaves in the opinion of the Inspector in a disruptive manner, he may be required by the Inspector to leave (r. 15).

(k)   The Inspector may make an unaccompanied site visit before or during the inquiry without giving notice of his intention to do so. Inspectors often visit the site on their own before the commencement of the inquiry. In addition, the rules provide that the Inspector may during an inquiry or after its close (and shall if requested to do so by the appellant or the local planning authority before or during the inquiry) inspect the land. On making such an inspection, the appellant, the local planning authority and statutory parties are entitled to accompany the Inspector, though he is not obliged to defer the inspection if a person entitled to accompany him is not present at the time appointed (r. 16).

The reason for site visits is to enable the Inspector to visually assess the impact of the proposed development on the immediate surroundings. No discussion of the merits of an appeal is allowed during a site inspection.

17.6.1.3 Procedure after the inquiry

(1) The rules provide that if, after the close of the inquiry, the Inspector proposes to take into consideration any new evidence or any new matter of fact (not being a matter of government policy) which was not raised at the inquiry and which he considers to be material to his decision, he shall not come to a decision without first notifying the persons entitled to appear at the inquiry who appeared at it of the matter in question; and affording them an opportunity of making representations to him in respect of it within three weeks of the date of notification or of asking within that period for the reopening of the inquiry (r. 17).

The genesis of this provision is to be found in the notorious *Chalk Pit* case in 1961. There, the owners of land in Essex applied for planning permission to develop land by quarrying chalk. The local planning authority refused the application on the ground that it would affect crops and livestock on neighbouring land. The owners appealed against the refusal to the Minister of Housing and Local Government, who appointed an Inspector to hold a local inquiry. Although the Inspector recommended that the appeal be rejected, the Minister allowed it and granted planning permission. It then became known that after the Inspector had made his recommendations, the Minister had had discussions with the Ministry of Agriculture, Fisheries and Food, who had convinced him that with proper safeguards the quarrying could be carried out without adversely affecting the neighbouring land. Adjacent landowners then applied to the High Court to set aside the Minister's decision. In *Buxton* v *Minister of Housing & Local Government* [1961] 1 QB 278, the court held that the statutory review procedure available under the Act to challenge the decision of the Minister was only available to a person aggrieved by that decision, and that Buxton (one of the neighbours affected) did not have the necessary standing to challenge the Minister's decision because he had not been aggrieved in the legal sense. Although the authority of that decision has since been progressively weakened, the landowners, having been defeated on a preliminary issue, secured detailed consideration of the problem by the Council on Tribunals, which led to a subsequent special report by the Council and the adoption of their proposals to amend the Inquiry Procedure Rules in the manner indicated above. This particular provision, however, has not been a fertile field of litigation. This is because Inspectors (and also the Secretary of State in recovered cases) are meticulously careful to ensure that they do not take into account new evidence or new issues of fact in breach of the rules.

(m) The Inspector is required to notify his decision and his reasons for it, in writing, to all persons entitled to appear at the inquiry who did appear, and to any other person who, having appeared at the inquiry, had asked to be notified of the decision (r. 18).

The obligation to state reasons for the decision has given rise to a considerable volume of litigation. In *Givaudan & Co. Ltd* v *Minister of Housing*

& Local Government [1967] 1 WLR 250, it was held that reasons must be adequate and intelligible. The obligation to give reasons was not met where they were scanty, uninformative and unintelligible.

In *Kent Messenger Ltd* v *Secretary of State for the Environment* [1976] JPL 372, an application had been made for listed building consent for the demolition of a listed building. Following an inquiry into an appeal against the refusal to grant consent, the Inspector had recommended to the Secretary of State that consent be granted on the ground that it would be uneconomic for the appellants to repair the building and to maintain it when repaired. The Secretary of State did not accept the recommendation and rejected the appeal. In his decision letter he dealt with the issue of the cost of restoring the building but not with the utility of the restoration. The court quashed the decision on the ground that the reasons stated were neither proper nor adequate.

The case raises the very important question of the extent to which the decision must deal with every point raised on appeal. In *Mountview Court Properties Ltd* v *Devlin* (1970) 21 P & CR 689, it was said:

> What reasons are sufficient in any particular case must, of course, depend upon the facts of the case . . . reasons are not deficient merely because every process of reasoning is not set out . . . reasons are not insufficient merely because they fail to deal with every point raised . . .

This approach was echoed in *Elliot* v *Southwark London Borough Council* [1976] 1 WLR 499, where it was said that a statement of reasons must be something more than a mere statement of conclusions. It must certainly state the salient reason, though it is not necessary to deal with every point of detail and every issue raised by the parties.

In *French Kier Developments Ltd* v *Secretary of State for the Environment* [1977] JPL 30, a challenge was made to the decision of the Secretary of State to dismiss an appeal against a refusal of the local planning authority to grant planning permission for residential development in the green belt. The Inspector conducting the inquiry had recommended (in a recovered case) that permission be granted. The Secretary of State decided otherwise, because he took a different view of policy considerations than that taken by the Inspector. Unfortunately, he did not say this in his decision letter, with the result that the decision was quashed because his reasons were inadequate. According to Willis J nothing could have been vaguer than the words used in the decision letter.

There is no doubt that landowners have sought to use the requirement to give reasons as a convenient peg on which to hang a judicial challenge to the decision made. In doing so, they have sought to show that the decision letter has failed to deal with one of the contentious issues raised by them on appeal. For their part, the courts are alert to the danger of subjecting decision letters to a hypercritical analysis. In the *French Kier* case, Willis J thought that a decision letter was not to be construed like a statute or a philosophical treatise, but the appellants and the local planning authority were entitled to a clear and intelligible statement of the reasons for the decision.

In the *Kent Messenger* case it was said that a decision letter must not be approached with 'niggling pedantry'. It cannot be impugned merely because it does not refer to or take into account every submission made to the Inspector or every point that is controversial.

In *Preston Borough Council* v *Secretary of State for the Environment* [1978] JPL 548, it was said that the court would not indulge in a 'nook and cranny exercise'. If it was shown that there was something of such importance that the applicant's or authority's case had not been properly put to the Secretary of State, the court might in a proper case say there had been a breach of the Inquiry Procedure Rules if they applied or the rules of natural justice.

In considering the obligation to state reasons it seems that the Secretary of State (or the Inspector) must not just give some reasons, but must give reasons which deal with the substantive matters which go to produce the eventual decision. The test is whether on a reasonably fair reading of the decision letter, the appellant and the local planning authority are given reasons dealing with all the essential issues raised in the appeal, and against a background that recipients of a decision letter are well-tutored.

In a more recent case, the House of Lords held that the three criteria of propriety, intelligibility and adequacy were regarded as essential for compliance with the rule. Their lordships then went on to hold that in planning cases an alleged inadequacy of reasons will afford ground for quashing only if the court is satisfied that the interests of the applicant have been substantially prejudiced by it. In *Save Britain's Heritage* v *Number 1 Poultry Ltd* [1991] 1 WLR 153, the respondents sought to challenge the Secretary of State's decision to allow appeals, by Number 1 Poultry Ltd and City Acre Property Investments Trust Ltd, from the non-determination of applications by the City of London Corporation for the grant of planning permission for the erection of offices and shops and listed building consent and conservation area consent for the demolition of buildings on land at 1-19 Poultry, 2-38 Queen Victoria Street and 3-9 and 35-40 Bucklersbury. The respondents alleged, *inter alia,* that the Secretary of State had failed to give sufficient reasons for his decision. The Court of Appeal had earlier found in favour of *Save* on the ground of the failure by the Secretary of State to comply with the requirement to notify the reasons for his decision. The question at issue was whether the reasons given by the Secretary of State (the notification of which, Lord Bridge of Harwich considered, 'lacks the clarity and precision which one would have wished to see') substantially incorporated the conclusions and recommendations made by the Inspector to the Secretary of State on all that was material to the appeal. A unanimous House agreed that the Secretary of State's decision letter did do so, and allowed the appeal from the decision of the Court of Appeal which had held otherwise. Lord Bridge of Harwich, who gave the main speech said this:

> Whatever may be the position in any other legislative context, under the planning legislation, when it comes to deciding in any particular case whether the reasons given are deficient, the question is not to be answered *in vacuo*. The alleged deficiency will only afford a ground for quashing the decision if the court is satisfied that the interests of the applicant have been substantially prejudiced by it. This reinforces the view I have already expressed that the adequacy of reasons is not to be judged by reference to

some abstract standard. There are in truth not two separate questions: (1) were the reasons adequate? (2) if not, were the interests of the applicant substantially prejudiced thereby? The single indivisible question, in my opinion, which the court must ask itself whenever a planning decision is challenged on the ground of a failure to give reasons is whether the interests of the applicant have been substantially prejudiced by the deficiency of the reasons given. Here again, I disclaim any intention to put a gloss on the statutory provisions by attempting to define or delimit the circumstances in which deficiency of reasons will be capable of causing substantial prejudice, but I should expect that normally such prejudice will arise from one of three causes. First, there will be substantial prejudice to a developer whose application for permission has been refused or to an opponent of development when permission has been granted where the reasons for the decision are so inadequately or obscurely expressed as to raise a substantial doubt whether the decision was taken within the powers of the Act. Secondly, a developer whose application for permission is refused may be substantially prejudiced where the planning considerations on which the decision is based are not explained sufficiently clearly to enable him reasonably to assess the prospects of succeeding in an application for some alternative form of development. Thirdly, an opponent of development, whether the local planning authority or some unofficial body like *Save,* may be substantially prejudiced by a decision to grant permission in which the planning considerations on which the decision is based, particularly if they relate to planning policy, are not explained sufficiently clearly to indicate what, if any, impact they may have in relation to the decision of future applications.

17.6.2 Recovered cases (SI 1992 No. 2038)

Where the Secretary of State has used his power to recover jurisdiction over the determination of the appeal, the Inspector, instead of determining the appeal himself, makes recommendations to the Secretary of State as to how the appeal should be determined. The procedure is regulated by the Town and Country Planning (Inquiries Procedure) Rules 1992 (SI No. 2038) and, of course, by the rules of natural justice. The Inquiries Procedure Rules relating to recovered cases differ from transferred cases in the following ways:

(a) The Secretary of State may cause a pre-inquiry meeting to be held if it appears to him desirable. Where this is done, the Secretary of State must serve with the relevant notice a statement of the matters which appear to him to be likely to be relevant to his consideration of the application or appeal (r. 5).

(b) Where a pre-inquiry meeting is held, the local planning authority and the appellant must, not later than eight weeks after the relevant date, each serve an outline statement on the other and on the Secretary of State (r. 5(4)).

(c) The pre-inquiry meeting must be held not later than 16 weeks after the relevant date (r. 5(7)).

(d) Where a pre-inquiry meeting has been held, the local planning authority must serve a statement of case on the Secretary of State, the applicant and any statutory party no later than four weeks after the conclusion of the meeting. If no pre-inquiry meeting has been held, the statement of case must be submitted no later than six weeks after the relevant date (r. 6(1)).

(e) Where a pre-inquiry meeting has been held, the applicant must also submit a statement of case no later than four weeks after the conclusion of the meeting. If no pre-inquiry meeting is held, the period is nine weeks after the relevant date, unless it is a referred application under s. 77 of the 1990 Act, in which case the applicant must submit his statement of case within no later than six weeks before the relevant date (r. 6(3)).

(f) Unless he considers such a date impracticable, the Secretary of State must fix a date for the holding of an inquiry no later than 22 weeks after the relevant date, or where a pre-inquiry meeting has been held, no later than eight weeks after the conclusion of that meeting (r. 10).

(g) After the close of the inquiry, the Inspector must make a report in writing to the Secretary of State which must include his conclusions and his recommendations or, if he makes no recommendations, his reasons for not doing so (r. 16). Before he determines the appeal, the Secretary of State may take into account new evidence or new matters of fact. He may also, however, decide to differ from the Inspector on a matter of fact. The latter situation can only occur, of course, in recovered cases where the Secretary of State is considering the Inspector's report prior to making his decision. Accordingly if the Secretary of State does decide to:

(i) differ from the Inspector on any matter of fact mentioned in or appearing to him to be material to a conslusion reached by the Inspector,

(ii) takes into consideration any new evidence or new matter of fact,
and is for that reason disposed to disagree with a recommendation made by the Inspector, he shall not come to a decision at variance with that recommendation without first notifying the persons entitled to appear at the inquiry and who appeared at it of his disagreement and reasons for it; and affording them an opportunity of making written representations to him within three weeks, or where new evidence or new matters of fact have been taken into consideration, of asking for the re-opening of the inquiry (r. 16(4)).

The rules which impose obligations on the Inspector or Secretary of State respectively to give the parties an opportunity to make further representations, are concerned with findings of fact, not statements of opinion or the planning merits. The distinction has caused difficulty in the past, particularly in recovered cases.

In *Lord Luke* v *Minister of Housing & Local Government* [1968] 1 QB 172 the Inspector in his report to the Minister had made two statements. The first was that the site of the proposed development was clearly defined behind walls. The second was that a well-designed house would add to the charm of the setting. He accordingly recommended that the appeal be allowed. In his decision letter, however, the Minister said he accepted the Inspector's findings of fact, but could not accept the Inspector's conclusions or recommendation. He consider-ed the proposed development would lead to sporadic development in open countryside. He then dismissed the appeal, without giving the appellant the opportunity to make further representations. The appellant argued that in disagreeing with the second statement of the Inspector, the Minister had differed from him on a finding of fact. Although the High Court upheld the appellant's contention, the Court of Appeal held that the Minister's difference of opinion with the Inspector was not on a finding of fact, but on a question of opinion on the planning merits of the proposed development, and that he was not obliged to give the appellant a further opportunity to make representations.

In *Pyrford Properties Ltd* v *Secretary of State for the Environment* (1977) 36 P & CR 28, the policy of the local planning authority was to restrict office development in its area, though exceptions were to be made for 'local firms'. The appellants were a firm with international ramifications, but the business had started in the locality. On an appeal against the refusal of planning permission, the Inspector had found that the appellants were and remained a local firm and recommended that the appeal be allowed. In his decision letter upholding the authority's refusal to grant planning permission, however, the Secretary of State said that he agreed with the Inspector's findings of fact but not his conclusions that the firm remained a local firm. Quashing the Secretary of State's decision for failing to comply with the relevant procedural rule, by providing the appellants with an opportunity to make further representations, Sir Douglas Frank QC, sitting as a deputy judge of the High Court, recognised that it was not easy to draw from the *Lord Luke* decision any firm rules for distinguishing findings of fact from expressions of opinion on the planning merits, unless it were that the former depended on evidence of an existing state of affairs and the latter upon a subjective opinion of what would result from the proposed development.

17.7 Statutory review

The 1990 Act contains a number of provisions under which the decision of the Secretary of State may be challenged in the courts. The procedures are often referred as proceedings for statutory review, in order to distinguish them from judicial review proceedings which are normally available to a person wishing to question the validity of a public authority's actions.

Section 288 of the 1990 Act provides the only means whereby a person may question the validity of a decision made by the Secretary of State on an appeal under s. 78. This is because s. 284(1) prescribes that, except in so far as may be provided by this part of the Act, the validity of any decision on an appeal under s. 78 'shall not be questioned in any legal proceedings whatsoever'. Once a decision has been made on a s. 78 appeal, therefore, whether it be a transferred or recovered case, the decision can only be questioned by using the machinery available under s. 288.

Section 288 (1) provides:

If any person—
    (a)   is aggrieved by any order to which this section applies and wishes to question the validity of that order on the grounds—
        (i)   that the order is not within the powers of this Act, or

(ii)   that any of the relevant requirements have not been complied with in relation to that order; or

(b)   is aggrieved by any action on the part of the Secretary of State to which this section applies and wishes to question the validity of that action on the grounds—

(i)   that the action is not within the powers of this Act, or

(ii)   that any of the relevant requirements have not been complied with in relation to that action,

he may make an application to the High Court under this section.

Section 288(3) provides that an application under the section must be made within six weeks from the date on which the action is taken.

It will be seen that action must be commenced within six weeks of the decision. In *Griffiths* v *Secretary of State for the Environment* [1983] 2 AC 51, it was held that time begins to run from the date the Secretary of State takes an irreversible step in relation to the decision, as by typing, signing and dating the decision letter, and not when it is received by the appellant.

The period of six weeks means precisely six weeks, and there would appear to be no discretion available to the court to extend the period. Thereafter, for reasons of public policy, the decision is immune from judicial attack, even if the appellant alleges fraud (see *Smith* v *East Elloe Rural District Council* [1956] AC 736 and *R* v *Secretary of State for the Environment (ex parte Ostler)* [1977] QB 122, both of which were cases of compulsory purchase with an identical time bar). More recently, the finality of the six-week time bar has been approved by the Court of Appeal in *R* v *Secretary of State for the Environment, ex parte Kent* [1990] JPL 124 and applied by the High Court in *R* v *Cornwall County Council, ex parte Huntington* [1992] 3 All ER 566.

Not everyone may use s. 288 to challenge the Secretary of State's decision. The section gives the right to 'any person aggrieved'. That clearly includes the appellant and the local planning authority. The position of others, particularly third parties, is not clear. In *Buxton* v *Minister of Housing & Local Government* [1961] 1 QB 278 it was held that an aggrieved person is not one dissatisfied with an act or decision, but one wrongfully deprived of something to which he is legally entitled. The appellant, a neighbour, was therefore denied review. A somewhat different view was taken by Ackner J in *Turner* v *Secretary of State for the Environment* (1973) 28 P & CR 123, where the chairman of a local amenity society was held to be an aggrieved person and able to apply for the review of the Secretary of State's decision. In *Bizony* v *Secretary of State for the Environment* [1976] JPL 306 the court were prepared to regard a neighbour (Bizony) as a person aggrieved, but held, before dismissing a weak case, that if it had been necessary to do so they would have required further argument on the question of whether or not he had the necessary standing.

Since the *Bizony* case there has been little further judicial discussion of the scope of the term and whether or not people such as neighbours fall within it. In the light of the relaxation of the rules relating to *standing* in judicial review proceedings, however, it is thought the courts are now prepared to take a more expansive view of the term than previously. Note, however, that *in Greater*

London Council v *Secretary of State for the Environment* [1985] JPL 868, the council had applied under the earlier provision equivalent to s. 288 to quash a decision made by an Inspector to dismiss an appeal by the developers against the failure of the Harrow London Borough Council to determine an application for planning permission. Although the Greater London Council had supported the dismissal of the appeal, it had sought review because it feared adverse consequences would flow from the reasoning of the Inspector. Granting leave to strike out the action, the court held that the council was not a person aggrieved in relation to the Inspector's decision, but that it might challenge the decision by judicial review proceedings.

The decision of the Secretary of State under s. 288 may be challenged either on the ground that 'the action is not within the powers of this Act' or, that 'any of the relevant requirements have not been complied with.' Relevant requirements means any requirements of the Act or of the Tribunals and Inquiries Act 1992, or of any order, regulations or rules made under either Act (s. 288(9)). It would include, therefore, a failure to comply with the Inquiry Procedure Rules. Where a challenge is made on the grounds that the relevant requirements have not been complied with, the person aggrieved must, if he is asking for the order to be quashed, also show that he has been substantially prejudiced by the failure to comply with those requirements.

Traditionally, the two grounds of challenge available are referred to as substantive *ultra vires* and procedural *ultra vires*. In practice, however, there is some overlap, since allegations that there has been a breach of natural justice (as opposed to a breach of the Inquiry Procedure Rules) may properly be regarded as being outside the powers of the Act rather than a failure to comply with any relevant requirements.

The principles on which the court will act in deciding whether or not to quash a planning decision under s. 288 is contained in the judgment of the Forbes J in *Seddon Properties Ltd* v *Secretary of State for the Environment* (1978) 42 P & CR 26 approved by the Court of Appeal in *Centre 21* v *Secretary of State for the Environment* [1986] JPL 915. Although the application made in *Seddon* was a challenge of a Secretary of State's decision, the principles laid down in the case apply equally to decisions of Inspectors. The principles stated by Forbes J were:

(1)   The Secretary of State must not act perversely. That is, if the court considers that no reasonable person in the position of the Secretary of State, properly directing himself on the relevant material, could have reached the conclusion that he did reach, the decision may be overturned, see, for example, *Ashbridge Investments Ltd* v *Minister of Housing and Local Government* [1965] 1 WLR 1320, *per* Lord Denning MR and Harman LJ at pp.1326 and 1328. This is really no more than another example of the principle enshrined in a sentence from the judgment of Lord Greene MR in *Associated Provincial Picture Houses Ltd* v *Wednesbury Corporation* [1948] 1 KB 223 at p.230: 'It is true to say that, if a decision on a competent matter is so unreasonable that no reasonable authority could ever have come to it, then the courts can interfere.'

(2)   In reaching his conclusion the Secretary of State must not take into account irrelevant material or fail to take into account that which is relevant, see, for example, again the *Ashbridge Investments* case *per* Lord Denning MR at p. 1326.

(3)   The Secretary of State must abide by the statutory procedures, in particular by the Town and Country Planning (Inquiries Procedure) Rules 1974 (now the Inquiries Procedure Rules 1992). These rules require him to give reasons for his decision after a planning inquiry, and those reasons must be proper and adequate reasons that are clear and intelligible and deal with the substantial points that have been raised, *Re Poyser and Mills' Arbitration* [1964] 2 QB 467.

(4)   The Secretary of State in exercising his powers which include reaching a decision such as that in this case must not depart from the principles of natural justice: *per* Lord Russell of Killowen in the *Fairmount Investment* case.

Section 288(5) of the Act provides that:

On any application under this section the High Court—

(a)   may ... by interim order suspend the operation of the order or action, the validity of which is questioned by the application, until the final determination of the proceedings;

(b)   if satisfied that the order or action in question is not within the powers of this Act, or that the interests of the applicant have been substantially prejudiced by a failure to comply with any of the relevant requirements in relation to it, may quash that order or action.

Despite the wording of the subsection, the courts have held that they have a residual discretion not to quash a decision where an application is made under this section. The general rule, however, is that unless the grounds of challenge are purely technical, or the applicant has suffered no real harm, the decision of the Secretary of State should be quashed. Where a decision of the Secretary of State is quashed under these provisions, its effect is to leave the appeal outstanding, so that a further lawful decision has then to be made. The action then taken by the Secretary of State will depend upon the defect that caused the original decision to be quashed. An unintelligible decision letter can be corrected by the issue of an intelligible decision letter. A failure to allow the parties to comment on new issues of fact taken into account after the close of the inquiry or to ask for the inquiry to be reopened, can be cured by giving them that opportunity or by reopening the inquiry. In *Kingswood District Council* v *Secretary of State for the Environment* [1988] JPL 248, it was held that following the quashing of a decision under this provision, the Secretary of State was obliged to deal with the matter *de novo* with a clean sheet, and that he had to have regard to the development plan and to any other material considerations, and thus to any further material considerations arising after the date of the original decision.

17.8   Award of costs

In England and Wales the award of costs is governed by s. 250(5) of the Local Government Act 1972, and is applied to planning appeals and other proceedings under the 1990 Act by s. 320(2) and sch. 6 to the 1990 Act. Section 250(5) empowers the Secretary of State to 'make orders as to the costs of the parties at the inquiry and as to the parties by whom the costs are to be paid, and every such order may be made a rule of the High Court on the application of any party named in the order'. The purpose in making an order as to costs a rule of the High Court is to enable a party to sue and be sued on an award. Similar provisions are to be found in s. 89 of the Planning (Listed Buildings and Conservation Areas) Act 1990.

Prior to 1986, the Secretary of State's powers to make an award of costs were limited to local inquiries. The power has since been extended and under s. 322 of the 1990 Act the Secretary of State has the same powers to make orders as to costs with regard to hearings and written representations as apply to local inquiries. An order has been made applying this power to hearings. It is the government's intention to make awards of costs available in all written representation appeals also, as soon as resources allow. In addition, Inspectors have now been given the right to exercise the Secretary of State's power to award costs.

The principles on which the power to award costs are exercised are based substantially on the general principles set out by the Council on Tribunals in 1964 in their *Report on the Award of Costs at Statutory Inquiries* (Cmnd 2471).

The award of costs in planning appeals is becoming more common. The view is taken that the award of costs should not necessarily follow the decision on the planning merits of the appeal, so that the appellant would be awarded costs if his appeal was successful and would have costs awarded against him if he was unsuccessful. Costs of a planning appeal will normally be borne, therefore, by the party that incurs them.

Before the Planning and Compensation Act 1991, the Secretary of State was able to make an award of costs against a party, requiring that party to pay the costs of another party, only where an inquiry or hearing had taken place. He had no power to do so where an inquiry or hearing had been cancelled as a result of the appellant abandoning the appeal or the local planning authority abandoning their case. The abandonment of an appeal by the appellant, or an objection to the development by the authority, could lead to the party not at fault incurring considerable costs preparing for the appeal which had now been aborted. Accordingly, the Planning and Compensation Act 1991, s. 30, introduced a new s. 322A into the 1990 Act giving the Secretary of State power to make an award of costs where an inquiry or hearing has been arranged, but does not then take place.

The criteria the Secretary of State uses in exercising his power to award costs, both in relation to cases where an appeal or hearing has taken place and where it has not, are now set out in Circular No. 8/93. The Circular contains seven annexes each dealing with specific circumstances. The annexes are:

Annex 1: general principles for awards of costs for unreasonable behaviour.
Annex 2: general procedural requirements of appeals: unreasonable behaviour.
Annex 3: unreasonable behaviour relating to the substance of the case, including action prior to submission of appeal.
Annex 4: application of costs policy to third parties in proceedings.
Annex 5: the costs application.
Annex 6: costs in respect of compulsory purchase and analogous orders (including a list of examples of analogous orders).
Annex 7: list of proceedings in which costs may be awarded where an inquiry or hearing is held.

The following is a brief summary of the criteria for awards of costs on grounds of unreasonable behaviour contained in the Circular.

Appellants are at risk of an award of costs against them if, for example, they:

(a)   fail to comply with normal procedural requirements for inquiries or hearings; do not provide a pre-inquiry statement when asked to do so, if the proceedings have to be adjourned or are unnecessarily prolonged; or are deliberately or wilfully uncooperative, such as refusing to discuss the appeal or provide requested, necessary information;

(b)   fail to pursue an appeal or attend an inquiry or hearing;

(c)   introduce new grounds of appeal, or new issues, late in the proceedings;

(d)   withdraw the appeal, or legal grounds in an enforcement appeal, after being notified of inquiry or hearing arrangements, without any material change in circumstances;

(e)   pursue an appeal which obviously had no reasonable prospect of success, including one which clearly 'flies in the face' of national planning policies.

Planning authorities are at risk of an award of costs against them, on appeal, if, for example, they:

(a)   fail to comply with normal procedural requirements for inquiries or hearings, including compliance with relevant regulations;

(b)   fail to provide evidence, on planning grounds, to substantiate each of their reasons for refusing planning permission, including reasons relying on advice of statutory consultees; or to demonstrate that they had reasonable grounds for considering it expedient to issue an enforcement notice;

(c)   fail to take into account relevant policy statements in Departmental guidance or relevant judicial authority;

(d)   refuse to discuss a planning application or provide requested information, or seek additional information, as appropriate;

(e)   refuse permission for a modified scheme when an earlier appeal decision indicated this would be acceptable, and circumstances have not materially changed;

(f)   fail to carry out reasonable investigations of fact, or to exercise sufficient care, before issuing an enforcement notice;

(g)   at a late stage, introduce an additional reason for refusal, or abandon a reason for refusal, or withdraw an enforcement notice unjustifiably;

(h)   impose conditions which are unnecessary, unreasonable, unenforceable, imprecise or irrelevant;

(i)   pursue unreasonable demands or obligations in connection with a grant of permission;

(j)   fail to renew an extant or recently expired planning permission, without good reason;

(k)   unreasonably refuse to grant permission for reserved matters or pursue issues settled at outline stage.

Applications for award of costs should normally be made to the Inspector at the inquiry. Later claims will be entertained only if the party claiming costs can show good reason for not having made the claim earlier. If an award of costs is made, the parties endeavour to agree on the amount to be recovered. If agreement is not possible (and even if it is), either party can refer the matter to the Supreme Court Taxing Office. An application to the Taxing Office is in two stages. The first involves applying to have the costs award made a rule of the High Court. This act will enable the party in whose favour the award has been made to sue upon it if necessary. It also enables the party to claim interest on the amount of the award from that date. The second stage involves applying to the court to commence taxation proceedings. Under the Rules of the Supreme Court, an award of costs under s. 250(5) of the Local Government Act 1972 is taxed on what is known as the 'standard basis'.

It was held in *R* v *Secretary of State for the Enviroment, ex parte North Norfolk District Council* [1994] EGCS 131, that the Inspector must give clear and intelligible reasons for a decision on costs, just as he must do on the issues in the appeal.

EIGHTEEN

Enforcement

18.1 Introduction

Under the British system of planning control, to develop land without planning permission is not a criminal offence. Nevertheless, there has to be a sanction to ensure that unauthorised development can be prevented. The sanction provided by the law is the enforcement notice machinery contained in Part VII of the 1990 Act. Under this machinery, once an enforcement notice takes effect, the development which is unauthorised must cease or be removed. If it is not, then, and only then, is a criminal offence committed of failure to comply with the enforcement notice.

The law relating to enforcement notices has been strengthened over the years on numerous occasions, the latest being in 1991.

The provisions of Part I of the Planning and Compensation Act 1991 supplemented and amended the enforcement provisions contained in Part VII of the 1990 Act. The new provisions, which strengthen and improve the enforcement of general planning control, are based on the recommendations of a report by Robert Carnwath QC, *Enforcing Planning Control,* published by the Department of the Environment in April 1989.

According to Baroness Blatch, Parliamentary Under-Secretary of State at the Department of the Environment in introducing the Planning and Compensation Bill in the House of Lords on 27 November 1990, the report showed that there is a small minority of people who are determined contraveners of planning regulations. According to Baroness Blatch:

> it is those people who bring the system into disrepute; and it is their damaging and unwelcome activities ... which the enforcement amendments are intended to deter or, failing that, to remedy through increased penalties; new methods of enforcing planning conditions; and improved powers of local authority officers to enter private land for enforcement purposes.

Part I of the 1991 Act supplements the provisions in Part VII of the 1990 Act by providing a new procedure for local planning authorities to obtain information relating to suspected breaches of planning control (planning contravention notices); for enforcing planning conditions (breach of condition notices); and for obtaining injunctions to restrain breaches of planning control (planning injunctions). The remainder of Part I of the 1991 Act amends Part VII of the 1990 Act to alter the time-limits on the taking of enforcement action; to provide for greater flexibility in the drafting and service of enforcement notices; to revise the power of the Secretary of State on appeal; to extend the power of a local planning authority to execute works required by an enforcement notice; to increase the penalties for non-compliance with an enforcement notice; to revise the provisions relating to stop notices; to provide for a new certificate of lawful use or development; and to give authorities greater rights of entry to property for enforcement purposes.

18.2 Planning contravention notices

In deciding whether or not to serve an enforcement notice, the local planning authority must, as far as possible, be sure of its facts. Accordingly, s. 324 of the 1990 Act gives power to local planning authorities to enter land, subject to at least 24 hours notice of intention to do so, for the purposes of surveying it in connection with the service of notices, including enforcement notices. In addition, s. 330 enables a local planning authority to demand information from the occupier of land as to his interest. The Carnwath report recommended that there should be a new optional statutory procedure, not only to enable authorities to obtain information, but to secure cooperation from an owner without recourse to enforcement action. This was done by s. 1 of the Planning and Compensation Act 1991, which inserted new ss. 171C and 171D into the 1990 Act providing for the service of planning contravention notices. Under s. 171C(1), where it appears to the local planning authority that there may have been a breach of planning control in respect of any land, the authority may serve a notice to that effect (called a 'planning contravention notice') on any person who is the owner or occupier of the land or has any other interest in it, or who is carrying out operations on the land or using it for any purpose. Where a notice is served, s. 171C(2) provides that the notice may require the recipient to give such information as may be specified in the notice about any operations being carried out on the land, any use of the land and any other activities being carried out on it, and any matter relating to conditions or limitations subject to which any planning permission has been granted in respect of the land. In addition, s. 171C(3) provides that, without prejudice to the generality of s. 171C(2), the notice may require the recipient, so far as he is able to do so, to state whether or not the land is being used for any purpose specified in the notice, or whether any operations or activities specified in the notice are being or have been carried out on the land; to state when any use, operations or activities began; to give the names and addresses of any persons known to him to use or have used the land for any purpose or to be carrying out or have carried out any operations or activities on the land; to give any information in his possession as to any planning permission for any use or operations or any reason for planning permission not being required for any use or operations; to state the nature of his interest (if any) in the land and the name and address of any other person known to him to have an interest in the land.

Under s. 171C(5), a planning contravention notice must inform the recipient of the likely consequences of his failure to respond to the notice and, in particular, that enforcement action may be taken. In addition, the recipient must also be informed that in the event of enforcement action being taken, failure to respond to the notice may affect his entitlement to compensation in the event of a stop notice also being served. It should be noted that the service of a planning contravention notice in no way prejudices any other action the planning authority may take in respect of a breach of planning control. If a local planning authority is already in possession of all the information necessary, it may decide to take enforcement action without the earlier service of a planning contravention notice.

Subsection (1) of s. 171D provides that if any person fails to comply with any requirement of a planning contravention notice within a period of 21 days, he shall be guilty of a criminal offence. The section goes on to provide that if at any time after conviction that person continues to fail to comply with any requirement of the notice, he may be convicted of a second or subsequent offence, thereby ensuring that the requirement is eventually complied with. Under s. 171D(3), it is a defence for a person charged with an offence to prove that he had a reasonable excuse for failing to comply with a requirement in the notice. In addition to the above, a person is guilty of an offence if the information he gives in response to a planning contravention notice is false or misleading in a material particular, or he recklessly makes a statement which is false or misleading in a material particular.

Under s. 17IC(4), a planning contravention notice may give notice of a time and place at which any offer which the recipient of the notice may wish to make to apply for planning permission, or to refrain from carrying out any operations or activities or to undertake remedial works, and any representations which he may wish to make about the notice, will be considered by the authority. The authority must give the recipient an opportunity to make any such offer or representations, in person, at a specified time and place.

It will be seen that the refusal of the person served with a planning contravention notice to make an offer (as opposed to providing the information required by the notice) is not a criminal offence. The recipient of the notice may well decline to do so without fear of any penalty. Hence, there must be considerable uncertainty as to the extent to which an offer would be made by that 'small minority of determined contraveners' mentioned by Baroness Blatch.

18.3   Additional rights of entry on property

The rights of local planning authorities in the 1990 Act to enter on land did not distinguish between the power to enter land for the purposes of investigating a breach of planning control and other powers to enter land for planning purposes, such as in connection with development plan preparation; the consideration of applications for planning permission or the making, for example, of a revocation or modification order. It was often difficult, therefore, for a local planning authority to obtain the precise information needed in order to take formal and effective enforcement action. Mention has been made above of the powers now available to a local planning authority under the amended 1990 Act to obtain information by means of the new 'planning contravention notice'. In addition, however, the 1991 Act has now introduced into the 1990 Act three new sections, 196A, 196B and 196C, in order to give local planning authorities more specific rights of entry on to land to be exercised where enforcement action is foreseen.

Subsection (1) of new s. 196A provides that any person duly authorised in writing by a local planning authority may at any reasonable hour enter land to ascertain whether there has been any breach of planning control on land; to determine whether any of the powers conferred by the Act on a local planning authority should be exercised; to determine how any such power should be exercised; and to ascertain whether there has been compliance with any requirement imposed as a result of any such power being exercised. The power of entry given by this subsection is subject to the proviso that there must be reasonable grounds for entering the land for any of those purposes. In the case of any building used as a dwellinghouse, the subsection provides that admission to the building shall not be demanded 'as of right', unless 24 hours' notice of the intended entry has been given to the occupier of the building. It would appear that this 24 hours' notice is not necessary if the authority wish to enter upon land adjoining a dwellinghouse or on land within its curtilage.

If entry in accordance with these provisions is refused, s. 196B(1) provides that if it is shown to the satisfaction of a justice of the peace, on sworn information in writing, that there were reasonable grounds for entering any land for the purposes of ascertaining whether there has been a breach of planning control or for determining whether enforcement action should be taken, and that admission to the land has been refused, or a refusal is reasonably apprehended, or the case is one of urgency, the justice may issue a warrant authorising any person duly authorised in writing by the local planning authority to enter the land. It should be noted that the warrant authorises entry on to the land in question on one occasion only, and entry must be within one month from the date of issue of the warrant, and at a reasonable hour, unless the case is one of urgency.

The new s. 196C of the 1990 Act contains provisions which are supplementary to the new ss. 196A and 196B discussed above. All the provisions in this new section replicate provisions previously found in the 1990 Act, being applicable to the exercise of rights of entry for a whole range of planning purposes. The new s. 196C groups those supplementary provisions in one section to be exercised in connection with the enforcement of planning control.

18.4   Enforcement notices

18.4.1   Time-limits on enforcement action
Under subsection (2) of a new s. 171A of the 1990 Act, enforcement action may be taken by the issue of an enforcement notice or by the service of a breach

of condition notice. Such enforcement action may only be taken in relation to a breach of planning control, defined in s. 171A(1) as carrying out development without the required planning permission, or failing to comply with any condition subject to which planning permission has been granted.

The Planning and Compensation Act 1991 makes important amendments to the provisions in the 1990 Act with regard to the time-limits for the bringing of enforcement action by a local planning authority. Under the old law, where the breach of planning control was the carrying out without planning permission of operational development, no enforcement action could be taken after the end of a period of four years from the date the operations were completed. No change has been made in that provision, save that the period is now made to run for four years from the date on which the operations were substantially completed. Similarly, under the old law, no enforcement action could be taken in relation to a change of use of any building to use as a single dwellinghouse if the use has subsisted for more than four years. Again no change is made to this provision.

Where the contravening development involved some other change of use there was no time-limit on the period within which an enforcement notice could be served. This has now been changed, since subsection (3) of a new s. 171B, inserted into the 1990 Act by s. 4 of the 1991 Act, provides that in the case of any other breach of planning control (i.e., other than operational development or a change of use to a single dwellinghouse), no enforcement action may be taken at the end of a period of *10 years* beginning with the date of the breach.

There is one further change to the time-limits for the bringing of enforcement action. Under the old law, where there had been a breach of a condition in a planning permission not involving a change of use to use as a single dwellinghouse, the condition could only be enforced on action taken within four years of the date of the breach. The effect of subsection (3) of the new s. 171B of the 1990 Act, is that the time-limit for enforcement action in such cases is now raised from four years to 10 years. A further important change should also be noted. Under the old law, where an enforcement notice had been issued and was subsequently held to have been defective, further enforcement action had to be taken before the period of immunity commenced. Now under s. 171B(4)(b) if an enforcement notice is held to be defective, the authority is given a further four years to issue another effective enforcement notice.

18.5   Issue of enforcement notices

Under a new s. 172 of the 1990 Act, a local planning authority may *issue* an enforcement notice where it appears to them:

(a)   that there has been a breach of planning control; and
(b)   that it is expedient to issue the notice, having regard to the provisions of the development plan and to any other material considerations.

The provision in para. (b) above is, of course, now to be read in conjunction with the new s. 54A of the 1990 Act (see Chapter 4), which has given the development plan a position of primacy over other material considerations.

Once issued, a copy of the enforcement notice is now required to be *served*. Subsection (2) of the new s. 172 provides that a copy shall be served:

(a) on the owner and occupier of the land to which it relates, and

(b) on any other person having an interest in the land, being an interest which, in the opinion of the authority, is materially affected by the notice.

The term 'owner' in s. 172(2) causes no problems. Section 336(1) of the 1990 Act defines an owner to mean:

... a person, other than a mortgagee not in possession, who, whether in his own right or as trustee for any other person, is entitled to receive the rack rent of the land or, where the land is not let at a rack rent, would be so entitled if it were so let.

The Act, however, does not define the term 'occupier'. The term has, therefore, given rise to some litigation, particularly over the question of whether caravan dwellers come within the term. In *Munnich* v *Godstone Rural District Council* [1966] 1 WLR 427, it was considered that they did not. In *Stevens* v *Bromley London Borough Council* [1972] Ch 400, it was considered that they did. In a later case, *Scarborough Borough Council* v *Adams* [1983] JPL 673, caravan dwellers were again held to be occupiers and entitled, therefore, to be served with a copy of the enforcement notice. Note however, that a person who occupies the land to which a notice relates by virtue of a licence, is given a right of appeal to the Secretary of State against the notice under s. 174 of the 1990 Act.

Where a person entitled to be served with a copy of an enforcement notice is not served, the position can be quite complicated. Before 1968, the position was that if an enforcement notice was challenged in the courts on the ground that a person required to be served with a notice had not been served, the court had no option but to quash the notice. This led to a practice known as 'shuffling of interests', whereby, after the local planning authority had made inquiries about the nature of a person's interest in land prior to the service on him of the enforcement notice, that person transferred his interest to a friend or relative, so that when the notice was eventually served it was served on a person who was not the owner of an interest in the land, and was not served on the person who now was the owner. Similar transfers sometimes took place between associated 'one-man' companies.

To meet this difficulty, the 1968 Act introduced a number of new provisions into the law. One, which is now found in s. 176(5) of the 1990 Act, provides that where it would otherwise be a ground for determining an appeal in favour of the appellant that a person required to be served with a copy of the enforcement notice was not served, the Secretary of State may disregard that fact if neither the appellant nor that person has been substantially prejudiced by the failure to serve him.

This may meet the case of a transfer made between spouses prior to service of a copy of the enforcement notice. But it is not likely to meet the case of an innocent purchaser who knows nothing of the notice and is unable, therefore, to appeal to the Secretary of State before the notice has taken effect. Accordingly, the 1968 Act made a further change in the law which is now found in s. 285 of the 1990 Act. Normally, the validity of an enforcement notice cannot be questioned in the courts on any of the grounds on which a person may bring an appeal against it to the Secretary of State (see below). Since one of the grounds of appeal to the Secretary of State is that copies of the enforcement notice were not served on those required to be served by the Act, this provision would, by itself, mean that a person not served would be unable to question the legality of the notice if he were subsequently prosecuted under s. 179(6) to (8) of the Act for a failure to comply with the notice.

Accordingly s. 285 provides that the embargo on questioning the validity of an enforcement notice shall not apply to proceedings brought under s. 179(6) to (8) of the 1990 Act against a person who:

(a)   has held an interest in the land since before the enforcement notice was issued . . .;

(b)   did not have a copy of the enforcement notice served on him . . .; and

(c)   satisfies the court—

(i)   that he did not know and could not reasonably have been expected to know that the enforcement notice had been issued; and

(ii)   that his interests have been substantially prejudiced by the failure to serve him with a copy of it.

Despite those elaborate provisions, however, it may still be possible for a person to be bound by an enforcement notice of which he has no notice. Section 285 does not seem to anticipate that a local planning authority might choose not to prosecute under s. 179(6) to (8) but to exercise its powers under s. 178(1) to enter the land and carry out the work which is required to be done by the enforcement notice. In *R* v *Greenwich London Borough Council (ex parte Patel)* (1985) 51 P & CR 282, the applicant sought (by way of judicial review) an order of prohibition against the local planning authority prohibiting them from entering his land and demolishing a shed which had been erected on the land by his wife without the grant of planning permission. The enforcement notice had been served on the applicant's wife as the person 'owning the land'. It was in fact owned by the applicant. There had been no appeal against the notice to the Secretary of State. Earlier, it appears, the applicant's wife had been refused planning permission to erect the shed on the land which she had stated she owned; and an appeal against the refusal had been dismissed by the Secretary of State. The applicant claimed he first knew of the notice when his wife received a letter from the local planning authority informing her of their intention to enter the land and demolish the shed.

In withholding the relief applied for, the Court of Appeal refused to hold that the failure to serve the enforcement notice in accordance with what is now

s. 172(2) rendered it a nullity. In doing so, it felt able to distinguish the Scottish case of *McDaid* v *Clydebank District Council* [1984] JPL 579, where the Court of Session had held to the contrary. In that case, however, the local planning authority had erred in that they had been aware of the identity of the owner but had still failed to serve him. In the *Patel* case, the Court of Appeal found that there had been no deliberate disregard of the statutory requirement by the local planning authority; nor had they failed to show due diligence. Furthermore, there was no reason to suppose that the applicant had suffered any real prejudice.

The case shows that despite the changes made in 1968, there may still be situations where the failure to serve an enforcement notice in accordance with the provisions of s. 172(2) will render the notice a nullity. For that to happen, however, it appears that not only must the owner or occupier have been prejudiced by the failure to serve the notice on him, but there must also have been some malfeasance on the part of the authority.

Subsection (3) of the new s. 172 of the 1990 Act provides also a strict time-limit for service of copies of the enforcement notice. According to the subsection, the service of the notice shall take place:

(a)   not more than 28 days after its date of issue; and
(b)   not less than 28 days before the date specified in it as the date on which it is to take effect.

The importance of this provision is that s. 173(8) of the 1990 Act provides that any enforcement notice must specify the date on which it is to come into effect; after which date no appeal will lie.

Two key dates, therefore, are the date when the enforcement notice is issued (i.e., made by the authority) and the specified date in the notice as the date on which it is to come into effect. The effect of s. 172(3) is to ensure that within that time period all copies of an enforcement notice that have to be served are served within 28 days of the date of its issue, and that any recipient of a copy of such an enforcement notice has it in his possession for at least 28 days before it comes into effect. The effect can be shown thus:

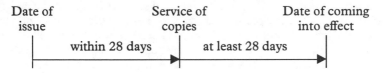

Date of	Service of	Date of coming
issue	copies	into effect
within 28 days	at least 28 days	

The purpose of the first period, introduced into the law by the Local Government and Planning (Amendment) Act 1981, was to overcome a problem that sometimes arose when an enforcement notice was served on different persons on different days. In *Bambury* v *Hounslow London Borough Council* [1966] 2 QB 204, enforcement notices were served on three new occupiers of land on 22 August 1964. Each notice required the unauthorised development to be discontinued within 28 days from the date on which the notice took effect. All stated that the notice should take effect on the expiration of 28 clear days after service of the notice.

Then on 8 September 1964 a further enforcement notice in similar terms was served on the owner. On appeal to the High Court the enforcement notices were quashed. The occupiers successfully contended that there could not be two dates for the coming into force of the same enforcement notice. If there were two separate dates, there were in effect two separate enforcement notices, neither of which had been served as required by the law on both the owners *and* occupiers of the land to which they related.

Under the new provisions, the procedure is commenced not when the enforcement notice is served by the authority, but when it is *issued* by them; and it enables the authority to serve *copies* of the notice, on persons required to be served, on any number of different dates, so long as all persons are served within the time span set out in s. 172(3).

The purpose of the second period is to give the recipient of the notice a minimum period of 28 days in which to decide whether or not to appeal against the notice. If he decides not to appeal, the notice takes effect on the date stated. If, however, he decides to appeal against the notice to the Secretary of State, s. 175(4) provides that it shall be of no effect pending the final determination or withdrawal of the appeal.

18.6 Content of enforcement notices

Section 173(1) of the 1990 Act provides that an enforcement notice shall state:

(a)   the matters which appear to the local planning authority to constitute the breach of planning control; and
(b)   the paragraph of s. 171A(1) within which, in the opinion of the local planning authority, the breach falls.

The 1990 Act originally provided that an enforcement notice should 'specify' the matters alleged to constitute the breach. By requiring the notice now to 'state' these matters, the drafters of the 1991 Act hope that notices will be less likely to be challenged as being a nullity because the breach has not been specified correctly. In addition, the effect of subsection (2) of the new s. 173 is that as long as the recipient of an enforcement notice understands from the notice what the matters are which the local authority consider to be a breach of planning control, the notice is not to be regarded as defective on the ground that it did not state the breach with sufficient clarity or particularity.

Having stated the breach of planning control, subsection (3) of section 173 then requires the notice to specify the steps which the authority require to be taken, or the activities which the authority require to cease, in order to achieve, wholly or partly, any of the following purposes:

(a)   remedying the breach by making any development comply with the term of any planning permission granted in respect of the land, by discontinuing any use of land or by restoring the land to its condition before the breach took place; or

(b)   remedying any injury to amenity which has been caused by the breach.

Subsection (5) provides the following examples of what an enforcement notice may require:

(a)   the alteration or removal of any building or works;
(b)   the carrying out of any building or other operation;
(c)   any activity on the land not to be carried on except to the extent specified in the notice;
(d)   the contour of a deposit of refuse or waste materials on land to be modified by altering the gradient or gradients of its sides.

In addition, where an enforcement notice is issued in respect of a breach of planning control consisting of demolition of a building, the notice may require the construction of a 'replacement building', as similar as possible to the demolished building.

If the notice could have required any buildings or works to be removed or any activity to cease, but does not do so, or requires the construction of a replacement building, and the notice is complied with, planning permission is deemed to be granted for the buildings, works, activity or replacement building.

Having stated what has to be done to remedy the breach, the notice must also specify the period at the end of which the steps required to be taken must be taken or any activities required to cease must cease. In this connection, s. 173(9) provides that a notice may specify different periods for the taking of different steps or activities.

An enforcement notice must specify such additional matters as may be prescribed, and regulations may require every copy of an enforcement notice to be accompanied by an explanatory note giving information about rights of appeal.

The new provisions in the 1990 Act relating to the steps which the recipient of the notice must take to remedy the breach were redrafted by the 1991 Act in order to give local planning authorities greater flexibility in the choice of those steps including, if the authority wish, the power to 'under-enforce'.

It should also be noted that local planning authorities are now given the power to waive or relax any requirement of an enforcement notice, including, in particular, power to extend the time specified in the notice for compliance with it (s. 173A(3)). When using this power, however, the authority must give notice of its exercise to every person served with a copy of the enforcement notice.

18.7   Appeals against enforcement notices

Section 174(1) of the 1990 Act provides that:

A person having an interest in the land to which an enforcement notice relates or a relevant occupier may appeal to the Secretary of State against the notice, whether or not a copy of it has been served on him.

It should be noticed that the persons entitled to appeal under s. 174(1) are not coterminous with the persons who are required to be served with a copy of the notice under s. 172(2). The right of appeal to the Secretary of State is restricted to those having an interest in the land and relevant occupiers. A 'relevant occupier' is a person who:

(a)   on the date on which the enforcement notice is issued, occupies the land to which the notice relates by virtue of a licence, and

(b)   continues so to occupy the land when the appeal is brought.

An appeal must be made by notice in writing to the Secretary of State before the specified date (i.e. the date specified in the notice as the date on which it is to take effect). Failure to appeal by that date may be fatal for any person wishing to do so, since, as was confirmed by the Court of Appeal in *Howard* v *Secretary of State for the Environment* [1975] QB 235, the Secretary of State has no jurisdiction to extend that date. After that date if no appeal has been made the enforcement notice will come into effect and must be complied with, unless that is, the notice is a nullity.

Section 174(2) provides that an appeal may be brought on any of the following grounds:

(a)   that, in respect of any breach of planning control which may be constituted by the matters stated in the notice, planning permission ought to be granted or, as the case may be, the condition or limitation concerned ought to be discharged;

(b)   that those matters have not occurred;

(c)   that those matters (if they occurred) do not constitute a breach of planning control;

(d)   that, at the date when the notice was issued, no enforcement action could be taken in respect of any breach of planning control which may be constituted by those matters;

(e)   that copies of the enforcement notice were not served as required by section 172;

(f)   that the steps required by the notice to be taken, or the activities required by the notice to cease, exceed what is necessary to remedy any breach of planning control which may be constituted by those matters or, as the case may be, to remedy any injury to amenity which has been caused by any such breach;

(g)   that any period specified in the notice in accordance with section 173(9) falls short of what should reasonably be allowed.

It will be seen that ground (a) relates to the merits of the development, grounds (b) to (e) to question of law or fact or mixed question of law and fact and grounds (f) and (g) to remedial measures required to be taken by the notice.

The real purpose of setting out the grounds of appeal in s. 174(2) is not merely to list the likeliest grounds on which an appeal will be brought. Its significance lies in the restrictive provisions of s. 285(1) of the 1990 Act. That subsection provides:

> Subject to the provisions of this section, the validity of an enforcement notice shall not, except by way of an appeal under Part VII, be questioned in any proceedings whatsoever on any of the grounds on which such an appeal may be brought.

The effect of this provision is to prevent the validity of the notice being challenged on any of the grounds specified in s. 174(2) except by way of appeal to the Secretary of State. It prevents a person from questioning the validity of the notice on those grounds by way of proceedings for judicial review or (save for the one exception previously mentioned) in proceedings brought against that person for a failure to comply with the enforcement notice. The provision, however, does not prevent a person from questioning the validity of the notice by judicial review or by way of defence to a prosecution for failure to comply with the notice on grounds not specified in s. 174(2). A person is not precluded, therefore, from challenging the legality of an enforcement notice other than by way of appeal, if he can show the notice to be a nullity. This would be done, for example, if a person can show that the notice failed to specify the date on which it was to take effect, or failed adequately to state the matters alleged to constitute the breach, or failed to specify the steps required to be taken to comply with the notice.

In order to avoid the Secretary of State being unable to consider an appeal against an enforcement notice because, perhaps due to postal delays, the notice of appeal was not received before the date on which the enforcement notice was expressed to take effect, s. 174(3) provides that an appeal shall be made either by giving written notice to the Secretary of State before the date specified in the notice as the date on which it is to take effect, or by sending such notices to him in a properly addressed and prepaid letter posted to him at such time that, in the ordinary course of post, it would be delivered to him before that date.

18.7.1 Appeal procedure

As already stated, an appeal must be made by notice in writing to the Secretary of State, before the date specified in the notice as the date on which it is to take effect. In order to determine the appeal properly, however, the Secretary of State needs to know the grounds upon which a person is appealing against the notice, as well as the facts upon which the appeal is based. He will also need to know the reason why the authority served the notice in the first place. Prior to the Local Government and Planning (Amendment) Act 1981, it was difficult for the Secretary of State to move to a speedy determination of the appeal if the parties concerned failed to provide this information, and in the absence of a power to make regulations requiring this to be done, his only course was to determine the appeal without that information. The 1981 Amendment Act resolved much of this difficulty by reformulating the obligation on the appellant to specify his grounds of appeal and to give the Secretary of State the power to make regulations with regard to enforcement notice appeals.

Section 174(4) and (5) of the 1971 Act now provides:

(4)   A person who gives notice under subsection (3) shall submit to the
Secretary of State, either when giving the notice or within the prescribed
time, a statement in writing—

(a)   specifying the grounds on which he is appealing against the
enforcement notice; and
(b)   giving such further information as may be prescribed.

(5)   If, where more than one ground is specified in that statement, the
appellant does not give information required under subsection (4)(b) in
relation to each of those grounds within the prescribed time, the Secretary of
State may determine the appeal without considering any ground as to which
the appellant has failed to give such information within that time.

Under s. 175(1) of the 1990 Act the Secretary of State may by regulations
prescribe the procedure which is to be followed on appeals under section 174
and, in particular, but without prejudice to the generality of this subsection,
may—

(a)   require the local planning authority to submit, within such time as may
be prescribed, a statement indicating the submissions which they propose to
put forward on the appeal;
(b)   specify the matters to be included in such a statement;
(c)   require the authority or the appellant to give such notice of such an
appeal as may be prescribed;
(d)   require the authority to send to the Secretary of State, within such
period from the date of the bringing of the appeal as may be prescribed, a copy
of the enforcement notice and a list of the persons served with copies of it.

Under these provisions the Secretary of State has made the Town and
Country Planning (Enforcement Notices and Appeals) Regulations 1991
(SI No. 2804). These regulations require the appellant to specify (in addition
to his grounds of appeal) the facts upon which the appeal is based. He must do
this within 28 days of being required to do so. In practice, if the appellant has
not supplied this information within one week of the end of the 28-day period,
the Department of Environment sends a warning letter to the appellant setting
out the powers of the Secretary of State at the end of that period. Section
176(3) provides that the Secretary of State:

(a)   may dismiss an appeal if the appellant fails to comply with section
174(4) within the prescribed time; and
(b)   may allow an appeal and quash the enforcement notice if the local
planning authority fail to comply with any requirement of regulations made
by virtue of paragraph (a), (b) or (d) of section 175(1) within the prescribed
period.

Furthermore, s. 174(5) provides that:

> if where more than one ground is specified in that statement, the appellant does not give information required under subsection (4)(b) in relation to each of those grounds within the prescribed time, the Secretary of State may determine the appeal without considering any ground as to which the appellant has failed to give such information within that time.

Under these provisions the local planning authority can also be required to provide information relevant to the appeal, and if they fail to do so, the Secretary of State is empowered to allow the appeal and quash the notice.

It will be seen that enforcement notice machinery now contains a rigorous timetable within which each particular stage must be completed. In particular, the recipient of the notice has to ensure:

(a)   that if he wishes to appeal he does so before the enforcement notice takes effect;

(b)   that if he does appeal he specifies his grounds and the facts upon which each ground of appeal is based and in any event within 28 days of being required to do so;

(c)   that in the event of the enforcement notice taking effect he takes, within the period or periods stated in the notice, the steps required by the notice to be taken to remedy the breach of planning control.

For its part, the local planning authority have to ensure:

(a)   that copies of the notice are served on those required to be served within 28 days of issue by the authority;

(b)   that each recipient is in possession of a copy of the notice for at least 28 days before it takes effect; and

(c)   that if an appeal is made against the notice, they provide the Secretary of State, within the period prescribed for doing so, with the information required to be provided under the regulations.

Under s. 175(3), the Secretary of State is required, if either the appellant or the local planning authority so desire, to give to each of them an opportunity of appearing before, and being heard by, a person appointed by the Secretary of State for the purpose. This may be done by a public local inquiry, although it is open to both parties to agree that the matter shall be dealt with by way of written representation procedure. Where an inquiry is held the procedure is governed by the Town and Country Planning (Enforcement) (Inquiries Procedure) Rules 1992 (SI No. 1903).

It has been estimated that evidence is given on oath in about half the cases involving appeals based on grounds (c), (d) or (e) of s. 174(2).

Section 177 of the 1990 Act provides that on determination of an appeal under s. 174, the Secretary of State may:

(a)   grant planning permission in respect of the matters stated in the enforcement notice as constituting a breach of planning control, whether in relation to the whole or any part of those matters or in relation to the whole or any part of the land to which the notice relates;

(b)   discharge any condition or limitation subject to which planning permission was granted;

(c)   determine whether, on the date on which the appeal was made, any existing use of the land was lawful, any operations which had been carried out in, on, over or under the land were lawful or any matter constituting a failure to comply with any condition or limitation subject to which planning permission was granted was lawful and, if so, issue a certificate under s. 191.

Indeed, s. 177(5) provides that where an appeal against an enforcement notice is made, the appellant shall be deemed to have made an application for planning permission in respect of the matters stated in the enforcement notice as constituting a breach of planning control. Accordingly, the Secretary of State has power to grant planning permission, even though no appeal has been made on ground (a) of s.174(2), that planning permission ought to be granted for the matter alleged to be a breach of planning control. Under the section and the appropriate regulations, the planning application fee must be paid at the time written notice of appeal is given to the Secretary of State or within such period as is specified by the Secretary of State. If the appropriate fee is not paid, the deemed application, or the appeal to the extent to which it is based on ground (a) of s. 174(2) will lapse. This latter provision is intended to overcome the problem where in the past the Secretary of State could quash the enforcement notice on the ground that planning permission for the contravening development should be granted, but was unable to grant planning permission because no planning application fee had been paid. That in effect left the planning status of the land in 'limbo'; without any planning permission existing for the development which had taken place, and enforcement powers being no longer available.

18.7.2   The power to vary

As the statistics mentioned in Chapter 2 show, many enforcement notices, although upheld by the Secretary of State, are varied by him on appeal. Power to do this is given by s. 176(1) of the 1990 Act, which provides that on an appeal under s. 174 the Secretary of State may:

(a)   correct any defect, error or misdescription in the enforcement notice; or
(b)   vary the terms of the enforcement notice.

if he is satisfied that the correction or variation will not cause injustice to the appellant or the local planning authority.

The powers of the Secretary of State under this provision are limited. An enforcement notice must tell the recipient clearly what he has done wrong and what he must do to remedy it. If it fails to do this, the notice is a nullity and beyond correction. The best known consideration of the scope of this power was by Lord Denning MR in *Miller-Mead* v *Minister of Housing & Local Government* [1963] 2 QB 196 where he said, at p. 221:

> The Minister has power . . . to correct any informality, defect or error in the enforcement notice if he is satisfied that the informality, defect or error is not a material one. This seems to me to be wider than the 'slip rule'. I think that it gives the Minister a power to amend, which is similar to the power of the court to amend an indictment. He can correct errors so long as, having regard to the merits of the case, the correction can be made without injustice. No informality, defect or error is a material one unless it is such as to produce injustice. Applied to misrecitals, it means this: if the misrecital goes to the substance of the matter, then the notice may be quashed. But if the misrecital does not go to the substance of the matter and can be amended without injustice, it should be amended rather than that the notice should be quashed or declared a nullity. In this way the legislature has disposed of the proposition that there must be a 'strict and rigid adherence to formalities'.

The statutory provisions considered by Lord Denning have been significantly reformulated in s. 176(1) to reflect the construction placed by him on the earlier provisions, and also to restrict the power of correction or variation to cases where this can be done without injustice to the authority as well as to the appellant. The power is often used to delete from an enforcement notice land falling outside the planning unit, to alter the steps required to remedy the breach, and to extend the time for compliance with the notice. It cannot be used to turn a nullity into a valid enforcement notice.

The terms of an enforcement notice (and thus the power to vary), cannot require action to be taken beyond that of remedying the breach. It cannot be used to bring to an end an existing lawful use. In *Mansi* v *Elstree District Council* (1964) 15 P & CR 153 the Divisional Court remitted to the Minister for variation a notice which required the discontinuance of sales of goods from premises, where it was clear that there was an established use for retail sales of produce from a garden nursery, and this use would have been lost if the notice in its original form had been upheld. A more recent example of the application of the *Mansi* principle can be seen in the case of *John Kennelly Sales Ltd* v *Secretary of State for the Environment* [1994] 1 PLR.

Where the Secretary of State determines to allow the appeal he may quash the enforcement notice. He may also give any directions necessary to give effect to his determination on the appeal.

From the decision of the Secretary of State on appeal against an enforcement notice, the appellant or the local planning authority or any other person having an interest in the land may, according as rules of court provide (under s. 289 of the 1990 Act) appeal to the High Court against the decision on a point of law or require the Secretary of State to state and sign a case for the opinion of the High Court. Under the Rules of the Supreme Court, this action must be taken within 28 days of the Secretary of State's decision (unless the period is extended by the court).

Because appellants have sometimes used the litigation process to delay or frustrate the implementation of an enforcement notice by submitting unmeritorious appeals, the Planning and Compensation Act 1991 introduces a new subsection (6) into s. 289 of the 1990 Act. The subsection introduces an entirely new 'leave' requirement, by providing that 'No proceedings in the High Court shall be brought ... except with the leave of that court and no appeal to the Court of Appeal shall be so brought except with the leave of the Court of Appeal or of the High Court.'

Section 175(4) provides that where an appeal is brought under s. 174, the enforcement notice shall be of no effect pending the final determination or withdrawal of the appeal. In *London Parachuting Ltd* v *Secretary of State for the Environment* (1985) 52 P & CR 376, it was held that this meant final determination of the appeal by the Secretary of State. Once this determination had been made, the enforcement notice, if upheld, was required to be obeyed. In *R* v *Kuxhaus* [1988] QB 631, however, the court disapproved of that decision, holding (with reluctance) that where an appeal was made to the court, this had the effect of further suspending the operation of the enforcement notice until the courts had finally determined the matter. This decision meant, therefore, that it was possible to frustrate the effect of an enforcement notice for a considerable length of time by pursuing an appeal to the Secretary of State, then beyond that to the courts. At that stage, it was not uncommon for the appellant then to withdraw the appeal.

To deal with this problem, s. 6 of the Planning and Compensation Act 1991 inserts a new subsection (4A) into s. 289 of the 1990 Act (the section which deals with appeals to the High Court against enforcement notices). The effect of the new subsection is that where an appeal is made to the courts against the decision of the Secretary of State in relation to an enforcement notice, the High Court or Court of Appeal may order that the notice shall have such effect or have effect to such extent as may be specified in the order, pending the final determination of the proceedings and any rehearing and determination by the Secretary of State. This provision will thus allow the courts, in dealing with the enforcement notice appeal, to decide whether, pending the determination of the appeal, the appellant should be made to comply with the enforcement notice and, if so, to what extent, or whether the notice should continue to be of no effect.

Although in determining an appeal against an enforcement notice, the Secretary of State has power to quash an enforcement notice, the powers of the court in dealing with an appeal are limited to remitting the matter to the Secretary of State with the opinion of the court for his rehearing and redetermination. There is no power available to the court, therefore, to quash or set aside an enforcement notice.

It appears that a decision made by the Secretary of State to allow an appeal against an enforcement notice on one of the grounds mentioned in s. 174 of the 1990 Act is capable of giving rise to an estoppel *per rem judicatam* or to an issue estoppel. In *Thrasyvoulou* v *Secretary of State for the Environment* [1990] 2 AC

273, a number of enforcement notices alleging breaches of planning control had been issued in 1981. On appeal, an Inspector had decided that no material change of use had taken place. Following a second batch of enforcement notices issued in 1985, an Inspector hearing the appeals decided that he was not bound by the decision reached by the earlier Inspector in relation to the 1981 notices. The House of Lords held that there was an important distinction between an issue raised by an appeal against an enforcement notice on ground (a) of what is now s. 174(2) of the 1990 Act, where the question is whether planning permission should be granted, and the issues raised by grounds (b) to (e). In the former case the public have a right to attend an inquiry and be heard as objectors, whereas in the latter case they have no *locus standi* as objectors, although they may be heard as witnesses of fact. Their Lordships thought that Parliament must have intended the determination of any issue arising under grounds (b) to (e) of s. 174(2) in favour of an appellant to be conclusive. Any such determination gives rise to an estoppel *per rem judicatam*. Such 'cause of action' estoppel will arise whenever the determination of the ground decided in favour of the appellant on an appeal against one enforcement notice can be relied on in an appeal against a second enforcement notice which is in the same terms and is directed against the same alleged development as the first.

In related proceedings (*Oliver* v *Havering London Borough Council*) the House ruled that where on one enforcement notice appeal an Inspector had ruled that land was immune from enforcement proceedings (because the use had been established before 1964), a second Inspector on a subsequent enforcement notice appeal was bound by issue estoppel to accept the ruling.

18.8 Stop notices

At one time one of the difficulties with the enforcement of planning control was that a person could begin to develop without planning permission and, when an enforcement notice was served, use delaying mechanisms (including the right of appeal) to postpone its operation; whilst at the same time continuing with the development. The effects of this were twofold. First, where the development involved the erection of a building, the Secretary of State, in determining the appeal, was less likely to require the demolition of a building which had been completed than one in the early stages of erection; secondly, the adverse environmental effects of the unauthorised development could continue for a longer period than necessary if the enforcement notice were finally to take effect.

The statutory provisions relating to stop notices are now contained in s. 183 of the 1990 Act. Subsection (1) of that section provides:

> (1) Where the local planning authority consider it expedient that any relevant activity should cease before the expiry of the period for compliance with an enforcement notice, they may, when they serve a copy of the enforcement notice or afterwards, serve a notice (in this Act referred to as a 'stop notice') prohibiting the carrying out of that activity on the land to which

the enforcement notice relates, or any part of that land specified in the stop notice.

Subsection(2) of s. 183 defines 'relevant activity' to mean any activity specified in the enforcement notice as an activity which the local planning authority require to cease and any activity carried out as part of that activity or associated with that activity. This provision makes it clear that a stop notice may be directed not merely to an activity specified in an enforcement notice as an activity the authority require should cease, but also to any use of land which is ancillary to its main use.

It should be noted that a stop notice may now be served on a person at the same time as the person is served with an enforcement notice, thus reversing the decision in *R* v *Southwark London Borough Council ex parte Murdoch* (1990) 155 JP 163, that a local planning authority had no power to serve an enforcement notice and stop notice simultaneously.

One limitation, however, is that a stop notice must be served before the related enforcement notice takes effect. This is because, once an enforcement notice takes effect, non-compliance with its terms is itself a criminal offence. Stop notices operate to prevent unauthorised development prior to that point of time. Hence, s. 187(1) of the 1990 Act provides for a criminal sanction if any person contravenes, or causes or permits the contravention of, a stop notice; and he may thereafter be convicted of a second or subsequent offence under the section. The Planning and Compensation Act 1991 amended the penalties for contravening a stop notice by raising the maximum fine from £2,000 to £20,000 on summary conviction. The 1991 Act also requires the court in imposing a fine to have regard to any financial benefit which has accrued or is likely to accrue to the wrongdoer in consequence of the offence.

The stop notice may be served by the local planning authority on any person who appears to them to have an interest in the land or to be engaged in any activity prohibited by the notice.

Section 183(4) of the 1990 Act provides that a stop notice shall not prohibit the use of any building as a dwellinghouse. Prior to the 1991 Act, this exclusion applied also to the use of land as the site for a caravan occupied by any person as his main residence. Because of the potential harm to local amenities caused by unauthorised residential caravan sites, the 1991 Act removed the prohibition against service with regard to caravans.

In addition, s. 183(5) prohibits the use of a stop notice to prohibit the carrying out of any activity if that activity has been carried out (whether continuously or not) for a period of more than four years ending with the service of the notice. Prior to the 1991 Act, a stop notice could not be used to prohibit the carrying out of any activity on land begun more than 12 months earlier unless it was, or was incidental to, building, engineering, mining or other operations or the deposit of refuse or waste materials. Although the 1991 Act extended the limitation period for service of a stop notice from 12 months to four years, it has maintained the right of a local planning authority to serve a stop notice within that period for activities amounting to operational development or the deposit of refuse or waste, or activities incidental thereto. The general extension from 12 months to four years reflects the fact that a use of land may at first be seen to be non-objectionable, but may become otherwise because of intensification.

18.8.1 Service of stop notices

A stop notice must refer to the enforcement notice to which it relates and have a copy of that notice annexed to it. It must also specify the date on which it will take effect. Before the Planning and Compensation Act 1991, the date on which a stop notice was specified to take effect was not to be earlier than three and not later than 28 days from the date of service. The purpose of giving three days' grace before the stop notice took effect was to cushion those affected from losses incurred by having to bring work to an immediate standstill. It was believed, however, that some activities, such as the depositing of waste, mineral extraction etc., could be sufficiently damaging to require them to be stopped immediately. Accordingly the 1991 Act amended the 1990 Act by substituting a provision to allow a stop notice to specify an earlier date than three days for its coming into effect, if the authority consider there are special reasons for so doing and a statement of those reasons is served with the stop notice. A stop notice will cease to have effect where the enforcement notice to which it relates is withdrawn or quashed, or the period for compliance with the enforcement notice has expired, or the local planning authority withdraw it.

18.8.2 Compensation for loss due to stop notices

Local planning authorities have often claimed they are deterred from serving stop notices because of the risk that is run of them having to pay compensation to the person on whom the notice is served, if he is successful in an appeal to the Secretary of State against the related enforcement notice. In fact the liability to pay compensation is much restricted, compensation only being payable if the enforcement notice is quashed on grounds other than that planning permission ought to be granted for the development to which the notice relates; or where the authority decide to withdraw the stop notice; or it is varied on appeal so that the matter alleged to constitute a breach of planning control is no longer included in the notice.

Despite attempts to explain these statutory provisions in Circular No. 4/87, local planning authorities have remained confused by the provisions relating to compensation. Accordingly, the Planning and Compensation Act 1991 amended the 1990 Act by substituting a new subsection (5) of s. 186 to clarify the circumstances in which compensation is not to be payable where a stop notice ceases to have effect. It is now provided that no compensation is payable in respect of any prohibition in a stop notice of any activity which, at any time when the notice is in force, constitutes or contributes to a breach of planning control. In addition, it should be noted that under various other statutory provisions (e.g., planning contravention notices in the new s. 171C of the 1990 Act; or the power to require information about interests in land under s. 330 of the 1990 Act), a person may be required to provide a local planning authority with relevant information. If that person fails to provide that information, or otherwise fails to cooperate with the local planning authority when responding to the notice, no compensation is payable in respect of any loss or damage which would otherwise have been avoided. The justification for this provision is that the local authority should not be liable if insufficient information has been given to them to enable them to decide whether to take enforcement action, and if they do so, to draft the notice with complete precision.

The philosophy behind the compensation provisions is that no compensation should be payable merely because the landowner and the local planning authority have taken a different view on whether or not planning permission for development should be granted. The correct procedure for the landowner is to submit an application for planning permission to the local planning authority and on refusal to appeal to the Secretary of State. If he develops first, is served with an enforcement notice and related stop notice, and then the enforcement notice is quashed solely on the ground that planning permission for the development should be granted, no compensation for loss due to the stop notice is payable. The owner is the victim of his own actions. Compensation becomes payable, therefore, where for some reason other than the merits of the development proposed, the local planning authority has in the view of the Secretary of State made a mistake.

Mention has already been made of the case of *Malvern Hills District Council* v *Secretary of State for the Environment* (1983) 46 P & CR 58, where compensation had to be paid for loss caused by service of a misconceived stop notice. Another example occurred in *Sample (Warkworth) Ltd* v *Alnwick District Council* (1984) 48 P & CR 474. Here, an enforcement notice was quashed on the ground that there had been no breach of planning control. The award made (of £3,122) included rent for temporary accommodation, the cost of idle time of workmen and for additional work necessary to rectify deterioration caused by delay in completing the development.

18.8.3   Execution of works required by enforcement notices

Under s. 178 of the 1990 Act as originally enacted, if any steps which an enforcement notice required to be taken *other* than the discontinuance of a use of land had not been taken, the local planning authority were entitled to enter the land and take those steps and recover from the owner of the land any expenses reasonably incurred in doing so. It has been felt that the inability of authorities to use this power to secure the discontinuance of a use was a serious obstacle to their efforts to secure the cessation of illegal uses of land. Hence, the Planning and Compensation Act 1991 strengthens s. 178 of the 1990 Act by removing that disability. Under the new provision, a local planning authority can enter land where *any steps* which an enforcement notice required to be taken have not been taken within the period for doing so and recover the expenses of so doing from the owner of the land.

Note that it may sometimes happen that the owner is prevented from taking the steps required to be taken by the notice because some other person (such as a tenant) has an interest in the land. In such cases, s. 178(3) allows the owner to apply to the magistrates' court for an order under the Public Health Act 1936 that that other person should permit those steps to be taken.

18.8.3.1 Offence where enforcement notice not complied with   Under s. 179 of the 1990 Act, where, at any time after the end of the period for compliance with an enforcement notice, any step required by the notice to be taken has not been taken, or any activity required by the notice to cease is being carried on, the person who is then the owner of the land is in breach of the notice and guilty of an offence.

Prior to the Planning and Compensation Act 1991, the person guilty of the offence of non-compliance with the notice was the person who was the owner of the land in respect of which the enforcement notice had been served. Where the person responsible for non-compliance was a subsequent owner, the original owner was entitled to have the subsequent owner brought before the court in any prosecution. Under the new s. 179 it is now the owner of the land at any time after the end of the period for compliance with the notice who has primary responsibility for securing compliance with the notice. The section recognises, however, that the owner of the land may not be responsible for the failure to comply with an enforcement notice if, for example, another person (such as a tenant) occupies the land and is responsible for non-compliance. The new section (which here corresponds to similar provisions in the old section)   provides that a person who occupies the land or has an interest in it (other than the owner) must not carry out any activity on it which is required by the notice to cease. If he should do so, the section makes this a criminal offence. It is also made clear that when an owner of land is in breach of an enforcement notice he shall be guilty of an offence, and he may be guilty of a second or subsequent offence if he continues in breach.

The new section provides that where a person charged with non-compliance with an enforcement notice has not been served with a copy of it, and the notice is not contained in the statutory register of enforcement and stop notices kept under s. 188 of the 1990 Act, it shall be a defence for him to show that he was not aware of the existence of the notice.

The maximum penalty that a magistrates' court may impose on a person guilty of non-compliance with an enforcement notice has been increased under the Planning and Compensation Act 1991 from £2,000 to £20,000. In addition, however, in determining the amount of any fine to be imposed on a convicted person, the court (whether the offence was tried summarily or on indictment), must have regard to any financial benefit which has accrued or is likely to accrue to that person in consequence of the offence.

Even though an enforcement notice may have been complied with, it continues to have effect as against any subsequent unauthorised development covered by the notice. Section 181(1) of the Act provides that:

Compliance with an enforcement notice, whether in respect of—

(a)   the completion, removal or alteration of any buildings, or works;
(b)   the discontinuance of any use of land; or
(c)   any other requirements contained in the notice,

shall not discharge the notice.

This provision ensures that once a person has taken the steps required to be taken by the notice, the enforcement notice will continue to bite if the unauthorised development is recommenced.

As regards unauthorised development involving the reinstatement or restoration of buildings or works which have previously been removed or altered in compliance with an enforcement order, the Act deems the enforcement notice to apply to such development, even though the terms of the notice are not apt to cover that development. Accordingly, the local planning authority may prosecute the person responsible and exercise their right to enter the land to secure compliance with the notice. The authority, however, cannot prosecute under s. 179(2) for any failure of a person to take steps required by the enforcement notice by way of removal or alteration of what was reinstated or restored, since to do so would be to impose a penalty both for doing the act and for failing to undo it.

It is not uncommon, once an enforcement has come into effect, for an occupier of land to proceed to lodge an application for planning permission for the contravening development which is the subject of the enforcement notice. Then, on prosecution for failure to comply with the notice, the occupier will ask for the criminal proceedings to be adjourned pending determination of the application for planning permission and/or any subsequent appeal. Magistrates have been advised not to adjourn such proceedings save in wholly exceptional circumstances. In *R v Beaconsfield Magistrates (ex parte South Buckinghamshire District Council)* (1993) 157 JP 1073, Staughton LJ said:

> As a general rule, magistrates should . . . proceed to hear and determine the guilt or innocence of the defendant, notwithstanding that a planning application has recently been presented. If the defendant has a defence or claims to have a defence, it should be tried and determined whether he is guilty or not. If he does not have a defence and does not claim to have one, he should be convicted. . . other than in exceptional cases . . . where the fate of the planning application is expected to be determined shortly, the magistrates should also deal with sentence in such cases and not adjourn them. They can, of course, take into account in considering the severity or lenience of any penalty the fact that a planning application is pending. . . .
>
> I do not think that the magistrates are absolutely deprived of all discretion in such a case where compassionate circumstances exist. Section 179(5) of the Town and Country Planning Act 1990 provides that if after a person has been convicted he does not as soon as practicable do everything in his power to secure compliance with the enforcement notice, he should be guilty of a further offence. Thus a conviction has the effect that the defendant, besides being guilty of failing to comply with the notice in the first place, becomes liable to a fine of up to £200 for each day after that. The magistrates were entitled to consider the effect that the subsection would have on Mrs K and Mrs S. They had outstanding planning applications which had not yet finally been determined. If they were convicted and did not thereafter comply with the previous enforcement notices they were liable to a daily fine. Bearing in mind the particular circumstances of the ladies, their age, means, state of

health and the substantial period of time when the local authority had taken no action consequent on the breach of the enforcement notices, the justices were entitled to take a very unusual course in the wholly exceptional circumstances of the case.

18.9 Breach of condition notices

Under s. 171A of the 1990 Act, failure to comply with any condition or limitation subject to which planning permission has been granted constitutes a breach of planning control. Accordingly, an enforcement notice may be served specifying the steps to be taken to remedy the breach.

In 1989, evidence was given to the review of enforcement procedure conducted by Robert Carnwath QC that the enforcement notice procedure was insufficiently flexible to secure the enforcement of conditions. The view was expressed that '... enforcement action was very rarely an efficient means of dealing with breaches of conditions relating to the period of construction of a project on such things as noise or working hours, since a stop notice would be too drastic in most cases and enforcement is too slow and unsure'. It was thought that there was a need for a summary remedy which would enable conditions to be enforced without enabling the merits to be reopened through the full panoply of an enforcement notice appeal.

Accordingly, the Planning and Compensation Act 1991 introduced a new s. 187A into the 1990 Act to give local planning authorities a new procedure for the summary enforcement of a breach of a condition or a limitation subject to which a planning permission has been granted. The procedure provides local planning authorities with an independent method of dealing with breaches of a condition or limitation as an alternative to the service of an enforcement notice or obtaining an injunction.

The new s. 187A applies where planning permission for the carrying out of any development of land has been granted subject to conditions; and any of the conditions are not complied with. In such cases subsections (1) and (2) of the new s. 187A empower a local planning authority to serve a notice (called a breach of condition notice) on any person who is carrying out or has carried out the development, or any person having control of the land, requiring him to secure compliance with such of the conditions as are specified in the notice. The notice, which the authority have power to withdraw, must specify the steps which the authority consider ought to be taken, or the activities which the authority consider ought to cease, to secure compliance with conditions specified in the notice. In this context, the word 'conditions' is expressed to include limitations.

Under s. 187A(7), the breach of condition notice must specify the period allowed by the authority for compliance with it, which must be not less than 28 days from the date of service of the notice, or that period as extended by any further breach of condition notice served by the authority on that person.

Then, if at the end of that period any of the conditions specified in the notice are not complied with and the steps specified in the notice have not been taken, or the activities specified have not ceased, the recipient of the notice will be in breach and be guilty of an offence. Furthermore, if at any time after conviction the recipient of the notice continues to be in breach of the notice, he may be convicted of a second or subsequent offence, thereby ensuring that eventually he ceases to be in breach.

It should be noted that no right of appeal to the Secretary of State is provided where this new procedure is used. This is because the merits of the condition are not in issue. If the recipient does not comply with the notice, a criminal prosecution in the magistrates' court for being in breach of the notice should follow. The local planning authority will, of course, have to prove all the elements in the offence, though s. 187A(11) recognises a defence that the recipient took all reasonable measures to secure compliance with the conditions specified in the notice; or if he was served with the notice as the person having control of the land, that he no longer had control.

Judicial review may be sought, however, if in issuing a breach of condition notice the local planning authority has acted outside its statutory powers. In *R v Ealing London Borough Council ex parte Zainuddin* [1994] EGCS 130, the High Court quashed a breach of condition notice relating to the attendance of 500 people at a ceremony to lay a foundation stone for a mosque, on the ground that it breached conditions in a grant of planning permission that 'no religious or ceremonial gatherings or acts of worship shall take place within the site except within the building' and that 'no part of the development shall be occupied until both the community building and the residential units have been satisfactorily completed in accordance with the terms of the consent'.

18.10 Injunctions

Injunctions have been used by local planning authorities in the past as an aid to the enforcement of planning control. One of the earliest cases in this area was *Attorney-General* v *Bastow* [1957] 1 QB 514, where the Attorney-General, at the relation of the local planning authority, obtained an injunction restraining the defendant from using land or causing or permitting it to be used as a caravan site contrary to the terms of an enforcement notice. The defendant had continuously disregarded the notice and been prosecuted and convicted on a number of occasions for that offence.

A year later, in *Attorney-General* v *Smith* [1958] 2 QB 173, the Attorney-General, again at the relation of the local planning authority, was granted an injunction restraining the defendant from using or causing or permitting to be used as a caravan site, any land within the boundaries of the authority without the prior grant of planning permission. The evidence was that the defendant, by moving caravans from one unauthorised site to another, was using the machinery of the Planning Act not for the purpose of making genuine applications for planning permission, but for the purpose of delay in order to evade the provisions of the Act for as long as possible. The fiat of the Attorney-General to pursue such cases is now no longer needed by local planning authorities that are also local authorities. Under s. 222 of the Local Government Act 1972:

Where a local authority consider it expedient for the promotion or protection of the interests of the inhabitants of their area ... they may prosecute or defend or appear in any legal proceedings and, in the case of civil proceedings, may institute them in their own name.

This power has been used on a number of occasions. Reference has previously been made to the case of *Bedfordshire County Council v Central Electricity Generating Board* [1985] JPL 43. Another case, where a local planning authority obtained an injunction to restrain a contravening use against which enforcement notice proceedings had been taken, was *Westminster City Council v Jones* [1981] JPL 750. In this case, the local authority acted to prevent the operation of an amusement arcade causing nuisance and disturbance in a residential area. The defendant had known when he took a lease of premises that he needed planning permission for the new use but he had elected to proceed before he had got the permission or before he took adequate steps to ascertain the authority's attitude. The authority had served both an enforcement notice and a stop notice on the defendant; and a summons for failure to comply with the latter was shortly due to be heard. Rather than wait just under one month for the criminal proceedings to be heard, however, the court was prepared to grant the injunction asked for.

In certain cases it may be possible to obtain an injunction to restrain a threatened or actual breach of planning control even before an enforcement notice or stop notice is served. In *London Borough of Southwark v M.L. Frow* [1989] JPL 645 property had originally been used by members of the same family as two informal flats. Minor and superficial building works had taken place and the property was being prepared for occupation as nine bedsit flats. The owner was contacted and told that a planning application was required, but that it was likely that such an application would be refused. Additionally, he was informed that enforcement action was being considered and that the units should not be occupied.

It needed to be established whether a material change of use had occurred, and whether enforcement and stop notices could be served. However, the use as bedsits was dependent upon occupation and thus the authority could not serve the notices as no change of use had yet occurred. As the premises began to become occupied, it became imperative that further occupation be prevented, although allowing the existing tenants to remain. It was the authority's opinion that full occupation of the building as bedsits was undesirable due to the effect of adjoining neighbours, the extremely poor quality of the accommodation itself and possible traffic implications in an already heavily parked and trafficked area.

As the use, usefulness and legality of using enforcement notices and stop notices were in doubt, and as the warnings and advice to the owner were being ignored, an injunction was sought as a solution.

The injunction was granted on the following basis:

(a)   that it was expedient for the promotion and protection of the interest of the inhabitants of the council's area;

(b)   that the council was reasonable in considering it expedient to seek an injunction;

(c)   that an injunction was appropriate in the case;

(d)   that the breach was deliberate and flagrant in that there had been a clear breach and that the owner had ignored the council's warnings and a breach would occur if not restrained by injunction.

The report *Enforcing Planning Control* in 1989 considered that injunctions had proved a useful back-up to the statutory system in difficult cases. In the view of Robert Carnwath QC there were doubts about the circumstances in which the remedy was available, particularly the extent to which it was available to restrain an actual or threatened breach of planning control before it had become a criminal offence following service of an enforcement notice or stop notice.

The review recommended that an authority should be able to apply for an injunction in respect of any breach or threatened breach of planning control, whether or not an enforcement notice or stop notice has been served. Such a remedy could be used in urgent cases where there was a serious threat to amenity and time was of the essence; or as a back-up for other remedies where they had failed to secure the termination of a breach. Accordingly, the Planning and Compensation Act 1991 introduces a new s. 187B into the 1990 Act, to give local planning authorities an express right in planning law to obtain from the High Court or a county court an injunction. The section provides that where the authority '. . . consider it necessary or expedient for any actual or apprehended breach of planning control to be restrained by injunction, they may apply to the court for an injunction, whether or not they have exercised or are proposing to exercise any of their other powers under this Part'.

The use of the new power to seek an injunction to remedy a breach or threatened breach of planning control has recently been considered by the Court of Appeal in two decisions given on the same day. In *Croydon London Borough Council* v *Gladden* [1994] JPL 723, it was held that the power enabled the court to issue a mandatory injunction requiring an occupier to remove a replica Spitfire aeroplane from the garden of a dwellinghouse. In *Runnymede District Council* v *Harwood* [1994] JPL 724 the court granted an injunction which sought to restrain an occupier from using his land for the storage of motor vehicles contrary to the requirements of an enforcement notice. If the court were to withhold an injunction it would have given temporary planning permission for the continuance of an activity for which the local planning authority had consistently refused permission. It was held that s. 187(B) of the 1990 Act was much wider than the power previously available to a local planning authority. It was no longer necessary to show that criminal penalties were not enough to deter the defendant from infringing planning law.

A recent decision by the House of Lords in *Kirklees Metropolitan Borough Council* v *Wickes Building Supplies Ltd* [1993] AC 227 that an injunction granted to enforce the law did not need to be supported by an undertaking in damages, may further encourage the use of this new provision.

18.11 Reversion to earlier use

When an enforcement notice has taken effect, the question may arise as to what use the land can henceforth be put. Section 57(4) of the 1990 Act provides that where an enforcement notice has been issued in respect of any development of land, planning permission is not required for the use of that land for the purpose for which it could lawfully have been used if that development had not been carried out.

18.12 Certificates of lawfulness of existing use or development and certificates of lawfulness of proposed use or development

The report by Robert Carnwath QC, *Enforcing Planning Control*, recommended that a new single procedure be introduced to replace the former 'established use' certificate provisions in ss. 191 to 196 of the 1990 Act and the provisions in s. 64 of the 1990 Act that enabled a local planning authority to determine whether a proposal to carry out operations on land or make any change in the use of land was development and, if so, whether an application for planning permission in respect of the development was required. Section 10 of the Planning and Compensation Act 1991, however, established not one but two new procedures. First, a procedure to enable anyone who wishes to do so to apply to the local planning authority to determine whether *existing* operational development on land or an existing use of land, or any other matter constituting a failure to comply with any condition or limitation subject to which planning permission has been granted, is lawful, and, if so, to be granted a certificate to that effect. Secondly a procedure to enable anyone who wishes to ascertain whether any *proposed* operational development or use of land would be lawful, to apply similarly to the local planning authority for a determination of this question, and, if it would be, to obtain an appropriate certificate to that effect. As with the old s. 64 procedure, neither of the two new procedures give a local planning authority power to answer a general question as to what use or operational development would be lawful for an owner to carry out on his land.

18.12.1 Certificate of lawfulness of existing use or development (CLEUD)

The main purpose of this new certificate procedure is to simplify and modernise the old provisions in the 1990 Act which enabled the owner of land to obtain from the local planning authority a certificate of established use which granted him immunity from the subsequent enforcement action. That procedure dates from the Town and Country Planning Act 1968 when it was decided to change the rule that any development that had taken place more than four years previously should be immune from enforcement action, to a rule which limited that immunity to development of an operational nature and a change of use of any building to use as a single dwellinghouse. Any other change of use however, was not to acquire immunity from enforcement action by the passage of time, and thereafter, enforcement action could be taken at any time. The changes made to the law by the 1968 Act created problems. The position was that any change of use made on or before 31 December 1963 without a grant of planning permission continued to be immune from enforcement notice procedure, whereas a change of use made on or after 1 January 1964 could, apart from the one exception mentioned, never acquire that immunity. Although immediately after 1968 it may not have been too difficult to prove the precise date on which a change had actually taken place, the difficulty of doing so was bound to increase with the passage of time and the frequency with which property is bought and sold. Hence the 1968 Act introduced a procedure for an owner to obtain an 'established use' certificate. The certificate was a procedural innovation designed to assist a vendor to sell his property with the aid of something like a guarantee that no enforcement notice would be served in respect of the use stated in the certificate.

Unfortunately, many owners of land did not apply, preferring to wait until the land was sold or doubts were raised about the lawfulness of the existing use. Now, as 1964 becomes more remote, it has become progressively more difficult to operate the established use certificate procedure satisfactorily. Reliable evidence as to the state of affairs in 1964 is now difficult to obtain, with the result that many applications for such certificates have to be decided on the basis of a 'balance of probabilities'. The decision to phase out the established use certificate procedure is linked, of course, to the change in the law relating to the period when immunity from enforcement action is acquired, which was made by s. 4 of the Planning and Compensation Act 1991 and has been referred to earlier.

Section 10 of the 1991 Act amends the 1990 Act by substituting new ss. 191 to 194. Subsection (1) of the new s. 191 provides that if any person wishes to ascertain whether any existing use of buildings or other land is lawful; any operations which have been carried out in, on, over or under land are lawful; or any other matter constituting a failure to comply with any condition or limitation subject to which planning permission has been granted is lawful; he may apply to the local planning authority specifying the land and describing the use, operations or other matter.

Subsections (2) and (3) of the new s. 191 specify the circumstances in which development or the failure to comply with a condition is to be regarded as lawful. Under s. 191(2), operations are lawful at any time if no enforcement action may then be taken in respect of them (whether because they did not involve development or require planning permission or because the time for enforcement action had expired or for any other reason) and they do not constitute a contravention of any of the requirements of any enforcement notice then in force.

Under s. 191(3) any matter constituting a failure to comply with any condition or limitation subject to which planning permission has been granted, is lawful at any time if the time for taking enforcement action in respect of the failure has then expired and it does not constitute a contravention of any of the requirements of any enforcement notice or breach of condition notice then in force.

Subsection (4) of the new s. 191 provides that if, on an application under this section, the local planning authority are provided with information satisfying them of the lawfulness at the time of the application of the use, operations or other matter described in the application, or that description as modified by the local planning authority or a description substituted by them, they must issue a certificate to that effect; and in any other case they must refuse the application.

It should be noted that, as with the old certificates of established use, the local planning authority have no discretion as to whether or not to issue a certificate. If the applicant can satisfy the local planning authority of the lawfulness of development carried out, he will be entitled to be issued with the certificate. Once issued, s. 191(6) provides that the lawfulness of any use, operations or other matter for which a certificate is in force shall be conclusively presumed. It will not, therefore, be possible for the authority to take enforcement action against any use, operations or other matter specified in the certificate. Thus in order to ensure that a high degree of precision is achieved in describing the particular lawful use or development specified in the certificate, s. 191(5) provides for a certificate to specify the land to which it relates, describe the uses, operations or other matter in question (including, if appropriate, the relevant Use Class), give the reasons for determining the use, operations or other matter to be lawful, and specify the date of the application for the certificate.

18.12.2   Conversion of existing established use certificates

Following the repeal of the provisions which enabled a landowner to apply for an established use certificate and its replacement by the certificate of lawfulness of existing use or development, s. 10(2) of the Planning and Compensation Act 1991 provides that an order under s. 84 of that Act may provide for established use certificates to have effect as certificates of lawfulness of existing use or development, in such circumstances and to such extent as may be specified in the order. Orders made so far contain no provision to enable existing use certificates to be converted automatically into certificates of lawfulness of existing use or development. The position, therefore, is that an existing use certificate retains its former effect and value, so that it continues to remain conclusive as respects any matters stated in it for the purpose of an appeal against an enforcement notice issued after the date specified in the certificate. As in the past, of course, the use described in the certificate may no longer be immune from enforcement action if, since the date of the certificate, there has been in respect of the land some subsequent unlawful material change of use or the established use has been abandoned. The Act does, however, allow the holder of an established use certificate to 'convert' it into a certificate of existing use or development. The application to 'convert' however, must be made like any other application for a certificate of lawfulness of existing use or development. Where an application to convert is made, the established use certificate may be used in support of the application for the certificate of lawfulness of existing use or development. Before issuing the certificate, however, the local planning authority may need to be satisfied that the 'established use' cited in the certificate has continued to subsist, and may decide in issuing the certificate of existing use or development to describe the use more precisely than that stated in the (old) established use certificate.

18.12.3 Certificate of lawfulness of proposed use or development (CLOPUD)

Subsection (1) of the new s. 192 of the 1990 Act provides that if any person wishes to ascertain whether any proposed use of buildings or other land, or any operations proposed to be carried out in, on, over or under land, would be lawful, he may apply for that purpose to the local planning authority specifying the land and describing the use or operations in question.

Subsection (2) of the new s. 192 provides that if, on an application under the section, the local planning authority are provided with information satisfying them that the use or operations described in the application would be lawful if instituted or begun at the time of the application, they must issue a certificate to that effect, and in any other case they must refuse the application. An application may be granted and a certificate issued, therefore, if the proposed use or operation does not constitute development, or if it does but the development is 'permitted development' under the General Development Order or carrying it out would be in accordance with an existing planning permission.

As with the certificate of lawfulness of existing use or development described earlier, the onus of proof will be on the applicant, who will need to describe his proposal in sufficient detail and with sufficient precision to enable the authority to make their decision. As is the case with the certificate of lawfulness of existing use or development, any certificate issued must, by virtue of s. 192(3), specify the land to which it relates, describe the use or operations in question, give the reasons for determining the use or operation to be lawful, and specify the date of the application for the certificate. As regards a proposed use, if the use is to fall within a Use Class, the certificate must specify that particular Class. Where a certificate has been issued, s. 192(4) provides that it shall be conclusively presumed that the use or operations described in the certificate, if subsisting or being carried out at the time of the application, would be lawful. Hence, no enforcement proceedings could be taken if the proposed use or development specified in the certificate became a reality.

The new procedure is similar to the procedure for obtaining a s. 64 determination under the 1990 Act which it replaces. Now this procedure is available s. 64 ceases to have effect.

The new s. 193 of the 1990 Act contains various provisions to enable the form of application and the procedure for dealing with applications for both of the above certificates to be prescribed by development order, for a certificate to be issued in respect of whole or part of the land specified in any application, for applications to be entered in the planning register, for certificates to be revoked if based on an application containing a falsehood in some material particular and for offences to be created where a person gives false information in order to obtain a certificate.

NINETEEN
Listed buildings and conservation areas

Until 24 August 1990, the law relating to listed buildings and conservation areas was contained substantially in the Town and Country Planning Act 1971. Under the measures taken to consolidate the law relating to town and country planning in 1990, it was decided to consolidate those statutory provisions relating to listed buildings and conservation areas. They are now contained in the Planning (Listed Buildings and Conservation Areas) Act 1990.

19.1 Listed buildings

Listed building control is a special form of control applicable to buildings of special architectural or historic interest. This special form of control, which is additional to that exercised over the development of land, is intended to prevent the unrestricted demolition, alteration or extension of a listed building without the express consent of the local planning authority or the Secretary of State. The control does not depend upon whether the proposed activity constitutes development under s. 55 of the 1990 Act. It extends to *any works* for the demolition of a listed building, or for its alteration or extension in any manner likely to affect its character as a building of special architectural or historic interest.

It should be emphasised that it is not just works for the alteration or extension of a listed building that is subject to control, but works for the alteration or extension of a listed building in a way which affects its character 'as a building of special architectural or historic interest'. In a Ministerial decision in 1972 the Secretary of State decided that the painting in yellow of the front door of a dwelling in a famous Georgian Royal Crescent in Bath amounted to unauthorised work altering the character of a listed building and was subject, therefore, to listed building control. But in *Royal Borough of Windsor and Maidenhead* v *Secretary of State for the Environment* [1988] JPL 410, the Secretary of State had taken the opposite view in finding that painting the Georgian stucco of a listed building black was not an alteration and was therefore outside listed building control. The High Court, however, held that having regard to the meaning of the word 'alteration' in ordinary language, and having regard to the relevant statutory provisions, repainting was capable of being an alteration. It was also held that the critical question was whether the repainting in any particular case affected the character of the building as one of special architectural or historic interest, and that was a matter for the Secretary of State to decide. It seems, therefore, that simple cleaning work to a listed building would not normally require listed building consent. There is probably no difference between the painting and repainting of a listed building, though repainting (in the same colour) may not affect its character as a building of special architectural or historic interest. In a Ministerial decision in 1989, it was held that the removal of the original-type glass forming the top glazed panels showing the word 'Telephone' in maroon on a white background, and their replacement with panels showing the word 'Phonecard' in white on a green background on a number of listed telephone kiosks in Cheltenham affected their character as buildings of special architectural or historical importance.

The law relating to listed building control is found in the Planning (Listed Buildings and Conservation Areas) Act 1990 (LBCA Act 1990) and the Town and Country Planning (Listed Buildings and Buildings in Conservation Areas) Regulations 1990 (SI No. 1519).

Under s. 1 of the LBCA Act 1990, the Secretary of State (since May 1992, this responsibility falls on the Secretary of State for National Heritage) is required to compile lists of buildings of special architectural or historic interest or approve, with or without modifications, such lists compiled by the Historic Buildings and Monuments Commission in England (the Commission) or by other persons or bodies of persons. Furthermore, s. 1(4) provides that before compiling, approving or amending any list, the Secretary of State shall consult with the Commission in relation to buildings situated in England and with such other persons or bodies of persons as appear to him appropriate as having special knowledge of, or interest in, buildings of special architectural or historic interest.

The current criteria for listing are contained in Appendix 1 to Circular 8/87. They cover four groups:

(a) All buildings built before 1700 which survive in anything like their original condition are listed.

(b) Most buildings built between 1700 and 1840 are listed, though selection is necessary.

(c) Between 1840 and 1914 only buildings of definite quality and character are listed, and the selection is designed to include the principal works of the principal architects.

(d) Between 1914 and 1939, selected buildings of high quality are listed.

The criteria for selecting buildings of the 1914-39 period for listing cover two issues: the range of buildings which may be considered, and the quality of the individual buildings actually selected.

The criteria are designed to enable full recognition to be given to the varied architectural output of the period. Three main building styles (broadly interpreted) are represented: modern, classical and others. The building types which may be considered cover nine categories, as follows:

(a) Churches, chapels and other places of public worship.
(b) Cinemas, theatres, hotels and other places of public entertainment.
(c) Commercial and industrial premises including shops and offices.
(d) Schools, colleges and educational buildings.
(e) Flats.
(f) Houses and housing estates.
(g) Municipal and other public buildings.
(h) Railway stations, airport terminals and other places associated with public transport.
(i) Miscellaneous.

The selection includes the work of the principal architects of the period.
In choosing buildings for listing, particular attention is paid to:

(a) Special value within certain types, either for architectural or planning reasons or as illustrating social and economic history (for instance, industrial buildings, railway stations, schools, hospitals, theatres, town halls, markets, exchanges, almshouses, prisons, lock-ups, mills).
(b) Technological innovation or virtuosity (for instance cast iron, prefabrication, or the early use of concrete).
(c) Association with well-known characters or events.
(d) Group value, especially as examples of town planning (for instance, squares, terraces or model villages).

In April 1987 the government announced that in future all buildings over 30 years old would qualify for listing, and that in exceptional circumstances, buildings of outstanding quality (i.e., grade I and II*) which were under threat would be listed, provided they were at least 10 years old. As a result of this change, a number of postwar buildings have now been listed. These include the Royal Festival Hall, the Jodrell Bank Radio Telescope, Coventry Cathedral, the Commonwealth Institute, the Runcorn-Widnes Transporter Bridge, Cripps Hall at the University of Nottingham and the Royal National Theatre.
Buildings are classified in grades to show their relative importance. The grades are:

Grade I. These are buildings of exceptional interest (only about 2 per cent of listed buildings are in this grade).
Grade II*. These are particularly important buildings of more than special interest, but not in the outstanding class (probably some 4 per cent of listed buildings).
Grade II. These are buildings of special interest, but are not sufficiently important to be counted among the elite.

Section 1(3) of the LBCA Act 1990 provides that:

In considering whether to include a building in a list compiled or approved under this section, the Secretary of State may take into account not only the building itself but also —

(a)   any respect in which its exterior contributes to the architectural or historic interest of any group of buildings of which it forms part; and

(b)   the desirability of preserving, on the ground of its architectural or historical interest, any feature of the building consisting of a man-made object or structure fixed to the building or forming part of the land and comprised within the curtilage of the building.

In other words, although an individual building may not in itself be worthy of listing in its own right, it becomes worthy and may be listed if in its setting it contributes to the architectural or historic interest of a group of buildings of which it is just one.

There are now 440,000 entries in the statutory lists in England and about 500,000 individual buildings protected as listed buildings. About 5,800 are classified as grade I. It is thought (because they have never been counted) that about 15,000 listed buildings are classified as grade II*.

Occasionally listed buildings have their status withdrawn because either they have lost their qualifying features through alteration, fire, etc., their architectural or historic merits prove to have been misjudged, or they have been listed in error. In 1988 for example, a building at Sea Palling, Norfolk, was added to the lists as a 16th century house. It had in fact been built in the preceding five years. The roof had come from an old barn; lintels and doors from a demolition site; and the bressummers over the inglenook fireplaces from a scrapyard. For authenticity, the owner had built in settlement. It was subsequently claimed that the building deserved to be listed on grounds of its rarity and eccentricity if not antiquity! In addition, a building may be deleted from a list following demolition, with or without listed building consent.

There is no statutory provision requiring consultation with either the local planning authority or the owner or occupier of a building before it is added to a statutory list though those responsible for surveying properties with a view to listing are instructed to make efforts to contact the owners and occupiers of the buildings concerned and cooperate with them as far as possible. Once a building is listed, the Department writes to the owner. This is in the nature of an early warning, because local planning authorities are required formally to notify owners and occupiers that a building has been included in a statutory list as soon as they receive notification of that fact from the Department. No formal machinery exists at this stage for an owner or occupier to challenge the inclusion of a building in a list.

There is, however, an informal mechanism to challenge the listing of a building. If an owner or occupier makes representations to the Department, the matter is referred to a different Inspector from the one who made the original recommendation. A second opinion is obtained, and the Department may in the light of that second opinion decide that the building should not be listed after all. In 1986, in answer to a Parliamentary question, it was revealed that out of 23,000 buildings listed in the preceding year, only three dozen had been the subject of representations and of those only five had been found to be justified and the buildings removed from the lists.

19.2 What can be listed

Under s. 1(5) of the LBCA Act 1990, a listed building means a building which for the time being is included in a list compiled or approved by the Secretary of State under the section. It will be recalled that under s. 336(1) of the 1990 Act, a building 'includes any structure or erection, and any part of a building, as so defined, but does not include plant or machinery comprised in a building'. Section 1(5) of the LBCA Act 1990 amplifies that definition by providing that the following shall be treated as part of a building:

(a)   any object or structure fixed to the building;

(b)   any object or structure within the curtilage of a building which, although not fixed to the building, forms part of the land and has done so since before 1 July 1948.

The effect of paragraph (a) is to enable control to be applied to both internal and external features of a building which are part of its historic fabric or of architectural interest, such as wall panelling, chimney-pieces and wrought-iron balconies.

The effect of paragraph (b) is to exclude from control any free-standing buildings erected within the curtilage of a listed building after 1 July 1948, unless, of course, the building has been listed in its own right.

A problem may arise as to precisely what is covered by the term 'object or structure fixed to the building'. The problem was considered by the House of Lords in *Debenhams plc* v *Westminster City Council* [1987] AC 396. There, the respondents owned a hereditament comprising two separate buildings on opposite sides of a street but joined by a footbridge over and a tunnel under the street. One of the buildings (the Regent Street building) was listed in its own right. The other building (the Kingly Street building) was not listed. A dispute arose as to whether the respondents could claim listed building exemption from rates under the General Rate Act 1967 for the period the hereditament had been unoccupied. The magistrate had held that the respondents were not entitled to the listed building exemption because the Kingly Street building was not a listed building. The respondents contended that the whole hereditament was listed because the Kingly Street building was a 'structure fixed to a [listed] building'. The House of Lords, in supporting the magistrate's view that the respondents were not entitled to the exemption, held that the term 'structure fixed to a [listed] building', only encompassed a structure which was ancillary and subordinate to the listed building itself and which was either fixed to the main building or within its curtilage, as, for example, in the case of the stable block of a listed mansion house or the steading of a listed farmhouse. The fact that one building was subordinate to another for the commercial purposes of the occupier or that a completely distinct building was connected to a listed building to which it was not subordinate, did not make the building a structure fixed to a listed building.

The *Debenhams* decision was followed in a later case, *Watts* v *Secretary of State for the Environment* [1991] JPL 719, where a successful challenge was made to the decision of the Secretary of State to dismiss an appeal against a listed building enforcement notice in respect of the demolition of part of a garden wall in order to provide a vehicle access. The question for the High Court to consider was whether the wall was subject to listed building control as being a 'structure fixed to a [listed] building' within the meaning of what is now s. 1(5)(c) of the LBCA 1990.

In 1985, the adjacent Bix Manor House and adjoining barn had been specifically listed, but other buildings within the curtilage of the manor house and the garden wall were not specifically referred to. At the date of the listing, the section of the wall now demolished had formed part of the curtilage of an adjacent property separate from the Manor in terms of both ownership and physical occupation. In quashing the decision of the Secretary of State and remitting the matter to him for further consideration, the court held that although historically and physically the wall had been associated with Bix Manor, at the time of listing, the part of the wall demolished was ancillary to another separate (unlisted) building and not a structure ancillary to Bix Manor. The structure was not, therefore, subject to listed building control.

It should be emphasised that every part of a listed building is in law equally 'listed', so that listing may protect the interior of a building as much as its exterior, regardless of any special architectural or historic interest which any particular part may have. It is, of course, common for the Secretary of State to provide a description of each building listed. That description, however, does no more in law than provide an aid to its identification, and any features not noted in the description are also part of the listing. Following recognition of the problems that this may cause, and comments by Lord Ackner in the *Debenhams* case on the power of the Secretary of State to list part of a building, it is believed that more use of that power is now being made.

A further difficulty concerns the extent to which control may be exercised over 'objects' fixed to a listed building. In 1989 the Secretary of State announced that in the light of legal advice, the statue of the *Three Graces*, believed to have been carved by Canova in 1817, which for many years had stood in a temple in Woburn Abbey, was subject to listed building control as being an 'object' fixed to a listed building. He had decided, however, not to take listed building enforcement action to secure its return to the temple.

Then in 1990, the Secretary of State announced that in the light of further information he had received, the better view was that the *Three Graces* was not part of the listed building and therefore not subject to listed building control ([1991] JPL 401). The Secretary of State's view was that the test to be applied was (as Lord Mackay had stated in the *Debenhams* case) the same test as applied at common law to decide whether an article was a fixture.

It appeared that the statue was installed in the *tempietto* in 1819 and remained there until 1872, when it was removed for exhibition at the Royal Academy. It was returned to Woburn Abbey in 1973 and remained installed in the *tempietto* until 1985. In that year it was sold and removed from Woburn Abbey. In his decision the Secretary of State said that the common law test, although easily stated, was not so easily applied. As regards the degree of annexation, the Secretary of State found it not to be great. The plinth on which the statue had stood had not been fastened to the floor in such a way as to make removal of the statue, which was free-standing, particularly difficult.

As regards the purpose of annexation, the Secretary of State said he now took the view, on further consideration, even accepting that the *tempietto* was specifically built or modified to house the statue, that this did not of itself mean that the statue became part of the building.

In his decision the Secretary of State said that in reaching his judgment on the question he had to decide, he attached importance to the following matters:

(a)   the *Three Graces* was expressly commissioned by the 6th Duke from a sculptor of prominence and has always been regarded as a major work of art;

(b)   the statue appears to have been commissioned before steps were taken to add the *tempietto* to the gallery;

(c)   the *tempietto* formed part of the gallery which was being converted and added to by the 6th Duke for the display or exhibition of sculpture;

(d)   the relative importance of the statue in its own right and the nature and character of the building;

(e)   the unlikelihood that sculpture put in a gallery for display is intended to become part of the building;

(f)   the probability that it was the *tempietto* which was designed to display or 'show off' the statue rather than the statue which was commissioned and installed as part of the architectural design of the building;

(g)   the physical nature and degree of annexation.

According to the Secretary of State, he considered that even if the degree of annexation, looked at in isolation, could have been sufficient to satisfy the relevant test (which he doubted), the purpose of annexation in this case was not such as to make the statue part of the building. He thought that if the position was judged objectively, and without regard to the way in which the owners had regarded and treated the statue, it seemed that the object or purpose of installing the statue in the *tempietto* was not to dedicate it to the land or to incorporate it into the land, but to show off the statue. That, he felt, was consistent with the treatment of the *Three Graces* by the 'owners' of the land and the statue, and by the Revenue authorities, on the deaths of the 11th and 12th Dukes, when such owners chose to treat the statue as a chattel and not as a fixture.

A little later [1991] JPL 1101, the Secretary of State decided that an 18th-century sundial, which had rested on a listed terrace but without being fixed to it, had not become part of the land and was not subject, therefore, to listed building control.

19.3 The protection

The special control over listed buildings is secured in the main by a criminal sanction. Section 7 of the LBCA Act 1990 provides that subject to the following provisions of the Act, no person shall execute or cause to be executed any works for the demolition of a listed building or for its alteration or extension in any manner which would affect its character as a building of special architectural or historic interest, unless the works are authorised. Section 9 provides that if a person contravenes s. 7 he shall be guilty of an offence. It is a defence to the prosecution, however, to prove the following matters:

(a)   that works to the building were urgently necessary in the interests of safety or health or for the preservation of the building;

(b)   that it was not practicable to secure safety or health or, as the case may be, to preserve the building by works of repair or works for affording temporary support and shelter;

(c)   that the works carried out were limited to the minimum measures immediately necessary; and

(d)   that notice in writing justifying in detail the carrying out of the works was given to the local planning authority as soon as reasonably practicable.

Following changes introduced by the Planning and Compensation Act 1991, the maximum fine on summary conviction for executing, or causing to be executed, without listed building consent, any works for the demolition of a listed building or for its alteration or extension in a manner affecting its character as a building of special architectural or historic interest, or for the failure to comply with any conditions attached to listed building consent to carry out works to a listed building, has been increased from £2,000 to £20,000. Furthermore, in determining the amount of any fine, the court is required to have regard to any financial benefit which has accrued or appears likely to accrue to the wrongdoer in consequence of the offence. This extends a requirement previously applicable only where a person was convicted on indictment. In addition, the maximum term of imprisonment on conviction on indictment has been increased from six months to two years.

The offence is an offence of strict liability, so that the prosecution do not have to prove *mens rea* in order to establish criminal liability (*R v Wells Street Metropolitan Stipendiary Magistrate (ex parte Westminster City Council)* [1986] 1 WLR 1046).

19.4 Buildings in ecclesiastical use and scheduled ancient monuments

Section 60(1) and (2) of the LBCA Act 1990 provides that ecclesiastical buildings which are for the time being used for ecclesiastical purposes are not subject to sections 3, 4, 7 to 9, 47, 54 and 59 of the Act. These relate to listed building control, including building preservation notices, restrictions on works of demolition, alteration or extension, compulsory acquisition of buildings in need of repair, urgent preservation works by a local authority, the Historic Buildings and Monuments Commission for England and the Secretary of State, and offences in relation to intentional damage. Section 75 of the Act provides that ecclesiastical buildings which are for the time being used for ecclesiastical purposes are not subject to section 74 of the Act which relates to the control of demolition of buildings in a conservation area. These exemptions are commonly collectively referred to as the 'ecclesiastical exemption'.

It follows that although ecclesiastical buildings can be listed under s. 1 of the LBCA Act 1990, no criminal offence can be committed under s. 9 for unauthorised works for the demolition, alteration or extension of an ecclesiastical building which is for the time being used for ecclesiastical purposes or would be so used but for the works. Some limited control over unauthorised work to ecclesiastical buildings, however, has been recognised following the decision of the House of Lords in *Attorney-General* v *Howard United Reform Church Trustees, Bedford* [1976] AC 363. In that case their Lordships decided that the exemption does not apply to the total demolition of a church, as it would then be impossible for the building to be used any longer for ecclesiastical purposes. Following this ruling, therefore, works for the total demolition of a church are not authorised and the appropriate consent must be obtained.

In 1984, following general concern over what is known as the 'ecclesiastical exemption', the Department of the Environment issued a consultation paper inviting comments on whether the exemption should be maintained. Following consideration of the responses to the paper, it was decided in general to retain the exemption. The Housing and Planning Act 1986, however, introduced a new provision to give the Secretary of State power to make orders for restricting or excluding the operation of s. 60(1) to (3) in relation to ecclesiastical buildings in particular cases. These provisions are now contained in s. 60(5) and (6) of the LBCA Act 1990.

Further consultation papers on the scope of the ecclesiastical exemption then followed in March 1989 and February 1992. Finally, in July 1994, the Government announced that as from October 1 1994 it would use its powers to bring religious bodies within the normal secular controls over both internal and external works to their listed buildings, except for those bodies who have an approved control system of their own which conforms with a Government Code of Practice. Those bodies which have, or are about to adopt approved control systems such as the Church of England, the Church in Wales, the Roman Catholic Church, the Methodist Church and the Baptist Union of Great Britain, the Baptist Union of Wales and the United Reformed Church will continue, therefore, to benefit from exemption from listed building control. After October 1 1994, however, all other religious bodies will be subject to normal listed building and conservation controls.

The relevant subordinate legislation giving effect to the above, the Ecclesiastical Exemption (Listed Buildings and Conservation Areas) Order 1994 (SI No. 1771), does, however, somewhat reduce the scope of the exemption. In future, the exemption is to apply only to buildings whose primary use is as a place of worship, and to objects or structures attached to their exterior or within their curtilage to the extent that they are not listed in their own right. It is also provided that special arrangements will apply to cathedrals of the Church of England. In that case the exemption will cover not only the cathedral itself and buildings, but objects or structures which are located within an area designated by the Secretary of State after consultation with the Cathedrals Fabric Commission for England and which fall within a Precinct indicated by the Commission under the Care of Cathedrals Measure 1990. The special arrangements will also cover places of worship elsewhere within the precinct and tombstones elsewhere within the precinct which are not listed in their own right.

19.5   Listed building consent

Under s. 8 of the LBCA Act 1990, works for the alteration of a listed building are authorised if:

(a)   written consent for their execution has been granted by the local planning authority or the Secretary of State; and
(b)   they are executed in accordance with the terms of the consent and of any conditions attached to it.

The section also provides that:

Works for the demolition of a listed building are authorised if—

(a)   such consent has been granted for their execution;
(b)   notice of the proposal to execute the works has been given to the Royal Commission;
(c)   after such notice has been given either—

(i)   for a period of at least one month following the grant of such consent, and before the commencement of the works, reasonable access to the building has been made available to members or officers of the Royal Commission for the purpose of recording it; or
(ii)   the Secretary of the Royal Commission, or another officer of theirs with authority to act on their behalf for the purposes of this section, has stated in writing that they have completed their recording of the building or that they do not wish to record it; and

(d)   the works are executed in accordance with the terms of the consent and of any conditions attached to it.

It will be seen that works for the demolition, alteration or extension of a listed building can only be authorised by a specific grant of listed building consent. This is so even though the works do not constitute development, as in the case of works for the maintenance, improvement or other alteration of a building which affect only the interior of the building. It will often happen, however, that before development or redevelopment can take place, both listed building consent and planning permission will be required. In such cases, both may be applied for at the same time. Sometimes, however, an applicant will wish to establish the planning position first before applying later for listed building consent. Whichever method is adopted, the local planning authority is required, in considering whether to grant planning permission for development or listed building consent for any works, to have special regard to the desirability of preserving the building or its setting or any features of special architectural or historic interest which the building possesses (s. 66(1) and s. 16(2) of the LBCA Act 1990).

19.5.1 Procedure for obtaining listed building consent The procedure for obtaining listed building consent is set out in s. 10 of the LBCA Act 1990 and in the Town and Country Planning (Listed Buildings and Buildings in Conservation Areas) Regulations 1990 (SI No. 1519). Application must be made to the local planning authority on a form obtainable from the authority, and must be accompanied by sufficient particulars to identify the building to which it relates, including a plan; such other plans and drawings necessary to describe the proposed works; and such other particulars as may be required by the authority. It is not possible for an owner to make an application for 'outline' listed building consent; he is required to give sufficient details to enable the impact of the works on the building to be assessed at this one stage. Nevertheless under s. 17(2) of the LBCA Act 1990, the local planning authority may still decide to grant listed building consent subject to a condition reserving specified details of the works for their subsequent approval.

Under s. 19 of the LBCA Act 1990 there is a procedure for varying or discharging conditions which have previously been attached to a listed building consent. The section, however, restricts the right to apply for variation or discharge of the conditions to any 'person interested in a listed building'. It seems that the purpose of this restriction is to prevent 'third parties' seeking an alteration to the earlier consent, where they would have no responsibility for carrying out the work if the conditions were to be varied or discharged.

The application form must be accompanied by certificates similar to those required by the General Development Order in relation to applications for planning permission made by persons other than the owner of the land to which the application relates. In addition, the regulations generally require local planning authorities to publish in a local newspaper circulating in the locality a notice regarding the application, display a site notice on or near the land to which the application relates and take into account any representations received as a result before determining the application.

Under s. 15(5) of the LBCA Act 1990, the Secretary of State has power to direct local planning authorities to notify specified persons of any applications for listed building consent and the decision taken by the authority on them. Extensive use has been made of this power. Directions given in Circular 8/87 require all applications for consent to *demolish* a listed building and decisions taken thereon to be notified to the Ancient Monuments Society, the Council for British Archaeology, the Georgian Group, the Society for the Protection of

Ancient Buildings, the Victorian Society and the Royal Commission on Historical Monuments (England). A further direction requires that notice of all applications for listed building consent to alter, extend or demolish a building, be given to the Historic Buildings and Monuments Commission for England where the building is grade I or II* outside Greater London, and any grade within Greater London. Another direction contains provisions with regard to applications for listed building consent made to the London Docklands Development Corporation.

The obligation of the local planning authority to comply with these directions, does not affect the provisions in s. 13 of the LBCA Act 1990 under which a local planning authority is required to notify the Secretary of State of any application for listed building consent which they propose to grant. The purpose of the provision is to enable the Secretary of State to call in any applications for listed building consent for his own determination. The Secretary of State, however, is empowered under s. 15 of the LBCA Act 1990 to direct that notification to him shall not apply to a specified application. He also has power to withdraw that exemption from notification in individual cases. (Slightly different notification arrangements apply within Greater London.)

Circular 8/87 contains directions absolving local planning authorities from the obligation to notify the Secretary of State of certain applications for listed building consent which they are proposing to grant. The absolution from the need to notify reflects the growing number of applications that are now being made as the number of listed buildings increases, and the fact that many of the applications relate to minor works to grade II (unstarred) listed buildings.

Notification to the Secretary of State is still required where the local planning authority propose to grant consent for applications involving works to grade I and grade II* listed buildings; for applications affecting buildings in receipt of grants under the Historic Buildings and Ancient Monuments Act 1953; and for most applications for the demolition of grade II (unstarred) listed buildings.

19.5.2 Determination of applications

Unless the Secretary of State has exercised the right to call in the application for his own determination, the local planning authority are free to determine the application after having considered any representations received. As with applications for planning permission, there is a right of appeal to the Secretary of State if the application is not determined within eight weeks (s. 20(2) of the LBCA Act 1990). As previously stated, s. 16(2) of the LBCA Act 1990 provides that, in considering whether to grant listed building consent, the local planning authority must have special regard to the desirability of preserving the building or its setting or any features of special architectural or historic interest which it possesses. Furthermore, in deciding whether or not to grant listed building consent, it appears now to be an undisputed proposition that the quality of any replacement buildings may be a relevant consideration to be taken into account (see the speech by Lord Bridge of Harwich in *Save Britain's Heritage* v *Number 1 Poultry Ltd* [1991] 1 WLR 153).

19.5.3 Conditions

Section 16(1) of the LBCA Act 1990 provides that listed building consent may be granted subject to conditions. Section 17(1) provides that without prejudice to this general power, listed building consent may be granted subject to conditions with respect to:

(a) the preservation of particular features of the building, either as part of it or after severance therefrom;

(b) the making good, after the works are completed, of any damage caused to the building by the works; and

(c) the reconstruction of the building or any part of it following the execution of any works, with the use of original materials so far as practicable and with such alterations of the interior of the building as may be specified in the conditions.

In addition, s. 17(3) provides that

listed building consent for the demolition of a listed building may be granted subject to a condition that the building shall not be demolished before

(a) a contract for the carrying out of works of redevelopment of the site has been made; and

(b) planning permission has been granted for the redevelopment for which the contract provides.

The purpose of this condition is to ensure that a listed building is not demolished prematurely before redevelopment is ready to take place. It should also be noted that although (as with planning permission) listed building consent enures for the benefit of the land, s. 16(3) allows the authority to impose a condition limiting the consent to a specified person or persons.

As with the grant of planning permission, listed building consents must include time-limits. Section 18(1) of the LBCA Act 1990 provides that every listed building consent shall be granted subject to a condition that the work to which it relates must be begun not later than the expiration of (a) five years from the date on which the consent is granted; or (b) such other period (whether shorter or longer), being a period which the authority considers appropriate having regard to any material considerations. By subsection (2), if the authority fail to grant consent subject to such a condition, the consent is deemed to be granted subject to the five-year time period.

19.5.4 Listed building consent for work already executed

As in the case of general planning control under Part III of the 1990 Act which allows, by virtue of s. 73A, an application for planning permission to be made to retain buildings or works or continue the use of land, s. 8(3) of the LBCA Act 1990 enables an application to be made for listed building consent after work to a listed building has taken place. Such applications must be made in the same way as any other application for listed building consent. It should be noted, however, that the work is only authorised from the actual date the consent is given, so that a prosecution for executing or causing to be executed works for the demolition of a listed building or for its alteration or extension in a way which would affect its character can still be maintained.

19.5.5   Appeals

Where a local planning authority refuse to grant listed building consent or grant consent subject to conditions, the applicant may appeal to the Secretary of State within a period of six months.

The appeal procedures correspond closely with those for ordinary planning appeals under s. 78 of the 1990 Act.

It should be noted that the appeal procedure provides an owner with one of the few opportunities he has to object formally to the listing. Under s. 21(3) of the LBCA Act 1990, among the grounds in which an appeal may be brought is the ground that the building concerned is not of special architectural or historic interest and ought to be removed from any list compiled or approved by the Secretary of State. In determining the appeal, the Secretary of State may, if he thinks fit, remove the building from the list.

19.6   Listed building enforcement notices

As well as taking criminal proceedings for unauthorised works to a listed building, a local planning authority may, under s. 38 of the LBCA Act 1990, issue a 'listed building enforcement notice'. Because of the existence of the criminal offence, there is no necessity for the related stop notice procedure as exists with general planning control.

As well as specifying the alleged contravention, a listed building enforcement notice must require such steps as may be specified in the notice to be taken within such period as may be specified in the notice:

(a)   for restoring the building to its former state; or

(b)   if the authority consider that such restoration would not be reasonably practicable or would be undesirable, for executing such further works specified in the notice as they consider necessary to alleviate the effect of the works which were carried out without listed building consent; or

(c)   for bringing the building to the state in which it would have been if the terms and conditions of any listed building consent which has been granted for the works had been complied with.

It seems that a listed building enforcement notice can be served in respect of a listed building which has been demolished, so long as a substantial part of it is available for rebuilding. In *R v Leominster District Council, ex parte Antique Country Buildings Ltd* [1988] JPL 554 a 'cruck barn', a grade II listed building with a timber frame which had been erected before 1620, was dismantled without listed building consent being obtained. Some 70 to 80 per cent of the barn's timbers had been sold by the owner in a condition which rendered them suitable for re-erection elsewhere. The intention of the purchasers had been to export the timbers to the United States, where they would there be reassembled. On the question of whether a local planning authority had power to serve a listed building enforcement notice requiring the cruck barn to be re-erected on its original site notwithstanding that the building had been demolished, the High Court held that where the components of a building were substantially extant, its restoration was possible and could lawfully be required by the local planning authority.

Such action would not be an option, however, if a listed building were demolished and it were not possible to put its parts together again. If a listed building were accidentally demolished, as recently occurred when a motor vehicle demolished a listed telephone kiosk ([1990] JPL 444), enforcement action would not be available to the local planning authority. In this particular case, the accident had destroyed the kiosk, which was lost forever.

The *Leominster* case also established that a listed building enforcement notice could be served on the owners of the disassembled parts of the listed building, though the ownership of 70 to 80 per cent of the component parts was thought to be a necessary threshold for this to be possible.

As with the enforcement procedure for general planning control, there is a right of appeal against the notice to the Secretary of State. The appeal procedures are similar. Two important differences, however, should be mentioned. First, there is no four-year rule as exists in general planning control. Secondly, the grounds of appeal to the Secretary of State include the ground 'that the building is not of special architectural or historic interest'.

Section 25 of the Planning and Compensation Act 1991 made various amendments to the LBCA Act 1990. As far as possible, the amendments replicate parallel amendments made by the 1991 Act in the field of the enforcement of general planning control. The main amendments made by s. 25 of the 1991 Act to the LBCA Act 1990 are as follows:

(a)   The existing power of a local planning authority to withdraw a listed building enforcement notice before it has taken effect has been extended to include a power to withdraw a notice after it has taken effect.

(b)   In order to prevent appeals against listed building enforcement notices being invalidated due to postal delays, it is now provided that an appeal may be validly made if sent to the Secretary of State in a properly addressed and prepaid letter posted to him at such time that, in the ordinary course of post, it would be delivered to him before the date specified in the notice as the date on which it is to take effect.

(c)   Section 39(3) of the LBCA Act 1990 provides that 'where . . . an appeal is brought the listed building enforcement notice shall be of no effect pending the final determination or withdrawal of the appeal'. In *R* v *Kuxhaus* [1988] QB 631 (a decision on the related s. 175(4) of the 1990 Act) the Court of Appeal held that the words 'final determination' meant that the enforcement notice was suspended not only up to the time the decision of the Secretary of State had been given on appeal, but until any appeal from his decision to the courts had been decided. This meant that an owner could delay having to comply with the enforcement notice by appealing to the Secretary of State and then to the courts before withdrawing his appeal to the courts at the last moment. In that way, the owner was able to use the procedure to continue to use his land in contravention of planning control for a longer period than would otherwise have been the case.

Accordingly sch. 3 to the 1991 Act amends s. 39(3) of the LBCA Act 1990 by making this provision subject to any order made by the court.

(d)   In order to prevent unnecessary appeals from decisions of the Secretary of State to the High Court, many of which are withdrawn before trial, the 1991 Act makes two changes to s. 65 of the LBCA Act 1990. First, a new subsection (3A) now provides that:

in proceedings brought by virtue of this section, the High Court or, as the case may be, the Court of Appeal may ... order that the listed building enforcement notice shall have such effect, or have effect to such extent as may be specified in the order, pending the final determination of those proceedings and any rehearing and determination by the Secretary of State.

This provision is necessary as a result of the amendment referred to in (c) above, so that a listed building enforcement notice may not be suspended by the taking of legal proceedings. Under the new s. 65(3A), the court is now given the power to decide the effect of the enforcement notice during the period before it comes to a final judgment on the appeal.

Secondly, sch. 3 to the 1991 Act makes a further change to s. 65 of the LBCA Act 1990, by substituting within it a new subsection (5). The new subsection provides that:

No proceedings in the High Court shall be brought by virtue of this section except with the leave of the court and no appeal to the Court of Appeal shall be so brought except with the leave of the Court of Appeal or of the High Court.

This provision in relation to listed building enforcement notices, replicates a similar provision introduced by the 1991 Act in relation to the enforcement of general planning control.

(e)   On an appeal against a listed building enforcement notice, the Secretary of State has been given an additional power to correct any 'misdescription' in the notice, so long as he is satisfied that the correction or variation will not cause injustice to the appellant or the local planning authority. Previously, his power to correct a notice on appeal was limited to the correction of any 'informality, defect or error in the notice'.

(f)   Where the steps required to be taken by a listed building enforcement notice are not taken, it is now provided that the person who is the current owner of the land is the person in breach of the notice. This, of course, may not be the same person as the owner on whom the notice was served.

(g)   Where an owner of land does not take the steps required to be taken by the listed building enforcement notice within the prescribed time, he is guilty of an offence. If at any time after conviction he still does not take those steps, he may be guilty of a second or subsequent offence.

(h) As previously mentioned, the maximum penalty for failure to comply with a listed building enforcement notice has been increased on summary conviction from £2,000 to £20,000. In addition, in determining the amount of any fine, the court is now required to have regard to any financial benefit which has accrued or appears likely to accrue to the wrongdoer in consequence of his offence.

(i) A local planning authority is now given an express power to apply to the court for an injunction where it considers it necessary or expedient to restrain any actual or apprehended breach of listed building control. The power is available whether or not the authority has exercised or is proposing to exercise any of its other powers under the LBCA Act 1990.

Furthermore, where the rules of court so provide, an injunction may be issued against persons whose identity is unknown.

(j) Under s. 88 of the LBCA Act 1990, the various authorities are given power to enter land at any reasonable time for certain specified purposes connected with listed building control. These purposes include ascertaining whether a breach of listed building control has taken place and whether a listed building is being maintained in a proper state of repair. The 1991 Act provided an opportunity to bring together in one section of the LBCA Act 1990 all the statutory provisions authorising 'rights of entry' to land in relation to listed building control. However, the 1991 Act, by adding a new s. 88A to the LBCA Act 1990, strengthens the power of the authorities to obtain information needed for a proper discharge of their listed building control functions. The new section now allows a local planning authority, the Secretary of State or, in Greater London, the Historic Buildings and Monuments Commission for England, to enter on land for any of the purposes set out in s. 88 of the 1990 Act without prior notice under the warrant of a magistrate. The applicant for a warrant must show to the satisfaction of the magistrate that there are reasonable grounds for entering the land for any of the purposes set out in s. 88, and that admission to the land has been refused (or refusal is reasonably apprehended), or the case is one of urgency.

19.7 Listed building purchase notices

If listed building consent has been refused or granted subject to conditions, an owner of land may serve on the council of the district or London borough in which the land is situated a notice, called a listed building purchase notice, requiring the council to purchase his interest in the land. In order to do so, however, he must be able to show that the land has become 'incapable of reasonably beneficial use'. The statutory provisions, which are contained in ss. 32 to 37 of the LBCA Act 1990 are similar to the provisions in Part VI of the 1990 Act which enable the owner of an interest in land to serve a purchase notice where an application for planning permission to develop land is refused or granted subject to conditions.

19.8   Compensation for the refusal of listed building consent

Prior to the Planning and Compensation Act 1991, in certain limited circumstances a person could claim compensation if his interest in land had been depreciated by the refusal or conditional grant of listed building consent.

The philosophy behind this right to compensation was that the owner of a non-listed building may carry out works which do not constitute development or which is permitted by development order. Since the only reason the owner of a listed building cannot avail himself of this right is the failure to obtain the necessary listed building consent, he should be compensated for that failure. Now, with the repeal by the Planning and Compensation Act 1991 of all provisions in the 1990 Act providing for the payment of compensation in respect of losses incurred as a result of adverse planning decisions, this limited right is also abolished.

19.9   Certificates of immunity

Prior to 1980, one of the difficulties that occurred with listed building control was that a landowner might apply for and obtain planning permission for the redevelopment of land on which there stood a building of some architectural or historic interest, but one not protected by inclusion in the lists. The planning permission obtained was often an outline permission, which left the landowner with the obligation to obtain approval of reserved matters before the redevelopment could actually be commenced. Then, before approval of reserved matters had been obtained, the building would be added to a list compiled or approved by the Secretary of State. Since this would generally mean the redevelopment could not then take place, or at best could not take place in the way originally envisaged, the landowner might have spent a considerable sum of money in preparing the plans, etc. needed for detailed approval which would then be wasted.

To meet this difficulty the Local Government, Planning and Land Act 1980 added a new provision whereby, where an application has been made for planning permission for development involving the alteration, extension or demolition of a building, or planning permission has been granted for such development, any person may apply to the Secretary of State for a certificate stating that he does not intend to list the building. This provision is now to be found in s. 6 of the LBCA Act 1990.

Once a certificate is issued, the building cannot be listed for a period of five years or be the subject of a building preservation notice made by the local planning authority during that period (see later). If a certificate should not be granted, the building will almost certainly be added to the list. Although the law does not require that step to be taken, a failure to add it to the list at the same time as the decision is taken not to issue a certificate, might well lead to the building's immediate demolition.

A recent use of the certificate procedure occurred in 1992, when the Secretary of State issued a certificate in relation to buildings in the South Bank Centre, including the Hayward Gallery, the Queen Elizabeth Hall, the Purcell Room and associated walkways. The Royal Festival Hall was already listed.

19.10 Listed buildings in need of repair

Under s. 54 of the LBCA Act 1990, local authorities have power to execute any works which appear to them to be urgently necessary for the preservation of unoccupied listed buildings in their area. Before doing so, they must give the owner of the building not less than seven days' notice in writing of their intention to do so. Such a notice can also be served in respect of the unused part of a partly occupied listed building, and the works executed may consist of or include works for providing temporary support (such as scaffolding or props) for the building.

Under s. 55 of the LBCA Act 1990, a local authority may recover the expenses incurred by them in carrying out such work (including continuing expenses in providing temporary support), subject to the right of the owner to make representation to the Secretary of State if he considers that the amount sought to be recovered is unreasonable or would cause him hardship or was for work unnecessary for the building's preservation, or that in the case of works for affording temporary support or shelter, the temporary arrangements have continued for an unreasonable length of time.

These provisions do not apply to ecclesiastical buildings or to ancient monuments. The arrangements are subject to some modification in the case of listed buildings in Greater London, where the Historic Buildings and Monuments Commission for England has extensive powers.

19.10.1 Compulsory purchase of listed buildings in need of repair

Under s. 47 of the LBCA Act 1990, the Secretary of State may authorise a local authority (or the Historic Buildings and Monuments Commission for England in Greater London) to acquire compulsorily any listed building (other than an ecclesiastical building or ancient monument) where it appears to him that reasonable steps are not being taken for the building's proper preservation.

A condition precedent to the exercise of this power is the service on the owner of the building of a 'repairs notice' under s. 48, specifying the works which the authority consider reasonably necessary for the proper preservation of the building and explaining that if the works required by the notice are not carried out compulsory purchase proceedings may be taken.

In *Robbins* v *Secretary of State for the Environment and Ashford Borough Council* [1989] 1 All ER 878, the House of Lords rejected the argument that a repairs notice could only require the carrying out of works that were necessary for the proper preservation of a building as it subsisted at the date on which the notice was served, and that the notice could require the owner to restore the building to the condition it was in at the date the building was listed.

Should the notice contain any items which are invalid because they require works to be done which are not for preservation, the notice remains valid and the invalid items may simply be disregarded. There is no right of appeal against the repairs notice. If the owner complies with it the authority need do no more. If, however, after two months from the date of service of the notice, reasonable steps have not been taken for properly preserving the building, the authority may commence compulsory purchase proceedings. If the authority proceed to do so, two special points should be noted. First, the compulsory purchase has to be authorised by the Secretary of State, who may not do so unless satisfied that it is expedient to make provision for the preservation of the building and to authorise its compulsory acquisition for that purpose. Hence, in objecting to the compulsory purchase order, the owner may claim that the building is not of special architectural or historic interest and should not be preserved, or that the work specified in the repairs notice is unnecessary for the preservation of the building. Secondly, any person having an interest in the land may apply within 28 days of service of notice of the order to a magistrates' court for an order staying further proceedings on the compulsory purchase order; and if the court is satisfied that reasonable steps have been taken for properly preserving the building, the court must order a stay.

The Secretary of State may also use the powers available under s. 48 to local planning authorities. In 1992, the Secretary of State served a repairs notice on the owners of the former St Ann's Hotel in the Crescent, Buxton, a grade I listed Georgian building. Following dissatisfaction with the lack of any significant progress being made to repair the building, and in order to halt any further deterioration through neglect and indecision, the Secretary of State later used his powers under s. 48 of the LBCA Act 1990 to serve a compulsory purchase order on the owner. The building was subsequently purchased, however, by the local planning authority, who, with the help of funding from the National Heritage Memorial Fund, are hoping to carry out all necessary repairs.

Some light on the use of listed building repair notices has now been shed by a recent report [1992] JPL 609. The report, based on a survey of local planning authorities in England, shows that over a six-year period between 1984 and 1990, local planning authorities authorised the issue of 287 listed building repair notices. That step alone led the owners of 125 buildings affected either to commence repairs to the building or to sell it for others to do so. Of the 162 repair notices that were actually served by local planning authorities, repairs were started by the original owner in 87 cases, though in 14 of the cases the repair work did not begin until the compulsory purchase order inquiry stage had been reached.

19.10.2 Compensation

Where a listed building is compulsorily acquired as part of the normal process of land acquisition for public purposes, compensation is assessed on the normal market value basis. By s. 49 of the LBCA Act 1990, for the purposes of assessing compensation for the compulsory acquisition of a listed building, it is to be assumed that listed building consent would be granted for any works for the alteration or extension of the building. No assumption may be made, however, that listed building consent would have been granted for works of the demolition of the building, apart from any works for the purposes of the limited development of any class specified in sch. 3 to the 1990 Act. It will, of course, still be possible for an owner to claim that, but for the acquisition, listed building consent would have been granted for the demolition of the building and planning permission granted for redevelopment of the land.

Where a listed building in need of repair is acquired in order to preserve it, and it can be shown that the building was deliberately allowed to fall into disrepair for the purposes of justifying its demolition and the development or redevelopment of the site or adjoining site, the local authority may acquire the building at a substantially lower price. In order for this to happen, s. 50 of the LBCA Act 1990 requires the compulsory purchase order to contain an application for a 'direction for minimum compensation', and the Secretary of State must include such a direction in the order when confirmed by him. Where a direction for minimum compensation is made, compensation for the acquisition is to be assessed on the basis that it is to be assumed that, but for the acquisition, listed building consent would *not* be granted for any works to the building other than works necessary for restoring it to and maintaining it in a proper state of repair, and that planning permission would *not* be granted for any development or redevelopment of the site.

The owner of an interest in the land subject to a direction for minimum compensation may appeal to the Secretary of State against the direction at the time he appeals against the compulsory purchase order. Alternatively, he may apply to the magistrates' court for an order that the direction be not included in the order on the ground that the building has not been deliberately allowed to fall into disrepair for the purposes of justifying demolition and the development or redevelopment of the site.

In the report referred to in 19.10.1, it is disclosed that there has been a final decision about minimum compensation by the Secretary of State in only six cases. He confirmed the order for minimum compensation in three cases. In three cases the Secretary of State rejected the order for minimum compensation but this did not affect the case for acquisition; and in these cases the order was in any event confirmed by the Secretary of State.

Two minimum compensation cases were taken to the magistrates' court. In one, the magistrates rejected the claim for minimum compensation although the owner had previously been refused listed building consent to demolish. The compulsory purchase order was one of those already cited which were subsequently confirmed by the Secretary of State. In another case, the authority was successful in convincing the magistrates that a direction for minimum compensation should be included in the compulsory purchase order but the Secretary of State ultimately rejected the compulsory purchase order entirely. In five cases the issue was never resolved because the owner's action obviated the need to pursue compulsory purchase; the other cases remained current.

19.11 Building preservation notices

If it appears to a local planning authority that a building, which is not a listed building, is of special architectural or historic interest and it is in danger of demolition or of alteration in such a way as to affect its character as a building of such interest, they may, under s. 3 of the LBCA Act 1990, serve on the owner and occupier a 'building preservation notice', stating that the building appears to them to be of special architectural or historic interest and that they have requested the Secretary of State to consider adding it to a statutory list. The notice must also explain its effect. A building preservation notice cannot be served if a certificate of immunity is in operation.

The effect of the notice is to apply to the building most of the provisions of the Act relating to listed buildings, so that it becomes a criminal offence to execute or cause to be executed works for the demolition of the building or for its alteration or extension in a manner which would affect its character as a listed building without listed building consent.

A building preservation notice remains in effect for six months from the date of its service (though it may be renewed), unless it has previously lapsed through the inclusion of the building in a statutory list, or the earlier notification by the Secretary of State to the authority that he does not intend to so include it. If the Secretary of State gives notice that he does not intend to include the building in a list compiled or approved by him, no further building preservation notice may be served within the following 12 months.

Once the notice has lapsed, all proceedings arising from the application of listed building control will also lapse, save for any criminal liability under ss. 9 (execution of works to a listed building without consent) or 43 (penalties for non-compliance with a listed building enforcement notice).

A fetter on the exercise by the local planning authority of their power to issue a building preservation notice, is that under s. 29 of the LBCA Act 1990 compensation must be paid for any loss or damage which is directly attributable to the effect of the notice if the building is not subsequently listed by the Secretary of State. The compensation may include any sum for which the applicant has become liable in respect of any breach of contract caused by the requirement of the notice.

Building preservation notices should be distinguished from what is known as 'spot listing'. This occurs when an approach is made to the Secretary of State by a local authority (or other body or person), without any service of a building preservation notice, to have a building added to the statutory lists. It is claimed that the listing process, which may take months or years when done as part of a general survey of buildings of architectural or historic interest, can be completed within 24 hours by the spot-listing method. Statistics show that of 3,574 buildings added to the statutory lists in 1990, 1,330 (37.2 per cent) were added as a result of spot listing, whereas only 49 (1.3 per cent) were added following service of a building preservation notice. In evidence given by English Heritage to the Committee of Public Accounts of the House of Commons in November 1992, it was disclosed that over 2,500 requests for spot listing were made each year, and that in 50 per cent of cases recommendations for listing were made.

19.11.1 Buildings threatened by development proposals

Public concern for the preservation of buildings has led to increasing problems when proposals are made for the development of land which includes a building which is not protected by listing. An application for planning permission may generate considerable public pressure for the preservation of existing buildings on the land, which, if achieved, would prevent the development proposed going ahead. Faced with an application for planning permission which generates such pressure, the local planning authority may decide to serve a building preservation notice. As stated, however, if the building is not subsequently listed, the local planning authority will be liable to pay compensation for any loss or damage suffered. If, on the other hand, the building is listed, the application for planning permission would have served the purpose of alerting people's attention to the need to preserve the buildings on the site.

It must be recognised that the act of listing may well diminish the landowner's prospects of developing or redeveloping the site and the possible loss of its value for that purpose. In *Amalgamated Investment & Property Co. Ltd v John Walker & Sons Ltd* [1976] JPL 308, the parties had entered an agreement for the sale and purchase of a disused warehouse. The purchase price of £1,700,000 reflected the potential of the site for redevelopment. On the day after contracts were exchanged, the Secretary of State added the building to the statutory list. As a result, the market value of the property (with no redevelopment potential) was no more than £200,000. The purchasers thereupon sought rescission of the contract on the ground of common mistake, claiming that the parties believed at the time of the contract that the property was capable of development, or alternatively, that the listing had frustrated the purposes of the contract so that it was void and of no effect and ought not to be enforced. Dismissing the application, the Court of Appeal held that loss must lie where it fell; that the only mistake made was one relating to the expectations of the parties and that a risk of listing was inherent in the ownership of all buildings. Although this case was concerned with which of the two parties should bear the loss, it illustrates the loss that any owner may suffer as the result of a building being listed.

In these circumstances, it is not surprising that an owner wishing to redevelop land on which stands a non-listed building, may decide first to demolish the building, and then to apply for planning permission for redevelopment. In this connection, although the definition of development now includes the demolition of buildings, the demolition of any building other than a dwellinghouse is excluded by virtue of s. 55(2)(g) of the 1990 Act; and in relation to dwellinghouses, demolition of most is permitted development under the General Development Order. It should however be noted, that demolition of a building in a conservation area requires 'conservation area consent.'

The effect of listing on the value of an owner's interest in land, helps to explain why penalties for contravention of listed building control may reflect the benefit obtained by the wrongdoer and why the law contains provisions relating to the payment of minimum compensation where buildings in need of repair are compulsorily acquired.

19.12 Conservation areas

Under s. 69 of the LBCA Act 1990, every local planning authority must from time to time determine whether any parts of their area are areas of special architectural or historic interest the character or appearance of which it is desirable to preserve or enhance, and shall designate those areas as conservation areas. It would appear that in deciding to designate such an area, a local planning authority can consider as one entity the whole of an area which gives rise to special architectural or historic interest and that not every part of that area need have in it something of interest. In *R v Canterbury City Council ex parte Halford* [1992] 2 PLR 137, the High Court held it could only interfere with a decision to designate if there had been an infringement of the *Wednesbury* principles. Land in a conservation area may not be included in a simplified planning zone (s. 87(1) of the 1990 Act). The designation of a conservation area has the following consequences:

(a)   Under s. 71 of the LBCA Act 1990, the local planning authority must from time to time formulate and publish proposals for the preservation and enhancement of such areas.

(b)   Under s. 72 of the LBCA Act 1990, in the exercise with respect to any buildings or other land in a conservation area of any powers under any of the provisions of the Planning Acts or Part I of the Historic Buildings and Ancient Monuments Act 1953, 'special attention should be paid to the desirability of preserving or enhancing the character or appearance of that area'.

This provision is derived from s. 277(8) of the Town and Country Planning Act 1971. Its scope was first considered by the courts in *Steinberg v Secretary of State for the Environment* (1988) 58 P & CR 453, where the main issue for decision was whether the Inspector, in allowing an appeal against the decision of the local planning authority to refuse planning permission to erect a two-storey house in a conservation area, had correctly applied s. 277(8) of the Town and Country Planning Act 1971. In his decision letter the Inspector had said that from his observations of the site and its surroundings and from representations received, he considered the main issue to be decided was whether the proposal would constitute overdevelopment of the site and whether the proposed development would harm the character of the conservation area. In quashing the decision, the High Court held that the Inspector had misdirected himself on a point of law. The duty imposed by s. 277(8) was 'to pay special attention to the desirability of preserving or enhancing the character or appearance of the conservation area'. The court held that there was a world of difference between what the Inspector had defined for himself — whether the proposed development would 'harm' the character of the conservation area — and the need to pay special attention to the desirability of preserving or enhancing the character or appearance of the area. Harm was one thing, preservation or enhancement another. The concept of avoiding harm was essentially negative, the underlying purpose of s. 277(8) essentially positive.

The *Steinberg* decision was later considered by the High Court in *Unex Dumpton Ltd v Secretary of State for the Environment* [1990] JPL 344. According to the court, the duty under s. 277(8) did not relieve the Secretary of State or his Inspector of the need to consider whether harm would be caused by proposed development in a conservation area or if so, whether the benefits of the proposed development would outweigh that harm. Important though the provisions of s. 277(8) were, they were only one of the material considerations that had to be taken into account and only required that 'special attention' be paid to the matters set out in s. 277(8).

The *Steinberg* decision was also considered by the Court of Appeal in *Ward* v *Secretary of State for the Environment* [1990] JPL 347. There, the court held, *inter alia,* that by failing properly to consider whether proposed development in a conservation area would preserve or enhance the area, the Inspector had fallen short of the statutory requirement imposed by s. 277(8). Although the Court of Appeal appeared to endorse the *Steinberg* principle, its application continued to give rise to difficulties. It seems that the positive duty imposed by s. 277(8) is a material consideration in determining planning applications. It is, however, merely one material consideration, though one given a certain pre-eminence by the section. It may be, for example, that the decision-maker, having paid special attention to the desirability of preserving or enhancing the character or appearance of the conservation area, may decide nevertheless that the application should be refused because of insuperable highway objections.

This approach was confirmed when the meaning of the provision was further considered by the House of Lords in *South Lakeland District Council* v *Secretary of State for the Environment* [1992] 2 AC 141. There, their Lordships had to consider a decision by an Inspector to allow an appeal against a refusal of outline planning permission for the erection of a new vicarage on a site within a conservation area. The Inspector had allowed the appeal and granted planning permission for the development on the ground that, provided the proposed vicarage did not cause harm 'to the character of the conservation area', it would not damage the appearance of the village. The local planning authority then successfully applied to quash the Inspector's decision on the ground that he had failed to discharge the duty imposed on him by s. 277(8) of the Town and Country Planning Act 1971 to pay special attention to the desirability of 'preserving or enhancing' the character or appearance of the conservation area.

The Secretary of State appealed to the Court of Appeal which reversed the decision of the High Court on the ground that the Inspector had indeed discharged his duty under s. 277(8) by his finding that, since the character and appearance of the conservation area would not be harmed by the development, the area's character and appearance would remain preserved. The planning authority appealed to the House of Lords.

In his speech dismissing the appeal, Lord Bridge of Harwich approved the interpretation placed upon the provision by Mann LJ, in the Court of Appeal below, in which he said:

In seeking to resolve the issue I start with the obvious. First, that which is desirable is the preservation or enhancement of the character or appearance of the conservation area. Second, the statute does not in terms require that a development must perform a preserving or enhancing function. Such a requirement would have been a stringent one which many an inoffensive proposal would have been inherently incapable of satisfying. I turn to the words. Neither 'preserving' nor 'enhancing' is used in any meaning other than its ordinary English meaning. The court is not here concerned with enhancement, but the ordinary meaning of 'preserve' as a transitive verb is 'to keep safe from harm or injury; to keep in safety, save, take care of, guard': *Oxford English Dictionary*, 2nd ed. (1989), vol. 12, p. 404. In my judgment character or appearance can be said to be preserved where they are not harmed. Cases may be envisaged where development would itself make a positive contribution to preservation of character or appearance. A work of reinstatement might be such. The parsonages board never advocated the new vicarage on that basis. It was not a basis which the Inspector was invited to address but importantly he did not have to address it because the statute does not require him so to do. The statutorily desirable object of preserving the character or appearance of an area is achieved either by a positive contribution to preservation or by development which leaves character or appearance unharmed, that is to say, preserved.

After agreeing with the construction placed upon the provision by Mann LJ Lord Bridge concluded:

We may, I think, take judicial notice of the extensive areas, both urban and rural, which have been designated as conservation areas. It is entirely right that in any such area a much stricter control over development than elsewhere should be exercised with the object of preserving or, where possible, enhancing the qualities in the character or appearance of the area which underlie its designation as a conservation area under s. 277. But where a particular development will not have any adverse effect on the character or appearance of the area and is otherwise unobjectionable on planning grounds, one may ask rhetorically what possible planning reason there can be for refusing to allow it. All building development must involve change and if the objective of s. 277(8) were to inhibit any building development in a conservation area which was not either a development by way of reinstatement or restoration on the one hand ('positive preservation') or a development which positively enhanced the character or appearance of the area on the other hand, it would surely have been expressed in very different language from that which the draftsman has used.

The approach of Inspectors to the interpretation of this provision can now be seen in a recent Ministerial decision where the Inspector held that the erection of a rose trellis and structure on the top of a wall in a conservation area would enhance the character of the area; but refused planning permission on the ground that it would lead to a loss of light to the first floor bedroom of an adjoining property.

(c)   Under s. 73 of the LBCA Act 1990, the local planning authority must give publicity to any applications for planning permission where the development would, in the opinion of the authority, affect the character or appearance of a conservation area.

Under s. 67(4) of the LBCA Act 1990, local planning authorities must send a copy of any notice published in accordance with this provision to the Historic

Buildings and Monuments Commission for England. The Secretary of State has power, after consultation with the Commission, to make a direction modifying the requirement. The effect of a recent direction (contained in Circular No. 8/87) is to restrict, *inter alia,* the requirement of notification to the commission to development exceeding 3,000 cubic metres, or where the area of ground covered by the development would exceed 1,000 square metres.

(d) Under the provisions of art. 4 of the General Development Order, directions are often made in relation to specified classes of development in conservation areas, thus restricting permitted development rights under the order in those areas.

(e) Land in a conservation area is within the definition of art. 1(5) land in the General Development Order. The significance of this is that the permitted development in such areas is not as wide as development which is permitted by the order in respect of non-art. 1(5) land.

(f) Under the provisions of s. 211 of the 1990 Act, a person proposing to cut, top or lop a tree in a conservation area (other than a tree already protected by a tree preservation order) is required to give six weeks' prior notification to the local planning authority of his intention to do so. The purpose of this provision is to enable the authority to make a tree preservation order if it considers it necessary to do so.

(g) Under the Town and Country Planning (Control of Advertisements) Regulations 1992 (SI No. 666), the local planning authority may submit to the Secretary of State for his approval an order designating the whole or part of a conservation area as an area of special control of advertisements (see Chapter 22).

(h) Under s. 74 of the LBCA Act 1990, the *demolition* of buildings in conservation areas is controlled by applying, with modifications, many of the provisions relating to the control of listed buildings found in Part I of the LBCA Act 1990. Anyone seeking to demolish a building to which these provisions apply must first obtain 'conservation area consent' to do so from the local planning authority. Conservation area consent is not needed for the demolition of a listed building (which, of course, requires listed building consent) an ancient monument or an ecclesiastical building. In addition the Secretary of State may direct that the section shall not apply to descriptions of buildings specified in the direction. A direction in Circular 8/87 provides that (among other buildings which are exempt) the section shall not apply to:

(i)　any building with a total cubic content not exceeding 115 cubic metres;

(ii)　any gate, wall, fence or railing erected before 1 July 1948 which is less than 1 metre high where abutting on a highway or public open space, or 2 metres high in any other case;

(iii)　any building erected since 1 January 1914 and used or last used for the purposes of agriculture or forestry; and

(iv)　any part of a building used for an industrial process provided that the part does not exceed 10 per cent of the whole or 500 square metres, whichever is the greater.

In general, the procedure for applying for conservation area consent for demolition of a building in a conservation area is similar to that for applying for listed building consent. It should be noted, however, that there is no certificate of immunity procedure as exists with listed buildings. But a person may be prosecuted for breach of the provisions and the local authority may take listed building enforcement proceedings.

It has been estimated that there are around 7,500 conservation areas designated in England and Wales, containing four per cent of the nation's building stock.

In April 1994, the Secretary of State for National Heritage announced that he was to give local planning authorities additional powers to control external alterations to domestic buildings in conservation areas. The new powers are likely to give authorities power to withdraw permitted development rights under the General Development Order without the need to seek the consent of the Secretary of State in relation to certain aspects of the external appearance of dwellinghouses such as doors, windows, roofs and frontages. Precise details of the change were still being awaited at the end of August 1994.

TWENTY

Ancient monuments and areas of archaeological importance

Statutory protection of ancient monuments has existed since 1882. Today the protection is secured in varying degrees by the Ancient Monuments and Archaeological Areas Act 1979 (the 1979 Act). Section 61(7) of the 1979 Act defines a 'monument' as meaning:

(a)   any building, structure or work, whether above or below the surface of the land, and any cave or excavation;

(b)   any site comprising the remains of any such building, structure or work or of any cave or excavation; and

(c)   any site comprising, or comprising the remains of, any vehicle, vessel, aircraft or other moveable structure or part thereof which neither constitutes nor forms part of any work which is a monument within paragraph (a) above;

and any machinery attached to a monument shall be regarded as part of the monument if it could not be detached without being dismantled.

20.1   Scheduled monuments

The degree of protection given to a monument under the 1979 Act depends upon whether it is classified as a 'scheduled monument' or as an 'ancient monument'. Under the Act the Secretary of State is required to compile and maintain a 'schedule of monuments'; hence a scheduled monument is defined in terms of inclusion within that schedule. A monument can only be included in the schedule where it appears to the Secretary of State to be of national importance. An 'ancient monument', on the other hand, is defined in wider terms than a scheduled monument and means any scheduled monument and 'any other monument which in the opinion of the Secretary of State is of public interest by reason of the historic, architectural, traditional, artistic or archaeological interest attached to it.'

The Act gives the greatest degree of protection to monuments which are scheduled monuments. Under s. 2 of the Act, a criminal offence is committed where a person executes or causes or permits to be executed prescribed works to a scheduled monument without first having obtained 'scheduled monument consent' for the works. The works referred to in the section include demolition, destruction or damage to a scheduled monument, removing or repairing a scheduled monument or any part of it, altering or adding to it, or flooding or tipping operations on land in, on, or under which there is a scheduled monument. Scheduled monument consent may be granted subject to conditions.

Under s. 3 of the 1979 Act, the Secretary of State may make an order granting scheduled monument consent for the execution of works of any class or description specified in the order. The order currently in force is the Ancient Monuments (Class Consents) Order 1994 (SI No. 1381). As with the General Development Order in relation to the development of land, this order removes the need for an express application to be made for scheduled monument consent where the work involved is of a minor nature.

Section 5(1) of the 1979 Act provides that where any works are urgently necessary for the preservation of a scheduled monument, the Secretary of State may enter the site and carry out these works, but at his own expense.

At present there are some 13,800 entries in the schedule of monuments in England, representing about 20,000 individual monuments subject to protection. These include ecclesiastical ruins, megalithic monuments, crosses and inscribed stones, as well as famous sites such as Stonehenge, the Tower of London and Hadrian's Wall. The Historic Buildings and Monuments Commission for England (known as English Heritage), has recently embarked on a ten-year re-survey programme, which is expected to result in significant additional numbers (perhaps 50,000) being given protection by the Secretary of State as scheduled monuments.

One difficulty with the provisions relating to the scheduling mechanism is that the definition of the term 'monument' presupposes some definable and identifiable entity. It is difficult, therefore, to schedule 'general urban debris' from an earlier age which may be spread over a large area. For that reason, few monuments have been scheduled in urban areas.

20.2 Ancient monuments

The 1979 Act also contains powers for the protection of 'ancient' monuments. As previously indicated, the term 'ancient monument' includes all scheduled monuments, but is not restricted merely to that category.

Under the Act, the Secretary of State is given power to acquire compulsorily any ancient monument for the purpose of securing its preservation. In addition, he is given power to acquire an ancient monument by agreement or by gift.

As an alternative to acquisition of an ancient monument, the Secretary of State may by s. 12 of the 1979 Act be constituted its guardian. Guardianship provides a means whereby the Secretary of State can assume responsibility for maintaining an ancient monument where the owner or occupier is unable or unwilling to do so, but without disturbing the existing ownership of the monument. Where an ancient monument is taken into guardianship, a duty is placed on the guardian to maintain the monument, for which purpose he is given control and management powers. An obligation is also placed on the guardian to permit public access to the monuments under his guardianship.

20.3   Areas of archaeological importance

In addition to the powers relating to scheduled and ancient monuments, s. 33 of the 1979 Act provides for the designation by the Secretary of State of what are called 'areas of archaeological importance.' Areas designated so far are the historic centres of Canterbury, Chester, Exeter, Hereford and York. Designation, however, does not protect the site from damage or destruction. Its purpose is merely to allow time for a site which is threatened by development proposals to be excavated and recorded. Under s. 35 of the Act, it is a criminal offence for any person to carry out or cause or permit to be carried out on the designated land any operation involving disturbance of the ground, flooding or tipping, without first having served a notice of that operation (called an 'operations notice') on the local authority in whose area the land is situated. The notice must be served at least six weeks before the operation is due to commence. After receiving an operations notice, the local authority or other investigating authority (such as a University Archaeological Unit) may enter and inspect the site, observe any operations and carry out excavations. An authority can only carry out excavations, however, if within four weeks of service of the operations notice, it has itself given notice of its intention to carry out excavations. In such a case, the authority is given four months and two weeks from the end of the six week period to carry out the excavation, during which period no operation involving disturbance of the ground, etc. (i.e. development) can be carried out. Thus under these provisions, development can be delayed for a maximum period of six months.

Although more relevant to the field of movable artefacts, s. 42(4) of the 1979 Act also contains a provision making it a criminal offence for a person to use a metal detector in a protected place without consent. A protected place means any place which is either the site of a scheduled monument or any monument in the ownership or guardianship of the Secretary of State or situated in an area of archaeological importance.

20.4   Protection under planning legislation

Ancient monuments and sites of archaeological interest may also be protected under town and country planning legislation. Development plans may contain policies for the protection of ancient monuments and sites of archaeological interest and the effect of development on a scheduled monument may be a material consideration to be taken into account in determining applications for planning permission.

According to a Planning and Policy Guidance Note 'Archaeology and Planning', PPG16, issued by the Department of the Environment in

November 1990, detailed development plans (i.e., local plans and unitary development plans) should include policies for the protection, enhancement and preservation of sites of archaeological interest and their settings. According to this guidance, archaeological remains identified and scheduled as being of national importance should normally be earmarked in development plans for preservation. The guidance goes on to state that the desirability of preserving an ancient monument and its setting is a material consideration in determining planning applications whether the monument is scheduled or unscheduled. (See *Hoveringham Gravels Ltd* v *Secretary of State for the Environment* [1975] QB 754.) Where the proposed development would affect a monument which is not a scheduled monument, the authority may impose a condition in a grant of planning permission placing an embargo on any development taking place until specified archaeological facilities have been provided. A model condition, which the Secretary of State has advised should be used in appropriate circumstances (Circular No. 1/85 Appendix A, para. 38), provides that the developer shall afford access at reasonable times to any archaeologist nominated by the local planning authority, and shall allow him to observe the excavations and record items of interest and finds. Whilst the model condition does not require the developer to pay for these facilities, if the condition imposed is that 'no construction work shall be carried out until an archaeological investigation has taken place to the satisfaction of the local planning authority', the condition effectively means that the developer will have to fund such excavation before he is able to proceed. (See [1990] JPL 87.)

In addition, PPG16 suggests (at para. 30) that:

> In cases when planning authorities have decided that planning permission may be granted but wish to secure the provision of archaeological excavation and the subsequent recording of the remains, it is open to them to do so by the use of a negative condition, i.e. a condition prohibiting the carrying out of development until such time as works or other action, e.g. an excavation, have been carried out by a third party. In such cases the following model is suggested:

> No development shall take place within the area indicated (this would be the area of archaeological interest) until the applicant has secured the implementation of a programme of archaeological work in accordance with a written scheme of investigation which has been submitted by the applicant and approved by the planning authority.

As an alternative to the imposition of conditions in the grant of planning permission, s. 106 of the Town and Country Planning Act 1990 enables a person interested in land, by agreement or otherwise, to enter into an obligation for the purpose of restricting the development or use of land. Under this provision, a developer may undertake to provide not only archaeological facilities on the site, but also the funding of those facilities.

In addition to the statutory provisions protecting ancient monuments described above, it should be emphasised that voluntary cooperation between archaeologists and developers for the protection of ancient monuments and archaeological sites has become a well-established practice in the UK.

This cooperation has been formalised in a voluntary Code of Practice drawn up by the British Property Federation and the Standing Conference of Archaeological Unit Managers. Experience has shown that this voluntary cooperation is preferable when the objective sought is physical preservation — particularly where it concerns the preservation of buried remains *in situ*. Thus, where development of land is to be allowed, it may be possible to minimise damage to a monument by raising ground levels under the proposed new buildings, by using foundations which minimise any damage, or by sealing archaeological remains underneath the new buildings in order to secure their preservation for the future. Where preservation *in situ* is not possible, however, the only acceptable alternative may be archaeological excavation for the purposes of 'preservation by record'. Preservation by record is a general term used to describe the process of documentation by means of photographic record, written report and, where appropriate, the display of the important artefacts/remains which have been uncovered in the course of an excavation.

A recent example of this cooperation may be seen in the dispute over the remains of Rose Theatre, in Southwark, London, where it is believed two of Shakespeare's plays received their first performance. The remains of the theatre were discovered in the course of preliminary works connected with re-development. Despite requests to do so, the Secretary of State refused to exercise his powers under the 1979 Act to make the site a scheduled monument, which had he done so, would have then required scheduled monument consent to be obtained before the redevelopment could proceed.

Under the existing law, compensation for loss of development value of land is not payable where loss results from a site being made a scheduled monument. If, however, planning permission for development of land has been granted and the development is then frustrated because the site is subsequently scheduled, compensation for loss of development value becomes payable. In *R* v *Secretary of State for the Environment, ex parte Rose Theatre Trust Co.* [1990] 1 QB 504, an action was brought challenging the decision of the Secretary of State not to make the site and remains of the theatre a scheduled monument. Dismissing an application for judicial review to quash the decision, the High Court held that the risk that compensation might be payable was a relevant factor for the Secretary of State to consider in coming to his decision. The court also found that in deciding whether or not to exercise his powers, the Secretary of State was entitled to take into account the developer's desire to cooperate in preserving the remains. As a result of this cooperation, the developers agreed at a cost to them of over £10m, to redesign their proposed development in order to protect the site, to remove all piling from the area, to contain remains of the theatre footings and to provide sufficient headroom over the remains to allow for their future display. Following the development of the Rose Court building, which included those proposals, the Secretary of State decided to include the site of the remains in the schedule of ancient monuments.

In April 1991, the government issued a consultation paper proposing a number of minor amendments to the Ancient Monuments and Achaeological Areas Act 1979 when a suitable legislative opportunity arose. The amendments included clarifying the definition of 'damage' in the 1979 Act and making it an offence to remove objects from scheduled sites. No such amendments had been made by the end of August 1994.

TWENTY ONE

Minerals

21.1 Introduction

Because of the particular nature and effect of mineral working, special provisions are considered necessary to control its environmental effects. Following the report of a Committee on Planning Control over Mineral Working, the government implemented many of the report's recommendations in the Town and Country Planning (Minerals) Act 1981. The main features of that Act, which are now incorporated in the 1990 Act, are as follows:

(a)   It established 'mineral planning authorities' to be responsible for all planning control over mineral working, including the service of enforcement notices and stop notices. Since the winning and working of minerals is a 'county matter' under sch. 16 to the Local Government Act 1972, the mineral planning authority (MPA) will be the county planning authority except in respect of a site in a metropolitan district or London Borough, when it will be the local planning authority (s. 1(4) of the 1990 Act).

(b)   It amplified the definition of development to bring within its scope activities relating to mineral working which may not previously have been regarded as being included within the definition (s. 55 (4) of the 1990 Act).

(c)   It provided that owners of 'mineral rights' should be notified of applications for planning permission for the mining and working of minerals in the same way as other owners are required to be notified.

(d)   It authorises the MPA, in a grant of planning permission for mineral working, to impose both 'restoration' and 'aftercare' conditions. A restoration condition secures that any or all of subsoil, topsoil and soil-making materials are replaced after the completion of the mineral working and the site contoured in an appropriate manner. An aftercare condition imposes an obligation to bring the land back to a required standard where the land is to be restored to agricultural, forestry or amenity use after the working has ceased (para. 2, sch. 5 to the 1990 Act). An aftercare condition, which can only be used in conjunction with a restoration condition, becomes operative after the restoration condition has been complied with. Aftercare may also be secured by the imposition of a condition in the planning permission requiring the subsequent approval by the MPA of an 'aftercare scheme'.

(e) It made every planning permission for mineral working subject to a time-limit upon its life. Where the MPA fail to impose a time-limit, a 60-year time-limit is deemed to be imposed. The 60-year time-limit is also made to apply to existing planning permission granted before 22 February 1982 and to run from that date (paras. 1-6 of sch. 5 to the 1990 Act).

(f) It imposed a duty on the MPA to review every site in their area of current or former mineral working to determine whether they should revoke or modify a planning permission; order the discontinuance of a use or the alteration or removal of buildings; prohibit the resumption of mining and the working of minerals; or order the suspension of mineral working (s. 105 of the 1990 Act).

(g) It authorised the MPA to prohibit by order the resumption of mineral working which has not been carried on for at least two years and it appears to them that the resumption of such development is unlikely (paras. 3 and 4, sch. 9 to the 1990 Act). Any order made may impose requirements to alter or remove plant, etc. and restoration and aftercare conditions. Apart from Kent County Council, which by July 1993 had made nine prohibition orders under this provision, little use has been made of the new power.

(h) It authorised the MPA to suspend by order the winning and working of minerals where the development has begun but has not been carried on for at least 12 months, and it appears that a resumption is likely. The order must specify a period during which specified steps must be taken for the protection of the environment (paras. 5 to 10, sch. 9 to the 1990 Act). The purpose of this provision is to secure the temporary restoration of the site before mineral working is resumed.

(i) Where a local planning authority revoke or modify planning permission, compensation becomes payable where any person has incurred expenditure in carrying out work rendered abortive by the revocation or modification or has otherwise sustained loss directly attributable to that restoration or modification. The Act authorises the Secretary of State to make regulations which in some circumstances will reduce the amount of compensation for which MPAs will be liable when revoking or modifying a planning permission for mineral working, or making a discontinuance order relating to such development or making a prohibition or suspension order under the Act (s. 116 of the 1990 Act).

21.2 Old mining permissions

Towards the end of 1990 concern began to be expressed over old permissions for mineral working, granted before 1946 under a then legislative scheme, known as interim development orders (IDOs). Under the Town and Country Planning Act 1947, permissions granted under IDOs before 22 July 1943 ceased to be effective on 1 July 1948. However, where consent for development had been granted on or after 22 July 1943, permission for that development (insofar as it had not been carried out before 1 July 1948) was deemed to be granted under the 1947 Act and no fresh application was needed. The existence of such permissions led to the following problems:

(a)   Unlike planning permission granted after the 1947 Act came into force, there was no requirement that such permissions be registered. Hence, many people (including local planning authorities) were ignorant of the existence or the precise details of a permission.

(b)   Because such permissions were not registered, long dormant workings could be reactivated without warning.

(c)   The permissions were not subject to the type of conditions that are normally attached to present-day permissions.

(d)   The extension of existing works covered by these permissions could have a significant adverse impact on the environment and amenity.

To meet this problem s. 22 and sch. 2 of the Planning and Compensation Act 1991 introduced new procedures for dealing with permissions for the winning and working of minerals or the depositing of mineral waste originally granted under IDOs. They are referred to in the Act as 'old mining permissions'. The main effect of these provisions was that a landowner or mineral owner with planning permission for development consisting of the winning and working of minerals or involving the depositing of mineral waste authorised by interim development orders made after 21 July 1943 could, within six months of the new provisions being brought into operation, apply to the MPA to have the permission registered. If no application for registration of the permission was made by 25 March 1992, therefore, the permission will have ceased to have effect and no compensation will have been payable. Any dispute about the validity of the permission in respect of which the application to register was made, has to be determined by the Secretary of State. It is believed that 508 applications were made for the registration of interim development order permissions. Many decisions about the validity of the permission sought to be registered are now being dealt with on appeal by the Secretary of State.

The 1991 Act also provided that, in the case of permissions where no operations for the winning and working of minerals or the depositing of minerals waste have been carried out to any significant extent in the two years preceding 1 May 1991 ('dormant' permissions), development may not recommence until a scheme of conditions has been determined by the MPA. In any other case (i.e., 'active' permissions), an application for determination of conditions is required to be made to the MPA within 12 months (or such longer period as the MPA agree) of the application for registration of the original permission having been granted by the MPA or finally determined by the Secretary of State on appeal.

This distinction is intended to prevent the reactivation of dormant permissions without proper planning conditions; avoid applicants having to prepare and submit schemes of conditions too far in advance of their need to work the site; ensures that schemes that are prepared and submitted are appropriate to the circumstances pertaining at the time; and ensures that the workload for both applicants and MPAs is more evenly spread.

The purpose of these provisions is to ensure that eventually the extent and terms of old mining permissions will be publicly known; that where old mining permissions are being implemented, conditions imposed on the permissions ensure that operational activity complies with modern standards; and that operations cannot be recommenced on sites which have recently been lying dormant without first proving the validity of an old mining permission and having conditions relating to operating and restoration aspects attached to it.

However, notwithstanding the measures taken in the Town and Country Planning (Minerals) Act 1981 and in the Planning and Compensation Act 1991 relating to old mineral permissions, concern continues to be expressed about the inadequacy of planning controls over development involving mineral working.

21.3   Mining permissions granted between 1948 and 1981

The changes to the law relating to mineral working made by the Town and Country Planning (Minerals) Act 1981 and by the Planning and Compensation Act 1991 in relation to old mining permissions (see 21.2), left unaffected those planning permissions for mineral working which had been granted between 1948 and 1981.

In March 1992, the government issued a consultation paper which made a number of proposals for reforming those permissions. In March 1994, the government issued a further consultation paper containing firm proposals for dealing with them. Under that consultation paper the government is now proposing:

(a)   a timetable for reviews of all active sites in two stages, dependent upon the date of the grant of planning permission;

(b)   the reviews to include ancillary mining development, but that any conditions imposed following a review should not affect the economic structure of the operation;

(c)   that there should be no blanket revocation of mineral permissions in SSSIs, National Parks or Areas or Outstanding Natural Beauty, that dormant sites should not be reactivated without full modern conditions and active sites should be made subject to modern 'sensory' conditions (i.e., those relating to environment, amenity, restoration and after-care) without compensation;

(d)   that dormant tipping permissions should not be reactivated without full modern conditions being imposed and that there should be no compensation for the cost of complying with those conditions (in the case of active tipping permissions, there should be no compensation for the imposition of sensory conditions);

(e)   that the current expiry date of 2042 for pre-1982 permissions granted before 22 February 1982 should be brought forward to 2012.

The overall aim of the government proposals is to establish between mineral operators a 'level playing-field' regardless of the date on which their permissions were granted. The present position is that holders of modern permissions and of 'reformed' IDO permissions granted between 1943 and 1948 are seen to be at a disadvantage compared to others.

TWENTY TWO
The control of outdoor advertisements

22.1 Introduction

The source of the power to control advertisements is found in s. 220 of the 1990 Act. That section gives the Secretary of State power to make regulations for restricting or regulating the display of advertisements, so far as it appears to him to be expedient in the interests of amenity or public safety. The present regulations are the Town and Country Planning (Control of Advertisements) Regulations 1992 (SI No. 666). Guidance on advertisement control and advertising appeals procedure is given in Circular 5/92. Planning Policy Guidance Note PPG19 gives advice on how advertising control should be exercised.

The power to control advertisements can only be exercised in the interests of amenity or public safety. As the content of an advertisement can only be considered from an amenity or public safety aspect, the control cannot be used as an instrument of censorship. Under the regulations, the local planning authority are required to exercise their powers only in the interests of amenity and public safety, taking account of any material factors and in particular:

(a)   in the case of amenity, of the general characteristics of the locality, including the presence of any feature of historic, architectural, cultural or similar interest, disregarding, if they think fit, any advertisements being displayed there;

(b)   in the case of public safety—

(i)   the safety of any person who may use any road, railway, waterway (including coastal waters), docks, harbour or airfield;

(ii)   whether any display of advertisements is likely to obscure, or hinder the ready interpretation of, any road traffic sign, railway signal, or aid to navigation by water or air.

Section 224 of the 1990 Act contains provisions relating to enforcement. Under the section, the regulations may make provision to enable the local planning authority to require the removal of any advertisement displayed in contravention of the regulations, or the discontinuance of the use for the display of advertisements of any site which is being so used in contravention of the regulations. In addition s. 224(3) provides that if any person displays an advertisement in contravention of the regulations he shall be guilty of an offence and liable on summary conviction to a fine of such amount as may be prescribed, not exceeding level 3 on the standard scale and, in the case of a continuing offence, £40 for each day during which the offence continues after conviction.

In *Royal Borough of Kingston upon Thames v National Solus Sites Ltd* (1994) but so far unreported, the Queen's Bench Divisional Court held that where different posters, each advertising goods, were displayed on an advertising hoarding on different sites without consent, each display constituted a single and separate offence under the Control of Advertisement Regulations. The decision greatly increases the maximum sentence a court may impose where an authority lays multiple informations in respect of each advertisement poster.

The control system covers a wide range of advertisements and signs. Section 24 of the Planning and Compensation Act 1991 made three amendments to the definition of the word 'advertisement' in s. 336(1) of the 1990 Act. As amended, the definition (with the amendments in italics) now reads:

advertisement means any word, letter, model, sign, placard, board, notice, *awning, blind,* device or representation, whether illuminated or not, in the nature of, and employed wholly or partly for the purposes of, advertisement, announcement or direction, and (without prejudice to the previous provisions of this definition) includes any hoarding or similar structure used, *or designed,* or adapted for use, *and anything else principally used, or designed or adapted principally for use,* for the display of advertisements, and references to the display of advertisements shall be construed accordingly.

The purpose of each of the amendments is as follows:

(a) *Awning, blind.* These words bring two additional methods of displaying advertisements within the statutory definition. Before this amendment was made, it was not clear whether awnings and blinds on which an advertisement was displayed, but held in place by metal supporting arms secured to the wall of a building, were to be treated solely as an outdoor advertisement or whether, independent of the provisions in the Act granting deemed planning permission for advertisements displayed in accordance with the Advertisement Regulations, planning permission was needed for any development that they might involve. The amendment means that awnings and blinds can now be treated solely as an outdoor advertisement.

(b) *Or designed.* The purpose of this amendment is to make it clear that the definition of 'advertisement' includes hoardings and similar structures (such as rotating poster-panels) designed for use for the display of advertisements, even though no actual display is presently taking place.

(c)   *And anything else principally used or designed or adapted principally for use.*
The purpose of this amendment is to extend the definition of 'advertisement'
so that it includes objects such as gantries, pylons, or free-standing drums often
found in shopping precincts.

22.1.1   Exclusions from control

For the purposes of the regulations, however, advertisement does not include
anything employed wholly as a memorial or as a railway signal (reg. 2(17)).

Under reg. 3(2) of and sch. 2 to the regulations, no control is exercised by
the regulations over the following advertisements:

Class A	The display of a single advertisement on or consisting of a balloon not more than 60 metres above the ground on not more than 10 days in total in any calendar year.
Class B	An advertisement displayed on enclosed land and not readily visible from outside or from any place to which the public has a right of access.
Class C	An advertisement displayed on or in a moving vehicle.
Class D	An advertisement incorporated in the fabric of a building, other than a building used principally for the display of advertisements.
Class E	An advertisement displayed on an article for sale which is not illuminated and does not exceed 0.1 of a square metre in area.
Class F	An advertisement related specifically to a pending Parliamentary, European Assembly or local government election.
Class G	An advertisement displayed by Standing Orders of either House of Parliament or by any enactment.
Class H	A traffic sign.
Class I	The national flag of any country.
Class J	An advertisement displayed inside a building.

To benefit from this exclusion, advertisements in the above classes may also
have to comply with other conditions and limitations set out in the schedule.

22.1.2   The control

Advertisements subject to control by the regulations fall into two main groups,
namely, advertisements for which deemed consent is granted by the regulations
(22.2) and advertisements which require express consent from the local
planning authority or the Secretary of State (22.3).

22.2   Deemed consent

Under reg. 6 and part 1 of sch. 3, deemed consent is granted for the display of
the following broad category of advertisements subject to stated conditions and
limitations and the power of the local planning authority to serve a discontinuance notice:

Class 1	Functional advertisement of local authorities, statutory undertakers and public transport undertakers.

Class 2	Miscellaneous advertisements relating to the premises on which they are displayed, (e.g., advertisements relating to professions, businesses or trades carried on in premises).
Class 3	Miscellaneous temporary advertisements (e.g., advertisements relating to the sale or letting of premises).
Class 4	Illuminated advertisements on business premises.
Class 5	Advertisements (other than illuminated advertisements) on business premises.
Class 6	An advertisement on a forecourt of business premises.
Class 7	Flag advertisements.
Class 8	Advertisements on hoardings.
Class 9	Advertisements on highway structures.
Class 10	Advertisements for neighbourhood watch and similar schemes.
Class 11	Directional advertisements.
Class 12	Advertisements inside buildings.
Class 13	Sites used for the display of advertisements on 1 April 1974.
Class 14	Advertisements displayed after expiry of express consent.

The deemed consent granted to the display of the advertisements in the above classes is granted subject to any conditions and limitations stated in each class and to what is referred to as the standard conditions.

The standard conditions (set out in sch. 1 to the regulations) are:

1. Any advertisements displayed, and any site used for the display of advertisements, shall be maintained in a clean and tidy condition to the reasonable satisfaction of the local planning authority.
2. Any structure or hoarding erected or used principally for the purpose of displaying advertisements shall be maintained in a safe condition.
3. Where an advertisement is required under these Regulations to be removed, the removal shall be carried out to the reasonable satisfaction of the local planning authority.
4. No advertisement is to be displayed without the permission of the owner of the site or any other person with an interest in the site entitled to grant permission.
5. No advertisement shall be sited or displayed so as to obscure, or hinder the ready interpretation of, any road traffic sign, railway signal or aid to navigation by water or air, or so as otherwise to render hazardous the use of any highway, railway, waterway or aerodrome (civil or military).

The other conditions and limitations to which the deemed consent may be subject relate to such matters as size of the advertisement, size of characters or symbols on the advertisement, area and height of the advertisement and its position.

The deemed consent to the display of the above classes of advertisements may be restricted in two ways. First, under reg. 7, the Secretary of State, if satisfied upon a proposal made to him by the local planning authority that the display of advertisements of any class or description (other than Class 12 or 13) should not be undertaken in any particular area or in any particular case without express consent, may direct that the consent granted by the regulations for that class or description shall not apply in that area or case, for a specified period or indefinitely.

In the early part of 1990, following representations made by Camden Borough Council and Westminster City Council, the Secretary of State issued directions with regard to estate agents' notice-boards in a number of conservation areas within Central London. The directions were to last for five years. Similar directions have previously been made in relation to advertisements in the Royal Borough of Kensington and Chelsea and in the City of Bath. The directions mean that before displaying 'for sale' or 'to let' notices in those areas, specific consent for the display needs to be obtained.

Secondly, under reg. 8, a local planning authority may serve a notice requiring the discontinuance of the display of an advertisement, or the use of a site for the display of an advertisement for which deemed consent is granted under the regulations, if they are satisfied that it is necessary to do so to remedy a substantial injury to the amenity of the locality or a danger to members of the public. The notice must be served on the advertiser and on the owner and occupier of the site on which the advertisement is displayed. There is a right of appeal against the notice to the Secretary of State.

22.3 Express consent

Unless an advertisement has deemed consent for its display under reg. 6, express consent is required. An application for express consent is now made to the authority to whom it falls to determine them. The authority may then refuse consent, or grant consent, in whole or in part, subject to the standard conditions and to such additional conditions as they think fit. Regulation 13(5) provides that an express consent shall be subject to the condition that it expires at the end of a period of five years from the date of the consent, or such longer or shorter period as the authority may specify. The regulations give a right of appeal to the Secretary of State against a decision of the authority on an application for express consent.

Consequent upon the changes made to the 1990 Act by the Planning and Compensation Act 1991, the regulations now give to a local planning authority the same power to decline to determine an application for express consent to the display of an advertisement as they have to decline to determine an application for planning permission which is the same or substantially the same as one dismissed by the Secretary of State on appeal within the previous two years (see Chapter 10). In addition, the regulations now give to the Secretary of State the power to dismiss an application for express consent where there has been undue delay in the prosecution of an appeal, as is available with planning appeals (see Chapter 17).

22.4 Proposed changes

A consultation paper issued by the government in December 1993 proposed a number of deregulatory changes to the Control of Advertisements Regulations.

The paper proposed some relaxation in the current conditions for displaying three classes of 'deemed consent' advertisement, namely, Classes 4A and 4B (illuminated advertisements on business premises), Class 8 (temporary hoardings around construction sites) and Class 9 (advertisements on highway structures). These 'deemed consent' Classes are well-established, and it was thought that some relaxation of the original conditions now seems justified and unlikely to affect visual amenity adversely. Two new 'deemed consent' Classes were also proposed for, respectively, developers' advertising flags on house-building sites and 'gantry' or 'goalpost' signs at petrol-filling stations, each with suitable conditions to minimise any adverse effect on visual amenity.

22.5 Areas of special control

Under s. 221 of the 1990 Act, the advertisement regulations may make different provision with respect to different areas. In particular, the regulations may make special provision with respect to conservation areas, areas defined as experimental areas and areas defined as areas of special control.

An experimental area is an area prescribed for a period, for the purpose of assessing the effect on amenity or public safety of advertisements of a prescribed description.

As regards areas of special control, the effect of defining an area as such is to restrict the class of advertisement that may be displayed in that area.

Within an area of special control, no advertisements may be displayed unless they come within Classes B to J in sch. 2, Classes 1 to 3 and 5 to 7 and 9 to 14 in sch. 3, or are advertisements of the following descriptions displayed with express consent; namely those relating to local events or activities, those made for the purpose of announcement or direction or required in the interests of public safety. The procedure for defining an area of special control involves the local planning authority making an order that an area be an area of special control. This order requires to be approved by the Secretary of State, who must afford to any person making an objection to the order an opportunity of appearing before and being heard by an Inspector (sch. 5 to the regulations).

The purpose of requiring the Secretary of State's approval is to ensure that nationally applicable standards are applied in determining what areas are subject to this stricter control.

22.6 Development and the display of advertisements

Where the display of advertisements in accordance with the regulations involves the development of land, s. 222 of the 1990 Act provides that planning permission for that development shall be deemed to be granted and that no application shall be necessary for that development under Part III of the Act.

TWENTY THREE

Trees

Cutting down a tree does not appear to be development within s. 55 of the 1990 Act; hence it is not subject to general development control. The Act contains other provisions, however, to secure the preservation or planting of trees. Under s. 197 of the 1990 Act, a duty is imposed on a local planning authority to ensure, whenever it is appropriate, that in granting planning permission for development adequate provision is made, by the imposition of conditions, for the preservation or planting of trees. In addition, the authority may make orders under s. 198 of the 1990 Act in connection with a grant of such permission.

Under s. 198, if it appears to a local planning authority that it is expedient in the interests of amenity to make provision for the preservation of trees or woodlands in their area, they may for that purpose make a tree preservation order with respect to such trees, groups of trees or woodlands as may be specified in the order. In particular, the order may make provision for prohibiting the cutting down, topping, lopping, uprooting, wilful damage or wilful destruction of trees except with the consent of the local planning authority, and for securing the replanting of any part of a woodland area which is felled in the course of forestry operations permitted by or under the order.

The Act does not contain a definition of the word 'tree'. According to Lord Denning MR in *Kent County Council* v *Batchelor* (1976) 33 P & CR 185, a 'woodland' tree 'ought to be something over seven or eight inches in diameter'.

A tree preservation order cannot prohibit the cutting down, uprooting, topping or lopping of trees which are dying or dead or have become dangerous, or where the cutting down, uprooting, topping or lopping is in compliance with any obligations imposed under an Act of Parliament or is necessary for the prevention or abatement of a nuisance.

Sections 206 to 210 of the 1990 Act provide for the enforcement of tree preservation orders. Under s. 210, if any person, in contravention of a tree preservation order, cuts down, uproots or wilfully destroys a tree, or wilfully damages, tops or lops a tree in such a manner as to be likely to destroy it, he shall be guilty of an offence and may be fined on summary conviction to a fine not exceeding the statutory maximum or twice the value of the tree, whichever is the greater, or on conviction on indictment, to a fine which may reflect the financial benefit which has accrued or is likely to accrue to him in consequence of the offence. In *Maidstone Borough Council* v *Mortimer* (1980) 43 P & CR 67, it was held that the offence is an absolute offence and that proof of knowledge by the accused of the existence of an order is not required. The penalties may indeed be heavy. In one case ([1991] JPL 101), a property company was fined £50,000 for breach of a tree preservation order and ordered to pay the local authority's costs in the sum of £2,250. Under s. 206 of the 1990 Act, if any tree is removed, uprooted or destroyed in contravention of a tree preservation order the owner (unless the local planning authority dispense with the requirement) must plant another tree of appropriate size and species in the same place as soon as he reasonably can. In such a case, the tree preservation order will then apply to the replacement tree.

If a landowner fails to comply with the requirements of s. 206, s. 207 provides that the local planning authority may serve a notice on the owner of the land, within four years of the failure, requiring him to plant a tree or trees of such a size as may be specified in the notice. Under s. 208 there is a right of appeal against the notice to the Secretary of State. Once the notice has taken effect, the local authority may enter the land under s. 209 of the 1990 Act and take the steps required by the notice.

Section 23 of the Planning and Compensation Act 1991 made a number of changes to the provisions of the 1990 Act which related to the preservation of trees, in order to reflect, as far as practicable, the amendments made by the 1991 Act to enforcement notice procedure generally. The main changes are as follows:

(a)   Where an order has been made under s. 206 of the 1990 Act requiring replacement of a tree, or conditions of a consent given under a tree preservation order require the replacement of a tree and the replacement has not been effected, any order made by the authority under s. 207(1) to enforce that duty, is now *required* to specify a period at the end of which the notice is to take effect. In addition, the amending legislation provides that the specified period is to be one not less than 28 days beginning with the date of service of the notice.

(b)   Where a notice has been served under s. 207 of the 1990 Act to require the replacement of a tree, the person on whom the notice is served may now appeal against the notice on the additional ground that in all the circumstances, the duty to plant a replacement tree should be dispensed with.

(c)   In order to prevent appeals against an order requiring the replacement of a tree being invalidated due to postal delays, it is provided that an appeal is validly made if sent to the Secretary of State in a properly addressed and prepaid letter posted to him at such time that, in the ordinary course of post, it would have been delivered to him before the end of the period specified (see (a) above) as the date on which the notice is to take effect.

(d)   On appeal against an order requiring the replacement of a tree the Secretary of State has been given an additional power to correct any 'misdescription' in the notice, so long as he is satisfied that the correction or variation will not cause injustice to the appellant or the local planning authority. Previously, his power to do this on appeal was limited to the correction of any 'informality, defect or error' in the notice.

(e)   Under s. 209 of the 1990 Act, a local planning authority may enter land in order to plant trees required to be planted by a replacement order where the owner has not complied with that notice. Under an amendment made by the 1991 Act to that section it has been made a criminal offence for any person wilfully to obstruct a person acting in exercise of that power.

(f)   The maximum penalty on summary conviction for a breach of a tree preservation order has been increased from £2,000 to £20,000. In addition, the existing requirement that the court should have regard to any financial benefit which has accrued or appears likely to accrue to a person convicted on indictment of a breach of an order, has now been extended to include summary conviction.

(g)   The 1991 Act inserts a new s. 214A into the 1990 Act to give local planning authorities an express power to apply to the court for an injunction where they consider it necessary or desirable to restrain an actual or apprehended offence under s. 210 (non-compliance with a tree preservation order) or s. 211 (preservation of trees in conservation areas) of the 1990 Act.

(h)   A new power allows magistrates to issue a warrant giving a person duly authorised by the local planning authority or Secretary of State the right to enter land where admission to the land has been refused or refusal is reasonably apprehended, or where the case is one of urgency. This power may be useful where necessary to enter land in the middle of the night to prevent a tree subject to a preservation order being felled.

A tree preservation order is required to be made in the form, or substantially in the form prescribed by the Town and Country Planning (Tree Preservation Order) Regulations 1969 (SI No. 17). The regulations require the authority on making an order:

(a)   To place on deposit for inspection at a place or places convenient to the locality in which the tree, trees or woodlands are situated a certified copy of the order with an accompanying map showing the position of the trees or woodlands to be protected.

(b)   To serve a copy of the order and map on the owners and occupiers of land affected and on any other person known to be entitled to work minerals on the land or to fell any of the trees. A notice must also be served upon such persons stating the grounds for making the order and that objections and representations with respect to the order must be made in writing to the authority within a period of 28 days. Before proceeding to confirm the order, which they may do with or without modifications, the authority must take into account any objections and representations made. The order will not take effect until confirmed by the authority though, under s. 201 of the Act, the local planning authority may include in the order a direction that it shall take effect immediately, in which case it remains in force for a period of six months or until the order is confirmed, whichever is the earlier.

Once the order is confirmed, it cannot be questioned in any legal proceedings whatsoever, except by way of application made within six weeks to the High Court under s. 288 of the 1990 Act.

The model order contains a procedure for obtaining the consent of the local planning authority to do work which would otherwise be prohibited by the order. The person seeking consent, must make a written application to the authority stating his reasons for making the application. The authority may then grant consent, either unconditionally or subject to conditions as the authority think fit (e.g., require a replacement tree in the immediate vicinity), or refuse consent. The applicant may appeal to the Secretary of State against the refusal of the authority to grant an unconditional consent, or their failure to make a determination within the prescribed eight-week period.

As previously mentioned, protection is also given to trees not subject to a tree preservation order located in a conservation area.

In July 1994, the Government indicated that it proposed to reform the law relating to the preservation orders in England and Wales in a number of ways. This included:

(a)   a clarification of the present exemption given to trees causing a nuisance;

(b)   the introduction of a code of practice to promote the sensitive management of trees by satutory undertakers and utility companies;

(c)   the giving of a discretion to local planning authorities to determine the location of replacement trees;

(d)   the clarification of an owner's rights to compensation for loss or damage incurred as a result of local authorities' decisions on applications to carry out work on trees subject to a preservation order;

(e)   a limitation on the power of local authorities to make preservation orders over areas of trees other than woodlands;

(f)   the replacement of the present offence of 'wilful' destruction or damage of a tree by an offence based on 'recklessness';

(g)   the creation of a new offence of 'failing to comply with a tree replacement notice'; and

(h)   the repeal of the exemption allowing work to be carried out on a dying tree.

It is unlikely, however, that legislation to give effect to these proposals will be introduced in the foreseeable future due to pressure on Parliamentary time.

TWENTY FOUR
Conservation of natural habitats

The most recent impact on town and country planning law due to the country's membership of the European Community, has arisen from the need to implement the EC Council Directive on the Conservation of Natural Habitats and of Wild Fauna and Flora (92/43/EEC: The Habitats Directive). In order to do this, the Government has laid before parliament draft regulations under the provisions of s. 2 of the European Communities Act 1972. The draft regulations, the Conservation (Natural Habitats etc.) Regulations 1994, comprise a total 'implementation package' which strengthens all existing legislation dealing with nature conservation. Part IV of the regulations, however, specifically amends the Town and Country Planning Act 1990, in so far as it affects applications for planning permission, development orders, grants of deemed planning permission, approvals for development and other consents and to ensure that any permission, approval, order or consent given under the Act is subject to the provisions of the Directive.

The draft regulations, which are subject to affirmative resolution procedure, were laid before both Houses of Parliament on 4 July 1994. They were approved by the House of Commons on 19 July 1994, but due to the pressure on Parliamentary time, approval by the House of Lords had to be delayed until after the summer recess. It is expected, therefore, that the regulations will be in force by the early part of November 1994.

The regulations will apply to sites that will be designated as Special Areas of Conservation (SACs) under the Habitats Directive and also to sites classified as Special Protection Areas (SPAs) under the EC Council Directive on the Conservation of Wild Birds (79/409/EEC: The Birds Directive). The Habitats Directive applies a common protection regime to SACs and SPAs, and they are referred to collectively in the regulations as 'European sites'.

The regulations make four main amendments to planning legislation as follows:

(a)   they restrict the granting of planning permission for development likely to significantly affect a SPA designated under the Birds Directive or a SAC classified under the Habitats Directive.

Regulation 48(1) provides

> A competent authority, before deciding to undertake, or give any consent, permission or other authorisation for, a plan or project which—
>
> (a) is likely to have a significant effect on a European site in Great Britain (either alone or in combination with other plans or projects), and
> (b) is not directly connected with or necessary to the management of the site,
>
> shall make an appropriate assessment of the implications for the site in view of the site's conservation objectives.

The section provides that for the purposes of the assessment, the competent authority shall consult the relevant nature conservation body and, if they consider it correct, take the opinion of the general public, by such steps as they consider appropriate.

The competent authority (normally the local planning authority or Secretary of State) may agree to the plan or project only after having ascertained that it will not adversely affect the integrity of the European site. Regulation 49, however, provides that

> (1) If they are satisfied that, there being no alternative solutions, the plan or project must be carried out for imperative reasons of overriding public interest (which, subject to paragraph (2), may be of a social or economic nature), the competent authority may agree to the plan or project notwithstanding a negative assessment of the implications for the site.
> (2) Where the site concerned hosts a priority natural habitat type or a priority species, the reasons referred to in paragraph (1) must be either—
>
> (a) reasons relating to human health, public safety or beneficial consequences of primary importance to the environment, or
> (b) other reasons which in the opinion of the European Commission are imperative reasons of overriding public interest.

The regulation is made to apply to the grant of planning permission on an application under Part III of the 1990 Act, or an appeal under s. 78, or where it follows from the service of the purchase notice, enforcement notice or discontinuance order.

(b) they require the review of existing planning permissions which have not been fully implemented and which are likely significantly to affect a designated SPA or classified SAC; and if necessary, the taking of appropriate action.

The duty to review applies to any planning permission or deemed planning permission except that granted by development order or by virtue of the adoption of, or alterations to, a simplified planning zone scheme. Neither does it apply to a permission where the development has been completed, or which is granted for a limited period that has expired, or which was subject to a time condition relating to commencement and that time has elapsed without the development having begun.

Under reg. 56, where the competent authority ascertain that the carrying out or continuation of the development would adversely affect the integrity of a European site, it must consider whether any adverse effects could be overcome by a planning obligation made under s. 106 of the 1990 Act and, if so, invite those concerned to enter into such an obligation. If no such obligation is entered into, the competent authority must proceed to use its powers under the 1990 Act to either revoke or modify the planning permission or require the discontinuance of a use or the removal of buildings or works so as to overcome the adverse effects.

(c)   they prevent the General Development Order granting permitted development rights which adversely affect the integrity of a SAP or SAC.

Regulation 60 provides

(1)   It shall be a condition of any planning permission granted by a general development order, whether made before or after the commencement of these Regulations, that development which—
(a)   is likely to have a significant effect on a European site in Great Britain (either alone or in combination with other plans or projects), and
(b)   is not directly connected with or necessary to the management of the site,
shall not be begun until the developer has received written notification of the approval of the local planning authority under regulation 62.

(2)   It shall be a condition of any planning permission granted by a general development order made before the commencement of these Regulations that development which—
(a)   is likley to have a significant effect on a European site in Great Britain (either alone or in combination with other plans or projects), and
(b)   is not directly connected with or necessary to the management of the site,
and which was begun but not completed before the commencement of these Regulations, shall not be continued until the developer has received written notification of the approval of the local planning authority under regulation 62.

Regulation 61 provides for the opinion of the appropriate nature conservation body to be sought, that the development is not likely to have the effect mentioned in reg. 60(1)(a) or (2) above, and that such opinion shall be conclusive of that question for the purpose of relying on the planning permission granted by the order. Alternatively, reg. 62 provides that a person intending to carry out development in reliance on the permission granted by the order may apply in writing to the local planning authority for their approval (with the appropriate fee), which the authority must then consider after taking into account any representations made by the appropriate nature conservation body.

(d) they prevent existing and future simplified planning zone schemes granting planning permission for development which is likely significantly to affect a SPA or SAC.

Regulations 65 and 66 provide:

Simplified planning zones

65. The adoption or approval of a simplified planning zone scheme after the commencement of these Regulations shall not have effect to grant planning permission for development which—

(a) is likely to have a significant effect on a European site in Great Britain (either alone or in combination with other plans or projects), and

(b) is not directly connected with or necessary to the management of the site;

and every simplified planning zone scheme already in force shall cease to have effect to grant such permission, whether or not the development authorised by the permission has been begun.

Enterprise zones

66. An order designating an enterprise zone, or the approval of a modified scheme, if made or given after the commencement of these Regulations, shall not have effect to grant planning permission for development which—

(a) is likely to have a significant effect on a European site in Great Britain (either alone or in combination with other plans or projects), and

(b) is not directly connected with or necessary to the management of the site;

and where the order or approval was made or given before that date, the permission granted by virtue of the taking effect of the order or the modifications shall, from that date, cease to have effect to grant planning permission for such development, whether or not the development authorised by the permission has been begun.

TWENTY FIVE
Remedies for adverse planning decisions

25.1 Compensation for restrictions on development

The general principle of allowing compensation to owners who suffer loss through the exercise by a planning authority of its statutory powers to control development was recognised in early legislation.

Thus the Housing, Town Planning etc. Acts of 1909 to 1925, gave a right to compensation, with certain exceptions, for any injurious affection to an owner's interest in land due to the making of a town planning scheme. The Town and Country Planning Act 1932 also gave a right to compensation for injurious affection to land due to the coming into operation of any provisions in a town planning scheme, or the doing of any work under it, which infringed or curtailed the owner's legal rights.

These earlier Acts were concerned, however, with the effects of the coming into operation of a 'town planning scheme'. But when, under the Town and Country Planning Act 1947, the town planning scheme was replaced by the much more flexible 'development plan' and planning permission became obligatory for all forms of 'development', the right to compensation (if any) became related to the actual decision taken by the planning authority in any particular case and not to the provisions of the development plan.

By 1990, the law provided for the payment of compensation for adverse planning decisions in two distinct situations.

(a)   planning decisions restricting development other than 'new development' (s. 114 of the 1990 Act); and

(b)   restrictions on new development where land has an 'unexpended balance of development value' (Part V of the 1990 Act).

In 1991, the government decided, in s. 31 of the Planning and Compensation Act 1991, to repeal the right to compensation in both cases.

As regards (a) above, the repeal was made retrospectively to apply to cases where the relevant application for planning permission was made on or after 16 November 1990.

It was considered that the payment of compensation for restriction on development other than new development (often referred to as development within the 'existing use of land') was now regarded as outdated and gave rise to abuse by stimulating applications for planning permission simply in order to obtain compensation for any refusal. According to the government, the opportunities for developers to exploit the right to compensation under s. 114 of the 1990 Act was a matter of concern, particularly in conservation areas in parts of central London where property prices were high. The purpose in making the repeal of s. 114 retrospective to 16 November 1990 (the day following publication of the original 1991 Bill) was to prevent a flood of applications for planning permission being made in order to elicit payment of compensation before the law had been changed.

With regard to the repeal of the provisions for the payment of compensation for restrictions on new development, (b) above, the view taken by the government was that the number of successful claims had become very small, whilst the cost of administrative work in examining potential claims and in recovering any compensation paid where planning permission was subsequently granted for development was no longer justified.

25.2 Compensation for the revocation or modification of planning permissions under section 97 of the 1990 Act

Where an order revoking or modifying a planning permission has been made, s. 107 of the 1990 Act provides for the payment of compensation by the local planning authority under the following heads:

(a) expenditure in carrying out work which is rendered abortive by the revocation or modification; or

(b) loss or damage otherwise sustained which is directly attributable to the revocation or modification.

For the purposes of these provisions, any expenditure incurred in the preparation of plans for the purposes of any work, or upon other similar matters preparatory to it, are to be taken to be included in the expenditure incurred in carrying out that work. No compensation, however, can be paid for any work carried out before the grant of the permission which has been revoked or modified.

Compensation will include any depreciation in the value of an interest in the land. The measure of compensation will be the amount by which the value of the claimant's interest, with the benefit of the original planning permission, exceeded the value of that interest with the planning permission revoked or modified under the order. Values are based on the rules in s. 5 of the Land Compensation Act 1961, so far as applicable, and it must be assumed that planning permission would be granted for development falling within paras. 1 and 2 of sch. 3 to the 1990 Act.

The Act also provides that where planning permission for the development of land has been granted by a development order and that permission is withdrawn, whether by the revocation or amendment of the order or by the issue of directions, and on a subsequent application for planning permission for that development the application is refused, or is granted subject to conditions (other than those previously imposed by the development order), the provisions of s. 107 are to apply as if the planning permission granted by the development order had been expressly granted under the Act and then revoked or modified by an order under s. 97 (s. 108).

Section 108 further provides, however, that where planning permission granted by development order is withdrawn by revocation or amendment of the order, compensation will only be payable if the subsequent application for planning permission is made within 12 months of the date on which the revocation or amendment became operative.

The main purpose of this provision is to ensure that a right to compensation does not exist in perpetuity simply because a type of development was once permitted development under a development order. However, a one-year period of grace is allowed to provide compensation for a person who was in the process of undertaking a development for which permission under a development order was then withdrawn, and who may already have incurred expenditure in reliance on that permission.

25.3   Compensation for discontinuance of a use or the alteration or removal of buildings or works under section 102 of the 1990 Act

Any person who suffers loss in consequence of such an order, either through depreciation in the value of his land, or by disturbance, or by expense incurred in complying with the order, is entitled, under s. 115 of the 1990 Act, to compensation from the local planning authority, provided his claim is made within six months.

Compensation for depreciation in the value of land will be assessed in accordance with the rules in s. 5 of the Land Compensation Act 1961, subject to a reduction in respect of the value to the claimant of any timber, apparatus or other materials removed for the purpose of complying with the order.

25.4   Purchase notices

Sections 137 to 148 of the 1990 Act contain provisions enabling the owner of an interest in land affected by a planning decision or order to require the purchase of that interest. This has sometimes been described as 'compulsory purchase in reverse', since it is the owner who initiates the proceedings leading to the acquisition of his interest.

The Act provides that where, on an application for planning permission to develop any land, permission is refused or is granted subject to conditions, then if the owner of the land claims:

(a)   that the land has become incapable of reasonably beneficial use in its existing state; and

(b)   in a case where planning permission was granted subject to conditions or was modified by the imposition of conditions, that the land cannot be rendered capable of reasonably beneficial use by the carrying out of the permitted development in accordance with those conditions; and

(c)   in any case, that the land cannot be rendered capable of reasonably beneficial use by the carrying out of any other development for which planning permission has been granted or for which the local planning authority or the Secretary of State has undertaken to grant planning permission,

he may, within 12 months from the date of the planning decision, serve on the council of the district or London borough in which the land is situated, a notice requiring that council to purchase his interest in the land.

For the purpose of determining what is a 'reasonably beneficial' use of the land, no account shall be taken of any prospective use of the land which would involve the carrying out of development other than any development specified in paras. 1 or 2 of sch. 3 to the 1990 Act.

For instance, land let at a good agricultural rent cannot be regarded as 'incapable of reasonably beneficial use' merely because, if planning permission had not been refused, it could have been used much more profitably for residential development.

The council on whom a purchase notice is served shall, within three months of such service, serve a responding notice on the owner stating either:

(a)   that the council are willing to comply with it; or

(b)   that another local authority or statutory undertakers specified in the response notice have agreed to comply with it in their place; or

(c)   that, for reasons specified the council are not willing to comply with the purchase notice and have not found any other local authority or statutory undertakers who will agree to comply with it in their place, and that a copy of the purchase notice and of the response notice has therefore been sent to the Secretary of State.

In cases (a) and (b) above, the council on whom the purchase notice was served, or the other authority who have agreed to comply with it, as the case may be, will be deemed to be authorised to acquire the owner's interest in the land and to have served a notice to treat on him on the same date as the service of the response notice.

In case (c) the council on whom the purchase notice is served must send a copy of it and their response notice to the Secretary of State together with their reasons for being unwilling to comply with it.

Before confirming, or taking any other action, the Secretary of State must give notice of his proposed action to the person who served the notice, to the local authority on whom it was served, to the local planning authority and to any other local authority or statutory undertakers who might be substituted for the authority on whom the notice was served. He must also afford to any of these persons or authorities the opportunity of a hearing if they so require.

After such hearing the Secretary of State may decide to take action available to him under the Act, other than that specified in his notice to the parties concerned.

The following courses of action are open to the Secretary of State:

(a)   to confirm the purchase notice if satisfied that the land is in fact incapable of reasonably beneficial use;

(b)   to confirm the notice, but to substitute some other authority or statutory undertakers for the authority on whom the notice is served;

(c)   to refuse to confirm, on grounds that the necessary conditions are not fulfilled;

(d)   instead of confirming the notice, to grant permission for the development in question, or to revoke or amend any conditions imposed;

(e)   instead of confirming the notice, to direct that if a planning application is made, permission shall be given for some other form of development.

Where an owner of land which has a restricted use by virtue of a *previous* planning permission serves a purchase notice, the Secretary of State is not obliged to confirm the notice if he considers that the land ought to remain undeveloped in accordance with the previous planning permission or, as the case may be, remain or be preserved or laid out as amenity land in relation to the remainder of the larger area for which that previous planning permission was granted.

This provision was introduced by the Town and Country Planning Act 1968 to reverse the effect of the decision in *Adams & Wade Ltd* v *Minister of Housing & Local Government* (1965) 18 P & CR 60. There, planning permission had been granted for the development of part of an area of land subject to a condition which required the remainder to be preserved as amenity land for the benefit of the part developed. Application was then made for permission to develop the amenity land, and when the application was refused the owner served a purchase notice claiming it to be incapable of reasonably beneficial use. The Minister's contention that, having had the benefit of the previous permission, the purchase order procedure could not be used to avoid the burdens of that permission was rejected, and his decision not to confirm the notice held to be invalid.

The provision which gives the Secretary of State power to refuse to confirm a purchase notice served in respect of amenity land is now found in s. 142 of the 1990 Act. The power extends beyond the situation found in the *Adams & Wade Ltd* case, since it is expressed to cover not only cases where the preservation of amenity land is an express condition of a previous planning permission, but also where the application for the previous permission contemplated that the part not comprised in the development should be treated in that way.

Any party aggrieved by the decision of the Secretary of State on a purchase notice may, within six weeks, make an application to the High Court on the grounds that either (a) the decision of the Secretary of State is not within the powers of the Act, or (b) the interests of the applicant have been substantially prejudiced by a failure to comply with any relevant requirements (ss. 284 and 288).

The court has power to quash the Secretary of State's decision, in which case the purchase notice is treated as cancelled.

If, within nine months from the service of a purchase notice or six months from its transmission to the Secretary of State (whichever is the less), the Secretary of State has neither confirmed the notice, nor taken any other action, nor notified the owner that he does not propose to confirm, the notice is deemed to be confirmed at the end of that period.

Where a purchase notice is confirmed, or deemed to be confirmed, the effect is that the authority on whom it was served will be deemed to be authorised to acquire the owner's interest compulsorily and to have served a notice to treat either on such date as the Secretary of State may specify, if he confirms the notice, or otherwise at the expiration of the period referred to in the previous paragraph (s. 143).

In the above cases — and also where a local authority confirms a purchase notice without reference to the Secretary of State — since notice to treat is deemed to have been served, the owner may, if necessary, take the requisite steps to secure the assessment of compensation and the acquisition of his interest in the land, as in any other compulsory purchase case.

The usual power to withdraw a notice to treat, under s. 31 of the Land Compensation Act 1961, is not exercisable in these cases (s. 143(8) of the 1990 Act).

Compensation for land acquired under a purchase notice will, in general, be assessed on the same basis as that of any other land compulsorily acquired.

Where, instead of confirming a purchase notice in respect of the whole or part of the land, the Secretary of State directs that planning permission should be given for some other form of development then, if the 'permitted development value' of the interest in the land (or part of it) is less than its 'schedule 3 value', the owner may claim compensation equal to the difference, estimated in accordance with the rules of s. 5 of the Land Compensation Act 1961, so far as applicable. Any dispute about the compensation will be determined by the Lands Tribunal.

'Permitted development value' means the value of the owner's interest calculated on the assumption that planning permission would only be given in accordance with the Secretary of State's direction. 'Schedule 3 value' means open market value on the assumption that planning permission would only be given for the forms of development specified in paras. 1 and 2 of sch. 3 to the 1990 Act.

A purchase notice is also available in the case of the revocation or modification of a planning permission under s. 97 or the discontinuance of a use or removal etc. of buildings or works under s. 102.

Appendix A

Town and Country Planning Act 1990, Section 55

(1) Subject to the following provisions of this section, in this Act, except where the context otherwise requires, 'development' means the carrying out of building, engineering, mining or other operations in, on, over or under land, or the making of any material change in the use of any buildings or other land.

(1A) For the purposes of this Act 'building operations' includes —
    (a) demolition of buildings;
    (b) rebuilding;
    (c) structural alterations of or additions to buildings; and
    (d) other operations normally undertaken by a person carrying on business as a builder.

(2) The following operations or uses of land shall not be taken for the purposes of this Act to involve development of the land —
    (a) the carrying out for the maintenance, improvement or other alteration of any building of works which —
        (i) affect only the interior of the building, or
        (ii) do not materially affect the external appearance of the building,
and are not works for making good war damage or works begun after 5th December 1968 for the alteration of a building by providing additional space in it underground;
    (b) the carrying out on land within the boundaries of a road by a local highway authority of any works required for the maintenance or improvement of the road;
    (c) the carrying out by a local authority or statutory undertakers of any works for the purpose of inspecting, repairing or renewing any sewers, mains, pipes, cables or other apparatus, including the breaking open of any street or other land for that purpose;
    (d) the use of any buildings or other land within the curtilage of a dwellinghouse for any purpose incidental to the enjoyment of the dwellinghouse as such;

(e) the use of any land for the purposes of agriculture or forestry (including afforestation) and the use for any of those purposes of any building occupied together with land so used;

(f) in the case of buildings or other land which are used for a purpose of any class specified in an order made by the Secretary of State under this section, the use of the buildings or other land or, subject to the provisions of the order, of any part of the buildings or the other land, for any other purpose of the same class.

(g) the demolition of any description of building specified in a direction given by the Secretary of State to local planning authorities generally or to a particular local planning authority.

(3) For the avoidance of doubt it is hereby declared that for the purposes of this section —

(a) the use as two or more separate dwellinghouses of any building previously used as a single dwellinghouse involves a material change in the use of the building and of each part of it which is so used;

(b) the deposit of refuse or waste materials on land involves a material change in its use, notwithstanding that the land is comprised in a site already used for that purpose, if —

(i) the superficial area of the deposit is extended, or

(ii) the height of the deposit is extended and exceeds the level of the land adjoining the site.

(4) For the purposes of this Act mining operations include —

(a) the removal of material of any description —

(i) from a mineral-working deposit;

(ii) from a deposit of pulverised fuel ash or other furnace ash or clinker; or

(iii) from a deposit of iron, steel or other metallic slags; and

(b) the extraction of minerals from a disused railway embankment.

(4A) Where the placing or assembly of any tank in any part of any inland waters for the purpose of fish farming there would not, apart from this subsection, involve development of the land below, this Act shall have effect as if the tank resulted from carrying out engineering operations over that land; and in this subsection —

'fish farming' means the breeding, rearing or keeping of fish or shellfish (which includes any kind of crustacean and mollusc);

'inland waters' means waters which do not form part of the sea or of any creek, bay or estuary or of any river as far as the tide flows; and

'tank' includes any cage and any other structure for use in fish farming.

(5) Without prejudice to any regulations made under the provisions of this Act relating to the control of advertisements, the use for the display of advertisements of any external part of a building which is not normally used for that purpose shall be treated for the purposes of this section as involving a material change in the use of that part of the building.

Appendix B

Town and Country Planning (Use Classes) Order 1987 (SI No. 764) (as amended)

[Dated 28 April 1987. Made by the Secretary of State for the Environment under ss. 22(2)(f) and 287(3) of the Town and Country Planning Act 1971; now ss. 55(2)(f) and 333(3) of the Town and Country Planning Act 1990.]

Citation and commencement
1.   This order may be cited as the Town and Country Planning (Use Classes) Order 1987 and shall come into force on 1st June 1987.

Interpretation
2.   In this order, unless the context otherwise requires:—

'care' means personal care for people in need of such care by reason of old age, disablement, past or present dependence on alcohol or drugs or past or present mental disorder, and in class C2 also includes the personal care of children and medical care and treatment;
'day centre' means premises which are visited during the day for social or recreational purposes or for the purposes of rehabilitation or occupational training, at which care is also provided;
'industrial process' means a process for or incidental to any of the following purposes:—

(a)   the making of any article or part of any article (including a ship or vessel, or a film, video or sound recording);
(b)   the altering, repairing, maintaining, ornamenting, finishing, cleaning, washing, packing, canning, adapting for sale, breaking up or demolition of any article; or
(c)   the getting, dressing or treatment of minerals;

in the course of any trade or business other than agriculture, and other than a use carried out in or adjacent to a mine or quarry;

'Schedule' means the schedule to this order;

'site' means the whole area of land within a single unit of occupation.

Use classes

3.—(1)   Subject to the provisions of this Order, where a building or other land is used for a purpose of any class specified in the Schedule, the use of that building or that other land for any other purpose of the same class shall not be taken to involve development of the land.

(2)   References in paragraph (1) to a building include references to land occupied with the building and used for the same purposes.

(3)   A use which is included in and ordinarily incidental to any use in a class specified in the Schedule is not excluded from the use to which it is incidental merely because it is specified in the Schedule as a separate use.

(4)   Where land on a single site or on adjacent sites used as parts of a single undertaking is used for purposes consisting of or including purposes falling within any two or more of classes B1 to B7 in the Schedule, those classes may be treated as a single class in considering the use of that land for the purposes of this Order, so long as the area used for a purpose falling either within class B2 or within classes B4 to B7 is not substantially increased as a result.

[(5)   Revoked by SI 1992 No. 657.]

(6)   No class specified in the Schedule includes use —

(a)   as a theatre,
(b)   as an amusement arcade or centre, or a fun-fair,
(c)   as a launderette,
(d)   for the sale of fuel for motor vehicles,
(e)   for the sale or display for sale of motor vehicles,
(f)   for a taxi business or business for the hire of motor vehicles,
(g)   as a scrapyard, or a yard for the storage or distribution of minerals or the breaking of motor vehicles,
(h)   for any work registrable under the Alkali, etc., Works Regulation Act 1906,
(i)   as a hostel.

Change of use of part of building or land

4.   In the case of a building used for a purpose within class C3 (dwelling-houses) in the Schedule, the use as a separate dwellinghouse of any part of the building or of any land occupied with and used for the same purposes as the building is not, by virtue of this Order, to be taken as not amounting to development.

Revocation

5.   The Town and Country Planning (Use Classes) Order 1972 and the Town and Country Planning (Use Classes) (Amendment) Order 1983 are hereby revoked.

SCHEDULE

PART A

Class A1. Shops   Use for all or any of the following purposes —

(a)   for the retail sale of goods other than hot food,
(b)   as a post office,
(c)   for the sale of tickets or as a travel agency,
(d)   for the sale of sandwiches or other cold food for consumption off the premises,
(e)   for hairdressing,
(f)   for the direction of funerals,
(g)   for the display of goods for sale,
(h)   for the hiring out of domestic or personal goods or articles,
(i)   for the washing or cleaning of clothes or fabrics in the premises,
(j)   for the reception of goods to be washed, cleaned or repaired,

where the sale, display or service is to visiting members of the public.

Class A2. Financial and professional services   Use for the provision of—

(a)   financial services, or
(b)   professional services (other than health or medical services), or
(c)   any other services (including use as a betting office) which it is appropriate to provide in a shopping area,

where the services are provided principally to visiting members of the public.

Class A3. Food and drink   Use for the sale of food or drink for consumption on the premises or of hot food for consumption off the premises.

PART B

Class B1. Business   Use for all or any of the following purposes —

(a)   as an office other than a use within class A2 (financial and professional services),
(b)   for research and development of products or processes, or
(c)   for any industrial process,

being a use which can be carried out in any residential area without detriment to the amenity of that area by reason of noise, vibration, smell, fumes, smoke, soot, ash, dust or grit.

Class B2. General industrial   Use for the carrying on of an industrial process other than one falling within class B1 above or within classes B4 to B7 below.

[**Class B3.** This class, which was special industrial group A, is now excluded from the order by SI 1992 No. 610.]

Class B4. Special industrial group B Use for any of the following processes, except where the process is ancillary to the getting, dressing or treatment of minerals and is carried on, in or adjacent to a quarry or mine—

 (a) smelting, calcining, sintering or reducing ores, minerals, concentrates or mattes;
 (b) converting, refining, reheating, annealing, hardening, melting, carburising, forging or casting metals or alloys other than pressure die-casting;
 (c) recovering metal from scrap or drosses or ashes;
 (d) galvanising;
 (e) pickling or treating metal in acid;
 (f) chromium plating.

Class B5. Special industrial group C Use for any of the following processes, except where the process is ancillary to the getting, dressing or treatment of minerals and is carried on, in or adjacent to a quarry or mine—

 (a) burning bricks or pipes;
 (b) burning lime or dolomite;
 (c) producing zinc oxide, cement or alumina;
 (d) foaming, crushing, screening or heating minerals or slag;
 (e) processing pulverised fuel ash by heat;
 (f) producing carbonate of lime or hydrated lime;
 (g) producing inorganic pigments by calcining, roasting or grinding.

Class B6. Special industrial group D Use for any of the following processes—

 (a) distilling, refining or blending oils (other than petroleum or petroleum products);
 (b) producing or using cellulose or using other pressure sprayed metal finishes (other than in vehicle repair workshops in connection with minor repairs, or the application of plastic powder by the use of fluidised bed and electrostatic spray techniques);
 (c) boiling linseed oil or running gum;
 (d) processes involving the use of hot pitch or bitumen (except the use of bitumen in the manufacture of roofing felt at temperatures not exceeding 220°C and also the manufacture of coated roadstone);
 (e) stoving enamelled ware;
 (f) producing aliphatic esters of the lower fatty acids, butyric acid, caramel, hexamine, iodoform, naphthols, resin products (excluding plastic moulding or extrusion operations and producing plastic sheets, rods, tubes, filaments, fibres or optical components produced by casting, calendering, moulding, shaping or extrusion), salicylic acid or sulphonated organic compounds;

(g) producing rubber from scrap;

(h) chemical processes in which chlorphenols or chlorcresols are used as intermediates;

(i) manufacturing acetylene from calcium carbide;

(j) manufacturing, recovering or using pyridine or picolines, any methyl or ethyl amine or acrylates.

Class B7. Special industrial group E Use for carrying on any of the following industries, businesses or trades—

Boiling blood, chitterlings, nettlings or soap.

Boiling, burning, grinding or steaming bones.

Boiling or cleaning tripe.

Breeding maggots from putrescible animal matter.

Cleaning, adapting or treating animal hair.

Curing fish.

Dealing in rags and bones (including receiving, storing, sorting or manipulating rags in, or likely to become in, an offensive condition, or any bones, rabbit skins, fat or putrescible animal products of a similar nature).

Dressing or scraping fish skins.

Drying skins.

Making manure from bones, fish, offal, blood, spent hops, beans or other putrescible animal or vegetable matter.

Making or scraping guts.

Manufacturing animal charcoal, blood albumen, candles, catgut, glue, fish oil, size or feeding stuff for animals or poultry from meat, fish, blood, bone, feathers, fat or animal offal either in an offensive condition or subjected to any process causing noxious or injurious effluvia.

Melting, refining or extracting fat or tallow.

Preparing skins for working.

Class B8. Storage or distribution Use for storage or as a distribution centre.

PART C

Class C1. Hotels Use as a hotel or as a boarding or guest-house where, in each case, no significant element of care is provided.

Class C2. Residential institutions Use for the provision of residential accommodation and care to people in need of care (other than a use within class C3 (dwellinghouses)).

Use as a hospital or nursing home.

Use as a residential school, college or training centre.

Class C3. Dwelling-houses Use as a dwellinghouse (whether or not as a sole or main residence) —

(a) by a single person or by people living together as a family, or

(b) by not more than six residents living together as a single household (including a household where care is provided for residents).

PART D

Class D1. Non-residential institutions Any use not including a residential use —

(a) for the provision of any medical or health services except the use of premises attached to the residence of the consultant or practitioner,

(b) as a crèche, day nursery or day centre,

(c) for the provision of education,

(d) for the display of works of art (otherwise than for sale or hire),

(e) as a museum,

(f) as a public library or public reading room,

(g) as a public hall or exhibition hall,

(h) for, or in connection with, public worship or religious instruction.

Class D2. Assembly and leisure Use as —

(a) a cinema,

(b) a concert hall,

(c) a bingo hall or casino,

(d) a dance-hall,

(e) a swimming-bath, skating-rink, gymnasium or area for other indoor or outdoor sports or recreations, not involving motorised vehicles or firearms.

Index